D1796266

KEN PIESSE is one of Australia's leading sports writers and his articles on cricket and Australian football appear in newspapers and magazines around the country, including the *Sunday Herald-Sun* in his home town Melbourne. He has written or edited more than a dozen books on cricket and football; the most recent are *Hooked on Cricket* (with Max Walker), *Hooked on Football* (with Dermott Brereton), *Blues, Blinders and Ball-Bursters*, *Plugger: the Tony Lockett Story* (with Tony Lockett), and the best-selling *Ablett: The Gary Ablett Story*.

Ken was a notable suburban footballer himself, playing more than a hundred games with Beaumaris. He is married to Susan. They have five children.

Also by Ken Piesse in Sun
Hooked on Football (with Dermott Brereton)
Blues, Blinders and Ball-Bursters
Plugger: the Tony Lockett Story (with Tony Lockett)

THE COMPLETE GUIDE TO AUSTRALIAN FOOTBALL

KEN PIESSE

IRONBARK
Pan Macmillan Australia

Cover pictures: football heroes, young and old, clockwise from top. Collingwood's Bill Picken; South Australian born-and-bred stars Darren and Andrew Jarman; Allen Aylett and Ron Barassi after North Melbourne's historic 1975 premiership; members of Carlton's 1945 Bloodbath Grand Final side; Melbourne and Victorian champion Garry Lyon; Brisbane Bear Scott McIvor and North Melbourne captain Wayne Carey in battle with St Kilda's David Grant.

First published in 1993 in SUN by Pan Macmillan Australia Pty Limited
Level 18, St Martins Tower, 31 Market St, Sydney
Reprinted 1995

Copyright © Ken Piesse 1993

All rights reserved. No part of this book may be reproduced or transmitted in any form or by any means, electronic or mechanical, including photocopying, recording or by any information storage and retrieval system, without prior permission in writing from the publisher.

National Library of Australia
cataloguing-in-publication data:
Piesse, Ken.
The complete guide to Australian football.

Rev. ed.
ISBN 0 330 35712 3.

1. Australian football—Anecdotes. 2. Australian football—Miscellanea. 3. Football players—Australia—Biography. I. Title.

796.336

Typeset in 10/11 pt Plantin by Midland Typesetters
Printed in Australia by Australian Print Group

Every attempt has been made to source the photographs included in this book. Publishers that may have been inadvertently overlooked should contact the author.

To KCP and PARP

FOREWORD

I can't imagine life without football. Fourteen years and more than 200 games after playing for Hawthorn for the first time, the game still holds much of its fascination.

A lot has changed, though. I'm 30, married and at my third club, Collingwood.

I can still vividly recall my nervous beginnings at Hawthorn, though—including my first match as a 16-year-old against Melbourne at the MCG.

It was the first game of the 1982 season and I was on the bench. Far from impressed by our early efforts, our coach Des Meagher yelled at one bloke, 'Smithy, you'd better pull your finger out, otherwise I'll give the kid a go'.

Soon afterwards I was on and quickly into the action, flying across the front of a pack for a mark. As I was deliberately lining up at the shot at goal, Peter 'Crackers' Keenan, who was on the mark, started yelling at me in his own inimitable way. The printable parts went like this: 'Well done, son, your first kick in the big time. Now, mind you don't . . . up.'

He said a few other things too, but I was concentrating too hard on the shot to remember much more.

To my consternation, my kick slewed off the side of my boot, but Crackers, bless him, had overstepped the mark, giving me a penalty shot, 15 metres closer to goal. This one sailed through, post high. My first goal in the big-time and you can imagine how pleased 'the kid' was.

Coming into this, my twelfth senior season, I felt a little like a first-year recruit again. Having missed so much football in 1992 with a hip injury, I longed for the chance to play every Saturday again.

I'd been able to do virtually all the preseason work, even if it was at a far slower pace than the other blokes, and planned to go easy in the practice match period to give myself the best possible chance of lasting through the bulk of the 20-match program.

While I've played a lot of football and enjoyed more successes than most, the challenge of competition still burns just as brightly for me now as it did years ago that day against Crackers Keenan and going right back to my earliest days with the Bomber under-10s at Frankston.

Back then, every Sunday in season, my brother Paul and I would carefully lace up our boots and jog down to nearby Bruce Park, jumping as many concrete driveways as possible so as not to wear down our stops.

Mum would have given us each 20 cents for oranges and we'd treat the game as seriously as the big-time footballers we watched on television. Football was an all-consuming passion. We played at every opportunity, before school, at recesses, at lunchtimes and again afterwards.

I could never understand why my cousins shunned football. We'd visit on a weekend and I'd always be asking them to switch channels so I could watch 'Football Replay' at six o'clock. To me it was as natural as breathing.

We started barracking for Collingwood, having found out that one of Dad's workmates, Errol Hutchesson, had played in the '66 Grand Final. From the age of nine or 10, we started going to matches.

Apparently I'd been taken to the football when I was about two but you'll forgive me for not remembering who the game was between, where I was, or who won!

The first game I actually recall was the Collingwood-Footscray match at VFL Park in 1975. One of my mates had a membership and helped me get in. Footscray won but Phil Carman and his white boots made the biggest impression on me.

My friends and I also went to the MCG and Moorabbin a lot. Both grounds were on the Frankston train line and easily reached without having to change trains. One year I must have seen St Kilda play 10 or 11 times. I got a bit sick of hearing their supporters yelling out all the time. 'C'mon, someone beat them!' I'd say to myself.

Many are sorry that grounds like Moorabbin, the Junction oval and Windy Hill are no longer used for matches. But football today is all about progress, and if you can attract a crowd of 50,000 to the MCG or Waverley on a Sunday, the money to be made is two and three times more than even capacity crowds encouraged at the old suburban venues.

Often I'm asked how the best modern day national league footballers would do against the suburban champions of the yesteryear. I'd love to go in against a Teddy Whitten, recognised as one of the greatest two or three players of the postwar VFL era. Not only did Ted play in my position, centre half forward, he did it with flair and aggression. I've no doubt that the superstars like Ted, Ron Barassi, 'Polly' Farmer and Co would all be scene-stealers today.

I'm reminded of just how good these players were by reading their entries in *The Complete Guide to Australian Football,* expertly researched and written by my friend Ken Piesse.

I began reading the draft one weekend morning and was still reading, almost without a break, late on Sunday afternoon. It's an enthralling, epic work which will not only settle arguments, but will entertain and inform along the way.

I particularly enjoyed the stories revolving around the legends, Jack Dyer, Haydn Bunton, Barassi and my old mate, 'Little Lou Lou' Lou Richards. A common theme in their success was their commitment to winning. I liked Dyer's quote, 'Anything goes as long as you can get away with it', and Haydn Bunton makes pretty good sense, more than 50 years later, in telling players of his era to make the most of their playing careers while they can.

Had Bunton stayed in League football in Melbourne, he could well have become known as the Don Bradman of the sport. Even now his record of three Brownlow and three Sandover Medals will take some beating!

Stories such as his—and a wanting to get as much out of myself as possible—made me determined to play on at least for another year in 1995.

Much has changed about the game in my time. It's far more athletic. Players must not only be able to think quickly, anticipate and read the play—they must have the leg speed to get to the fall of the ball and the stamina to make contest after contest.

Having turned 30, I made one final big effort to get myself fit enough to play at the highest level. Some asked me why. It's simple. I still love the challenge. I reckon you're a long time retired.

DERMOTT BRERETON
Hawthorn's five-times premiership forward
April, 1995

CONTENTS

ACKNOWLEDGEMENTS

Col Hutchinson, statistician for the Australian Football League, has been most generous in providing data, research and answering queries. His knowledge of the game, tireless enthusiasm and records are unparalleled.

My thanks are also due to Geoff Poulter for providing the three Best-Ever post-war teams from WA, SA and Tasmania, freelance photographer Ken Rainsbury, the AFL, WAFL, the SANFL, ACTAFL, TFL Statewide League, QAFL and the NSWAFL, as well as the many footballers, young and old, who contributed.

Others who have assisted in various ways and whose help was very much appreciated include: Graham Arthur; Ed Biggs; Jenny Brown; Tom Carey; Santo Caruso; Ian Collins, Peter Cummiskey; Jenny Cooke; Col Dawson, Father Gerard Dowling; Alan East; Doug Gaff; Tony Greenberg; Peter Haby; Greg Hobbs; Paul Hogan; Ashley Hornsey; John Hook; Geoff Iles; KR Photographics; Ken Levy; Ian McDonald; Bill Meaklim; Melbourne Sports Books; Justion McCulloch; John O'Connell; Jack Pollard; Geoff Poulter; Peter Isaacson Publications; Michael Roberts; Neil Roberts; Norm Sowden; Graham Smith; The Age; The Herald & Weekly Times.

My thanks also to Dermott Brereton for his foreword, the great Jack Dyer for his encouragement, Russell Holmesby for the picture of St Kilda's '66 premiership side and to photographers Stephen Laffer, Sergio Dionisio and Phillip Stubbs for providing some of the new shots for the updated edition.

INTRODUCTION

Australian football followers have been a neglected race. Unlike their cricketing cousins who can indulge in a remarkable array of literature, guaranteed to see them through from season to season, footy fans have—until recently—had little reference reading.

A trip to the local library confirmed the disparity. Almost three shelves were devoted to cricket and another to golf and tennis. The football section was restricted to a mere three or four titles.

We believe the publication of this book will help satisfy the multitudes of followers who, with their enthusiasm and support, have helped to make the game so remarkable.

In addition to 500,000 regular players, millions more are attracted to the game, especially now that we have a national competition which has evened the imbalance between States, and fuelled interstate rivalries. The Australian Football League has drawn thousands of new devotees. The 1991 Grand Final was not just a showdown between club teams Hawthorn and the West Coast Eagles, but a winner-take-all battle between the best footballers from Victoria and Western Australia.

Earlier that season, WA thrashed Victoria with one of the most devastating wet-weather footballing displays ever seen. For years, the skills of Victorian and Tasmanian players in wet weather had been unsurpassed. Western Australia's victory was further proof of the game's advancement at all levels and in all States, a fact confirmed by the West Coast Eagles' historic premiership in 1992.

This book, updated to the start of the 1995 AFL season and incorporating many new features, celebrates more than 100 years of League football and salutes its champions from all over Australia who have helped to make it great.

While the emphasis is on VFL and AFL competition since 1897, many of the best players and teams from WA, SA, Tasmania, NSW, Queensland and the Northern Territory are all analysed. Players whose names appear in italics all have their own entries. The player-by-player biographies include those who have:
- Played or coached in 200 VFL/AFL games;
- Won a Brownlow Medal;
- Become illustrious League goalkickers;
- Played in four or more premierships.

No-one will dispute the right of legendary and influential players such as Darrel Baldock, Graham 'Polly' Farmer or Barry Cable to be included in this glittering Hall of Fame. Great administrators such as Sir Kenneth Luke have also made enormous contributions.

Club-by-club histories and many statistical tables, never before published, add dimension, while those with a taste for trivia will find an array of fascinating and off-beat facts.

Some of the game tallies differ from traditional sources; for example, Carlton's John Nicholls played 328, not 331 *club* games. Previous League records had included interstate games played concurrently with club fixtures in a player's overall games record. Peter Hudson, with 129 games, not 130, is similarly affected.

The statistics are complete to the start of the 1995 AFL season. A player's year of birth and, if applicable, his death year are included, where known.

The author welcomes additional information and comments. Please write to Ken Piesse, c/o Football Australia magazine, 2a Expo Crt., Mt Waverley, Vic., 3149.

KEN PIESSE

ABLETT, Gary (1961–   )

The youngest and most gifted of five footballing brothers, spring-heeled Gary Ablett made history with his spectacular goalkicking feats in the 1989 final series.

In four matches, he kicked 27 goals, including nine in the Grand Final, and won the Norm Smith Medal. Geelong legend *Bob Davis* called him the greatest player in club history, a champion with the ability to explode like a hand grenade.

Yet, just over a year later, he quit football, saying the pressures were too great. A born-again Christian, he concentrated on his studies to be a Baptist church pastor.

His comeback to football, half-way through the '91 season, triggered an incredible amount of publicity. But he failed to recapture his magical, breathtaking best. Some claimed his prime motivation in returning was to protect a $50,000 retirement fund nest-egg, part of a five-year contract signed in 1988.

Earning $105,000 a year, Ablett was one of football's best-paid players, but he needed to play at least 90 matches in five seasons to be eligible for the bonus. Until his temporary retirement, he had played only 61, but fulfilled the contractual criteria on the eve of the 1992 finals.

Thanks to Ablett's thrill-a-minute form, Geelong powered into the 1989 Grand Final, its first play-off for more than 20 years. Widely known as 'Gazza the Great', 'God' or 'Superman', Ablett kicked 87 goals—including 14.3 against Richmond in round nine.

Possessing superb aerial gifts, blistering speed off-the-mark and the ability to kick 60 metres with either foot, Ablett became the AFL's most exciting player.

He lifted his career average to more than four goals a match and to the start of the 1995 season, had kicked 839 goals in 209 matches, including, in 1993, a career-best 14.8 against eventual premiers Essendon at the MCG.

He'd also represented Victoria 10 times, for 39 goals, including eight on debut against Western Australia in Perth, in 1984.

Ablett's exceptional effort in the 1989 Grand Final was hailed as one of the most memorable of all time.

He had 12 kicks, eight marks and kicked 9.1, against Hawthorn's State defender *Chris Langford.*

On accepting his best-afield award, he said: 'I would like to congratulate Hawthorn and thank God for making it all possible.'

He played in another Grand Final in 1992 and again won All Australian status.

Ablett had originally played at Hawthorn, if only reluctantly, from the age of 17. After six maiden games with Hawthorn's senior side in 1982—he spent the rest of the season in the reserves—he was suspended for failing to train and spent the 1983 season with Ovens and Murray club Myrtleford.

He changed his ways on his return to the big-time with Geelong in 1984, and revelled under the coaching of *Tom Hafey*, who regarded him as one of the most talented players he'd ever handled.

Hawthorn received $60,000 in staggered payments for his release. Later, when

Gary Ablett's 'Mark of the Century' against Collingwood, at the MCG in 1994.

1

Ablett looked like he'd leave Geelong, the Hawks offered him $525,000 for five years.

Geelong's sports psychologist Dr Colin Davey says Ablett was so outstanding because of his 'fast twitch' muscles which enabled him to jump enormous heights from virtually a standing start and be quicker than almost any other player when sprinting for the ball.

Geelong coach *Malcolm Blight* extended Ablett's fabulous career by playing him as a virtual fulltime full-forward and reducing the amount of running he'd been doing. He trained him lightly and, in 1993–94, was rewarded as Ablett played some of the most consistent football of his career, kicking 124 and 129 goals in successive seasons and winning back-to-back John Coleman Medals.

In 1993, Ablett reached 100 goals for the season in 14 matches, just one short of Bob Pratt's 1934 record. Early in 1994, a skyscraping mark on the shoulders of Collingwood's Gary Pert was acclaimed as 'The Mark of the Century'.

Team-mate Garry Hocking said Ablett flew so high, 'he was rubbing shoulders with the air hostesses'.

'Gary is the one player capable of doing the unnatural,' said Blight. 'Quite out of the blue he'd come up with something special, usually at the right time. That's the quality that sets him apart from the rest of football humanity.'

Geoff Ablett and Kevin Ablett (36 games) also were prominent at League level. Len and Graham Ablett also played, while their uncle, Alf, represented Richmond from 1939–43. Gary's sister, Fay, married Hawthorn legend *Michael Tuck*.

ABLETT, Geoff (1955–)

The eldest of three brothers to play League football, Geoff Ablett's blistering pace helped Hawthorn to win dual premierships in 1976 and 1978.

A long-kicking wingman from Drouin, Ablett played more than 200 games in a decade with Hawthorn from 1973–82. He later also played briefly at Richmond and St Kilda, and finished with 229 matches. He represented Victoria in 1980.

ABORIGINAL PLAYERS

In 1932, when Fitzroy's roving legend *Haydn Bunton* noticed Aboriginal recruit Doug Nicholls changing by himself in a corner of the club dressing-rooms, he approached Nicholls and asked why he wasn't changing with the rest of the players. 'We-e-ll, you know how it is,' said Nicholls, then in his first year with the club.

Bunton immediately moved all his gear to the same corner and made a point of changing with Nicholls whenever possible.

Racial prejudice was a major barrier against Aboriginals successfully competing in Australian football, especially in Melbourne. Before Fitzroy gave Nicholls the opportunity, he was rejected by Carlton (they said he smelled) and forced to play for five years with Northcote.

Nicholls, from the Cumeroogunga Aboriginal settlement in NSW, was the first to break into League ranks. In 1935, aged 29, he became the first Aboriginal player to win Victorian selection.

He played until 1937 when he concen-

Aboriginal star Nicky Winmar leaps high in a Western Australia-Victoria State-of-Origin match.

2

trated fulltime on his church commitments.

As Pastor Douglas Nicholls, noted for his work with Aboriginal people, he was knighted in 1972. Later, he was appointed Governor of South Australia.

The very first Aboriginal to play League football was Joe Johnson, who figured in two Fitzroy premierships in his first two League seasons in 1904–05. His great grandson Trent Cummings also plays at Fitzroy. Team-mate Chris Johnson is also understood to be a descendant.

Among leading Aboriginals who played at League level in the post-war era are: Eddie Jackson (Melbourne), Norm McDonald (Essendon), *'Polly' Farmer* (Geelong), Syd Jackson (Carlton), Brian Peake (Geelong), Maurice Rioli (Richmond), Phil Egan (Richmond), Jim and Phil Krakouer (North Melbourne), Nicky Winmar (St Kilda), Chris Lewis (Eagles), Michael Long, *Gavin Wanganeen* and Derek Kickett (Essendon).

McDonald, the 'Black Bullet', who grew up in an orphanage in Geelong, was the first Aboriginal to play in a post-war Grand Final, in 1947. He played in six in a row, including Essendon's back-to-back premierships in 1949–50. He also won the Bendigo 1000 and ran second to Essendon team-mate Lance Mann in the 1952 Stawell Gift. Current Bomber Wanganeen, from the Northern Territory, now wears McDonald's famous No. 4 guernsey.

Most of the greatest Aboriginal players emerged from Western Australia, including Peake, who also captained Geelong; and Winmar, whose spring-heeled leaping and pinpoint passing to Sydney full forward *Tony Lockett* bordered on the miraculous.

Carlton's Syd Jackson was recruited via the Roelands Mission in Bunbury and East Perth. He was first signed by the Blues in 1965 but his clearance was stopped by the WAFL and Jackson had to stand out of football in 1968. He spent the season as *Ron Barassi's* runner.

Jackson made his debut the following year, aged 25. He played in three Grand Finals with Carlton, for two wins and a loss. A clever half-forward, whose temper

The durable and highly-decorated Stephen Michael representing WA against Victoria.

sometimes bubbled over, he also played in two grand finals with South Bunbury and three with East Perth.

In the 1970 second semi-final against Collingwood, he was reported for striking Lee Adamson. Pleading guilty, he claimed the provocation of racist remarks. Jackson was reprimanded, and was outstanding in the next two games, including the Grand Final.

Years later, he admitted that Adamson had not taunted him and his tribunal defence had been concocted by Carlton officials to help him beat the charge and play in the premiership side.

'Lee stepped on my hand when I was picking up the ball after being awarded a free kick,' Jackson said. 'It may or may not have been accidental. I said, "You bastard", and gave him a back-hander. The umpire ran in and said I was reported.'

Jackson's temper also landed him in trouble off the football field. At various times, he was charged with assault, resisting arrest and vagrancy. Once, Sir Douglas Nicholls acted as a character witness. 'I wish we had a few more people of the calibre of Sydney Jackson in this state,' he told the City Court in Melbourne. Jackson

LEADING ABORIGINAL PLAYERS IN LEAGUE FOOTBALL

	MATCHES
Chris Mainwaring (West Coast Eagles) 1987–94	161*
Michael McLean (Footscray) 1983–89 (Brisbane) 1991–94	157*
Nicky Winmar (St Kilda) 1987–94	153*
Chris Lewis (West Coast Eagles) 1987–94	153*
Phil Krakouer (North Melbourne) 1982–89 (Footscray) 1991	148
Jim Krakouer (North Melbourne) 1982–89 (Footscray) 1990–91	147
Syd Jackson (Carlton) 1969–76	130
Norm McDonald (Essendon) 1947–53	128
Phil Egan (Richmond) 1982–90 (Melbourne) 1991	125
Maurice Rioli (Richmond) 1982–87	118
Barry Cable (North Melbourne) 1970, 1974–77	116
Michael Long (Essendon) 1989–93	102*
Andy Lovell (Melbourne) 1988–94	101*
Graham 'Polly' Farmer (Geelong) 1962–67	101

* current player.

retired in 1976 and later became the executive director of the National Aboriginal Sports Foundation.

Rioli, a Melville Islander and one of 10 children, was the first Aboriginal to win the Norm Smith Medal for being best afield for Richmond in its losing 1982 Grand Final side. The game was umpired by another Aboriginal, Glenn James, who officiated at five day and night Grand Finals in an auspicious career.

Winmar, one of the most gifted of all the Aboriginal players, played his 150th game with St Kilda in 1994, despite an early-season walk-out in 1993 and a 10-match suspension in 1990. An All Australian player in 1991, he also won St Kilda's goalkicking in 1988 and was best and fairest in 1989. A born again Christian, a clause in his contract allowed him to leave St Kilda at any time to pursue a ministry in the Baptist Church.

Decorated WA ruckman Bill Dempsey played 343 games with West Perth from 1960–76 after being recruited from St Mary's, Darwin. In June, 1976, he was awarded the MBE for his services to Australian football. Another follower, Stephen Michael played more than 200 games in a row, winning two Sandover Medals in 1980–81.

The Krakouer brothers were dynamic influences at North Melbourne in the 1980s, after joining from Mt Barker via

Claremont, where they'd become the first brothers to both kick 50 goals in a senior season (1981). A third Krakouer brother, Andrew, also played League football, with North Melbourne, in 1989–90.

Keith and Phil Narkle were captain and vice-captain of Swan Districts in 1983. Phil Narkle also represented St Kilda and the Eagles, while Keith is one of the Swan's greatest players.

Another fine Aboriginal player was Irwin Lewis, who played in Claremont's 1964 premiership. His son, Chris, played in the 1992–94 Eagles premiership double, as did Peter Matera, a part-Aboriginal and one of the quickest players in the AFL. Matera won the Norm Smith Medal for being best afield in the 1992 Grand Final.

Other Aboriginal stars to represent the Eagles at premiership level include Craig Turley and Chris Mainwaring.

South Australia's most famous Aboriginal players include David Kintilla (South Adelaide), Roger Rigney (Sturt), Sonny Morey (Central Districts), Michael Graham (Sturt) and Gilbert McAdam (Central Districts).

Kintilla, a full-blood Aboriginal from the Bathurst Island Tiwi tribe, played 113 games at South Adelaide. Rigney played 212 games including the team's five consecutive premierships from 1966–70. Morey was also a 200-game player.

McAdam won SA's Magarey Medal in

1989 after being runner-up in 1988. He was one of the outstanding recruits to AFL football in 1991. He and his brother, Greg, who also represented St Kilda, come from Alice Springs.

'I have always felt footy is part of me,' said McAdam in an interview in 1991. 'I think it must be in our Aboriginal blood.'

Wanganeen, one of the most talented current Aboriginals, won All Australian status in 1992 and the Brownlow Medal in 1993.

ACKERLY, David (1960–)

Ackerly twice won South Melbourne's best and fairest award, in 1980 and 1982. Recruited from local team South Districts, he played 191 League games from 1979–89 with South and North Melbourne, mainly as a back-pocket player, before crossing to VFA club Williamstown. He also represented Victoria.

ADAMS, Frank (1935–)

A member of six Melbourne premiership teams, red-headed Frank 'Bluey' Adams was a livewire winger and an Australian professional sprint champion.

His spectacular head-on collision with Collingwood's Des Healey in the 1955 Grand Final remains one of the most famous incidents in League annals. Both were knocked out.*

Adams played 164 games, and appeared in 11 consecutive final series.

His happiest finals memories revolve around the 1956 Grand Final when he outplayed celebrated Thorold Merrett and the 1964 play-off when he was best afield, again against Collingwood.

Raised in Queensland, Adams was recruited to Melbourne via Prahran. He'd originally wanted to go to St. Kilda, thinking he had a better chance of playing regular senior football at the Junction. 'My address was 40 Chapel St., Windsor—Melbourne's territory—but it was put down as 40 Chapel St., St. Kilda,' he said. 'Unbeknown to me, Melbourne knew what

* see 'FIVE FAMOUS INCIDENTS'

the zoning situation was. I was residentially bound to Melbourne, so went down there at the start of '53 looking for a clearance. They wanted me to play in a couple of practice games and I got a game with the thirds which surprised me. At the end of the year, I was in the seniors. That was an even bigger surprise.

'If I had got that clearance, I would have played League footy for St. Kilda and not participated in any finals at all.'

ADELAIDE

The 15th club to join the Australian Football League was the Adelaide Crows, a composite South Australian team, in 1991. This meant the AFL was now made up of clubs in five States.

Despite the success of the Eagles, Adelaide authorities had been worried a SA team in the AFL would severely weaken their local competition. In May, 1990, the AFL was told SA would not consider being involved nationally until at least 1993.

Then the SANFL's most powerful club, Port Adelaide, began shock negotiations with the AFL. This triggered an almighty controversy and SA re-thought its anti-AFL stance. By September, 1990, negotiations had been completed allowing the entry of the Crows. The 14 AFL clubs shared a $2.8 million 'sweetener' ($200,000 each) as part of the arrangement.

The Crows immediately proved to be competitive, especially at their home ground at Football Park, Westlakes. They finished mid-list in their initial season in 1991 and enjoyed victories against powerful teams Hawthorn, Essendon and Melbourne. In 1992, they won five of their last six games to finish ninth and, in 1993, they made the finals for the first time, full forward Tony Modra kicking 129 goals.

Playing in navy-blue guernseys with red and gold hoops, the Crows attracted huge crowds from their stunning opening night on 22 March, when 44,902 fans saw Hawthorn—winner of two of the three previous premierships—thrashed in a boilover.

The club's inaugural coach was Graham Cornes. The equally legendary Neil Kerley

ADELAIDE: THE STATISTICS

JOINED LEAGUE: 1991
HOME VENUE: Football Park (1991–)
OFFICIAL COLOURS: Navy blue guernsey, with red and gold hoops
HOME VENUE DIMENSIONS: 180 metres × 145 metres
HOME VENUE RECORD ATTENDANCE: Football Park: 48,522, Adelaide v Collingwood, R.22, 1993.
RECORD ATTENDANCE IN ANY MATCH: 76,380 Adelaide v Essendon, MCG, PF, 1993
TOTAL FINALS MATCHES: 3 (1 win, 2 losses)
MOST FINALS: Greg Anderson 3, Mark Bickley 3, David Brown 3, Andrew Jarman 3, Scott Lee 3, Matthew Liptak 3, Chris McDermott 3, Tony McGuinness 3, Tony Modra 3, David Pittman 3, Shaun Rehn 3, Mark Ricciuto 3, Nigel Smart 3, Simon Tregenza 3, Mark Viska 3, Wayne Weidemann 3, Stuart Wigney 3.
YOUNGEST PLAYER: Ben Hart, 17 years 257 days (1991)
OLDEST PLAYER: Mark Mickan, 32 years 112 days (1993)
HIGHEST SCORE: 28.12 (180) v North Melbourne, R.24, 1991 (Football Park)
LOWEST SCORE: 4.7 (31) v St Kilda, R.7, 1991 (Moorabbin)
GREATEST WINNING MARGIN: 110 points v Richmond, R.16, 1993 (Football Park)
GREATEST LOSING MARGIN: 131 points v St Kilda, R.7, 1991 (Moorabbin)
LONGEST WINNING SEQUENCE: 5 (1992)
LONGEST LOSING SEQUENCE: 4 (1992)
MOST SEASONS AS COACH: Graham Cornes 4 (1991–94)
MOST SEASONS AS CAPTAIN: Chris McDermott 4 (1991–94)
MOST GOALS IN A MATCH: Tony Modra, 13, v Richmond, Football Park (R.16, 1993)
Tony Modra, 13, v Carlton, Football Park (R.1, 1994)
Scott Hodges, 11, v Geelong, Football Park (R.23, 1992)
LEADING LEAGUE GOALSCORERS: Tony Modra 129 (1993)

MOST GAMES		MOST GOALS	
Chris McDermott	88*	Tony Modra	220*
Tony McGuinness	84*	Scott Hodges	95
Scott Lee	78*	Matthew Liptak	93*
Rod Maynard	76*	Rod Jameson	78*
Nigel Smart	76*	Tony McGuinness	69*

* current player.

was manager of the club. Chris McDermott was the team's first skipper.

Tony McGuinness (Footscray), Bruce Lindner (Geelong) and Danny Hughes (Melbourne) all returned from stints in Victoria to play with the Crows. The club also retained many talented young SA players who had been signed to Melbourne teams, including speedster Simon Tregenza and utility Rod Jameson. Matthew Robran returned from Hawthorn.

In 1992, red-headed teenager Ben Hart was the rookie of the year and the youngest member, at 18, of the All Australian team. He was an All Australian again in 1993.

ALVES, Stan (1946–)

Initially told he was too small for League football, Alves became one of Melbourne's post-war greats. He played 236 games in 12 years from 1965–76. He never appeared in even one final in Demon colours.

A good leap—as a schoolboy he cleared 193 cm (6 ft 4 in.) in a high jump at a combined competition—Alves had pace, durability and the grace of a gazelle. His dashes around the wing at the Melbourne Cricket Ground made him one of the most popular post-war Demons.

Stan Alves: an inspirational captain at Melbourne from 1973–76.

First selected for Victoria in 1968, he was Melbourne's vice-captain in 1969 and captained the club from 1973–76 before his controversial transfer to North Melbourne, where he hoped to fulfil his dream of playing in a final.

Alves was to play in three consecutive Grand Finals for North Melbourne, two in 1977 and another in 1978, for one win, a tie and one loss. He retired after a third year at North, having played a total of 268 games. He coached St Kilda from 1994.

ALVIN, Tom (1962–)

Noted for wearing his long, dark hair in a ponytail, Tom Alvin was one of Carlton's most consistent running players throughout the 1980s, after being recruited from Bairnsdale, Footscray's zone.

Appearing in three Grand Finals, including the 1987 premiership, Alvin played 218 games in 11 years with the Blues before coaching VFA club Sandringham.

ARMSTRONG, Barry (1950–)

To earn a trial at a League club these days, it's by invitation only. But Carlton's premiership ruck-rover Barry Armstrong asked to have a run. 'I wrote a letter to Carlton asking them could I train and they said yes.'

Armstrong played 204 games from 1969–81 and appeared in Carlton's 1972 and 1979 premiership teams. He would have also played in the 1973 Grand Final but for a bout of appendicitis. In one game that season, he had 34 kicks, and was renowned as one of Carlton's most important on-ball players in a dominant era when the Blues figured in nine final series in his 12 years at the club.

ARTHUR, Graham (1936–)

Hawthorn's first premiership captain, 'Mort' Arthur was a prominent player from his very first season. The teenage debutant from Sandhurst won Hawthorn's 1955 best and fairest award, the first of his three club champion trophies.

One of the greatest half-forwards of his era, Arthur was an inspirational leader, becoming the club's longest serving captain from 1960–68. He also coached the Hawks in 1964–65. For years after his playing days ended, he remained closely involved with the club as Hawthorn's marketing manager.

The 180 cm Arthur played 237 games and kicked 202 goals in his 14 year career from 1955–68. His father, Alan, played League football at Essendon.

ASHMAN, Rod (1954–)

A skilled, courageous and team-oriented rover, Ashman failed by just one vote to win the 1981 Brownlow Medal, despite being the favourite. Ashman's disappointment was short-lived as Carlton not only took the 1981 premiership, but won again the following year. Ashman was first rover in both victories. He enjoyed an illustrious 236 game career from 1973–86, and represented Victoria four times.

ATTENDANCES

The record VFL attendance of 121,696 for the 1970 Collingwood–Carlton Grand Final is unlikely to be surpassed, unless the super stadiums, once planned for Melbourne, become a reality.

When the Melbourne Cricket Club's Great Southern Stand was completed in March, 1992, seating capacity was lifted to close to 100,000. Only a minimum of standing room now remains.

The capacity at Waverley Park is less than 80,000, though a crowd of more than 90,000 attended a mid-year holiday match between Collingwood and Hawthorn in 1981.

League attendances have lifted steadily in the last 20 years from 2.8 million in 1970 to 3.5 million in 1990. The inclusion of the Adelaide Crows in the national competition in 1991 provided a further increase. In 1992, four million attended for the first time.

The record attendance for a 'first round' match is 99,346 for the Melbourne-Collingwood round 10 game at the MCG in 1958. In April, 1995, a crowd of 94,825

LARGEST ATTENDANCE AT EACH VENUE

VENUE	HOME/AWAY MATCHES	FINALS
Football Park	48,522 Adel. v Coll., R.22, 1993	—
Carrara	22,684 Bris. v Fitz., R.4, 1987	—
Brisbane C.G.	20,351 Ess. v Hawth., R.14, 1981	—
Princes Park	47,514 Carlt. v Geel., R.6, 1963	62,986 Carlt. v South., GF, 1945
Victoria Park	47,224 Coll. v South., R.2, 1948	16,000 Carlt. v Ess., F, 1904
East Melb C.G.	35,791 Ess. v Coll., R.15, 1909	20,181 Melb. v Fitz., GF, 1900
Windy Hill	43,487 Ess. v Coll., R.3, 1966	22,300 Rich. v South., F, 1924
Brunswick St. Oval	34,765 Fitz. v Ess., R.14, 1923	16,600 Coll. v Carlt., SF, 1903
Western Oval	42,354 Foots. v Coll., R.12, 1955	—
Yarraville	14,000 Foots. v Rich., R.12, 1942	—
Corio Oval	26,025 Geel. v Coll., R.15, 1925	5,000* Geel. v Ess., F, 1897
Kardinia Park	49,107 Geel. v Carlt., R.19, 1952	—
Glenferrie Oval	36,000 Hawth. v Carlt., R.1, 1965	—
MCG	99,346 Melb. v Coll., R.10, 1958	121,696 Carlt. v Coll., GF, 1970
Motordome	13,000 Melb. v Rich., R.2, 1932	—
Arden St. Oval	35,116 North. v Carlt., R.19, 1949	—
Coburg	21,626 North. v Coll., R.10, 1965	—
Punt Rd. Oval	46,000 Rich. v Carlt., R.9, 1949	—
Junction Oval	46,973 St K. v Carlt., R.5, 1950	43,000 Fitz. v Rich., GF, 1944
Prahran	10,000 St K. v Rich., R.3, 1943	—
Moorabbin	51,370 St K. v Coll., R.1, 1965	—
Lake Oval	40,441 South. v St K., R.18, 1923	—
SCG	39,763 Sydn. v Hawth., R.19, 1986	—
Subiaco	42,209 West C. v St K., R.15, 1991	44,142 Hawth. v West C., QF, 1991
WACA	32,119 West C. v Geel., R.22, 1993	34,317 West C. v Melb., PF, 1994
AFL Park, Waverley	92,935 Coll. v Hawth., R.11, 1981	75,526 Coll. v Geel., PF, 1980
Brisbane E.G.	28,000 Ess. v Geel., R.8, 1952	—
North Hobart	18,387 Fitz. v Melb., R.8, 1952	—
Albury	15,000 South. v North., R.8, 1952	—
Euroa	7,500 Carlt. v Hawth., R.8, 1952	—
Yallourn	3,500 St K. v Foots., R.8, 1952	—

* approximate only.

Grand Final day, MCG, 1956. Collingwood's Neil Mann and Melbourne's Ian Ridley temporarily join the crowd which had spilled onto the boundary edge.

attended the Essendon–Collingwood match on Anzac Day.

Before the VFL introduced pre-booked seating in 1957, spectators often spilled onto the playing perimeters on Grand Final day.

In the 1937 premiership play-off between Geelong and Collingwood, hundreds of the 88,540 present viewed the game from the boundary line. In 1938, when Collingwood played Carlton, 96,834 attended, and many again took vantage spots in front of the fence.

Grand Finals in 1950, '52 and '56 were also witnessed by huge crowds which spilt onto the boundary edge. In 1956, when Collingwood played Melbourne in front of 115,802, the fans not only encroached onto the arena but some clambered onto the Southern Stand roof.

AUSTEN, Col (1920–   )

Awarded a Brownlow Medal retrospectively (in 1989) for his outstanding 1949 season, the Hawthorn half-back had initially lost the Medal on a countback to South Melbourne's *Ron Clegg*. This was

despite the fact that he polled votes in more matches and played fewer games.

'From the start I thought the system was completely incorrect,' said Austen. 'He scored more No. 1 votes and I have no animosity towards him. He was entitled to a Medal that year and so was I.'

Recruited from Kew, and originally appearing with Carlton reserves, Austen played 85 games from 1940–49. He was best and fairest in 1949. He also twice represented Victoria.

After the much-publicised sacking of club coach Alec Albiston, vice-captain Austen became involved in the off-field political brawl, and transferred to Richmond where he played 52 games in three seasons, and once finished fourth in the Brownlow voting.

In 1953, he won the Gardiner Medal, the reserves best and fairest, which, with his belated Brownlow, completed a rare 'double'.

AUSTIN, Rod (1953–   )

One of only three players to keep the great *Peter Hudson* goal-less (on 2 July, 1977), the dependable Carlton backman known as 'Curly' played 220 games from 1972–85. He was a member of the 1979 premiership team and missed two others (1981–82) with injury.

Recruited from St Dominics, he coached Fitzroy for two years in 1989–90 before taking a job with the Australian Football League. From 1994, he coached Victoria.

AUSTRALIAN CAPITAL TERRITORY

Canberra's association with Australian football dates back to the birth of *Thomas Wentworth Wills*, one of the founders of the game, on 11 January 1837 at the family's property at the head of the Molonglo River, 50 kilometres from Canberra. Wills spent some of his boyhood years in the district before being taken to England by his father in 1851 to be educated at the famous Rugby school.

On return, he was one of the founders and first captain of the Melbourne football club.

The first recorded match in Canberra was in 1911 at the newly established Royal Military College at Duntroon. Several of the cadets were from southern States and wanted to play Australian football.

Games were played regularly up until the start of World War One and resumed again in 1920 when Wesley College opposed the RMC. In 1922 a Canberra team played Western Australia and in 1924 the Federal Territory Australian Rules Football League formed, with four pioneering clubs: Acton, Canberra, Federals and Duntroon. Builder Jerry Dillon was its first president.

The influx of public servants to Canberra from Victoria, South Australia and Tasmania in the early 1920s provided players and supporters for the game to gain momentum.

Queensland played the first interstate game in Canberra in 1927, the year the Canberra league adopted a new title of the Canberra Australian National Football League.

John Mulrooney, born in St Kilda in 1894, was one of Canberra's foremost administrators. He became league presi-

dent in 1928. In that year Australian rules was introduced into Canberra schools. The following year Mulrooney became the league's delegate to the ANFC.

Mulrooney was the Canberra league's president for 17 years until 1946 (with the exception of 1935, when he was secretary). The Mulrooney Medal, awarded to the best and fairest player in the Canberra league, was instituted in 1936.

One of the biggest early names in Canberra football was much-travelled Tom Fitzmaurice, who helped Manuka to the premiership in his first season in 1938 by kicking 10 goals in the grand final against Queanbeyan. He joined Manuka, after playing 188 games with Essendon, Geelong and North Melbourne from 1918–35.

In 1939, two-thirds of Canberra's population—about 4000 fans—attended the Carlton-Hawthorn match at Manuka Oval.

Former Footscray premiership player Roger Duffy exerted enormous influence on the development of ACT football after the war. He played successfully in the VFL for seven seasons before joining Eastlake in 1959 and leading the club to an unprecedented five premierships in a row from 1962–66. Eastlake also won the flag in 1960, when the team was unbeaten for the season. Duffy played in every Canberra representative side from 1959–64, being captain in 1960–61.

Another former League star who coached with success was Geelong and South Melbourne goalkicker Lindsay White who lifted Queanbeyan-Acton to the 1956 premiership, kicking his 100th goal for the season in the grand final.

One of Eastlake's star juniors of the early 1960s was *Alex Jesaulenko*, whose brilliant career at Carlton made him the Territory's most celebrated export. In 1980, the Alex Jesaulenko trophy was awarded for the first time to the best player afield in the ACT grand final.

Eastlake, Manuka and Ainslie have won almost 50 senior premierships between them.

Hobart-born Neil Conlan coached Manuka to five premierships in six years from 1967 to 1972. In the only year he

MOST VFL/AFL GAMES BY PLAYERS FROM CANBERRA
(100 matches or more)

PLAYER	MATCHES	TEAMS	SPAN	RECRUITED FROM
Alex Jesaulenko	283	Carlton/St Kilda	1967–81	Eastlake
Michael Conlan	210	Fitzroy	1977–89	Manuka
Brett Allison	137*	North Melbourne	1987–94	Belconnen

* current player.

missed, 1970, Manuka was runner-up. His son, *Michael Conlan*, played more than 200 games at Fitzroy.

Other clubs, such as Royal Military College, have also had their stars. RMC's John Moody, the father of Australian Test cricketer Tom Moody, is one of the few to win two Mulrooney Medals, in 1957–58, playing as a ruckman.

Another dual Medallist was Ainslie centreman Barry Browning, who won in 1955–56 and earned an invitation to train with Geelong. Perth-born Roy Watterston won successive Medals in 1953–54 with Queanbeyan-Acton.

One of the competition's most popular stars was St Kilda powerhouse *Kevin 'Cowboy' Neale*, who in 1978 became Ainslie coach and captain of the ACT representative side.

In 1980, he led the ACT to a historic victory against the VFL, the locals winning 13.17 (95) to 11.16 (82).

Neale created a Canberra record in 1980 when he kicked 149 goals. He also booted 139 in 1981 and 125 in 1982. He led Ainslie into five consecutive grand finals

before shifting to Adelaide. The first winner of the annual Kevin Neale goal-kicking trophy, in 1984, was Ainslie's Paul Angelis, who booted 139 goals. He is the only man to kick 100 goals in three separate senior competitions: NSW, Canberra and the VFA. During the '84 season, he kicked an Australian record 29.9 from 40 shots against West Canberra, the most shots by a player in any senior game. Ainslie scored a massive 53.15 (333) to West Canberra's 6.5. (41).

In 1990, senior AFL football was played in Canberra for the first time when Hawthorn met the Sydney Swans at Bruce Stadium in a Foster's Cup match. Five players tied for first for the Mulrooney Medal. Three of them polled identical votes and were awarded Medals: Michael Swan (Manuka Weston), Tony Wynd and Steve Cornish (Queanbeyan). Beaten on a countback were Andrew Mills (Manuka Weston) and Glen Dickerson (Eastlake). The five-way tie is believed to be an Australian first in a major league. It was Wynd's third medal in succession and fourth overall.

AUSTRALIAN FOOTBALL LEAGUE

See: 'VICTORIA'.

AYLETT, Allen (1936–)

A talented all-round sportsman, who later combined his dentistry practice with his role as VFL president, 'Mick' Aylett's zeal and enthusiasm made him the most influential football administrator in the game.

Aylett's feats on and off the field for North Melbourne are outstanding. He

A five-way tie for Canberra's Mulrooney Medal in 1990: from left Michael Swan, Glen Dickerson, Tony Wynd, Andrew Mills and Steve Cornish.

Allen Aylett (left) with Ron Barassi after North Melbourne's historic 1975 premiership.

a game, North Melbourne's winning chances would suffer. He generally avoided the heaviest knocks but, in May, 1963, was knocked out against Hawthorn. He was unconscious for eight hours. Doctors told him he could have been killed if the impact on his head had been any lower.

He won North Melbourne's best and fairest award three years in a row from 1958–60 and captained the club from 1961–64. In that year he broke his arm in two places against Melbourne and retired, aged 30. For many years he took out special insurance on his hands so, in case of injury, his income from dentistry would not be affected.

Aylett replaced Tony Trainor as club president in 1971 and helped master-mind the recruiting of 'super coach' *Ron Barassi* in 1973. When North won its first premiership two years later, Aylett's administrative genius was a major factor.

In February, 1977, his abilities were recognised at VFL level when, after an election with Hawthorn's Phil Ryan to decide Sir Maurice Nathan's successor, Aylett became the League's ninth president in 80 years.

He immediately attacked his new job with trail-blazing enthusiasm, purpose and vision. He helped to shift the ailing South Melbourne club to Sydney in the first of the moves which by 1990 had broadened the borders of the VFL competition into almost every State in the country. He was also chiefly responsible for an independently-administered VFL, and showed an uncompromising commitment to the game he'd loved all his life and genuinely wanted to see played all over the world.

Aylett remained VFL president into a ninth year in 1985 when the VFL Commission was implemented. He also served as president of the National Football League for seven years. His contribution to football was recognised with an OBE.

AYRES, Gary (1960–)

The first to win two Norm Smith Medals for being the most outstanding player in a modern-day Grand Final, the powerhouse 187 cm defender played in all

made his debut, aged 17, in the opening match of 1952 when he was still at University High School. He played a club record 225 games and, in 1958, became the first VFL player to win the Tassie Medal for the best player in the centenary Australian carnival in Melbourne.

He never played a reserves or under 19s match. He won a Simpson Medal in 1960 and was All Australian in 1958 and 1961. His personal feats helped to add lustre to North Melbourne's generally mediocre performances of the period. In one game against Collingwood in 1962, he had 41 kicks. Most commentators agreed that he was in the class of *Bob Rose* and *Bobby Skilton* as the game's leading rover.

Aylett's skilful roving helped North into the 1954 final series. Four years later he was in the team which made it through to the 1958 preliminary final, only to be beaten by eventual premiers Collingwood.

His on-field presence made him a 'target' for opposing teams, who believed if they could restrict Aylett's influence on four of Hawthorn's premierships in the 1980s, including the 1986 and 1988 victories when he was named best afield. He played in another, in 1991, and in 1992–93 was Hawthorn's captain, before transferring to Geelong where he became senior coach in 1995.

Recruited from Warragul as a half-forward in 1978, he became renowned for his tough defensive work. His treetrunk legs, robust approach and commitment won him the nickname 'Conan', after the celluloid barbarian.

There have been few better marks for his size in the history of the game.

Champion team-mate *Dermott Brereton* said he'd never seen a more motivated player in important matches: 'You can count on the fingers of one hand the number of times he's been beaten over the years.' Long-time coach *Allan Jeans* said Ayres was 'a good driver in heavy traffic'.

Ayres often answered the challenge of lifting his team with inspirational play when shifted into the centre.

His domination of in-form Carlton winger David Rhys-Jones in the 1986 Grand Final was a catalyst for Hawthorn's victory after it had lost the second semi. Against Melbourne in 1988, he was again best afield, this time playing as a running defender, shadowing Melbourne skipper and first rover Greg Healy.

Ayres suffered a depressed fracture of the cheekbone in the first quarter—after a collision with Demon *Jim Stynes*—but he refused to go off and became the most important player on the ground even though Healy tried to run him around to exploit his apparent lack of pace. After the Hawks had clinched a record 96 point win, coach Alan Joyce paid tribute to his long-maned defender: 'There is no stronger or tougher man in football than Gary Ayres.'

His fourth premiership, in 1989, remains one of the most memorable—and certainly the most emotional. The Hawks finished with 13 fit players, and Ayres' thigh injury forced him from the field late in the third term.

In 1993, he appeared in his 12th final series in a row. Only five players have figured in more finals.

Among his distinctions in 16 seasons include Hawthorn's best and fairest in 1986, the Victorian 'B' team captaincy, five other state appearances and 269 club games. He played in five day and night premierships.

BALDOCK, Darrel (1938–)

No player in history is more revered for his ball-handling abilities than Tasmanian wizard Darrel John Baldock, whose anticipation, baulking and brilliance won him the nickname, 'Mr Magic.'

Captain of St Kilda's only premiership team in 1966, 'Doc' Baldock is a legend in two States as the unsurpassed master of groundplay. Later he returned to coach the Saints and help develop the massively-talented *Tony Lockett*.

Prematurely balding and tubby in appearance, the 177 cm Baldock remained in his home State until he was 23. He captained Tasmania at 21, won All Australian honours in 1961 and also played cricket for the Tasmanian XI.

Baldock joined the Saints in time for the start of the 1962 season. He was the most publicised Tasmanian import since *Laurie Nash*.

He had originally signed 'form fours' with Melbourne (1955) and South Melbourne (1957) before accepting St Kilda's invitation via the club's persuasive Tasmanian-born secretary Ian Drake.

He looked an unlikely hero dressed in his street clothes, but once he donned his famous No. 4 St Kilda guernsey and touched the ball, his magic was immediately evident.

In full flight he was unstoppable. He could control the ball miraculously, even in the muddiest conditions, making his opponents look like novices.

Baldock was one of the few players who was regularly applauded for his feats by opposing supporters.

Best and fairest in his first two seasons and again in 1965—when fellow Tasmanian *Ian Stewart* won the Brownlow Medal—Baldock captained St Kilda in five of his six seasons from 1963–68, helping to lift his side into consecutive Grand Finals in 1965 and 1966. The Saints' exciting one-point win against Collingwood in the '66 play-off ensured his immortality at Moorabbin.

Late in that memorable '66 season, with the club battling to remain in the finals fight, Baldock strained knee ligaments and it was decided to rest him until September. By round 18, though, the Saints were in danger of slipping out of the top four and named their far-from-fit skipper 19th man for the win-at-all-costs match with Hawthorn. With the Hawks clawing to the lead, he came on late in the third quarter, kicked an immediate goal and inspired his team to a crucial 10 point win, which clinched the double chance and a place in the second semi-final. If St Kilda had lost, Richmond, under first-year coach *Tom Hafey*, would have made the play-offs.

Baldock captained Victoria in the absence of injured *Ken Fraser* in the 1966 Australian Championships in Hobart and was captain again in 1967. Overall, he represented Victoria 10 times, winning his second All Australian blazer in 1966.

Born in Devonport on 29 September, 1938, Baldock's earliest coach was East Devonport full-back and skipper, Ted Viney. He represented the Tasmanian schoolboys in 1952, captained the team in 1953 and debuted, aged 16, in East Devonport's senior XVIII in the opening game of 1955.

Best afield in his first three games, Baldock was named in the North West Football Union's combined team and a year later, aged 17, represented Tasman-

Darrel Baldock: three years as St Kilda coach after more than 400 games in two States.

14

ia's senior team. Baldock won Easts' best and fairest in his first three senior years and, from 1959–61, coached Latrobe. He was Tasmania's captain in the 1961 Australian championships in Brisbane before joining the Saints.

Despite conceding height to most of his opponents, he cemented St Kilda's centre half-forward post. Coach *Allan Jeans* called him the most creative player he'd seen.

'St Kilda never lost when he (Baldock) played well at centre half-forward. He is one of the greatest, yet he wasn't fast. He had tremendous powers of anticipation and recovery,' said Jeans.

'Many times he played his game with injuries. We were warned not to play him in a very important game against Hawthorn at Moorabbin in 1966. He had knee trouble.

'So we named him as a reserve. If we had lost we would have missed the four. Baldock went onto the field during the game and helped win it for us. The win put us in second place and we went on to win the premiership.'

Runner-up in the 1963 Brownlow Medal, Baldock was equal fourth in 1966 and second in 1968.

On returning to Tasmania and Latrobe, Baldock helped the club win four premierships in a row, a North West record. He won his third Wander Medal for best and fairest in 1969. He represented the NWFU 20 times, was captain in 1960–61, vice-captain in 1969 and captain-coach from 1970–73. He was forced to retire from football and relinquish his captain-coach role at New Norfolk after just four games, since his duties as the Minister for Housing and Social Welfare took precedence.

He played 418 senior games in his illustrious career, including 71 with East Devonport, 127 with St Kilda, 184 at Latrobe and four at New Norfolk—not to mention all his State and representative games.

St Kilda tried to lure him back many times as coach. In 1987, the club finally succeeded when Baldock took the helm for three seasons. He suffered a partial stroke late in the '87 season but remained as coach in 1988–89 before returning to his

beloved farming property at Lower Barrington, near Tasmania's north-west coast.

BARASSI, Ron (1936–   )

Footballing immortal Ronald Dale Barassi overcame adversity to become one of the game's most inspirational champions. His record of six premierships as a player and four as a coach is unsurpassed.

His transfer late in his player career from Melbourne to Carlton created one of the game's mightiest sensations. Some thought his famous No. 31 guernsey was emblazoned to his body.

He was a magnificent ruck-rover who would often drive himself beyond his body's endurance. Barassi's never-say-die spirit and obsession with winning are legend.

He was born in hard times in the mid-1930s at a mining settlement at Guildford, near Castlemaine. Barassi's father, Ron snr, was also a player of note. After 53 games in four years with the Demons, including a telling contribution in the 1940 semi-final, Barassi snr was killed in action at Tobruk. Young Ron was just five.

When Barassi was 15 his mother remarried and went to live in Tasmania. Barassi remained in Melbourne. He lived with legendary Melbourne player *Norm Smith* and his family. Smith, who'd just become Melbourne coach, had been a great friend of Barassi's father. He realised young Ron's potential—and hunger to succeed. Smith was a strict disciplinarian. The two had many blow-ups but the man became a second father to the boy.

In 1953, at the age of 16, he was blooded in the seniors for six games. Wearing his father's No. 31 guernsey, Barassi played in the first of seven consecutive Grand Finals in 1954. He added an eighth in 1964. He and winger *Frank 'Bluey' Adams* were among the first players to appear in six premiership teams.

'Barassi was very focused,' said his premiership team-mate Geoff Tunbridge. 'He won stacks of games for us by taking the impossible mark, kicking the goals at the right time when the pressure was really on and giving us that edge.'

Barassi showed outstanding leadership abilities from his first years and refused to be bowed by injuries, even when doctors found that the sockets of all his joints were enlarged. He suffered frequent dislocations. Heavy, jarring knocks were agonising for him and his mentor Smith wondered if his outstanding career prospects would be fulfilled.

Barassi learnt to endure the pain and forced his dislocated joints back into place without aid. Calcifications of the joints complicated his agony, but somehow his headlining progress was unimpeded.

In 1956, he polled 13 votes to finish equal fourth in the Brownlow, eight votes behind the winner, Footscray's *Peter Box*. It was to be his best finish, as umpires didn't appreciate his volatile temperament. He was once suspended for a match after being found guilty of a charge of abusive language against field umpire Bob Nunn.

In 1963 he missed the finals, after a striking charge against Richmond's *Roger Dean* was upheld. 'It was the biggest court case of '63,' said Keith Dunstan in *The Sun*. Melbourne believed Dean had 'acted' to win a free kick, but the suspension remained. The tribunal refused to view videotape of the incident, which proved Barassi's innocence.

Barassi won two best and fairests at Melbourne, in 1961 and 1964, his final year—but many believe 1957 was his greatest season, when he was first appointed deputy captain to *John Beckwith*.

His efforts in the '57 preliminary and Grand Finals were extraordinary. Richmond legend *Jack Dyer* described how, in the play-off: 'Barassi played that last quarter like a man possessed and at long last the Demons clicked and raced home to a great win. Many rated that effort for sheer courage and determination as the finest individual game in the history of the finals . . . pound for pound, inch for inch, he's probably the greatest player the game has produced.'

But Barassi could also be beaten, as occurred in the boilover 1958 Grand Final when he was effectively shadowed by Collingwood's Barry 'Hooker' Harrison.

He won a premiership in his first year as captain in 1960 and another in his last, 1964—the famous game when Redlegs defender Neil Crompton kicked the winning goal after following his opponent upfield.

He appeared to have a Midas touch. In 1961 he won his third All Australian guernsey and was appointed team captain, the highlight of a representative record which included 18 State games.

His leadership abilities had attracted the interest of several clubs, notably Richmond and Carlton, but the Tigers lost enthusiasm. Carlton persisted, though, and after the club slumped to its lowest-ever finish, 10th, under ex-player *Ken Hands*, the old committee was sacked. The new regime immediately offered Barassi a small fortune: $20,000 for three years.

Smith conceded the offer was 'too good to refuse', but desperately tried to keep him at Melbourne. He even offered to stand down as coach. The Melbourne committee would not hear of this. After much acrimony and faction-fighting, Barassi was released.

Hundreds of youngsters who worshipped Barassi threw away their No. 31 guernseys that day. Letters condemning him flooded into newspaper offices. His switch went against the very loyalty he'd preached.

'I'm aiming to mould the perfect team,' he said on his appointment. 'No one has achieved this yet, but if you aim high enough, I think you have a better chance of success.' The Blues finished sixth in 1965, made the preliminary final in 1966, won the flag in 1968 and repeated their success in 1970.

Injuries had reduced Barassi's on-field effectiveness, but he still played 50 games with the Blues—his last in the seventh round of 1969.

The following year he pulled off his greatest achievement, Carlton's miraculous comeback which clinched the 1970 Grand Final against Collingwood, after the club trailed by 44 points at half-time.*

Carlton great *John Nicholls* said Barassi's natural instincts made him a formidable

* see 'GREAT GRAND FINALS'

16

coach. 'Over the years he learnt the importance of flexibility; of how players have to be able to play in as many positions as possible. He introduced smothering and tackling and a lot more skill work.'

After a brief stint in the VFA with Port Melbourne, under ex-Blue Ian Collins, Barassi was enticed to lowly North Melbourne, which in 1972 had finished last, winning just one game. Bringing *Norm Smith* with him as his right-hand man—before Smith's resignation through ill-health—Barassi lifted North immediately. The Roos finished sixth, just two points out of the finals in 1973, made the Grand Final in 1974 and won their first-ever flag in 1975.

Barassi's emotional speech after the losing '74 Grand Final was regarded as one of his best—and catalyst for the history-making year of '75.

Addressing the players, wives and girlfriends at the team's dinner at the Southern Cross, he lashed the players and accused them of being unprofessional.

'I'm not proud of you today,' he said. 'I'm afraid some players did not show enough desire to win . . . Today we tasted the ultimate in defeat in the ultimate match and I hope it stays with you until next year.

North won the '75 Grand Final by almost 10 goals and won again in 1977. It was Barassi's fourth flag as coach.

In 1981, he returned to Melbourne as the faithful had always predicted, but was not a success. The Demons lacked enough good players to rise above mediocrity. Barassi won just one game in his first year and six in his last, 1985.

After 253 games as a player and 458 as a coach, 'Barass' severed his active association with football before returning for one last time, to bail out ailing Sydney, after it had sacked Gary Buckenara early in the 1993 season.

His coaching was always dramatic and totally committed. He studied replays and analysed the game for hours. He wasn't always orthodox—or popular.

At North Melbourne he caused a ruckus when he dragged *Malcolm Blight* from the ground after Blight had kicked a magnificent left foot goal from the boundary line.

Barassi said Blight should have followed the team plan and centred the ball. To prove his point he asked Blight to repeat his efforts at training. After eight of Blight's first 10 shots sailed through, Barassi conceded he was wrong!

At Carlton he barred his players from having sex on the Friday night before a game. He claimed it was the equivalent of running eight to 12 kilometres and would remove a player's competitive edge.

One of Barassi's best players, the legendary *Alex Jesaulenko*, didn't agree. Jezza said that sex relaxed him and was an essential part of his big game preparation!

The wife of a well-known Carlton player was so annoyed by Barassi's policy that on the Saturday morning of a Grand Final, she served her husband breakfast in bed completely naked, a rose between her teeth. 'He made his way to the car as red as a beetroot,' said his wife. 'So weak that he could hardly carry his Gladstone bag. He played like a dog.'

While Barassi's much-publicised return to Melbourne proved unsuccessful, it satisfied his own desires.

'I always thought I'd come back,' he said, 'but as the years wore on I was getting less and less hopeful of this occurring. So when it did happen I suppose you could call it the makings of a dream.

'I certainly don't regret coming back. At the time of leaving North I could have gone elsewhere to teams with a greater chance of success . . . My roots were here and my sentimental heart was here.'

BARKER, Trevor (1956–)

A spectacular aerialist who served St Kilda proudly—and sometimes without pay—in his 231-game career from 1975–89, Barker was cruelly denied the opportunity of playing in a final. The Saints' best finishes in his years at the club were in 1975 and '78 when St Kilda finished sixth.

Captain from 1983–86, he became the darling of the Moorabbin crowds with his blond locks and virtuoso leaping. He twice won St Kilda's best and fairest award—in 1976 and 1981. He was a regular Victorian representative.

A run of injuries resulted in him missing more than four full seasons of football. For years he had to play with a screw implanted in his knee to help hold his knee-cap together. 'Everytime I go through an airport, the metal detector goes off and I have to say I haven't got a gun,' he'd joke.

Recruited from Cheltenham where he'd captained the club's under 18 premiership team, he made League football ranks while still at high school.

Trevor Barker: more than 200 games without playing in a final.

He had a lucrative mid-career opportunity to leave St Kilda and play under the legendary *Ron Barassi* at Melbourne. He remained loyal, despite the chance to more than double his income. In 1981 he donated a car he'd won for being best and fairest a second time back to the club. In 1984, when the cash-embarrassed Saints appointed a receiver after a succession of disastrous trading years, he waived his claim for a full settlement of a $17,500 debt, and agreed to the club's offer of 22.5 cents in the dollar.

Coaching for the first time in 1992, he piloted VFA club Sandringham to the premiership and won again in 1994, before rejoining St Kilda in 1995, as assistant coach.

BARTLETT, Kevin (1947–)

Few have achieved more in football than the wispy-haired Bartlett who remains Richmond's finest rover and one of the club's legendary performers.

The first man to amass 400 VFL games, he played in five Richmond premierships and seven Grand Finals, winning five best and fairests as well as heading the goal-kicking on four occasions.

In all, he played 440 senior matches, spanning 19 seasons from 1965–83. The breakdown is: club 403 (including 27 finals); State matches 20; night 12; national club championships five.

His tally of 778 goals is the best by a non-specialist full forward and included 21 goals in the memorable 1980 final series (six, eight and seven), a feat bettered by only two men, Geelong's *Gary Ablett* with 27 in 1989 and Collingwood's *Ron Todd* with 23 in 1939.

His speed and durability allowed him to avoid major injuries—despite his small stature. Just 175 cm and 71 kg, he missed fewer than 20 games in almost two decades. Between round 11, 1966 and round 13, 1972, he played 150 games in a row. From round two in 1975 to round 13, 1981, he managed a further 173 in succession.

He played in a record number of 199 matches on the famed Melbourne Cricket Ground.

Bartlett's kickwinning ability was extraordinary. Seven times he gathered more than 500 kicks in a season (an average of more than 25 a game) and twice was above 600. In 1973, he totalled 633 kicks and the following season, 605. In those years Richmond won back-to-back premierships.

He was so good at getting rid of the ball just as he was about to be tackled that umpires were forced to pay him a string of free kicks. Opposing coaches eventually complained and forced a rule amendment. But it mattered little. Bartlett adapted and remained an elite player, continuing in League ranks until he was 36.

'I always knew I would hate the day when I decided to retire as I loved the

The elusive Kevin Bartlett was nicknamed 'Hungry' because of his liking for kicking goals.

fastest players in the game and, in his third season, was best and fairest as well as a member of Richmond's '67 premiership team. In 1967 he also won the Portland Gift.

He represented Victoria 18 times and was State captain in 1980. He also led Richmond in 1979.

In the 1980 Grand Final, playing at half-forward, he booted seven goals to win the Norm Smith Medal for best afield.

His services to football were recognised in 1981 when he was awarded the Order of Australia.

Tiger fans hoped that one day he'd return and he did from 1988. He lifted Richmond to 10th in his first season after the club had been wooden-spooners for the first time in almost 30 years in 1987.

When the side failed to improve, he was replaced for the start of the 1992 season by renowned *Allan Jeans*, the former St Kilda and Hawthorn premiership coach.

BAYES, Mark (1967–   )

One of the finest kicks in the game in the 1990s, 185 cm Mark Bayes played his 200th game early in the 1995 season.

Recruited from Noble Park, the same southern club as *Darren Millane*, the *Morwood* brothers, Darren Bennett and *Steven Icke*, Bayes was used as an offensive, goalkicking forward early in his career before being shifted into defence where he won state honours.

BEAMES, Percy (1911–   )

The intervention of World War Two stopped Percy Beames from becoming an even bigger name in Victorian sport. He captained Victoria at cricket and had a highest score of 226 not out to his credit. He also made 989 District runs in a season. His peers considered him one of the game's most attractive players. Former Australian player Jack Hill said Beames would have played Test cricket but for the eight year gap between internationals from 1938–46.

A fearless footballer who roved in Mel-

game so much,' he said. 'And I always planned to play for as long as I could. You are a long time retired so I wasn't going to get out too early.'

In 1965, in the third-round game against St Kilda, he made his senior debut, as 19th man.

From his early days, he didn't smoke or drink—and still doesn't. He played the guitar in his spare time and was renowned for his good humour, his encyclopaedic sporting knowledge and his love of life.

He quickly became known as one of the

bourne's consecutive premierships from 1939–41, Beames was the first Redleg to amass 200 games. He played 213 from 1931–44 and also represented Victoria 11 times. He was captain-coach in his final three years, from 1942–44.

After retiring, he worked for *The Age* for 30 years as a cricket and football writer, covering 25 series including three tours to England, two to South Africa and one to West Indies.

He is the only man to have captained Victoria at football and cricket.

BECKWITH, John (1932–)

Captain of two of Melbourne's five premiership teams from 1955–60 and one of post-war football's finest back pocket players, Beckwith is best known for his skill in being able to clear the ball out of immediate danger, with long punt kicks, which invariably made it to, or over, the boundary line, without being considered 'deliberate' or subject to a free kick.

Recruited from federal league club Black Rock in 1951, Beckwith had 10 years and 176 games at Melbourne before coaching Colac.

He succeeded *Norm Smith* as Melbourne's senior coach from 1968–70.

BEDFORD, Peter (1948–)

One of the elite band to represent his State at football and cricket, the gifted South Melbourne centreman/rover won the 1970 Brownlow Medal by four votes from Footscray's *Gary Dempsey*.

Playing initially at Port Melbourne, a VFA power, 'Wheels' Bedford was a key member of Port's 1966 premiership team and played in the 'bloodbath' grand final of 1967.

He transferred to League ranks in 1968 for the first of his 192 League games in an 11 year VFL career which ended at Carlton.

A skilled, exciting player, who was a great opportunist, Bedford suffered from playing with a lowly club. He appeared in only one final series, in his Brownlow year.

Capable of matchwinning bursts, he

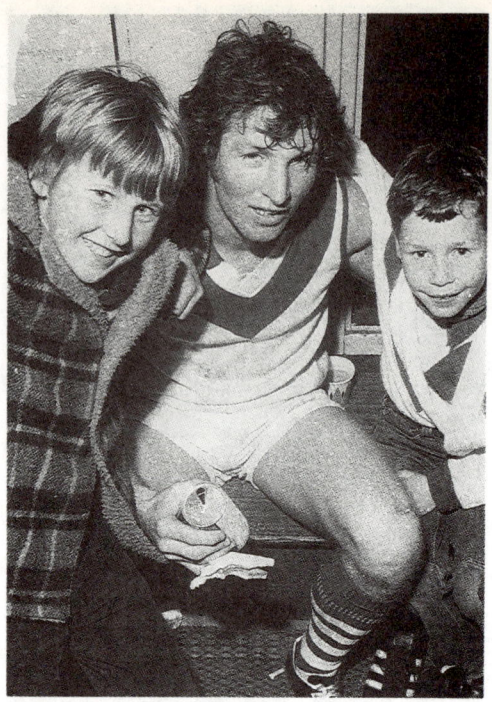

Peter Bedford with some young Swans fans after a game in 1973.

won South's best and fairest award five times and was skipper from 1973–76. He also led the club goalkicking three years in a row. In all, he kicked 331 VFL goals.

After an unsuccessful period at Carlton where he was often injured, Bedford returned to Port Melbourne briefly, the club where his father, Bill, had also played.

Bedford played 13 State games from 1969–75. He also represented the VFA at the 1966 carnival.

BELCHER, Vic

Captain-coach of South Melbourne from 1914–16, Belcher lifted South into the 1914 Grand Final in his first year, only to see his side kick 4.15 (39) to lose to Carlton 6.9 (45). He played 226 games with South from 1907–20, playing in South's 1909 and 1918 Grand Finals. He captained the club in 1913 and his farewell season, 1920. He represented Victoria twice.

BENNETT, George

Recruited from Camberwell and renowned for his brilliant defensive marking, he played 194 games with Hawthorn and Footscray from 1930–44. He had seven seasons and 92 games at Hawthorn and seven seasons and 102 games at Footscray. He won Footscray's best and fairest in 1935.

BENTLEY, Percy (1906–82)

Captain and the first ruckman in Richmond's 1932–34 premiership teams, Bentley played 263 games with the Tigers from 1925–40. He was captain-coach of the club in his final seven seasons. Tough and talented, he proudly captained Victoria against South Australia in 1933.

Born in Castlemaine, he joined Richmond from Burnley.

In lifting the Tigers to the centenary premiership in 1934, he cemented his standing as one of Richmond's finest coaches.

After asking, unsuccessfully, for a 10 shilling a week increase from seven pounds to seven pounds, 10 shillings in 1941, Bentley quit the club. *Jack Dyer* took over as playing coach. Bentley went to Carlton. He coached the Blues from 1941–55.

In all he coached 414 games in 20 consecutive years for 253 wins, 156 losses and five draws. Carlton won two premierships, in 1945 and 1947, under his firm guidance.

Bentley encouraged the introduction of country zoning and the building of the new League playing headquarters at Waverley.

BEVERIDGE, Jack (1907–86)

One of the most celebrated members of Collingwood's four consecutive premiership sides from 1927–30, Beveridge played 148 games from 1926–34. He appeared as a centreman in five straight Grand Finals, having some titanic battles with Melbourne great *Ivor Warne-Smith*. He was runner-up in the 1933 Copeland Trophy.

BEWS, Andrew (1964–)

A hard-hitting back pocket and on-baller renowned for his strength, Bews had 207 games with Geelong from 1982–93 before switching to Brisbane for his final seasons.

Originally from North Geelong, he was an All Australian player in 1987, captained the Cats in 1990–91 and played 12 times for Victoria.

BIRT, John (1937–)

A superb rover, originally from Ballarat, the 173 cm Birt played 196 games with Essendon from 1957–67. He won the best and fairest three times, in 1961, 1965 and 1967, when he was fourth in the Brownlow. He played in four Grand Finals including the 1962 and 1965 premierships. He also represented Victoria 11 times in five of his last eight VFL seasons.

He left the Bombers, aged 30, at the end of 1967 to captain-coach West Torrens for three seasons.

BISSET, George (1943–)

One of the most popular small men to play League football, Bisset played 11 of his 13 League seasons with Footscray before crossing to Collingwood for his final two years, under the 10-year rule in 1973.

As a rookie, Bisset sometimes rode a horse to training. Recruited from Braybrook, 'Wee Georgie' was just 164 cm and lacked natural pace but became a frontliner, winning Footscray's best and fairest award in 1969. He headed the goalkicking three times and was equal first on two other occasions. He was runner-up in the 1969 Brownlow Medal, his first season of two in which he represented Victoria.

Footscray people believe only a report—against Carlton in the 14th round—cost him the Medal that year. He'd been one of the best afield but was automatically passed over for votes. Later he was cleared of the striking charge—and lost the Medal by one, to Fitzroy's *Kevin Murray*.

Known as the 'Court Jester' of football, he played 207 League games from 1963–74 including 166 at Footscray.

BLIGHT, Malcolm (1950—   )

A football genius who played more than 300 games in almost two decades at Woodville and North Melbourne, the 182 cm Blight is—with *John Platten*—the only man to win a Brownlow (AFL) and a Magarey Medal (SANFL).

Later, a highly-successful and innovative coach at Geelong, the acrobatic Blight also captained both Victoria and South Australia and led the competition goalkicking in both states.

Named an All Australian in 1972, he also won the Magarey Medal. In 1974 he joined North Melbourne for the first of his nine VFL seasons.

He was struck down by a bout of glandular fever in his first season but became a frontline member of North's first two premierships in 1975 and 1977, played 196 games in nine seasons, was North's best and fairest and the Brownlow Medallist in 1978, and led the goalkicking four times including his superb final year in 1982 when he kicked a record-equalling 103 goals.

Malcolm Blight and his wife, Patsy, after he won the 1978 Brownlow Medal.

Blight is well remembered for kicking a 70-metre torpedo goal after the siren at Princes Park in 1976 to give North Melbourne a single kick victory over Carlton. He booted four goals in that memorable last quarter, including three in time-on.

Hawthorn legend *Leigh Matthews* regarded him as the greatest, most magical player of his era. 'He always seemed capable of doing just about anything: take the big mark, kick the long goal and kick the "impossible" one with his left foot.'

His highest tally with North was a record 11.6 against Footscray in 1981.

He played seven games with Victoria, being captain in 1979 and 1981.

Returning to Adelaide for the 1983 season as Woodville's captain-coach, he won the best and fairest and was leading goalkicker.

In his final year of football in Adelaide, he kicked 126 goals and captained South Australia, at the age of 35. In one match he kicked 14 goals straight and was again named an All Australian.

In 1989 the Malcolm Blight Cup was inaugurated for South Australia and Victoria's annual battles for supremacy in State-of-Origin football.

Blight was the last footballer at VFL level to mix playing and coaching duties, in 1981, when he lost 10 of his 16 games before resigning. He coached Woodville for five years before returning to Melbourne. In 1989, he became Geelong's coach and led the Cats into three losing Grand Finals in six years, including the 1989 classic against Hawthorn.

Always innovative and adventurous, Blight tried to keep as much fun in football as possible, his teams being renowned for the same flowing, attractive style he'd shown as a player.

'He was a coach in the Geelong tradition and liked his players to experiment,' said Geelong historian Col Hutchinson. 'He had team guidelines but he didn't overburden the players with details.'

During the 1994 final series, senior pair *Gary Ablett* and Stephen O'Reilly faced fitness tests. Instead of insisting on the normal, hard-competitive contests, Blight had them complete kick to kick, catching the ball with plastic rubbish bins!

Before announcing his resignation, after the 1994 Grand Final, he said, 'It's a pretty elite group of people I'm with now, three who have coached three losing Grand Finals ... and we all know where they finished.'

BOLGER, Martin (1907–91)

A dual premiership defender, Bolger played 185 games with Richmond from 1930–39. He helped to form a famous last line of defence with fellow 'Musketeers' Maurie Sheahan and *Kevin O'Neill*. They became known as 'The Invincibles', being unchanged for seven years including three consecutive Grand Finals from 1932–34.

'Kevin and I would pick up the rucks and rovers and Maurie was at full-back,' Bolger said in an interview in 1973. 'We had a great understanding because we played together for so long.'

BOS, Mark (1960–)

A footballer-farmer who returned home prematurely, the disciplined half-back with his imposing 185 cm physique played 195 games with Geelong from 1979–89. Bos won the Cats' best and fairest in consecutive years in 1987–88. His last game was in the memorable 1989 Grand Final.

BOURKE, Francis (1947–)

A committed and courageous team player whom many referred to as 'St Francis', Bourke played 302 games with Richmond from 1967–81. He figured in five premierships, before lifting the club into the 1982 Grand Final in the first of his two seasons as coach.

The son of Frank Bourke, who represented Richmond after the war before being sidelined by a knee injury, Bourke was a self-made champion. He was admired by his peers for his strength and unselfishness and loved by his coaches for his discipline and example.

So keen was he to play football that he'd nail wooden studs into his school shoes so he could join his mates in games for Nathalia State School. At 14 he was told to stop playing all sport because of a heart abnormality, but this was only a temporary scare.

To help cure a fumbling habit, he'd work before and after training with a team-mate who would belt the ball at him from 10 metres, as hard as he could. It was a routine Bourke insisted on every night at training throughout his 14 year career.

He started as a wingman, and combined with Bill Barrot and *Dick Clay* to form one of post-war football's greatest centrelines. The 185 cm Bourke later became a noted defender.

In 1968, his second full year, he made the first of his 13 State appearances. He was State captain in 1977 against Western Australia and in 1980 against Tasmania. He also captained Richmond in 1976–77, and in 1970 was best and fairest.

Team-mate Tony Jewell said: 'If somebody could give you a choice of how you'd like your son to be, it would be like "Bourkey". I don't know of any other man, apart from Jesus Christ himself—and

Francis Bourke defending for Victoria, ahead of WA's Geoff Blethyn in the early 1970s.

I don't know if he could play football—whom you'd like your son to emulate.'

On retirement in mid-season, 1981, Bourke said: 'I leave the game with an inner self-esteem that is satisfied by the thought that I couldn't have done much more in my efforts to be a League player.'

He is remembered most for his courage. Once he played on in a game at Hawthorn despite a broken bone in his leg.

In his second-last season, in a game against North Melbourne at Arden Street, he was shifted into the forward line after taking several sickening knocks in defence early on. With blood streaming from a cut above his eye, he threw himself into a pack without any regard for personal injury, received a free kick, and booted a 40 metre goal which helped trigger a magnificent victory. 'His eye was a terrible mess,' said team-mate *Kevin Bartlett*. 'It was so badly cut that I can still see the jagged skin around it covered in blood, but it was typical of his courage.' Bourke's son, David, debuted with Richmond in 1995.

BOWYER, Percy (1910–   )

A versatile winger/ruck-rover who played in four Collingwood premierships (1929, 1930, 1935, 1936), Bowyer played 155 games from 1928–38. 'I was fortunate to have got a guernsey in the early years, particularly when they were winning premierships,' he said.

BOX, Peter (1932–   )

An outstanding member of Footscray's only premiership team in 1954, Box played much of his early football at centre half-forward before winning the Brownlow Medal in 1956 as a centreman. He won by six votes, one of the most comfortable margins in post-war count.

Recruited from Cheltenham in the Federal league, he was one of the outstanding rookies of the 1951 season. He played 19 matches before being injured when his motor-cycle collided with a car. He was hospitalised for three months, and more than 50 stitches were inserted in his left leg. He also had four skin grafts.

When he resumed in 1953, his left leg was thinner than his right but he retained his prodigious spring and his strength which made him such a valuable ground player.

He played 107 games and had five matches with Victoria, including four at the 1956 carnival.

BRADLEY, Craig (1963–   )

One of South Australia's finest-ever players and one of the few to play more than 200 games at VFL/AFL level, Craig Bradley won three best and fairests at Carlton after crossing from Port Adelaide, where he also won three.

A speedy centreman/winger with exceptional disposal skills, the 182 cm Bradley played in Carlton's 1987 premiership side. He was an All Australian in 1987, 1993 and 1994.

He was originally tied to Essendon before joining the Blues at the start of the 1986 season along with fellow SA stars Peter Motley and *Stephen Kernahan*.

Craig Bradley (right) joins fellow South Australian Peter Motley for a training run at Carlton, December, 1985.

24

Barry Breen, the first St Kilda player to reach 300 games, watching training with specialist coaches, Jack Clarke (ex-Essendon) and Ross Smith.

A former Australian youth cricket representative, Bradley also played Sheffield Shield cricket with South Australia and Victoria. He continued to play both sports at an elite level into his late-20s.

BREEN, Barry (1949–)

A ragged old punt-kick which bounced through for a point to win St Kilda its one and only premiership in 1965 remains centre half-forward Barry Breen's crowning moment in a 300-game career which stretched from 1965–82.

The teenage forward from Mentone had accepted a hurried handpass from Collingwood's Ted Potter following a ball-up in the time-on period in the last quarter, and scored from 35 metres. The kick broke the deadlock.

Breen later said he had 'blazed away blindly'.

'I remember seeing the ball head towards the goals and bounce in the goal square, but it then changed direction and bounced through the behind post. It didn't really matter as long as it was a score.'

It was Breen's sixth consecutive point of the match. He missed three goals from deliberate shots earlier in the game.

Christened Richard Damien Finbar Breen, he was to play in only one more Grand Final, in 1971, when Hawthorn came from behind to defeat the Saints. But he remained a stalwart throughout the 1970s, being captain in 1979, representing Victoria and figuring in a total of 14 finals.

His loyalty to St Kilda was highlighted in the summer of 1982–83 when it was revealed he was owed $64,448 as the financially-stricken club's longest-serving player. Like other leading players and staff, he accepted only a fraction of the amount owing as the club traded under a scheme-of-arrangement until 1986.

BRERETON, Dermott (1964–)

One of the greatest forwards of the modern age and the highest-profile player since *Ted Whitten*, charismatic Dermott Brereton's feat of playing centre half-forward in seven consecutive Grand Finals and eight in nine years is unsurpassed.

25

Dermott Brereton (left) and Jason Dunstall embrace after Hawthorn's first AFL flag, at Waverley in 1991.

An aggressive matchwinner, known for intimidating both opponents and umpires, Brereton's athleticism, courage, flair and personality make him one of the game's topliners.

His importance was recognised in the late 1980s when he became one of the first Hawthorn players to receive more than $100,000 a year.

Regarded as a god by his loyal Hawthorn fans, he was the envy of opposition coaches for his brilliant, destructive bursts in the games that count most.

Asked, in 1991, to name the game's best player, Essendon's renowned coach *Kevin Sheedy* said: 'Brereton and *(Jason) Dunstall*. They are both great players, they really perform. They play in central forward line spots, are always in front and put their bodies in.'

Before turning 28, Brereton had figured in 12 Grand Finals, for nine wins and three losses, including day premierships in 1983, 1986, 1988–89 and 1991, and night flags in 1985–86, 1988 and 1991.

In the 1985 Grand Final against Essendon he kicked eight goals, the most in a play-off since *Gordon Coventry*'s nine in 1928–a record later equalled by one of his old team-mates, *Gary Ablett*, who kicked nine for Geelong in the 1989 Grand Final.

In that memorable '89 play-off, Brereton's match almost finished before it began. Seconds into the game, he was flattened by a charging Geelong defender, Mark Yeates, and suffered severe internal injuries.*

'The last thing I wanted was for Geelong to see me out of the game,' Brereton recalled. 'I remembered what (ex-team-mate) *Leigh Matthews* had said: "Never show them that you're hurt." In my case it was impossible.

'Georgie Stone, our runner, kept on saying to me: "Come off, come off."

'But I wanted to hang on in there. I desperately wanted recovery time. After the mark and goal, he came out again and said: "Inspirational. Stay on!"'

Brereton's aggressive tactics in the second semi-final a fortnight earlier, when he had downed Essendon pair Darren Williams and *Paul Van der Haar* triggered great controversy. Many said he'd gone outside the laws and was unnecessarily violent. A concussed Van der Haar returned to the ground but hardly knew where he was. Williams announced his retirement.

Recruited from Frankston Rovers, the 186 cm forward was just 15 when he played his maiden games with Hawthorn under 19s.

On his debut for Hawthorn's senior team for the 1982 first semi-final he was 18. He kicked five goals, against North Melbourne.

In 1985, he won Hawthorn's club championship, first represented Victoria and won All Australian status. He also topped Hawthorn's goal kicking.

Until injury forced him out of both 1991 State games, he had represented Victoria in every season from 1985.

* see 'FIVE FAMOUS INCIDENTS'

Accorded more publicity than probably any other player in history—*John Coleman* included—Brereton also became one of the most booked. By 1995, after a mediocre season with Sydney, he'd been reported 16 times, for eight 'guilty' verdicts and 37 weeks suspension. Hawthorn complained that Brereton was a 'marked man' and that umpires paid him undue attention.

Sydney was disappointed that he spent two thirds of the '94 season sidelined courtesy of two seven-week suspensions. Officials did not extend his contract beyond one year, Brereton returning to Melbourne to be drafted by Collingwood.

In *The Hard Way*, Hawthorn historian Harry Gordon described Brereton as football's 'swaggering buccaneer'.

'They called him "The Kid" and he was a cowboy in territory where cowboys don't normally roam. He wore dyed blond hair, an ear stud and, when the fancy took him, bright green and yellow boots; he modelled, drove a Ferrari, marketed bread and had his boisterous aggression celebrated by the Coodabeen Champions in a song called "Dermott Brereton is a Hood".'

In 1992, Brereton became Hawthorn's deputy captain, but missed most of the season with a hip injury, playing his first season's football in 10 years.

BRIGHT, Terry (1958–   )

A nephew of Geelong legend Billy Goggin, who coached him in his formative days at Geelong West, Terry Bright was a skilled and versatile flanker who played 210 games with Geelong from 1976–86.

In 1975, aged 17, Bright was a member of Geelong West's VFA first division premiership team. The 188 cm utility made his debut in the opening round in 1976.

A strong mark and heady ball-winner, he averaged almost 30 goals a year. His best season was in 1980 when he kicked 59 goals to top the goalkicking. In that year the Cats failed by less than a goal to make the Grand Final. Bright also was the leading goal-scorer in 1981 and 1983.

Bright represented Victoria three times and in 1985, his second-last season, captained Geelong in four matches.

BRISBANE

Joining the VFL competition in 1987 (along with the West Coast Eagles), the Bears finished no higher than 10th in their first five years. Like their nearest League neighbour, Sydney, the club struggled in a rugby stronghold and lacked support. Finances at one stage were so precarious that the club's existence was at risk.

Its initial teams were made up mainly of ageing players from the south. The first captain was South Australian Mark Mickan, making his debut in VFL ranks. The first coach was Hawthorn legend *Peter Knights*, who was sensationally sacked halfway through his third term, in 1989. His replacement, Paul Feltham, was dismissed before the start of the 1990 season.

Chunky Brownlow Medallist *Brad Hardie*, recruited from Footscray via WA, became the first Bear to reach 100 games. He topped the goalkicking three years in a row from 1989–91, before switching to Collingwood.

The recruitment of proven coach *Robert Walls* in 1991 was seen as a coup. He did not enjoy immediate success but the Bears began to play with more consistency. The club's reserve grade team made the finals for the first time in three years of competition, and hosted a final at Carrara—the Bears' administration centre and initial home ground, situated on the Gold Coast.

The Bears were football's third privately owned club (after Sydney and the Eagles) and developed Carrara to such an extent that Saturday night football games under lights became popular.

In 1991, four of the club's home games were at the more central Woolloongabba ground in Brisbane, where Test cricket matches are played. Keen to woo support in the State's capital city, the 'Gabba became the club's new base from 1993.

From its earliest games, Brisbane played in gold guernseys with a maroon yoke and a maroon stylised map of Queensland with an extended line depicting 'BB' for Brisbane Bears and featuring a bear head. A new striped uniform in Queensland maroon with gold V and white trim was introduced from 1992.

Brisbane Bear Brad Rowe proudly holds the AFL reserves premiership Cup after the Bears' victory in the 1991 grand final, the last reserves premiership contested.

BRISBANE: THE STATISTICS

FORMED: December, 1986

JOINED LEAGUE: 1987
HOME VENUE: Carrara (1987–92), The 'Gabba (1991, 1993–)
OFFICIAL COLOURS: Maroon guernsey, with gold 'V' and white trim
HOME VENUE DIMENSIONS: 165 metres × 145 metres
HOME VENUE RECORD ATTENDANCE: The 'Gabba: 18,881, Bris. v Coll., R.14, 1994
Carrara: 22,512, Bris. v Fitzroy, R.4, 1987
RECORD ATTENDANCE IN ANY MATCH: 42,759, Adel. v Bris., Football Park, R.6, 1992
YOUNGEST PLAYER: Michael Voss, 17 years 11 days (1992)
OLDEST PLAYER: Roger Merrett, 34 years 131 days (1994)
HIGHEST SCORE: 33.21 (219) v Sydney, R.8, 1993 (The 'Gabba)
LOWEST SCORE: 2.5 (17) v Hawthorn, R.12, 1988 (Princes Park)
GREATEST WINNING MARGIN: 162 points v Sydney, R.8, 1993 (The 'Gabba)
GREATEST LOSING MARGIN: 164 points v Geelong, R.7, 1992 (Carrara)
LONGEST WINNING SEQUENCE: 4 (1988)
LONGEST LOSING SEQUENCE: 12 (1990–91)
MOST SEASONS AS COACH: Robert Walls 4 (1991–94)
MOST SEASONS AS CAPTAIN: Roger Merrett 5 (1990–94)

MOST GAMES		MOST GOALS	
Roger Merrett	128*	Roger Merrett	221*
John Gastev	113*	Brad Hardie	192
Scott McIvor	110*	Warwick Capper	71
Marcus Ashcroft	104*	Cameron O'Brien	65

BRISBANE: THE STATISTICS (cont)

MOST GAMES		MOST GOALS	
Martin Leslie	103*	Marcus Ashcroft	64*
Brad Hardie	101	Laurie Schache	64
David Bain	86	Bernie Harris	58
Mike Richardson	81	Mark Williams	58
Matthew Campbell	79	Scott McIvor	52*
Richard Champion	75*		

* current player.

MOST GOALS IN A MATCH: Brad Hardie 9 v Carlton, R.10, 1989, Princes Park
Jim Edmond 8 v Geelong, R.2, 1987, Kardinia Park
Warwick Capper 8 v Richmond, R.11, 1988, Carrara
Roger Merrett 8 v Geelong, R.19, 1990, Carrara
John Hutton 8 v Geelong, R.7, 1992, Carrara
Rod Owen 8 v Fitzroy, R.18, 1992, Princes Park
John Hutton 8 v Sydney, R.23, 1992, Carrara
RECORD HOME VENUE ATTENDANCE: 22,512 v Fitzroy, R.4, 1987, Carrara.
12,764 v Geelong, R.4, 1991, The 'Gabba
RECORD ATTENDANCE IN ANY MATCH: 42,759 v Adelaide, R.6, 1992, Football Park

BRITTINGHAM, Bill (1923–   )

The VFL's leading goalkicker in 1946 with 66 goals, Brittingham played in three premierships at Essendon and was twice its leading goalkicker—but he is best remembered for the goals he missed, rather than the ones he kicked.

Playing in seven Grand Finals in a row from 1946–51—including two in 1948—he was full forward in four play-offs and full-back in three. His inaccuracy—and the arrival of the great *John Coleman*—forced him to adapt to a new role at the opposite end of the ground in mid-career.

Essendon won three and drew one of the Grand Finals, but if it had kicked straighter, it could easily have won five flags, lifting its post-war teams to rank beside Melbourne in the 1950s and Hawthorn in the 1980s as one of the best combinations of the last 40 years.

Essendon coach *Dick Reynolds* countered criticism of his failure to shift Brittingham once he started to kick inaccurately, saying he didn't want to hurt anyone's feelings. He believed there was no other player capable of winning the ball as often.

After Coleman was recruited, Brittingham was sent back into defence, where he was to stay until the end of the 1952 season when he retired, having played 171 games and kicked 181 goals.

Recruited from Warrnambool in 1943, Brittingham was 184 cm and 82 kg. He was a sticky-fingered mark. Tall, fast and agile, he played with confidence, using all his speed and height to worry opponents.

He was vice-captain in his final year with the Dons and the author of several limited-edition Essendon football books.

BROTHERS, Famous

(1) Victoria

Recruiting restrictions and the implementation of a national draft have seen many current footballing brothers play on opposing sides. Some—like the Worsfold brothers, John (West Coast Eagles) and Peter (Brisbane Bears)—were separated by the very width of Australia.

It's now commonplace for brothers to play against each other, but it was once a rarity. In 1912, Alan Belcher (Essendon) and his brother *Vic* (South Melbourne)

Joe (left) and Jim McShane were two of three brothers to represent Geelong in the VFL. They played from 1897–1901, James becoming the first player to kick 10 or more goals in a match when he booted 11 against St Kilda in 1899.

were the opposing captains in the second semi-final. Previously, the famous McShane brothers opposed each other. But there were few others.

In 1991, West Coast teenager Glen Jakovich jousted with his elder brother Allen (Melbourne), the pair swapping insults in the heat of the moment in Yugoslav! South Australians Darren Jarman (Hawthorn) and Andrew Jarman (Crows) started their AFL careers at opposing clubs and in different States. Their very first day game was at Football Park, Westlakes, where they lined up on each other at the opening bounce.

The record for the most brothers playing League football is five, held by the Rush brothers who were involved in the early days of the VFL, from 1899–1924. The most celebrated of them was Collingwood's Bob Rush, who appeared in the 1902–03 premierships. Brian, Gerald, Kelvin and Leo Rush also played League. Six McShane brothers played for Geelong but only three at VFL level.

The first brothers to figure in a premier-

ship team were the Daltons, Jack and Bill, with Fitzroy in 1898.

The Robertson brothers, Harold and Austin snr, are legendary at South Melbourne. Harold once kicked 14 goals in a game against St Kilda in 1919, while Austin was a star in the 'foreign legion' teams of the early 1930s. His son, Austin jnr, was also a brilliant player, in two States.

The *Coventry* and *Collier* brothers are the game's most revered footballing relations, being among only four sets of brothers to aggregate 200 VFL games each. All four were prominent members of Collingwood's most famous teams of all, the 1927–30 premiership sides.

Collingwood's *Wayne Richardson* (279 games) and *Max Richardson* (245), and Geelong's *Ian Nankervis* (326) and *Bruce Nankervis* (256) also mounted formidable records. Max Richardson ended his career at Fitzroy.

Brothers Frank and Len Murphy were among Collingwood's most prominent between-the-wars players. Frank played in four flags in a row, and Len in three, from 1928–30.

The Reynolds brothers at Essendon were also notables. Tom joined younger brother *Dick* in the winning 1942 Grand Final side.

Alan, Jack and Bob Collins all represented Footscray. Alan won the best and fairest in 1943 and Jack was the club's full forward in its only premiership in 1954. Their father, Jim, played at Essendon. At Fitzroy, Ivan, Bert and Alf Clay all played together, in the 1941 season.

Collingwood's revered Twomey brothers (*Bill*, Pat and Mick) became the first fraternal trio to play in a winning Grand Final side, in 1953. (Three Daniher brothers played in Essendon's 1990 losing Grand Final side.)

Magpies *Lou* and Ron Richards also figured in Collingwood's 1953 flag, along with *Bob* and Bill Rose. Another Rose brother, Kevin, was in Collingwood's 1958 premiership team.

Identical twins *Alistair* and Stewart Lord played in Geelong's 1963 premiership team, while Sted and Phil Hay were in Hawthorn's 1961 flag side. Another defender in that team was Graham Cooper, whose brother, Ian, played in St Kilda's historic 1966 premiership team.

Brian and *Sam Kekovich* also played in premierships at opposing clubs—Brian at Carlton in 1968 and Sam at North Melbourne in 1975.

Essendon was particularly well served by the *Daniher* brothers, *Terry*, Neale,

Geelong's identical twins Stewart (left) and Alistair Lord with a young fan, Darryl Warne.

Anthony and Chris. In 157 Essendon games from 1986–93, at least one Daniher brother played in each match. Terry captained Essendon's back-to-back premiership sides in 1984–85, while Chris was on the interchange bench in the 1993 victory.

Other notable brothers in modern-day Victorian football are: *Neil*, Graeme and Brian *Cordy*; Greg and Paul Dear; *Simon* and *Justin Madden*; *Leigh* and Kelvin *Matthews*; *Tony*, Paul and Shane *Morwood*; *Gerard* and Greg *Healy*; Steve and Garry Hocking; Ray, *Tony* and Neville *Shaw*.

(2) Interstate

Among the most famous Western Australian footballing brothers are:

- Jim, Don and Frank Conway from East Fremantle, who figured in several post-war premierships.
- Don, Pat and Barry Dalton, who played a total of 364 games for Perth from 1956–74. Pat won the 1970 Sandover Medal.
- The Doigs—'Scotty', 'Hookey', Charlie and Cleave—who all played in East Fremantle's 1910 premiership team. Later Edgar, Norman, William, Charlie and George Doig played in the same East Fremantle side in the 1930s.
- George, Tom (307 games), Don and John Grijusich, who all played with South Fremantle.
- Roy and Keith Harper, who played 441 games—Roy 213 with West Perth and Keith 228 with Perth.
- Graham, Laurie and Stephen Heal. Their father, Stan 'Pops' Heal played 180 games at West Perth and nine with Melbourne (in 1941–42, including Melbourne's 1941 premiership).
- Robert, Colin and Neville Hebbard who formed the entire West Perth centreline in 1965. Colin also played 86 games with Essendon.
- Otto, Ernest and 'Duff' Kelly who played in East Fremantle's 1904 premiership team.
- Jim and Phil Krakouer, the sensational Aboriginal brothers from Mt Barker, who starred at Claremont, before crossing to the VFL in 1982. Another brother, Andrew, also played League football.

- Don, Ray, Mick and Tom Marinko, whose father, Don, played 234 games with West Perth between the wars.
- The Tysons (Charles, Edward, George, 'Jock', Sam and 'Wally') who were early-century products of the tough Goldfields competition at Kalgoorlie.

South Australia's most renowned brothers include:

- Michael and Andrew Aish who, like their father, Peter, represented Norwood and South Australia. Michael won the 1981 Magarey Medal.
- Port Adelaide's John and Daryl Cahill, who played 538 games between them. John finished in the first three in the Magarey Medal three times and later coached Collingwood in 1983–84.
- 'Bos' and 'Bunny' Daly. Bunny was one of four Dalys to represent SA and Bos kicked 23 goals in one game for Norwood in 1893.

BROTHERS IN LEAGUE PREMIERSHIP SIDES

J. Dalton (*Fitzroy*) 1898; W. Dalton (*Fitzroy*) 1898–99

J. Grace (*Fitzroy*) 1898–99; M. Grace (*Fitzroy*) 1898–99, (*Carlton*) 1906–07

T. Collins (*Essendon*) 1897; 1901; M. Collins (*Essendon*) 1901

A. Leach (*Collingwood*) 1902–03; F. Leach (*Collingwood*) 1902

E. and G. Lockwood (*Collingwood*) 1902–03

L. Barker (*Fitzroy*) 1904–05; G. Barker (*Fitzroy*) 1905

J. Deas (*Fitzroy*) 1899; R. Deas (*Sth Melbourne*) 1909

F. Hiskins (*Essendon*) 1901; A. Hiskins (*Sth Melbourne*) 1909

V. Belcher (*Sth Melbourne*) 1909–18; A. Belcher (*Essendon*) 1912

R. F. Daykin (*Collingwood*) 1910; P. Daykin (*Carlton*) 1914–15

H. James (*Richmond*) 1920–21; W. James (*Richmond*) 1920

R. Weatherill (*Richmond*) 1920–21; G. Weatherill (*Richmond*) 1920

S. Morris (*Richmond*) 1920; M. Morris (*Richmond*) 1921

C. Pannam jnr (*Collingwood*) 1917–19; A. Pannam (*Collingwood*) 1935–36

S. Coventry (*Collingwood*) 1927–28–29–30; G. Coventry 1927–28–29–30–35

A. and H. Collier (*Collingwood*) 1927–28–29–30–35–36

F. Murphy (*Collingwood*) 1927–28–29–30; L. Murphy (*Collingwood*) 1928–29–30

L. and H. Hardiman (*Geelong*) 1931–37

L. Metherell (*Geelong*) 1931; J. Metherell (*Geelong*) 1937

G. Strang (*Richmond*) 1932–34; D. Strang (*Richmond*) 1932

J. Baggott (*Richmond*) 1932–34; R. Baggott (*Melbourne*) 1939–40–41

E. Cordner (*Melbourne*) 1941; Don Cordner (*Melbourne*) 1941–48; Denis Cordner (*Melbourne*) 1948–55–56

R. Reynolds (*Essendon*) 1942–46–49–50; T. Reynolds (*Essendon*) 1942

H. Lambert (*Essendon*) 1946–49–50; C. Lambert (*Essendon*) 1946–50

M. Twomey (*Collingwood*) 1953–58; W. Twomey (*Collingwood*) 1953; P. Twomey (*Collingwood*) 1953*

R. Rose (*Collingwood*) 1953; W. Rose (*Collingwood*) 1953; K. Rose (*Collingwood*) 1958

L. and R. Richards (*Collingwood*) 1953

S. and P. Hay (*Hawthorn*) 1961

A. and S. Lord (*Geelong*) 1963

G. Cooper (*Hawthorn*) 1961; I. Cooper (*St Kilda*) 1966

B. Kekovich (*Carlton*) 1968; S. Kekovich (*Nth Melbourne*) 1975

L. Matthews (*Hawthorn*) 1971–76–78–83; K. Matthews (*Hawthorn*) 1976

S. Madden (*Essendon*) 1984–85; J. Madden (*Carlton*) 1987

G. Dear (*Hawthorn*) 1986–88–89; P. Dear (*Hawthorn*) 1991

T. Daniher (*Essendon*) 1984–85; C. Daniher (*Essendon*) 1993

* three brothers in the same premiership side (1953) is a VFL record.

- Bob, Bill and Ray Hank, who played 224, 183, 169 games respectively with West Torrens. Bob won two Magarey Medals and nine best and fairest awards.
- Bernie, Tom and Vin Leahy who played for West Adelaide from 1906–09. Bernie was captain of the 1908–09 premiership teams. Tom and Bernie were also Australian handball champions.
- Bob and Peter Oatey, sons of the great player/coach Jack Oatey, who coached 10 premierships. Bob kicked 434 goals in 301 games with Norwood, being captain from 1968–73.
- Peter and Trevor Obst, who played almost 400 games between them at Port Adelaide. Peter also represented Woodville and was runner-up in the Magarey Medal in 1962, an award won by his brother in 1967.
- Glenelg's Fred and Wayne Phillis, who amassed 541 games between them. Fred kicked 100 goals in a season five times.
- Bob and Tom Quinn, whose father 'Cooper' Quinn also played SA league football. Bob, awarded the Military Cross during the Second World War, won two Magarey Medals and had 186 games from 1933–47 while Tom Quinn—who had 59 games with Port—crossed to Geelong where he played 168 games.
- The five brothers Ryan, who played with South Adelaide before and after the First World War. 'Bulla' Ryan was the most famous, playing 146 games.
- Johnny Taylor jnr and his brothers Don and Laurie had more than 500 games between them with West Adelaide and Glenelg. Don and Laurie also played League football briefly in Melbourne during the war.
- The four Williams brothers, Foster, Glynn, Alex and 'Slick' who belonged to one of the most dominant post-war footballing families. 'Fos' represented SA in five carnivals. His sons, *Mark*, Anthony and Stephen, all played league football.

Among Tasmanian football's best-known brothers are:
- Twins Simon and Paul Atkins, from Wynyard, who played AFL in 1992, Simon with Footscray and Paul with Sydney. Simon debuted in 1987. In 1995 he crossed to Fitzroy.
- Lance and Darren Crosswell from Launceston, who were northern Tasmanian champions. Darren's son, *Brent*, was later a champion VFL player with Carlton, North Melbourne and Melbourne. Darren's grandson, Tommy Kavanagh, also played.
- *Laurie* and Bob Nash starred with City-South before transferring to South Melbourne. In 1931, Laurie won the first of two Tasman Shields and Bob topped the NTFA goalkicking with 71. Their father, Bob, captained Collingwood and represented Victoria in the 1908 carnival, while their grandfather, Tom, represented Carlton.
- Graeme and Wayne Fox (New Norfolk) who finished second and third in the 1983 William Leitch Medal.

The Most Brothers to Play League Football

FIVE:

RUSH—Bob, 146 games (Collingwood, 1889–1908); Bryan, 17 (Collingwood, 1913–14); Gerald, 15 (Richmond, 1920); Kelvin, seven (Richmond, 1923–24) and Leo, eight (Melbourne, 1911 and Richmond, 1912).

FOUR:

CORDNER—Don, 166 games (1941–50); Denis, 152 (1943 and 1948–56); Ted 51 (1941–43 and 1946) and John, six (1951). All played with Melbourne.

STRANG—Doug, 64 games (Richmond, 1931–35); Gordon, 116 (Richmond, 1931–36, 1938); Colin, 2 (St Kilda, 1933); Alan, 16 (South Melbourne, 1947–48).

DANIHER—*Terry*, 313 games (South Melbourne, 1976–77 and Essendon, 1978–92); *Neale*, 82 (Essendon, 1979–81, 1985, 1989–90); *Anthony*, 216 (South Melbourne, 1981–86, Essendon, 1987–92); Chris, 40 (Essendon, 1987–92).

HISKINS—Fred, 50 games (Essendon, 1900–02, 1906); 'Paddy' 184 (South Melbourne, 1908–15, 1919–23); Stan, 66 (South Melbourne, 1913–14, 1912–21); Rupert, 74 (Carlton, 1920–24).

ROSE—*Bob*, 152 games (1946–55); Bill, 40 (1950–55); Kevin, 159 (1958–67); Ralph, 23 (1962–63). All played with Collingwood.

ROBINSON—William, 71 games (Essendon, 1901–06); Alex 10 (Essendon, 1904); Fred, 33 (Essendon, 1904–05); Gordon, 1 (St Kilda, 1911).

Twins in League Football

There have been six sets of twins to play League football, the most successful being the Lord twins, who appeared in Geelong's 1963 premiership team.

The footballing twins are:

CLAY—Bert and Ivor (Fitzroy), from Henty (NSW). Bert was 193 cm and Ivor 192 cm. Both played in the ruck, Bert in 157 games from 1940–51, including the 1944 premiership, and Ivor, 31 games from 1941–46. They played 10 matches together with Fitzroy's senior team.

COOK—Fred and Keith (Richmond), from Croydon. They debuted in round one of the 1944 season against Melbourne, 180 cm half-forward Fred playing 81 games from 1944–49 and 182 cm half-back, Keith, 26 games from 1944–46. They played 20 games together for Richmond seniors.

KOL—Michael and Nigel (Geelong), from Lara. Two of the quickest players at Kardinia Park in the early 1980s, both were 183 cm and played on the flanks. Michael had 63 games with Geelong from 1983–89 and Nigel two with the Cats in 1983 and 28 at Melbourne, from 1985–87. They played one day game and two night matches together.

LORD—*Alistair* and Stewart (Geelong), from Cobden. Centreman Alistair, who was slightly bigger and taller at 180 cm and 84.5 kg, played 122 games with the Cats from 1959–66. He won the Brownlow Medal in 1962. Stewart, a half-back flanker, played 74 games from 1960–64. They played 70 games together for Geelong seniors, including the 1963 premiership.

RICHARDSON—Mike and Steve. Both debuted in League ranks in 1983, having been recruited from Swan Districts.

Mike, a good running player and goal-sneak, played 60 games and kicked 117 goals with Collingwood from 1983–86, before joining Essendon for 15 games and finishing his League career at Brisbane from 1987–90 where he played 81 matches, for a total of 156. Steve, slightly taller at 180 cm, played just one match with Essendon before returning to WA.

STIBBARD—Neville and Robert (South Melbourne). From South Melbourne under 19s, 178 cm Neville had 23 games from 1973–75 and 180 cm Robert, 14, from 1972–74. They played eight games together for South Melbourne seniors.

At the start of the 1995 season, Shane Wakelin was joined by his twin brother, Darryl, on St Kilda's senior list.

BROWN, Norm (1943–   )

A steady, big-hearted ruckman, who played 183 games at Fitzroy from 1962–73, the 191 cm Brown had considerable success on transferring to the VFA. He led Port Melbourne to three premierships in five years. He won three best and fairests in consecutive years at Fitzroy from 1965–67 and represented Victoria four years in a row in the mid-1960s.

Recruited from North Heidelberg, Brown progressed from the under 19s into the seniors in the same year. He regularly conceded height to opponents, but compensated with his big leap and his marking ability, earning acclaim as one of the most valiant ruckmen of his time.

BROWNING, Mark (1956–   )

Sydney's substitute captain in its first ever finals series, in 1986, Mark Browning was deputising for the injured *Dennis Carroll*. It had been nine years between finals for the big-kicking left-footer, who had also played in the elimination final in 1977.

Captain of the club in 1984–85, Browning played 252 games from 1975–87 before transferring to Tasmania where he soon lifted Hobart to a premiership. Recruited from Beverley Hills, he was the

Swans' best and fairest in 1983, being most renowned as a centreman/half-back.

BROWNLOW, Charles (1862–1924)

One of the Australian sport's greatest administrators, Brownlow was a player, coach and administrator of note, a visionary and tireless worker whose influence was felt initially in Geelong, his home town, and later around the country.

As Geelong's coach in 1886 he was instrumental in devising a pattern of organised positions, where lighter, less-physical players were able to have an influence by moving up and down the perimeters of the ground. He also asked for his forward-line players to lead, a tactic so successful that the club provided five of the top seven goalkickers in the VFA competition that season and was undefeated in its 27 matches. It was such a dominant season that the game was revolutionised, with teamwork and open play being introduced in place of the milling packs which characterised the game's early history.

Brownlow had a 40-year association with Geelong, including one year when he captained the team to the VFA premiership. He was secretary from 1885–1923, Geelong's VFL delegate for 21 years, VFL vice-president from 1911–16, VFL delegate on the Australasian Football Council from 1911–16 and chairman of the permit and umpires committee from 1911–22.

In 1891, the VFA accepted his proposal that players must take up their allotted positions before matches commenced—rather than all being gathered around the ball—and that the central umpire should start the match by bouncing the ball in the centre of the ground and re-start the match after each goal is scored. These two rules still exist.

Soon after his death, aged 62, in January 1924, the VFL struck a medal to perpetuate his memory, the Charles Brownlow Medal for the fairest and best player of the season.

BROWNLOW MEDAL, The

The Brownlow Medal is the most highly-prized individual award in Austra-

Sir Rohan Delacombe, Governor of Victoria presents Ian Stewart with the 1971 Brownlow Medal, his third in seven years.

lian football, bestowed on the fairest and best player in each League season.

Field umpires are responsible for casting votes after each game. Their impartiality and ability to observe fair and brilliant play make them best qualified to decide the most deserving winner.

Some of the game's greatest players have not won it, including post-war champions such as *Bob Rose*, *John Coleman*, *Ted Whitten*, *Ron Barassi*, *Graham 'Polly' Farmer*, *Darrel Baldock*, *Leigh Matthews*, *Alex Jesaulenko*, *Gary Wilson* and *Barry Cable*.

Since the award's inception, however, in 1924, there had not been an unworthy winner.

Voting was suspended for four years during the war from 1942–45. According to Brownlow Medal historian Peter Blair, the best players of the seasons were: 1942—Ted Cordner (Melbourne), 1943—*Norm Smith* (Melbourne), 1944—*Jack Dyer* (Richmond) and 1945—*Jack Graham* (South Melbourne).

More than one third of the 62 champions to have won the Medal were reported at least once during their careers.

The much-travelled Greg Williams, who joined his third League club in 1992, is the most reported among Brownlow champions. In his first 11 seasons, he was booked 15 times, being found guilty on nine occasions for a total of 21 matches' suspension, a severe reprimand and a $3000 fine.

Hawthorn's *Robert DiPierdomenico*, who shared the award with Williams in 1986, is also among the most reported, having been

LEADING BROWNLOW MEDAL VOTEWINNERS: 1924–94
(100 or more in a career)

NAME	CLUBS AND SEASONS	VOTES
Gary Dempsey#	Footscray 1967–78; North Melbourne 1979–84	218.5
Bob Skilton	South Melbourne 1956–68, 1970–71	180
Leigh Matthews#	Hawthorn 1969–85	173.5
Bill Hutchison	Essendon 1942–57	172
Dick Reynolds	Essendon 1933–51	154
Keith Greig#	North Melbourne 1971–85	144
Ian Stewart	St Kilda 1963–70; Richmond 1971–75	139
Francis Bourke#	Richmond 1967–81	139
Gary Wilson#	Fitzroy 1971–84	138.5
Greg Williams	Geelong 1984–85; Sydney 1986–91; Carlton 1992–94	138*
Kevin Bartlett#	Richmond 1965–83	136.5
Robert Flower#	Melbourne 1973–87	130.5
Norman Ware	Footscray 1932–42, 1944–46	130
Len Thompson#	Collingwood 1965–78; South Melbourne 1979; Fitzroy 1980	127
Simon Madden#	Essendon 1974–92	125
Haydn Bunton	Fitzroy 1931–37, 1942	122
Barry Davis	Essendon 1961–72; North Melbourne 1973–75	121
David Cloke#	Richmond 1974–82, 1990–91; Collingwood 1983–89	121
Ron Clegg	South Melbourne 1945–54, 1956–60	120
Ross Glendinning#	North Melbourne 1978–86; West Coast 1987–88	120
Bernie Quinlan#	Footscray 1969–77; Fitzroy 1978–86	119.5
John Platten	Hawthorn 1986–94	118*
Alex Jesaulenko#	Carlton 1967–79; St Kilda 1980–81	116.5
Herbie Matthews	South Melbourne 1932–45	116
Jack Clarke	Essendon 1951–67	116
Laurie Dwyer	North Melbourne 1956–58, 1960–64, 1966–70	115
Justin Madden	Essendon 1980–82; Carlton 1983–94	115*
Ted Whitten	Footscray 1951–70	112
John Schultz	Footscray 1958–68	111
Jason Dunstall	Hawthorn 1985–94	107*
Greg Wells#	Melbourne 1969–80; Carlton 1980–82	106
Harold Bray#	St Kilda 1941–43, 1945–52	106
Barry Round	Footscray 1969–75; South Melbourne 1976–85	102
Peter Knights#	Hawthorn 1969–85	101
Peter Moore#	Collingwood 1974–82; Melbourne 1983–87	101
John Nicholls	Carlton 1957–74	101
Wilfred Smallhorn	Fitzroy 1930–40	100

* current player.
\# In 1976–77 each field umpire allocated 3-2-1 votes per match. Players' votes have been halved for those seasons to balance aggregates.

booked nine times for five 'guilty' verdicts and 18 weeks suspension.

On-ball players have dominated counting, ruckmen, centremen and ruck-rovers being the most decorated. Only one fullback, South Melbourne's *Fred Goldsmith* (1955) and one full-forward, St Kilda's *Tony Lockett* (1987) have won the Brownlow.

Top teams often supply the most-favoured players. Since the war, however, only five players have won the Medal as well as appearing in a premiership team in the same year: *Bert Deacon* (Carlton, 1947), *Bernie Smith* (Geelong, 1951), *Ian Stewart* (St Kilda, 1966), *Robert DiPierdomenico* (Hawthorn, 1986) and *Gavin Wanganeen* (Essendon, 1993).

Gary Dempsey, *Bob Skilton*, *Kevin Murray* and 'Lethal' *Leigh Matthews*—the only one of the quartet never to win a Medal—have polled the most Brownlow votes.

The youngest winner was 19-year-old *Dinny Ryan*, of Fitzroy, in 1936. *Dick Reynolds* was also 19 in 1934. The oldest winners were 31-year-olds *Kevin Murray* (Fitzroy, 1969) and *Barry Round* (South Melbourne, 1981).

A 3-2-1 voting system has been used since 1931, except in 1976–77 when both field umpires allocated six votes a match.

From 1924–30, only one vote was awarded in each match. The system was changed after Richmond's *Stan Judkins* won the 1930 Medal on a countback from Collingwood's *Harry Collier* and Footscray's *Allan Hopkins*. All had polled four votes. Judkins was awarded the Medal as he'd played fewer games.

From 1981, the countback system was abolished and in the last 10 VFL seasons, there have been three dual winners.

Eight players who had been beaten on a countback in earlier seasons were presented with retrospective Brownlows at a presentation dinner in August 1989.

Until 1991, players who had been reported were automatically ineligible to receive Brownlow votes.

Rules governing the Medals refer only to the home-and-away series where the votes are cast.

In 1994, moves by the AFL's law review panel for suspended players to become eligible to win the medal were rejected after a wave of protest from former winners and fans.

BRUNS, Neville (1958–   )

Involved in the sensational incident with *Leigh Matthews* in mid-June 1985 which resulted in his jaw being broken and the Hawthorn champion being deregistered for four weeks, red-headed Bruns played more than 200 games with Geelong and twice represented Victoria in his 15 year career.

Recruited from Leitchville, he was first chosen for the Cats in the seventh round in 1978. His pace and aggression at the ball helped him to win a place in Geelong's finals team of 1991. At 32, he was the oldest player in the side and continued for a further season in 1992, playing in his team's losing Grand Final side.

BUCKENARA, Gary (1958–   )

Hawthorn's master playmaker from the West figured in four premierships and five Grand Finals in a magnificent 154-game career from 1982–90, before knee injuries forced his premature retirement. After a season as assistant-coach at Fitzroy, he replaced Colin Kinnear as senior coach of the Sydney Swans in 1992.

Originally leased, at $210,000 for three years, from Subiaco, where his long kicking and magnificent marking won him WA State status as a rookie, he's best remembered for kicking the winning goal after the siren in the 1987 preliminary final which lifted Hawthorn into its fifth Grand Final in a row.

With just seconds to go, he was free-kicked and was lining up for a set shot from the 50-metre line when Melbourne recruit *Jim Stynes* ran across his mark, conceding a 15-metre penalty. His cool drop-punt split the big sticks before he was besieged by jubilant Hawthorn players.

Buckenara's starring performances in State-of-Origin matches won him the Western Australian captaincy and All Aus-

Gary Buckenara (left) with Chris Wittman after Hawthorn's 1989 Grand Final victory.

tralian honours in 1983, 1985 and 1986.

His team-mates regarded him as the game's master kick. Full-forward *Jason Dunstall* said Buckenara could pinpoint him from fifty metres. 'The only problem sometimes was hanging onto them. They went that fast, they'd knock the wind out of you,' he said.

Hawks coach *Allan Jeans* liked to play him in the centre where his creativity brought others into play. But his dicky knees often forced him to play a half-forward role where he was only marginally less effective. In the 1989 Grand Final, his four goal, twenty possession contribution was vital in Hawthorn's narrow win.

He'd seen only several minutes action in his first Grand Final, in 1983, when he twisted his knee and was forced to undergo a major operation. He lost so much weight after post-surgery complications that he wondered if he'd ever play again.

But an eight goal contribution in Hawthorn reserves' grand final win in 1985 relaunched his career.

He coached Sydney unsuccessfully in 1992–93.

BUNTON, Haydn (1911–1955)

The 'champion's champion', one of the all-time greats of the game, Bunton was a masterful ball-handler whose skills, judgement and anticipation won him three Brownlow Medals in Melbourne and three Sandover Medals in Perth—all in a remarkable 11-year span between 1931–41.

Born on 15 July, 1911 and raised in Lavington, Bunton's schoolboy sporting exploits around the Riverina were so extraordinary that seven clubs from Victoria pursued him. Geelong offered him a motor car and Fitzroy 100 pounds cash and a regular job.

First attracting the attentions of League scouts as a 14-year-old while representing the combined Albury schoolboys against Richmond Cubs, Bunton later trained with the Tigers. Essendon and Carlton were also in the race for his prized signature.

The very public bartering for his services did not impress the VFL, which had just implemented the Coulter Law aimed at regulating player payments. The chairman of the League's permit committee, Percy Page, withdrew Bunton's permit to play League football in 1930, saying that 'trafficking' and the 'offering of inducements' was against VFL rules.

Bunton was also a cricketer of note and played as a 17-year-old for a combined NSW Country XIII against 'Percy' Chapman's famed 1928–29 touring MCC side. An opening batsman, he'd earned selection by making two centuries in four NSW Country Week games earlier that season. On witnessing one of Bunton's centuries and other promising players from the country, former Australian captain M. A. 'Monty' Noble said he'd seen three possible Test players in action that day. 'In order of merit,' Noble said, 'I'll give you the names—Haydn Bunton, Don Bradman and Archie Jackson.'

In 1931, his sensational first season, Bunton won the Brownlow by one vote, one of only two Fitzroy players to play all 18 games for the season. He also represented Victoria, being best afield in the interstate clash with South Australia.

So impressed was Fitzroy that officials elected him captain for the start of the 1932 season, but he stood down after two matches, saying he wanted to concentrate only on his game. He won a second Brownlow, an unprecedented achievement. Runner-up in 1934, he won again in 1935, the first in League history to win three times.

He immediately spoke out against the 'fairness' of the voting system, saying the umpires should not be the sole arbiters of the best players each game. Bunton thought players near the centre of the ground had an unfair advantage over those who took up set positions.

During Bunton's seven seasons at Fitzroy, he tallied 122 Brownlow votes, or 17.4 a season.

'He was the greatest individualist who ever played,' said Fitzroy team-mate Mickey Sharp. 'But not the best team player. I don't think I've seen any player with his judgement and ability. He never seemed to get tired.'

Haydn Bunton: the game was a pleasure to him, not a hardship.

Another team-mate *Wilfred 'Chicken' Smallhorn* said Bunton possessed freakish abilities. 'I think he may have been a little psychic,' he said. 'He was a handball specialist; he had a magnificent stride—he never seemed to be running fast; and when running to the ball he wouldn't run to it and bend down; he would be bending as he ran and one hand would come out and he would pluck it in.'

Bunton was known to take high marks one-handed, in *Roy Cazaly* style. While not renowned as a brilliant kick of the ball, his torpedo punts travelled sizeable distances.

In 1935, he averaged almost 30 kicks and five handballs a game, a dominance unprecedented for years. The most kicks he had in one match was 45, against Footscray. In 1939, playing for Subiaco, he was reported to have had 60 kicks in one game.

He was always superbly fit. His philosophy was to 'make the game a pleasure, not a hardship'. He realised his own worth and at his farewell from Fitzroy he advised players: 'While you are playing for money you should get all you can out of the game. If you can improve your position through your ability as a footballer do so; because when you can't give your best any longer you will soon be forgotten, and you won't have anything to show.'

At 178 cm and 72 kg, Bunton was tall for a rover, being able to mark above the biggest players and outpace most of them. Sides tried to develop strategies to knock him out of a game, but Bunton's extraordinary reflexes and speed often stymied their plans.

To help protect him from the risk of opposition players deliberately aggravating the injuries he sometimes carried, Fitzroy medical staff developed elaborate strategies aimed at easing the pressure on their star. Once, when Bunton had injured his shoulder, his good shoulder was bandaged to confuse the opposition. The ruse worked. Only the good shoulder was bumped by the opposition.

The handsome rover was the game's first superstar, a great personality who cornered much of the game's publicity. Immaculately dressed in expensive suits off the field, he looked so clean on it that it was rumoured he even pressed his bootlaces!

'He has such a winning, unaffected personality that everyone likes him and is affected by his charm of manner,' said the *Australian Footballer* magazine. 'He knows that he is a great footballer and is willing to confess that he's a natural athlete, but he does not talk in any boastful spirit, but with the kind of quiet confidence of the man who knows his job.'

Bunton played 15 times for Victoria, and was captain in his last year, 1937. On moving to Perth, he reproduced all of his inspirational skills, winning the Sandover with Subiaco in 1938, 1939 and 1941.

He played the last of his 119 games with Fitzroy in 1942 when he returned to the team for two weeks while he was in Melbourne completing a physical education course in the Army. An ankle injury stopped him from playing more. In September, 1955, he died when his car crashed into three gum trees near Gawler, 58 km north of Adelaide. He was 44.

His eldest son, Haydn jnr, was also a fine footballer. He won the Sandover Medal in 1962 and coached successfully. Representing Swan Districts against South Fremantle in 1962, Bunton jnr is reputed to have had more than 85 kicks, a record for senior Australian football.

BYRNE, Ray (1953–   )

One of football's greatest characters, the Carlton cast-off gave exceptional service at Collingwood before finishing his career at Geelong. Byrne played 219 games from 1973–84, including three (losing) Grand Finals. He also represented Victoria.

Coach *Tom Hafey* regarded him as one of his most reliable players. Byrne followed Hafey to Geelong for his final League season in 1984. He always mixed his football with pleasure, and took delight in hiding Hafey's whistle on training nights.

When the balding *Kevin Bartlett* celebrated his 400th match in the 19th round, 1983, Byrne—his opponent for the day—presented the Richmond legend with a toothless comb.

As the teams lined up for the national anthem before a Collingwood–Geelong final, he casually rolled down his sock and produced a $50 bill. Yelling out to Geelong's *Mick Turner*, he said: 'Hey Mick, here's that $20 I owe you! Do you have any change?'

CABLE, Barry (1943–   )

A pocket dynamo who played 405 games in two States—a remarkable effort after he was rejected by his first WA club—Barry Thomas Cable became one of the post-war game's finest rovers.

A triple Sandover Medallist, he was best afield in each of Perth's consecutive grand final victories from 1966–68 before crossing to North Melbourne where he played in five Grand Finals in a row in the mid-1970s, including North's historic 1975 premiership.

Barry Cable: 18 senior seasons in WA and Victoria.

Known as 'The Little Master,' the 168 cm blond-headed left-footer possessed exceptional handball and kicking skills. He worked extremely hard, honing and perfecting his abilities until he was the most destructive small man in the game. He practised his handball at home, punching the ball into buckets.

He finished in the top four in the Brownlow Medal twice in his five VFL seasons. Among Cable's many other distinctions are winning the 1966 Tassie Medal at the Australian championships in Hobart, finishing in the first two in the Sandover Medal for five years in a row—including victories in 1964 and 1968—and twice being awarded All Australian status. In 1979 he was awarded an MBE for his services to football.

His performances rivalled those of another famous WA rover Billy Walker, who had beaten Cable for three consecutive Sandover Medals in the mid-1960s. Cable's brilliant field-kicking became a feature of his game. Like fellow West Australian *Graham 'Polly' Farmer*, he could handpass 20–25 metres with pinpoint precision. He worked tirelessly in gymnasiums to increase his upper body strength.

Six League clubs sought his services before he agreed to join North Melbourne in 1969. While North struggled, winning four games to finish last, Cable was best and fairest. He finished fourth in the Brownlow Medal. His sensational debut was rated superior to the first seasons of other interstate champions including 'Polly' Farmer, Denis Marshall, *Darrel Baldock* and *Ian Stewart*.

On his return to Perth in 1971, Cable won another club championship, his seventh in a row, a unique record in Australian senior football. In all, he won eight best and fairests in nine years—a feat equalled by only one other player, Fitzroy and East Perth's *Kevin Murray*.

After 13 seasons in Perth and five in Melbourne, Cable became one of the game's great ambassadors. He later coached in both cities, and coached WA in 1979.

He had 226 games at Perth, 116 at North Melbourne and 41 at East Perth, representing WA 22 times and Victoria once.

Soon after his 18th senior season in 1979, the 36-year-old was involved in a horrific farming accident. A tractor at his outer suburban farm at Orange Grove went out of control and tore his right leg to shreds. For many weeks it was feared Cable would die. Doctors considered amputation before transplanting a section of muscle and skin from his right thigh to save his leg. Fourteen weeks later he was released from hospital.

He had remained conscious throughout the accident. Despite his calls, it was an hour before help arrived and the tractor—which had wedged him against a wall—was turned off.

His career was over but he returned as a leading coach, including three and a half years at North Melbourne from 1981–84.

The Kangaroos finished on top in 1983, only to lose both finals. After the team tumbled to 11th the following year, Cable returned to WA. He was replaced by *John Kennedy snr*. His son, Shane, also played senior football, with the West Coast Eagles in the final year of VFL football in 1989.

CANBERRA

See: 'AUSTRALIAN CAPITAL TERRITORY'.

CAPPER, Warwick (1963–)

A high-flying, flamboyant full-forward, Warwick Capper became the highest-paid footballer in the League in 1987 when he signed a $350,000 three year agreement to play with the Brisbane Bears. His transfer fee was also a record: $425,000.

Having kicked almost 200 goals with Sydney in the 1986–87 seasons, Capper lost form in Brisbane and returned to Sydney, having played just 34 games for 71 goals.

Originally from Oakleigh Districts, Capper was noted for his spectacular marking ability, his long blond hair, white boots, deep suntan and ultra-tight shorts.

His kicking lacked the depth and accuracy of the greatest full-forwards. He could easily be upset, too, by aggressive opponents.

His most successful efforts were a 10 goal haul against Richmond in 1986 and nine against Collingwood in the opening round of 1987. From 1983–91, he played 123 games and kicked 388 goals, his best season being 1987 when he kicked 103 goals.

CAPTAINCY

When Hawthorn won the 1991 AFL premiership under the captaincy of *Michael Tuck*, it was the seventh time Tuck had led the Hawks to the flag, four during the day and three at night.

Collingwood's *Syd Coventry* and Essendon's *Dick Reynolds*—the most experienced captain of all—also led their teams to four League premierships.

Tuck led the Hawks in 139 games in his seven seasons from 1985–91. To the start of 1993, only 12 others have had more VFL captaincy experience, including Reynolds (220 games from 1938–50) and Footscray's *Ted Whitten* (212 from 1957–70).

North Melbourne's *Wayne Schimmelbusch* was captain for nine seasons from 1979–87. He was reappointed in 1988 but was unable to play because of injury. South Melbourne's *Bob Skilton* was also captain for nine years, from 1961–64, 1967–68 and 1970–71. He didn't play in 1969 because of an achilles tendon operation.

The record for most premierships as captain is six, held by Jack 'Dinny' Reedman—who led South Adelaide for 11 seasons and North Adelaide for five at the

Rival captains Charlie Tyson (Collingwood) and Cliff Rankin (Geelong) before the 1925 Grand Final. Geelong won the premiership, the first of three years under Rankin's leadership.

PLAYERS WHO HAVE CAPTAINED LEAGUE CLUBS IN 100 OR MORE MATCHES

PLAYER	MATCHES	TEAM
Dick Reynolds	224	Essendon (1938–50)
Ted Whitten	212	Footscray (1957–70)
John Nicholls	187	Carlton (1961–74)
Stephen Kernahan	174*	Carlton (1987–94)
Percy Bentley	168	Richmond (1932–40)
Bob Skilton	165	South (1959–71)
Danny Frawley	163*	St Kilda (1987–94)
Jack Dyer	160	Richmond (1940–49)
Kevin Murray	159	Fitzroy (1962–72)
Syd Coventry	153	Collingwood (1925–34)
Graham Arthur	153	Hawthorn (1956–68)
Wayne Schimmelbusch	150	North (1977–87)
Reg Hickey	142	Geelong (1930–40)
Des Tuddenham	142	Collingwood 73 (1966–76); Essendon 69 (1972–75)
Ron Barassi jnr.	141	Melbourne 92 (1958–64); Carlton 49 (1965–68)
Michael Tuck	139	Hawthorn (1985–91)
Henry Young	137	Geelong (1901–09)
Dan Minogue	136	Collingwood 41 (1914–15); Richmond 94 (1920–25); Hawthorn 1 (1926)
Dennis Carroll	131	Sydney (1986–92)
Arthur Olliver	127	Footscray (1943–50)
Robert Flower	127	Melbourne (1980–87)
Terry Daniher	127	Essendon (1983–88)
Don Scott	124	Hawthorn (1974–80)
Bill Hutchison	122	Essendon (1949–57)
Jack Clarke	121	Essendon (1958–64)
Bill Cubbins	119	St Kilda 87 (1992–30); Footscray 32 (1931–32)
Alan La Fontaine	119	Melbourne (1935–41)
Wayne Richardson	117	Collingwood (1970–75)
Leigh Matthews	112	Hawthorn (1975–85)
Barry Davis	111	Essendon 40 (1970–72); North 71 (1973–75)
Tony Shaw	111	Collingwood (1987–92)
Alan Ruthven	110	Fitzroy (1946–54)
Ian Nankervis	110	Geelong (1973–83)
Phonse Kyne	107	Collingwood (1938–50)
Ron Clegg	106	South (1949–60)
Darrel Baldock	104	St Kilda (1963–68)
Fred Hughson	103	Fitzroy (1942–47)
Des Rowe	103	Richmond (1950–57)
Herbie Matthews	101	South (1938–45)
Les Foote	101	North 68 (1946–51); St Kilda 33 (1954–55)
Mark Williams	100	Collingwood 88 (1983–86); Brisbane 12 (1988–89)

Totals include matches as acting captain.

* current player.

turn of the century—and Fos Williams, who was captain-coach in Port Adelaide's premiership successes in 1951 and from 1954–58.

The West Australian record is five, held by East Fremantle's Tom Wilson, who led his club in nine grand finals, including victories in 1900, 1904, 1906, 1908–09.

Haydn Bunton jnr is the most experienced interstate captain-coach, with 12

PLAYERS WHO HAVE CAPTAINED CLUBS FOR ALMOST ALL THEIR CAREERS

NAME	TEAM	YEAR	DETAILS
Jack Conway	Geelong	1897–99	Captain in each of his 51 League matches.
Bill Shaw	St Kilda	1897–99	Captain in each of his 27 matches for the Saints (no wins).
	Melbourne	1901	One match—not captain.
J. Wearmouth	St Kilda	1905	Acting captain in his second (and final) match.
Johnny Leonard	South	1932	Captain in each of his 12 League matches.
Ern Henfrey	Carlton	1944, 1947–52	Captain in all but the first two of his 84 League matches.
Mark Mickan	Brisbane	1987–90	Captain in his first 46 matches.
	Adelaide	1991–92	
Chris McDermott	Adelaide	1991–94	Captain in his first 88 matches.

years at the helm—four at Norwood (1958, 1965–67), four at Swan Districts (1961–64) and four at Subiaco (1968–70, 1972).

Fos Williams had nine consecutive seasons as Port Adelaide's captain-coach. *Jack Dyer* led Richmond for nine years and WA's Jack Sheedy was in charge at East Fremantle and East Perth for the same length of time.

Norwood's Jack Oatey was captain-coach in eight seasons, as was Neil Kerley—two years with West Adelaide, three with South Adelaide and three with Glenelg.

Tasmania's 'Prince of Coaches' was noted disciplinarian Bruce Carter who was captain-coach or vice-captain-coach of North Launceston, Mersey and Cananore from 1904–14. He won three flags in a row at North Launceston from 1904–06, a flag at Mersey in 1908 and captained Tasmania in the 1908 national championships. He led Cananore to three flags in a row, won a flag at North Launceston in 1912 and another at Cananore in 1913, his ninth in 11 years. He retired after leading Cananore into yet another grand final in 1914. More than 20 years later, in 1937, he was induced out of retirement to coach Cananore again, aged 55.

CAREY, Wayne (1971–)

Widely recognised as the premier player in the AFL as the 1995 season opened, the North Melbourne centre half-forward was on the verge of 100 games, having already won two best and fairests, played state football for New South Wales and South

Wayne Carey: the outstanding player of the mid-1990s.

Australia and been honoured with the All Australian captaincy.

North Melbourne's youngest captain since *David Dench*, Carey's instrumental leadership was primarily responsible for North making the 1994 preliminary final and going within a kick of qualifying through to the Grand Final.

In a thrilling match with Geelong, Carey kicked 6.4 and took 14 marks in a rare solo effort which has had few recent parallels.

Originally from Wagga Wagga, Carey played with North Adelaide as a 16-year-old before switching to North Melbourne in 1988 and playing in an under 19s premiership.

He debuted under *John Kennedy* in 1989 and with his superb athleticism and courageous marking—often with the flight of the ball—soon developed into one of the game's young stars.

Carlton clinched the 1972 premiership in the highest scoring Grand Final of all. Jubilant players, from left: Ian Robertson, Robert Walls, captain-coach John Nicholls (with cup), Adrian Gallagher and Paul Hurst.

CARLTON

Formed in 1864, Carlton was the dominant force in colonial football before the formation of the Victorian Football Association in 1877. Winning the very first VFA premiership, it became one of the VFA's 'super powers'. The club's original colours were blue and orange, before, in 1871, the orange was abandoned in favour of an 'oxford' dark blue.

At that time, Carlton was regarded as a remote part of Melbourne. Some streets were settled by affluent merchants and bankers but the area around Royal Park was little more than a scrubland. The club played its first football matches in an unenclosed area near the corner of Royal Parade and Gatehouse Street. Games were rough and ready affairs. Players often helped police control the crowds.

In 1864, Carlton won only one of its 10 matches but by 1867 it had defeated the great Melbourne side for the first time and in 1871 won its first premiership.

At one stage during the mid-1870s, the Blues had been defeated only once in three years.

A foundation member of the Victorian Football League, Carlton figured well in the first season in 1897. After a series of

poor seasons, the club became extremely successful and played in every final series, except two, between 1903–27.

Its League football home has always been Princes Park, now known as Optus Oval and regarded as one of the three showpiece football stadiums in Victoria.

The club's most prominent playing personality in the colourful and highly-competitive early years was George Coulthard, who was Victoria's 'Champion of the Colony' in three of his first four seasons from 1876–79. He was described as the 'grandest player' of his day. Coulthard also represented Australia at Test cricket and was a Test match umpire before dying of tuberculosis in 1883, aged 27.

Another Test cricketer, the legendary *Jack Worrall*, joined the club as secretary in 1902. He insisted he manage all team matters, including coaching. Recruiting, training and directing the players in ruthless style, he rid the club of its loser's tag. In the previous year Carlton had suffered the ultimate humiliation—a 13.16 to 0.7 defeat to Collingwood.

45

CARLTON: THE STATISTICS

FORMED: July, 1864

JOINED LEAGUE: 1897
HOME VENUE: Princes Park, 139.2 m × 152.3 m
COLOURS: Navy blue guernsey with white monogram.
TOTAL FINALS MATCHES: 120 (56 wins, 62 losses, 2 ties)
FINALS RECORD: Premiers, 15 (1906–07–08, 1914–15, 1938, 1945, 1947, 1968, 1972, 1979, 1981–82, 1987)
RUNNERS-UP: 12 (1904, 1909–10, 1916, 1921, 1932, 1949, 1962, 1969, 1973, 1986, 1993)
PREMIERSHIPS COACHES: Jack Worrall (3), Norman Clark (2), Brighton Diggins (1), Percy Bentley (2), Ron Barassi (2), John Nicholls (1), Alex Jesaulenko (1), David Parkin (2), Robert Walls (1).
NIGHT SERIES PREMIERSHIP: 1 (1983)
YOUNGEST PLAYER: Jim Buckley, 16 years 200 days (1967)
OLDEST PLAYER: Jim Flynn, 40 years (1910)
HIGHEST SCORE: 30.30 (210) v Hawthorn, R.2, 1969, Princes Park
LOWEST SCORE: 0.6 (6) v Collingwood, R.5, 1898, Victoria Park
LONGEST WINNING SEQUENCE: 15 (1907–08)
LONGEST LOSING SEQUENCE: 14 (1901–02)
MOST FINALS: Bruce Doull 29, Rod McGregor 25, John Nicholls 23, Peter Jones 23, Alex Jesaulenko 23, David McKay 22, Mark Maclure 21, Geoff Southby 20
MOST SEASONS AS COACH: Percy Bentley 15 (1941–55)
MOST SEASONS AS CAPTAIN: Stephen Kernahan, 9 (1987–95)

MOST GAMES		MOST GOALS	
Bruce Doull	359	Harry Vallence	722
John Nicholls	328	Stephen Kernahan	596*
Geoff Southby	270	Alex Jesaulenko	424
David McKay	263	Horrie Clover	398
Alex Jesaulenko	260	Ken Baxter	373
Peter Jones	249	Rod Ashman	369
Mark Maclure	243	Robert Walls	367
Justin Madden	241*	Vin Gardiner	338
Sergio Silvagni	238	Mark Maclure	327
Rod McGregor	237	John Nicholls	307
Rod Ashman	236	Peter Jones	284
Rod Austin	220	Wayne Johnston	283
Robert Walls	219	"Mick" Crisp	281
Tom Alvin	218	David McKay	272
Ken Hands	211	Jack Wrout	266
Wayne Johnston	209	Jack Howell jnr	246
Trevor Keogh	208	Ansell Clarke	242
Frank Gill	205	Adrian Gallagher	236
Barry Armstrong	205	Paul Schmidt	228
Harry Vallence	204		
Craig Bradley	201*		

* current player.

CARLTON: THE STATISTICS (cont)

MOST GOALS IN A MATCH: Horrie Clover, 13 v St Kilda, R.12, 1921, Junction Oval.
Greg Kennedy, 12 v Hawthorn, R.21, 1972, Princes Park.
Ross Ditchburn, 12 v St Kilda, R.16, 1982, Waverley Park

LEAGUE LEADING GOALSCORERS: Mick Grace, 50 (1906), Vin Gardiner, 47 (1911), Ern Cowley, 34 (1918), Horrie Clover, 56 (1922), Harry Vallence, 86 (1931), Tom Carroll, 54 (1961).

BROWNLOW MEDALLISTS: Bert Deacon (1947), John James (1961), Gordon Collis (1964), Greg Williams (1994).

RECORD HOME VENUE ATTENDANCE: 47,514 v Geelong, R.6, 1963, Princes Park
62,986 v South Melb., GF, 1945, Princes Park.

RECORD ATTENDANCE IN ANY MATCH: 121,696 v Collingwood, GF, 1970, MCG.

MOST RECENT PREMIERSHIP TEAM: 1987 Carlton 15.14 (104) d Hawthorn 9.17 (71).
B: T. Alvin, S. Silvagni, D. Glascott. H.B: I. Aitken, D. Rhys-Jones, P. Dean. C: M. Kennedy, C. Bradley, S. Robertson. H.F: R. Dennis, S. Kernahan (c), K. Hunter. F: P. Meldrum, J. Dorotich, M. Naley. R: J. Madden, W. Johnston. R: F. Murphy. Interchange: A. Gleeson, W. McKenzie.

Surviving a mid-career overthrow attempt, Worrall led the club to three consecutive premierships from 1906–08. A power club was forming, and in one match against Essendon at Princes Park, 32,000 fans attended—a phenomenal home-and-away attendance for the time.

In Carlton's first 95 years of competition, its lowest-ever finish was 10th, in 1964, the year before the great *Ron Barassi* was enticed from Melbourne in the most talked-about transfer of them all.

The Blues won seven premierships in two decades from 1968–87, playing in 10 Grand Finals, a record surpassed by only one other club, Hawthorn.

In all, the Blues have won a record 15 premierships, one more than Collingwood and Essendon, and have fielded some of the game's finest players including Brownlow Medallists *Bert Deacon, John James* and *Gordon Collis* and other post-war favourites, *John Nicholls, Alex Jesaulenko, Wayne Johnston, Geoff Southby* and *Stephen Kernahan*.

Among its distinguished array of No. 1 ticket holders are two former Prime Ministers of Australia, Malcolm Fraser and Sir Robert Menzies.

CARROLL, Dennis (1960–)

The leading member of one of the Riverina's most outstanding football families, Dennis Carroll captained the Swans, represented Victoria and NSW and, in his 11th season in 1991, played his 200th game.

Carroll's long kicking, skill and endeavour lifted him into Sydney's captaincy in 1986, the first of seven consecutive seasons as skipper. He'd been runner-up in the best and fairest in 1985, the first of many 'near-misses'.

Injury stopped him from leading the Swans into the 1986 finals. He had his opportunity in 1987, only to see the team again finish fourth after losing both play-offs.

Superbly built at 187 cm and 86 kg, Carroll could play successfully at either end of the ground. His best football was at half-back.

'I used to kick the football with my uncle ("Turkey" Tom) on the farm at Ganmain when I was nine or 10,' Carroll said. 'He helped me tremendously. I always had a ball with me. Tom would tell me: "You can kick right foot all right. Kick left foot."'

Carroll's field-kicking with both feet became a feature of his game. Few could kick as precisely or with the same consistent length. His achievements were all the more meritorious considering he played rugby league until he was 13.

'Turkey' Tom Carroll headed the VFL goalkicking in 1961, with Carlton.

CARTER, Rod (1954–)

A determined, dour full-back from Banyule who went within seven games of 300 (a unique milestone considering he never represented Victoria), Carter made the most of his second chance in League football after he was off-loaded in mid-career by Fitzroy.

He had six seasons and 76 games with the Lions before joining the Swans in 1980, via VFA club Port Melbourne, where he'd finished the 1979 season.

In 11 seasons with Sydney he played more than 200 games. Carter retired at the end of the 1990 season, on the eve of his 36th birthday. In 1983, he was runner-up in the best and fairest and in 1985 made the Victorian training squad.

Hawthorn's *Jason Dunstall* and other champion full-forwards considered Carter their tightest opponent. He'd stick rigidly to them, using every possible tactic to stop their run at the ball.

At the height of his career, Carter said: 'My job is to stop the bloke getting a goal, getting a kick and I just concentrate on the ball and don't let him get too far away. That might be frustrating to another player and he might decide to do something about it. My theory is if he belts you, then you belt him back.'

CARTER, Wally (1910–)

North Melbourne's only 200-game coach, Wally Carter followed his distinguished 12 year playing career by coaching the Kangaroos for 11 years and 208 games from 1948–53 and again from 1958–62.

North's inaugural best and fairest winner in 1937—the season he represented Victoria—Carter played 137 games from 1929–40, and was vice-captain in his final year.

He was coach of the North Melbourne reserves team which won the premiership in 1947 and impressed fans with his astute moves and enthusiasm. The following year he replaced Bob McCaskill as senior coach and in 1950 lifted the Roos into their first Grand Final. The club lost to Essendon 7.12 (54) to 13.14 (92). He also helped the club into final series in 1949 and 1958.

CAZALY, Roy (1893–1963)

A champion ruckman who thrilled crowds with his marking, Cazaly had a magnificent senior career which spanned 40 years, three VFL clubs and several in Tasmania.

His ability to mark the ball one-handed was legendary. The phrase, 'Up there Cazaly,' became a battlecry, celebrated in songs and poems, and even used by Australian troops in war zones.

Roy Cazaly dominates the ruck for South Melbourne in the game against Geelong in 1921.

It was first used on the football field shortly after World War One by Cazaly's South Melbourne team-mate, ruckman Fred 'Skeeter' Fleiter, who would allow Cazaly to fly for the ball while he shepherded opponents away. When Fleiter saw Cazaly was in position to mark he'd shout: 'Up there Cazaly,' to encourage his team-mate to fly for the ball.

Cazaly was a slim 180 cm and 79.5 kg. He had great anticipation and a prodigious leap, fine-tuned by a home training routine in which he took a big breath and exhaled mightily, while jumping as high as he could for a ball hung on the end of a string.

Born on 13 January, 1893, Cazaly was the youngest of 10 children. His father had been a champion British oarsman and young Roy was a gifted sporting all-rounder, particularly proficient at cricket and football. He also loved rowing.

In 1910, at the age of 17, he played for St Kilda—after an unsuccessful trial at Carlton—and spent 11 seasons at what was then an inner-city club before shifting to South Melbourne as playing coach. Here he formed a formidable following combination with Fleiter and rover *Mark Tandy*.

He also had a League football association with Hawthorn. He coached the Hawks to their first victory ever over Collingwood (in 1942 after 29 consecutive defeats) and lifted the club into fifth place in 1943.

Cazaly played 198 League games, 99 at both St Kilda and South Melbourne. He also represented Victoria 13 times from 1921–26 and played in the VFA with Preston (1931), Camberwell (1941) and three Tasmanian clubs, City, North Hobart and New Town.

For years it was thought he'd played 100 matches with St Kilda, but historian Stephen Rogers recently discovered that one match had inadvertently been credited to Cazaly, instead of his brother, Ernest.

It was also widely believed that Cazaly played 393 senior games, but his biographer, David Allen, says a more realistic figure is 414, without reference to matches with Minyip and in Melbourne's thriving mid-week competition.

Cazaly's final match was in Tasmania at the age of 58, for New Town against Glenorchy.

CHADWICK, Sir Albert (1897–1983)

Melbourne's captain-coach from 1924–27, 'Bert' Chadwick helped lift the club from bottom of the ladder in 1923 to premiers in 1926, its first flag in 26 years.

The son of a Tungamah chemist, Chadwick was an inspirational leader who enjoyed great success in his sporting and business life.

A tall, gifted player, who generally played at centre half-back, he was a brilliant mark and a noted strategist. He was runner-up to Geelong's *'Carji' Greeves* for

the 1924 Brownlow Medal. He also represented Hawthorn.

In all, he played 159 games from 1920–29.

He was chairman of the Melbourne football club through its glory reign from 1950–62 and Melbourne cricket club president from 1965–78. He was knighted in 1974.

CHESSWAS, Harry (1902–56)

A member of all four of Collingwood's consecutive premiership sides from 1927–30, Chesswas played 154 games from 1922–31. He appeared in six Grand Finals altogether, mainly as a winger or half-forward.

CLARK, Norman (1883–1931)

A 100-game Carlton player who was involved in the club's first three premierships from 1906–08, Norman 'Hackenschmidt' Clark, from North Adelaide, was a back-pocket player who later coached Carlton to the 1914–15 premiership double. In 1914, Carlton won 12 matches on end and defeated South Melbourne in the Grand Final by six points. From 1905–12, Clark played 125 games and kicked three goals. During 1907, he was captain in six matches.

The Blues won 102 of the 150 games he coached, in three separate stints: 1912, 1914–18 and 1920–22.

Clark coached three other League teams, Richmond in 1919, St Kilda in 1925–26 and North Melbourne in 1931, where he lasted only half a season and lost all 10 games before being replaced by renowned player John Lewis.

In all, he coached in 214 matches for 128 wins, 80 losses and six draws. He is also remembered as winner of the 1899 Stawell Gift.

CLARKE, David (1952–)

A three-time winner of Geelong's best and fairest—including his very first season as a 19-year-old in 1971—Clarke had immense natural skill which made him one of the champions of the game in the 1970s.

Recruited from Geelong College where he was captain of football, cricket and athletics in his final year, the 182 cm Clarke was a noted half-forward who in mid-career switched to defence with telling results.

He amassed 207 games in 12 seasons with Geelong from 1971–81. Clarke joined Carlton in 1982 but injury restricted him to just one senior season and, after a few games in the reserves in 1983, he announced his retirement. He'd been named in Carlton's 23 for the '82 Grand Final and, in a tactical ploy, actually ran out with the team for the warm-ups before heading back up the race and changing into his street clothes.

Clarke won Geelong's best and fairest awards in 1978 and 1979 and represented Victoria 14 times, winning All Australian status in 1972. He led Geelong's goalkicking in 1973 and 1979, and captained Geelong in 23 matches, playing a total of 216 games with Geelong and Carlton in his 12 senior seasons.

CLARKE, Jack (1933–)

The older brother of famous Australian athlete, record-breaking runner Ron Clarke, Jack Clarke played 266 games with Essendon from 1951–67 and represented Victoria 27 times, a feat surpassed by only one other Bomber, celebrated rover *Billy Hutchison*.

A smart centreman and rover who successfully combined football with his professional job as an architect, the 175 cm Clarke won All Australian selection three times, was Essendon's best and fairest twice and captained the club for seven consecutive years from 1958–64.

He played in the club's 1962 and 1965 premierships and also figured in three other Grand Finals.

Clarke joined the Bombers in 1947, aged 14, and played in the under 19s and reserves.

He made his debut in 1951 on his 18th birthday and had six games in that year, including the Grand Final when he sat on the bench alongside captain-coach *Dick Reynolds* for much of the match. It was the last of Reynolds' record 320 games.

Clarke's ballgetting ability and superb disposal was a feature of his game throughout his distinguished career. Few matched his artistry or were as courageous. He played for Victoria every year from 1953–62, and was captain in 1959 and 1960, when he was at his peak.

After Essendon lost the opening two games in 1967, Clarke and fellow veteran *Hugh Mitchell* were dropped. Both retired immediately and Clarke received $3257 from Essendon's testimonial fund.

He later coached Essendon for three years, lifting the Bombers into the 1968 Grand Final in his first season. He introduced a wide variety of training routines and took a scientific approach to coaching based on multiple measurements of player performance. His revolutionary techniques—some of them developed in tandem with brother Ron—were widely copied.

CLAY, Dick (1945–)

The subject of a VFL inquiry before he'd even played a League game, the teenage Kyabram goalkicking sensation became one of Richmond's greatest post-war players. He figured in four premierships in his 213-game League career from 1966–76.

Versatile, fast and with a thumping kick, the 185 cm Clay first played as a centre half-forward before switching to a wing and helping form a revered Richmond centreline with *Francis Bourke* and Bill Barrot.

He'd been wooed to Tigerland by his friend *Tom Hafey*, who took over as Richmond coach in 1966, having coached against Clay in the Goulburn Valley league.

Clay had become a hot country prospect. He'd grown 15 cm in six months, and developed from a forward flanker into a key position player.

North Melbourne signed him in 1964 after former player Les Mogg saw him in action in a practice match for Kyabram at Cobram.

He kicked 116 goals for the season and

Dick Clay shrugs off a Collingwood opponent at VFL Park in the early 1970s.

early the next year played in one of North's practice matches at Coburg, but decided to have another season of country football.

The day after North's hold on him expired, in early 1966, Clay signed with Richmond, believing the Tigers, under Hafey, were more likely to progress.

He also took immediate possession of a Holden motor car.

North accused Richmond of poaching and tried to block Clay's entry into League football. A special hearing of the VFL delegates voted in Richmond's favour. Clay was a Tiger, and made his debut at centre half-forward against the legendary *Ted Whitten* in the second round of 1966.

He played for Victoria in his second season. His aggression, aerial strength and prodigious field-kicking made him one of the game's elite running players.

Later he became a top defender. He played at full-back in Richmond's consecutive premierships in 1973 and 1974. He retired after six games in 1976, and headed to the VFA where he coached Prahran.

CLAYDEN, George (1903–90)

A tough rugged player who was a front-line defender in Collingwood's historic premiership teams from 1927–30, he played 134 games from 1924–33. He also represented Victoria 10 times, including two Australian carnivals.

CLEARY, Jim (1914–   )

A scrupulously fair full-back known as 'Gentleman Jim', Cleary played 216 games with South Melbourne from 1934–48, including two Grand Finals, in 1936 and 1945. He was twice best and fairest.

It was a major shock when he was reported during the 1945 'Bloodbath' Grand Final and outed for eight weeks. He later claimed he'd only been trying to defend himself.

He represented Victoria against South Australia in Adelaide in 1941.

CLEGG, Ron (1927–90)

Known as the 'champion's champion', Ron 'Smokey' Clegg won the 1949 Brownlow Medal, was second in 1951, fourth in 1948 and fifth in 1953.

A versatile, key-position player who was a magnificent mark, the 185 cm Clegg played 80 per cent of his 231 League games at centre half-forward, winning three club best and fairests and representing Victoria 15 times, the first time as an 18-year-old in his second season. He was also brilliant at centre half-back.

Clegg would practise one-handed marks at training and take them with breathtaking ease come matchday.

Many say he was unbeatable at his best. He made his debut in 1945 as a 17-year-old.

In 1951 against Fitzroy, he took 32 marks, an astonishing performance which became known as 'Clegg's day'. He was in such devastating form that Fitzroy's *Norm Johnstone* refused coach *Norm Smith's* directive to tag him. 'He's beaten four of us already. He's not beating five,' Johnstone was reported as saying.

On winning the '49 Medal, on a countback from Hawthorn's *Col Austen*—who was later to be awarded a Brownlow retrospectively—South Melbourne gave him a set of deluxe golf clubs. Months later, when the club was short of cash, it asked for them back!

Clegg polled six best-afield votes to Austen's five and became the first player to win on a countback since the Medal's 1930 'triple-tie'.

The great Ron Clegg. He was so good he could stop an army, according to Richmond legend Jack Dyer.

He played in the 'Bloodbath' Grand Final, and was knocked out in the vicious opening. Opposed by Carlton's great defender *Bert Deacon*, Clegg said all he remembered about the first half of that game was being told by the scrupulously-fair Deacon: 'Stick with me son, and you'll be right.'

'He was an unbelievable player,' said contemporary and triple-Brownlow Medallist *Bob Skilton*. 'Even in his last years he was doing things we never dreamt about.'

A self-taught guitarist, he was the life of South Melbourne footy parties for many years. He was so talented that he appeared at Caesar's Palace as an entertainer in the early 1970s.

His nickname Smokey came from his years as a cigarette salesman for Mandy stores.

Clegg was South Melbourne's captain-coach in 1958–59. His final season was in 1960, when he continued to play despite two broken ribs. His 231-game tally established a new South Melbourne club record, surpassing *Jack Graham*'s 227.

CLOKE, David (1955–)

A committed follower and forward with enormous pride and personal drive who had great influence at two clubs, David Malcolm Cloke played 333 games in 18 seasons of League football. His career ended in fairytale fashion in Richmond's final match of the 1991 season when Cloke, aged 36, kicked eight goals against Carlton to be best afield.

Only one ruckman, Essendon's Simon Madden, has played more games than Cloke.

The 196 cm Cloke played 217 games with the Tigers from 1974–82—he rejoined them in 1990–91—and 116 with Collingwood from 1983–89.

Recruited from Oakleigh fourths, Cloke was 18 when he played in Richmond's 1974 premiership team. He figured in another Tiger flag in 1980, kicking six goals. Cloke captained Richmond in 1982—another Grand Final year.

His cross to Victoria Park in 1983 was one of the most sensational clearance cases of the 1980s and worsened the feud between the two clubs. Richmond refused the original transfer fee of $130,000 and returned the cheque to Collingwood. Later the VFL appeals board allowed his release for $185,000.

Cloke became one of Collingwood's most valuable imports, not only providing crucial on-field contributions, but valuable leadership off the field as well.

He served for several years as deputy captain. Collingwood coach *Leigh Matthews* once called him 'ageless'—'he has never thought of himself as old and he plays that way'.

Richmond's David Cloke: eight goals in his final game against Carlton, 1991.

Cloke says his secret of longevity was all in the mind. 'If you really believe you can do something and you're willing to do it, you should get it done.'

After being told, late in 1989, that his services were no longer required at Collingwood, Cloke was drafted back to his old club, where his experience and consistency were great assets. The previous season he'd played his first matches in the reserves for more than a decade.

COACHES, Notable

Not only was *'Jock' McHale* the longest-serving coach in VFL history, he was also the most successful. He lifted Collingwood into the finals in 27 of his 38 years as coach, for eight premierships, including four in a row from 1927–30.

His Collingwood teams made the Grand Final 17 times. As a player and coach, he won 10 and lost 10 of his record 20 play-offs.

McHale is one of three men to coach in more than 500 games—along with *Allan Jeans*, who returned to football with his third club, Richmond, in 1992, and *Tom Hafey*, whose last year in an uninterrupted coaching period of 23 seasons was at Sydney in 1988.

Ron Barassi joined the elite group, coaching his 500th match early in the 1995 season.

McHale's record of eight premierships is unsurpassed. *Norm Smith* (Melbourne) won six, *'Checker' Hughes* (Richmond and Melbourne) five, and *Jack Worrall* (Carlton and Essendon) five.

Worrall, the game's first official coach, was also a coaching adviser—along with Alex Sloan—at Fitzroy in 1922, when the Lions came from behind to defeat Collingwood in an exciting play-off.

Barassi (Carlton, North Melbourne and Melbourne) won four flags. So did Hafey (Richmond, Collingwood, Geelong and Sydney) and *Dick Reynolds* (Essendon).

Hawthorn's Alan Joyce also won four, two day flags and two night flags, in his first two years of coaching, in 1988 and 1991. He won the night flag again in 1992, his fifth premiership in five attempts.

He's one of 11 men to coach a premiership in his first season. The others are: Charlie Ricketts (South Melbourne) 1909; Percy Parratt (Fitzroy) 1913; Dan Minogue (Richmond) 1920; Cliff Rankin (Geelong) 1925; Charlie Clymo (Geelong) 1931; Jack Bissett (South Melbourne) 1933; *Percy Bentley* (Richmond) 1934; Brighton Diggins (Carlton) 1938; John Nicholls (Carlton) 1972; and *Alex Jesaulenko* (Carlton) 1979.

Modern-day masters Hafey, Barassi and Jeans were not only successful in their own right, but many of their methods were adopted by their own players when they graduated into coaching ranks. A record 13 Hafey-coached players also became League coaches. Eleven of Barassi's players have coached at League level, and ten of Jeans'.

When naming a successor for legend *Kevin Bartlett* in late 1991, Richmond chose Jeans, saying his successful background at Hawthorn was crucial.

Of the five ex-Hawthorn players who coached in League ranks in 1992, Jeans had nurtured two at League level: *Leigh*

Jack Oatey celebrates a Sturt premiership.

Matthews (Collingwood) and *Gary Buck-enara* (Sydney Swans). Another Jeans protege, from his days at St Kilda, was *Mick Malthouse* (West Coast Eagles).

Clubs invariably prefer coaches with illustrious playing backgrounds. But the best players do not always make the best coaches. Footscray sacked Richmond star *Royce Hart* in mid-year 1982 after the club finished 10th and 11th in his only two full seasons.

St Kilda's *Darrel Baldock* was one of the mightiest post-war forwards but, despite an imposing coaching record in Tasmania, couldn't repeat his success in VFL football. The Saints finished no higher than 10th in his three years.

On 12 occasions clubs have chosen coaches who have not played League football. They include Hughie Thomas (St Kilda) 1944–45, Alan Miller (South Melbourne) 1967–68, and Colin Kinnear (Sydney) 1989–91. Thomas was a long-time seconds coach at Collingwood in the 1920s and 1930s, and was regarded by some as being almost as important as

McHale in helping to mould Collingwood's unparalleled successes.

Clubs prefer to have stability among their coaching ranks, but new administrations often trigger premature changes. Richmond's Tony Jewell, an inspirational and popular coach, lifted the Tigers to the 1980 flag but just over 12 months later was replaced by Francis Bourke.

Carlton's *Robert Walls* led the Blues to the 1987 flag, only to be sacked mid-season in 1989 in favour of *Alex Jesaulenko*.

Among the best-performed interstate coaches are South Australian legend Jack Oatey who won 10 premierships in his 37 years as coach, three with Norwood as playing coach in 1946, 1948 and 1950, and seven with Sturt as non-playing coach in 1966–70, 1974 and 1976.

Oatey coached a record 778 games in the SANFL between 1945–82. He also played 203 games with Norwood and represented SA seven times, captaining SA in 1949.

Fos Williams won nine premierships with Port Adelaide, including six as playing

200 MATCHES OR MORE AS A LEAGUE COACH

Name	Club/s	Span	Games	Wins	Losses	Draw	Total Seasons	Flags
Jock McHale	Collingwood	1912–49	714	467	237	10	38	8
Allan Jeans	St Kilda	1961–76	332	193	138	1	16	1
	Hawthorn	1981–87, 1989–90	221	159	61	1	9	3
	Richmond	1992	22	5	17	0	1	0
TOTAL			**575**	**357**	**216**	**2**	**26**	**4**
Tom Hafey	Richmond	1966–76	248	173	73	2	11	4
	Collingwood	1977–82	138	89	47	2	6	0
	Geelong	1983–85	66	31	35	0	3	0
	Sydney	1986–88	70	43	27	0	3	0
TOTAL			**522**	**336**	**182**	**4**	**23**	**4**
Ron Barassi	Carlton	1965–71	147	99	47	1	7	2
	North Melb.	1973–80	198	129	66	3	8	2
	Melbourne	1981–85	110	33	77	0	5	0
	Sydney	1993–94	37	5	32	0	2	0
TOTAL			**492**	**266**	**222**	**4**	**22**	**4**
Norm Smith	Fitzroy	1949–51	55	30	23	2	3	0
	Melbourne	1952–67	310	198	107	5	16	6
	South Melb.	1969–72	87	26	61	0	4	0
TOTAL			**452**	**254**	**191**	**7**	**23**	**6**
Dick Reynolds	Essendon	1939–60	420	277	137	6	22	4
Percy Bentley	Richmond	1934–40	133	86	46	1	7	1
	Carlton	1941–55	281	167	110	4	15	2
TOTAL			**414**	**253**	**156**	**5**	**22**	**3**
John Kennedy	Hawthorn	1960–63, 1967–76	296	181	113	2	14	3
	North Melb.	1985–89	113	55	55	3	5	0
TOTAL			**409**	**236**	**168**	**5**	**19**	**3**
'Checker' Hughes	Richmond	1927–32	120	87	31	2	6	1
	Melbourne	1933–41, 1945–48, 1965	254	157	95	2	14	4
TOTAL			**374**	**244**	**126**	**4**	**20**	**5**
Dan Minogue	Richmond	1920–25	105	59	45	1	6	3
	Hawthorn	1926–27	36	4	31	1	2	0
	Carlton	1929–34	117	85	32	0	6	0
	St Kilda	1935–37	54	30	24	0	3	0
	Fitzroy	1940–42	51	25	26	0	3	0
TOTAL			**363**	**203**	**158**	**2**	**20**	**3**
David Parkin	Hawthorn	1977–80	94	57	37	0	4	1
	Carlton	1981–85, 1991–94	211	131	78	2	9	2
	Fitzroy	1986–88	69	30	39	0	3	0
TOTAL			**374**	**218**	**154**	**2**	**16**	**3**

continued

200 MATCHES OR MORE AS A LEAGUE COACH (cont)

Name	Club/s	Span	Games	Wins	Losses	Draw	Total Seasons	Flags
Reg Hickey	Geelong	1932, 1936–40, 1949–59	304	184	117	3	18	3
Kevin Sheedy	Essendon	1981–94	329*	212	115	2	14	3
Robert Walls	Fitzroy	1981–85	115*	60	54	1	5	0
	Carlton	1986–89	84	56	28	0	4	1
	Brisbane	1991–94	86	20	65	1	4	0
TOTAL			**285**	**136**	**147**	**2**	**13**	**1**
Bob Rose	Collingwood	1964–71, 1985–86	192	121	69	2	10	0
	Footscray	1972–75	89	42	45	2	4	0
TOTAL			**281**	**163**	**114**	**4**	**14**	**0**
'Phonse' Kyne	Collingwood	1950–63	271	161	108	2	14	2
Jack Worrall	Carlton	1902–09	144	100	43	1	8	3
	Essendon	1911–15, 1918–19	123	60	60	3	7	0
TOTAL			**267**	**160**	**103**	**4**	**15**	**3**
Michael Malthouse	Footscray	1984–89	135*	67	66	2	6	0
	West Coast	1990–94	124	88	34	2	5	2
TOTAL			**259**	**155**	**100**	**4**	**11**	**2**
Bill Stephen	Fitzroy	1955–57, 1965–70, 1979–80	214	67	146	1	11	0
	Essendon	1976–77	44	16	27	1	2	0
TOTAL			**258**	**83**	**173**	**2**	**13**	**0**
John Northey	Sydney	1985	22*	6	16	0	1	0
	Melbourne	1986–92	167	90	76	1	7	0
	Richmond	1993–94	42	16	26	0	2	0
TOTAL			**231**	**112**	**118**	**1**	**10**	**0**
Ted Whitten snr.	Footscray	1957–66, 1969–71	228	91	137	0	13	0
Jack Dyer	Richmond	1941–52	225	134	89	2	12	1
Norman Clark	Carlton	1912, 1914–18, 1920–22	150	102	42	6	9	2
	Richmond	1919	19	12	7	0	1	0
	St Kilda	1925–26	35	14	21	0	2	0
	North Melb.	1931	10	0	10	0	1	0
TOTAL			**214**	**128**	**80**	**6**	**13**	**2**
Wally Carter	North Melb.	1948–53, 1958–62	208	96	111	1	5	0
Leigh Matthews	Collingwood	1986–94	202*	117	82	3	9	1

* current coach.

coach, in a 27-year association which ended in 1978 when he coached West Adelaide for the last time.

In 1994, John Cahill won his ninth premiership at Port Adelaide.

Tasmania's Bruce Carter won nine premierships as playing coach with three different clubs from 1904–13.

Another Tasmanian, Neil Conlan, won six premierships as a coach in Canberra as did the much-travelled Roger Duffy, who'd played in Footscray's 1954 premiership side.

Western Australia's most successful premiership coach is Phil Matson who won seven flags with East Perth from 1919–23 and again in 1926–27 after one with Subiaco, in 1913.

Two of the greatest VFL reserves and under 19 coaches are Ray Jordon and Denis Pagan. Jordon, a former Australian cricketer, coached 11 premiership sides in the two competitions, while Pagan led North Melbourne under 19s to five flags. Crossing to Essendon in 1992, he again won the flag, at Victorian State Football League level.

Finally given a chance at senior level, with North Melbourne, Pagan led the Roos into the finals in each of his first two seasons, in 1993–94.

COLEMAN, John (1928–73)

A goalkicking phenomenon and one of the game's most remarkable players, John Coleman was post-war football's first super-hero, the most publicised player of his and perhaps any era.

Recruited from Hastings, via Port Fairy, where he kicked 136 goals in his first senior year and 160 in his second, Coleman joined Essendon only after he had considered standing out of football for 12 months to join Richmond.

Lightly built, with a tremendous leap, he averaged almost six goals a game in five and a half seasons from 1949–54, adding an incredibly exciting dimension to League football.

'Never was there a more sensational player than the high-marking Coleman,' said Richmond legend *Jack Dyer*.

A trademark John Coleman leap, against North Melbourne in the early 1950s.

At 185 cm and 80.5 kg he was a superb and acrobatic mark, an expert lead, and a long and accurate kick. He was the first player since Collingwood forward *Gordon Coventry* to head the VFL goalkicking four or more times.

He would have also won the goalkicking in 1951, if not for his controversial four-week suspension, which remains one of the most famous tribunal cases in history.

In his first League season, he:
- Kicked 12 goals on debut.
- Was the first player to kick 100 goals in his maiden season.
- Won Essendon's best and fairest and broke its goalkicking record.
- Became the first player to head the VFL goalkicking in his first season.
- Won selection in two Victorian teams.

From his remarkable first game against Hawthorn, he was a box-office smash. Opposition supporters even deserted their own clubs to witness his thrilling marking.

His huge goal tallies made Essendon, already a post-war power, even more formidable.

Unfortunately Coleman's reign was all too brief. In the eighth round of the 1954 season he dislocated his knee in the final quarter against North Melbourne at Arden Street, while attempting to mark a pass from *Jack Clarke*. Spectators gasped in horror as they saw the ugly, unnatural angle of his dislocated leg. At 26, his career was over.

He attempted a comeback in 1956 but, after half a practice game, realised his attempts to play again were futile. Doctors discovered floating fragments of bone in his leg and placed it in a metal splint.

Later he was to coach the Bombers to two premierships in four years. He remained a magnetic personality and was one of the most popular stars of the early football shows on radio, the Kia-Ora Parade and the Pelaco Football Inquest.

Many regard him as the game's greatest full-forward: his goals-per-match average of 5.48 is marginally behind Hawthorn's *Peter Hudson* (5.64) and well ahead of between-the-war greats, Magpie stalwart Coventry (4.25) and South Melbourne's *Bob Pratt* (4.34).

'His spring was the main thing,' said Essendon legend *Dick Reynolds*. 'He took off from either foot and would soar straight up. Nobody could get near him for marks.'

Coleman led the League goalkicking in four of his five full seasons. His overall tally of 537 goals in 98 matches includes 12 'double figure' tallies. His best effort was 14 against Fitzroy in 1954, an incredible effort as he was kept goalless in the first term. Against Collingwood in 1950, he kicked 10 out of Essendon's 12 and against South Melbourne in 1953, 11 out of 13.

Like St Kilda's modern-day goalkicking colossus, *Tony Lockett*, Coleman drew huge crowds to his games. His No. 10 guernsey was the most famous on the field.

He was mobbed everywhere he went. Newspapers devoted columns to his habits, home life and what he ate for breakfast.

Country people used to ring Essendon secretary Bill Cookson from 7 a.m. on Saturdays asking: 'Will Coleman be playing?'

Alf Brown, *The Herald*'s distinguished and long-serving football writer, said Coleman was the greatest player he'd seen: 'He had all the football gifts. He was courageous, a long, straight kick, had a shrewd football brain and, above all, was a spectacular mark. Coleman, flying high above a pack, provided football's finest spectacle. He was a matchwinner—the player every coach and selection committee spent hours worrying about.'

In an odd twist, it was an article by Brown in early 1949 which triggered Coleman's emergence at Essendon, just when it appeared the 20-year-old might play elsewhere.

Brown blasted the Essendon players for ignoring the potential star recruit during trial matches. The Bombers had been in three straight Grand Finals and some felt keenly about the arrival of gifted newcomers who might endanger their own places.

Coleman had played practice games in the city for three consecutive years without being overly impressive. In one such game in 1947 he was shifted from the forward line into a back pocket. Established Essendon players selfishly shared the ball with their mates, rather than with the recruits.

After Brown's scathing article there was a remarkable transformation. Players started to look for the prodigy and even kicked the ball backwards to him. He booted a swag of goals and was named in the first match of '49. An unforgettable career was about to unfold.

Debuting against Hawthorn he equalled Ted Freyer's 1935 opening-round record by kicking 12 goals at Windy Hill.

Hawthorn tried three different opponents against him, including fellow first-gamer Fred Wain. Coleman kicked five goals in the first quarter and four in the last. It was a freakish effort.

He had hauls of eight and seven later in the season, amassing 85 in 18 matches as the Bombers qualified fourth. After impressive September wins against Collingwood and North Melbourne, in which Coleman kicked a total of nine goals, the Bombers made the Grand Final. Coleman needed six goals to reach his century. There was almost as much interest in his milestone as there was in whether Essendon could beat Carlton for the flag.

To three-quarter time, he'd kicked just two goals but Essendon led comfortably. Carlton defenders had paid the penalty of being 'Coleman-conscious' and not manning-up on Essendon's forward line.

With the premiership assured, Essendon players did everything possible to help Coleman reach his ton.

He kicked two early last-quarter goals, courtesy of Ted Leehane, but missed his next three shots. His 99th came via 'Whopper' Lane and then he accepted a pass from captain-coach Reynolds.

Only seconds remained as he carefully lined up for goal No. 100. Carlton's *Bert Deacon* ran down to Coleman and offered him some words of encouragement. The kick was true and the thunderous roar of acclamation lasted for several minutes.

As the siren sounded, Coleman snatched off his guernsey and exchanged it with his great opponent, Ollie Grieve. The crowd swept him off his feet and chaired him from the ground. Essendon was a clear winner by 73 points.

It was the Bombers' 11th straight victory. Coleman was an irresistible force and averaged five goals a game.

When he repeated his century triumph in 1950, kicking 120 goals in 19 games, many claimed it was an even superior effort to Pratt's record 150 in 1934. Goals tended to be harder to get after the war than before it as teams worked harder on their defensive skills.

Coleman's combination work with champion rover *Billy Hutchison* and centre half-forward Bill Snell became a feature of Essendon's game.

The Bombers were going for their third flag in a row in 1951 when, on the eve of the finals, Coleman was sensationally reported on a charge of striking Carlton follower Harry Caspar.

Opponents had pushed him to the limit with rough-house tactics. The tribunal found Coleman had been provoked but he was suspended for four weeks, effectively rubbing him out of the '51 finals.

A shocked Coleman fought his way out of the tribunal through a large crowd.

There were tears in his eyes. Caspar also received four weeks, but most felt Coleman's sentence was unnecessarily severe. As the retaliator, they believed he should have received only two weeks.

His suspension started a public protest against the tribunal. Letters flooded into clubs and newspaper offices demanding an overhaul of the system.

Perhaps the only flaw in Coleman's game was his temperament. He could not get on with umpires or his opponents, who reserved tough treatment for him which he resented.

After his suspension, he became even more of an umpire 'hater'. Team-mate Billy Hutchison once said: 'I used to shudder at the things he called them.'

Essendon would almost certainly have won the '51 flag with Coleman playing. Without him the Bombers did well to defeat Footscray by eight points and Collingwood by two, but lost the Grand Final to Geelong, by 11 points. It was Dick Reynolds' last match.

The Cats played the better football on the day, but Essendon supporters remembered how their club had thrashed Geelong the last time the two sides met, just a few weeks before.

Earlier that season, *Jack Dyer* classed Coleman with Bob Pratt, saying while Pratt was more spectacular, Coleman was a superior converter and more team-orientated. He was also taller, heavier and could protect himself better.

'Those sensational leaps of Pratt's could inspire a side but Coleman has a quality lacking in Pratt. As long as Essendon get the goals, Coleman doesn't worry who gets them. Pratt was an individualist and a brilliant one—but give me team-man Coleman every time.'

In 1952, he kicked 31 goals in his last three games to reach 103, including six in the last quarter against St Kilda at the Junction Oval, *after* he was knocked out earlier in the game.

In 1961, he replaced Reynolds as coach. In the next seven years, Essendon won the 1962 and 1965 flags.

Unlike Reynolds, he had no qualms about making moves or taking players from the field if he felt they weren't doing well enough. Some said he was heartless but two premierships and two other finals appearances proved his disciplinarian tactics worked.

Coleman coached Victoria in 1965. He also played 12 games for his State, from 1949–53, and was an All Australian in 1953. His best finish in the Brownlow was his fourth placing in 1949.

His death at his Dromana hotel on 5 April, 1973, was greeted with disbelief. He was just 44.

In 1981, the VFL moved to perpetuate his memory by awarding the leading home-and-away goal-kicker each season with the John Coleman Medal.

COLLIER, Albert (1909–88)

A three-time winner of Collingwood's Copeland Trophy, in 1929, 1934 and 1935, Albert 'Leeta' Collier also won the 1929 Brownlow Medal. A talented centre half-back who also played on the ball, he was recruited to Collingwood from Ivanhoe in 1925 as a 15-year-old forward.

Staunchly loyal to his five brothers, his mates and his guernsey, 84 kg Leeta was renowned as one of the roughest and toughest players of the Depression era. He played 14 State games for Victoria, 206 with Collingwood and 12 with Fitzroy (in 1941–42).

His effort of playing in six winning Grand Final sides has been surpassed by only one other, Hawthorn's *Michael Tuck* and equalled by only three others: his brother *Harry*, and post-war Melbourne players *Ron Barassi* and *Frank 'Bluey' Adams*.

Collingwood and interstate rovers boasted that the 179 cm Collier gave them so much protection in the ruck that he made their jobs easy. He loved to sprint clear of packs after taking a mark and met any challenge with a hip and shoulder.

Jack Dyer says Collier was Collingwood's greatest-ever player, with an on-field 'presence' matched by few. 'He could do anything,' his brother Harry told Michael Roberts in *A Century of the Best*. '(He could) run, mark, kick either foot,

The master of the blind turn, Collingwood's Harry Collier. He won a Brownlow and was 'Champion of the Colony'.

handball, turn—and to top it off he was just about the toughest player you'd ever see.'

COLLIER, Harry (1907–94)

Born in Turner Street, just across the railway line from hallowed Victoria Park, young Harry lived and breathed football, hoping that one day he'd represent Collingwood. He did so with distinction—his polished skills and determination helped him to figure in a record-equalling six Collingwood premierships from 1927–36.

Beaten for the Brownlow on a countback by Richmond's *Stan Judkins* in 1930, he was one of seven who were awarded their medals retrospectively. Playing as a centreman or rover, he captained the Magpies from 1935–39, when the club made five successive Grand Finals. He was best and fairest in 1928 and 1930 and 'Champion of the Colony' in 1936.

One of Collingwood's most popular champions, Collier considered it the greatest of privileges to be playing at Collingwood. 'I thought it was beaut just to be able to hold my place in the side each week. I was one of the lucky ones. Every week some really good players missed out and I always felt for them.'

His all time favourite finals memory was in 1935 when Collingwood reversed its second semi-final loss to South Melbourne to win the Grand Final, 11.12 (78) to 7.16 (58).

South led in the last quarter until Collier's desperate tackle on South Melbourne midfielder Jim Reid resulted in the ball spilling to winger Jack Carmody who helped set up a crucial, matchlifting goal.

Regarded highly for his ability to turn blind, the 172 cm Collier was described as 'as game as you can make them, persistent as a fox terrier after a rabbit and extremely skilful in extricating himself and teammates from awkward positions.' He also kicked 299 goals in 253 games over 15 seasons.

In 1938, Collier was involved in a sensational incident with Carlton's Jack Carney, whom he admitted striking after hearing an offensive remark at the end of the match. No umpire witnessed the incident but the Carlton committee complained and Collier was outed for the rest of the season (14 weeks, including the finals).

The VFL was swamped by protests. A petition for a rehearing was submitted to the League contained 1500 signatures. But it was ignored. Collingwood lost the Grand Final, to Carlton, by 15 points. 'I reckon I may have been able to make the difference,' said Collier. 'But I had to sit out in the crowd. It was painful.'

Collier's suspension was staggering considering his unblemished record in 13 previous years of League football.

'The Colliers provided the spirit (of the teams of the '30s),' said Collingwood historian Richard Stremski. 'They insisted on and valued teamwork more than anyone at Victoria Park except *"Jock" McHale*. It was the Colliers who tutored young players, took them under their wing, did not let them drink (!), made them feel at home in the team, looked after them in their early League games, made sure they got a kick, visited them in hospital and instilled in them the finest features of the Collingwood tradition.'

COLLING, Gary (1950–)

A stalwart half-back with St Kilda from 1968–81, 187 cm 'Cat' Colling played 265 games and was a member of the Saints' 1971 Grand Final side. Recruited from Frankston Peninsula, via Karingal High, he played in a final series in his first season, as an 18-year-old.

COLLINGWOOD

Australia's most famous sporting club, Collingwood revels in its working-class roots and, together with arch rivals Carlton and Essendon, is League football's most successful side, having won 14 premierships and been runners-up 23 times. The Magpies won the first Australian Football League premiership in 1990 and boast more supporters across Australia—and overseas—than any other team.

Formed in 1892—in part, to raise the dignity of one of Melbourne's more unfashionable suburbs—Collingwood was an offshoot of the nearby Fitzroy club. Its founders were the members of the old Brittannia and Normandy cricket and football clubs.

Collingwood played at Dight's Paddock at Studley Park. Owing to its lack of training quarters, the team had to change into their football gear in the Yarra Hotel in Johnston Street and run across to the ground, situated on the banks of the Yarra.

In its early days, the team was known as the 'Flatties' or 'Flatites' (after Collingwood's flat topography). Some called the club the 'Purloiners' before the more-acceptable nickname of 'the Magpies'—after the club's black and white uniform—came into being from 1894.

Collingwood played a major hand in football's surge in popularity. The Depression of the 1890s may have resulted in many losing their jobs, but it also led to growing numbers of men having more leisure time.

Football was a release for thousands from the tough economic times, according to Collingwood's historian Richard Stremski. Commenting on one of the club's earliest public meetings, he said: 'One thousand boisterous barrackers packed the Town Hall for the club's 1894 annual public meeting, even though less than 300 could afford the five shilling membership subscription. The supporters "were so light-hearted and bubbling over with enthusiasm that want of work and want of food one would imagine to be unknown" in depression-riddled Collingwood.'

Encouraged to join the VFA, Collingwood immediately attracted 400 'subscribers', mainly 'blue collar' industrial workers who already shared a united spirit for 'their' football club.

Sixteen thousand attended the club's first game at Victoria Park against Carlton on 7 May, 1892. It was a major social event. The fledgling team won only three games, but was encouraged by the generosity of many benefactors, including the MCC secretary Major Ben Wardill, who allowed his curator to assist Collingwood to select soil from Merri Creek. The MCC also supplied free grass seed to help bring Victoria Park up to Association standard.

Under the leadership of its first great captain, Carlton's Bill Strickland, Collingwood improved quickly, and won the VFA premiership in 1896 before being invited to join the breakaway Victorian Football League in 1897. Already it was becoming known for its discipline. Stremski said:

'Although the suburb may have been born with a wooden spoon in its mouth, the club founded on pride, discipline and leadership was predestined for greatness.'

Within six years, Collingwood had a 'top-three' finish and a premiership to its credit. Intense rivalries with neighbouring clubs Fitzroy and Carlton began to develop. From 1897 to 1911, Collingwood appeared in 15 consecutive final series, a record which still stands today.

One of its finest early players was centre-man *'Jock' McHale*, who joined in 1903 and played 261 games in the next 15 years, including a record 191 in a row. From 1925–30, McHale-coached Collingwood sides appeared in six Grand Finals in succession.

Collingwood's 1940 Brownlow Medallist, Des Fothergill.

Season 1929 was particularly memorable. The club lost only one game, the second semi-final to Richmond, before reversing the result in the Grand Final.

Opposition sides regarded the Magpies as the meanest, toughest side in the competition.

'No outsiders were welcome,' said legendary Tiger *Jack Dyer*. 'In the early thirties Geelong beat them and the Magpie vice-president, Rosey Dummett, took the Geelong president over to the club rooms for a drink. The door was opened by Collingwood secretary (Frank) Wraith, probably the most outstanding secretary they had. He was a taciturn, nasty character who did more to build the Collingwood

Collingwood
Football Club.

PREMIERS.
1930

COMMEMORATIVE PICTURE.
4 SUCCESSIVE PREMIERSHIPS.
1927 · 1928 · 1929 · 1930

The revered Collingwood team which won the 1930 premiership, the club's fourth flag in a row, a feat unequalled in VFL history.

tradition than any other man. Dummett said he had brought the Geelong official over for a drink. Wraith snarled: "I don't care if he's the president of the British Empire, he can't get a drink here." '

The club's proud record of four premierships in a row may never be broken. Melbourne went close, on two occasions winning three flags on end. In 1958, Collingwood stopped the Demons from equalling its record with a surprise win in the Grand Final.

In the club's first 43 years to the Second World War, it finished no lower than seventh and made the finals 37 times.

In the first 92 years of VFL competition, the Magpies appeared in the finals 69 times, 12 more times than the second-most successful club, Carlton.

Collingwood teams figure in the best-attended games ever. In mid-year 1958, 99,346 saw the Queen's Birthday match with Melbourne, a record for home-and-away football. On Anzac Day, 1995, the Collingwood–Essendon game drew 94,825. The 1970 Grand Final against Carlton attracted 121,696, another record.

Club insiders say that a quarter of football's annual income is generated by Collingwood. Newspaper editors love the Magpies to win as it leads to thriving next-day sales.

Though always competitive, the club went three decades without a flag after '58, finishing runner-up eight times in a row. Critics claimed the club suffered a bad case of stage fright each September. The term 'Colliwobbles' was born.

In 1990, it ended the 32-year premiership drought with a magnificent victory against Essendon in the first AFL Grand Final.

Five Collingwood players have won the Brownlow, the most recent being ruckmen *Len Thompson* (1972) and *Peter Moore* (1979).

The club resisted pressure to shift its home games to Waverley and initially won a guarantee to have seven home matches a year at Victoria Park. But as the 1995 season opened, that number had decreased to three, Collingwood joining four other co-tenants at the MCG for most of its major matches.

COLLINGWOOD: THE STATISTICS

FORMED: February, 1892

JOINED LEAGUE: 1897

HOME VENUES: Victoria Park (1897–), MCG (1993–)

CURRENT HOME VENUE DIMENSIONS: Victoria Park: 164 metres × 133 metres; MCG: 161 metres × 140 metres

COLOURS: Vertical black and white striped guernsey.

TOTAL FINALS MATCHES: 151 (63 wins, 84 losses, 4 ties)

FINALS RECORD: Premiers: 14 (1902–03, 1910, 1917, 1919, 1927–28–29–30, 1935–36, 1953, 1958, 1990)

Runners up: 22 (1901, 1905, 1911, 1915, 1918, 1920, 1925–26, 1937–38–39, 1952, 1955–56, 1960, 1964, 1966, 1970, 1977, 1979–80–81)

PREMIERSHIP COACHES: Lardie Tulloch (2), George Angus (1), Jock McHale (8), 'Phonse' Kyne (2), Leigh Matthews (1).

NIGHT SERIES PERMIERSHIP: 1 (1979)

YOUNGEST PLAYER: Keith Bromage, 15 years 287 days (1953)

OLDEST PLAYER: Les Hughes, 38 years 144 days (1922)

HIGHEST SCORE: 32.19 (211) v St Kilda, R.17, 1980, VFL Park

LOWEST SCORE: 0.8 (8) v South Melb., R.11, 1897, Victoria Park

LONGEST WINNING SEQUENCE: 20 (1928–29)

LONGEST LOSING SEQUENCE: 9 (1982)

MOST FINALS: Gordon Coventry 31, Harry Collier 27, Albert Collier 26, 'Dick' Lee 22, Len Thompson 22, Tony Shaw 22, Syd Coventry 21, 'Phonse' Kyne 21, Bill Picken 21, Ron Wearmouth 21, Charlie Dibbs 20, Wayne Richardson 20, Peter Moore 20, Ray Shaw 20

MOST SEASONS AS COACH: 'Jock' McHale 38 (1912–49)

MOST SEASONS AS CAPTAIN: Syd Coventry 8 (1927–34)

MOST GAMES		MOST GOALS	
Tony Shaw	313	Gordon Coventry	1299
Gordon Coventry	306	Peter McKenna	838
Wayne Richardson	278	Dick Lee	707
Len Thompson	270	Peter Daicos	549
'Jock' McHale	261	Albie Pannam junior	455
Harry Collier	253	Lou Richards	424
Lou Richards	250	Brian Taylor	371
Peter Daicos	250	Des Fothergill	337
'Phonse' Kyne	245	Ron Todd	327
Dick Lee	230	Wayne Richardson	324
Syd Coventry	227	Harry Collier	299
Les Hughes	225	Murray Weideman	262
Charlie Dibbs	216	Craig Davis	251
Max Richardson	214	Des Tuddenham	250
Ross Dunne	213	Rene Kink	240
Bill Picken	213	Ross Dunne	238
Albert Collier	205	'Phonse' Kyne	237
		Len Thompson	217
		Bob Rose	214
		Ray Shaw	201

COLLINGWOOD: THE STATISTICS (cont)

MOST GOALS IN A MATCH: Gordon Coventry 17 v Fitzroy, R.12, 1930, Victoria Park.
Gordon Coventry 16 v Hawthorn, R.13, 1929, Victoria Park.
Peter McKenna 16 v South Melb., R.19, 1969, Victoria Park.
Gordon Coventry 15 v Essendon, R.11, 1933, Victoria Park.
Gordon Coventry 14 v Hawthorn, R.14, 1934, Victoria Park.

BROWNLOW MEDALLISTS: Syd Coventry (1927), Albert Collier (1929), Harry Collier (1930), Marcus Whelan (1939), Des Fothergill (1940), Len Thompson (1972), Peter Moore (1979).

COLEMAN MEDALLISTS: Brian Taylor (1986)

LEAGUE LEADING GOALSCORERS: Archie Smith 31 (1898), Ted Rowell 33 (1902), Teddy Lockwood 35 (1903), Charlie Pannam snr 38 (1905), Dick Lee 47 (1907), Dick Lee 54 (1908), Dick Lee 58 (1909), Dick Lee 58 (1910), Dick Lee 57 (1914), Dick Lee 66 (1915), Dick Lee 54 (1917), Dick Lee 56 (1919), Dick Lee 64 (1921), Gordon Coventry 83 (1926), Gordon Coventry 97 (1927), Gordon Coventry 89 (1928), Gordon Coventry 124 (1929), Gordon Coventry 119 (1930), Gordon Coventry 72 (1937), Ron Todd 120 (1938), Ron Todd 121 (1939), Ian Brewer 73 (1958), Peter McKenna 130 (1972), Peter McKenna 84 (1973), Brian Taylor 100 (1986).

HOME VENUE RECORD ATTENDANCE: Victoria Park: 47,224, Coll. v South Melb, R.2, 1948.
MCG: 94,825, Coll. v Essendon, R.4, 1995

RECORD ATTENDANCE IN ANY MATCH: 121,696 v Carlton, GF, 1970, MCG.

MOST RECENT PREMIERSHIP TEAM: 1990—Collingwood 13.11 (89) d Essendon 5.11 (41).
B: S. Kerrison, M. Christian, M. Gayfer. H.B: S. Morwood, C. Kelly, G. Crosisca. C: D. Millane, T. Shaw (c), G. Wright. H.F: D. Banks, J. Manson, D. Barwick. F: S. Russell, G. Brown, P. Daicos. R: D. Monkhorst, M. McGuane. R: T. Francis. Interchange: J. Turner, C. Starcevich.

COLLIS, Gordon (1940–)

In a career restricted to 97 games because of injury, Carlton centre half-back Collis was a fine mark and thumping kick who won the 1964 Brownlow Medal by eight votes from Essendon's *Ken Fraser* and Hawthorn's Phil Hay.

The Blues won the signature of the Healesville kid ahead of Fitzroy. The Lions were desperately unlucky. He'd originally signed with the club, but Carlton committeeman George Woodward visited Collis, convinced him the agreement with Fitzroy was worthless, and tore it up.

Collis signed a new agreement with Carlton only minutes before Fitzroy officials arrived to collect the original document.

He soon showed rare ability in his debut games at centre half-forward.

He was selected for Victoria against Tas-

Carlton's Gordon Collis possessed exceptional talent.

65

mania in 1962, the first of his three State games. He missed the finals because of illness, and had several games late in the year in the reserves.

He was given an opportunity to play centre half-back early in 1964 and had a magnificent year, even though the Blues slipped to 10th, their lowest ever ranking.

The 187 cm Collis also won Carlton's best and fairest in '64. In the Brownlow count, his 27 votes was 23 ahead of the next best Carlton player, Ian Collins.

In 1965, he injured his ankle and was restricted to just eight games. He missed the whole season in 1966 and retired at the end of 1967, having never regained his eye-catching Brownlow form.

COMBEN, Bruce (1930–)

A tough, no-nonsense Carlton stalwart who played 187 games from 1950–61, Bruce 'Bugsy' Comben captained the Blues from 1958–60, twice being best and fairest, in 1957–58.

He represented Victoria nine times from 1957–60, as a proud and successful State defender. But his most-remembered Big V appearance was in Launceston in 1960, when he led the Victorian team which lost to Tasmania for the first time.

In a memorable match, the Victorians lost *Hugh Mitchell* with a knee injury early and *Bill Goggin* broke his collarbone. Comben ran into a goalpost and later had 10 stitches inserted in a cut over his eye. Tasmania won by seven points in front of more than 15,000 delirious fans.

Comben's opposing captain was Stuart Spencer, the former Melbourne premiership rover. There was one former Tasmanian in the VFL line-up, *Verdun Howell*, who was among his team's best, along with St Kilda team-mate and centreman Lance Oswald.

COMEBACK KIDS

Big marking Ian 'Humper' Cooper was one of post-war football's most courageous players and one of the most notable to make a comeback after time out of the game.

Best afield in St Kilda's 1966 premiership, the spindly blond was forced to retire at 21 after the opening match of the 1968 season. He was suffering from rheumatic fever and had subsequent trouble with a leaking heart valve.

But he returned in 1969 and extended his League career to 69 games, before shifting to Swan Districts in 1970–71 and for part of 1972.

Returning to Melbourne, he had four highly successful seasons at Sandringham, where he kicked 282 goals in 56 matches, his spectacular leaping a highlight.

Melbourne's *Don Williams* and Fitzroy's *Kevin Murray* also spent time interstate in mid-career.

Brownlow Medallist *Ron Clegg* crossed to North Wagga in 1955 before returning to the VFL and being named South's captain in 1957.

Melbourne's Dr Brian Roet went overseas after 71 games with the Demons from 1961–66, including the 1964 premiership, before returning in 1968 and playing several more seasons.

More recently, Hawthorn's *Chris Mew* and Essendon pair Shane Heard and *Tim Watson* returned to the game after late-career 'retirements'.

Others to play again after sizeable gaps include Andrew Merryweather (almost six years in between games for Fitzroy and Essendon), Paul O'Brien, Craig Davis, Andrew Taylor, Peter Melesso, Neale Daniher, Tim Barling and Graeme Schultz.

Full forward Davis had almost a four and a half year gap in between his final League season at Collingwood in 1983 and his first (and last) with Sydney in 1988.

CONLAN, Mick (1958–)

An aggressive, free-running half-forward who played in Tasmania and in the VFA after his 13-season League career had finished, Conlan amassed 210 games from 1977–89.

He was renowned for his devastating bursts. It was not unusual for 'Crash' Conlan to take three or four bounces as he charged downfield, knocking his way past

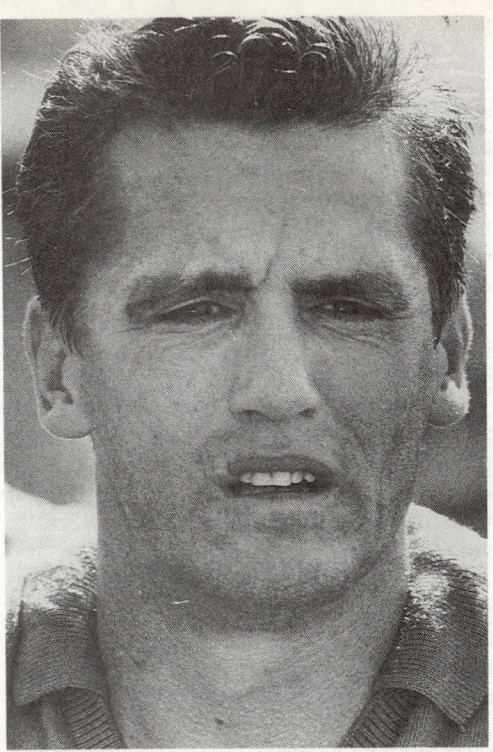

Mick Conlan: devastating speed.

opposing players. He combined blistering speed with awesome strength and a temper which at the end of his career often saw him on report.

In one game against North Melbourne in 1983 he kicked seven goals, all in the second half, after having just one kick in the opening two quarters. Against Footscray in 1984 he kicked 10 goals, a personal best.

His early coaches at Fitzroy told him he must increase his physical strength to play League football. For years he worked out in a gymnasium before dawn, five times a week, and increased his weight from a spindly 73 kg to a robust 89 kg.

He played in only one grand final in his time at Fitzroy, the 1978 night play-off when Fitzroy defeated North Melbourne. He also represented Victoria four times.

Conlan's father, Neil, was one of Tasmania's greatest players. In 1953, at 17, he became the youngest ever Tasmanian State representative. He played in three Australian carnivals, amassing a record 25

appearances. Neil Conlan was signed by Richmond as a 16-year-old but remained in Tasmania, playing more than 250 games.

CORDNER, Denis (1924–90)

A leading member of one of Victoria's most remarkable football families, Denis Cordner played in five Grand Finals in his nine years at Melbourne, including two in successive weeks, in 1948, after the Grand Final was sensationally tied.

A player in three premiership sides, he was centre half-back in 1948 and first ruckman in the 1955–56 flags.

On debut for Melbourne against Richmond in 1943, he was flattened at the opening bounce by Tiger toughman *Jack Dyer*. 'Welcome to the League, son,' Dyer was heard to remark. Cordner, then 19, recovered to kick two goals, showing the courage he was to be renowned for.

Like his brothers, Ted, *Don* and John—who all played League football—Cordner played as an amateur. His commitments with the Royal Australian Navy during the war kept him out of the game and it wasn't until September 1948, after three consecutive premierships with University Blacks, that he returned to Melbourne.

A replacement had to be found for suspended centre half-back Alan McGowan and Cordner agreed to play. He was among Melbourne's best six in the tied Grand Final and held his place for the replay, which Melbourne won easily.

He maintained his links with Melbourne until 1956, and became a fine key-position player and ruckman. In 1950 and 1954 he was Melbourne's best and fairest player.

Captain of the Redlegs from 1951–53, he also represented Victoria three times, in 1949, 1951 and 1952.

He had an impressive career in business and diplomacy. For almost 25 years he was head of ICI Australia and, in the early 1980s, was Australia's Consul-General in New York.

The three eldest Cordner brothers, Don, Denis and Ted, all represented Victoria. John 'Jock' Cordner had six games in 1951 before leaving for England, where he worked as an industrial chemist. John was also a fine cricketer and represented Victoria in the Sheffield Shield.

CORDNER, Don (1922–   )

The only amateur to win the Brownlow Medal, the 192 cm doctor of medicine triumphed in 1946 when he won by a vote from fellow bigmen, Richmond's *Bill Morris* and Carlton's Jack Howell.

He made his VFL debut in the second semi-final against Carlton in 1941, when the Redlegs were minus almost a dozen regular players—seven were in the services and four were injured.

Best and fairest in 1943, Cordner played 166 games, and retired after the 1950 season. He captained Melbourne in 1948 and 1949, seasons in which he also represented Victoria. In 1948 he captained Victoria against South Australia.

His father, Dr Edward Cordner, represented University at VFL level. The four boys, Ted, Don, *Denis* and John amassed a combined tally of 376 games with Melbourne.

The three eldest brothers, Ted, Don and Denis figured in Melbourne premiership sides. They first played in the same team against Richmond in 1943.

Don and Denis were very alike and at one stage during this game *Jack Titus* was slow in climbing off a player he thought was the youngest Cordner. When Don complained, Titus said: 'Sorry, Don, I thought it was Denis.'

Dr Cordner maintained close ties with the Melbourne Football and Cricket Clubs. In early 1992, as president of the Melbourne Cricket Club, he opened the new $140 million Great Southern Stand at the Melbourne Cricket Ground. He has been a member since 1936 and served as president for eight years.

See: 'BROTHERS, Famous'

CORDY, Neil (1959–   )

The most prominent of three footballing brothers from Traralgon, all of whom played League football, Neil amassed 236 games in 15 seasons from 1979–93.

A fine high mark, the 188 cm defender began at Footscray in 1979 and had eight seasons and 140 games before joining Sydney in 1987. In 1985, he and his brothers Graeme and Brian achieved the rare feat of playing together in three Footscray matches. In 1987 Graeme Cordy played with Neil for Sydney, against Brian Cordy, representing Footscray.

COUCH, Paul (1964–   )

Geelong's first Brownlow Medallist in 27 years, Couch won the 1989 count by three votes from Hawthorn's *John Platten*. A Geelong committeeman, who backed Couch at the pre-season odds of 330/1, won $10,000.

On joining Geelong after an unsuccessful trial at Fitzroy, he became a front-line player almost immediately. He was the Cats' best first-year player in 1985 and their most-improved player and club champion in 1986. But in 1988 he lost form playing as a winger cum half-forward and was dropped. He was back to his best against Sydney in the 18th round that season when, selected in the centre, he had 47 possessions against the great *Greg Williams*.

In 1989, under new coach *Malcolm Blight*, Couch's inspirational play in the pivot helped Geelong into the Grand Final. He was one of the Cat's best in their six point loss. He again won the best and fairest.

He'd gained extra fitness during the season by running 20 kilometres each day as a garbage collector with the Corio council.

He played in two more (losing) Grand Finals in 1992 and 1994.

COULTER LAW, The (and player payments)

Player payments were first made legal in 1911. Regulations were introduced in 1930, during the Depression, to limit these sums. Players received £3 a game, and playing coaches £4, under the Coulter Law, named after its deviser Gordon

Coulter, a VFL administrator and former Melbourne player.

This law was maintained for almost 40 years. The standard match payment was adjusted in line with increases in average weekly earnings and cost-of-living rises.

By 1960, the maximum fee was £6. In 1968, players were paid $25 per game.

During the 1960s and 1970s, the law became increasingly difficult to enforce and it was clear that it was being deliberately flouted.

Melbourne was just one of the leading clubs accused of making 'under-the-table' payments for players' educational expenses.

Other clubs were said to be offering recruits huge, undeclared signing-on fees. Further loopholes involved travelling expenses and compensation for lost wages, as well as payments to injured players.

From the outset, player payments were a constant source of worry for clubs, who relied mainly on gate receipts and donations from beneficiaries to stay solvent.

The richer and most popular clubs like Collingwood, Essendon and Carlton regularly drew the best crowds of the round and could afford to pay players more than other clubs.

The Coulter Law was designed to assist the struggling clubs to remain afloat. But it was the centre of continual criticism and, in the end, clubs refused to abide by it.

In 1960, Collingwood agreed to pay its players £10 a game, £2 more than was officially allowed.

Under new president Tom Sherrin, the club instigated a provident fund payment, with bonuses for 50, 100 and 200 game milestones. In 1964, Collingwood claimed it paid its players more than any other club.

By 1970, the Coulter Law was obsolete and clubs were able to offer their best players the largest contracts in history.

During the 1970 pre-season period, two of Collingwood's most senior players, inspirational skipper *Des Tuddenham* and rising young rucking star *Len Thompson* threatened to strike unless the club was prepared to contract them at fees equivalent to those being paid to blond West Australian import Peter Eakins, who had received a signing-on fee of $5000, and the promise of lucrative benefits.

Tuddenham wanted $24,000 over three years and 22-year-old Thompson $20,000 for five. Collingwood doubled the pair's pay which met them 'half-way', but both players remained on strike for three weeks. Just hours after they'd resumed training in early March, Collingwood officials—obviously peeved at Tuddenham and Thompson's stance—announced a new on-field leadership team. Terry Waters was the new captain and *Wayne Richardson* vice-captain.

Soon afterwards, five Essendon players refused to play in the initial home-and-away match as a protest against their level of payment.

The VFL made several concessions and introduced a more attractive player-payment schedule with bonuses for captains, vice-captains and deputy-captains. Players with at least seven years' experience could also enter into contracts.

In 1975, payments for the least-experienced and those in non-leadership roles were set at between $45 and $65. Reserve grade players received $7 a week. At the top end of the scale, however, salaries reached record levels.

In 1979, Hawthorn rover *Leigh Matthews* was re-signed for $40,000. The next highest paid Hawk was ruckman *Don Scott*, on $23,000.

As payments rose, more clubs struggled to make ends meet and ran up huge deficits.

The salary cap and the salary cap commissioner were introduced in 1986. The standard player contract was drawn up in 1987. These moves helped the lower clubs, but were considered 'unnecessarily socialistic' by the well-to-do teams like Carlton and Hawthorn.

Hawthorn's chief executive John Lauritz said: 'A player is entitled to be paid what he is reasonably worth as a footballer, if his club can afford it. It's unfair for a player to have to leave his club because he can't be accommodated within the salary cap when the club can and is prepared to pay him.'

In 1991, it was estimated that the AFL's 15 clubs spent $25 million on player salaries. In 1990, Collingwood paid out $1.8 million after providing bonuses for a successful premiership campaign.

At the start of 1992, *Greg Williams* was deregistered for six weeks after it was found he and his former club, Sydney, had deliberately flaunted salary cap regulations. Both were fined $25,000.

COVENTRY, Gordon (1901–68)

A shy and gentle strongman, Gordon Richard James Coventry is one of the elite members of football's Hall of Fame, and acclaimed as the greatest goalkicker in VFL history.

In 18 seasons with Collingwood from 1920–37, he amassed 1299 goals from 306 games. He kicked more than 100 goals on four occasions, and in 1930 against Fitzroy he kicked a club and League record of 17 goals—a feat topped only by Melbourne's *Fred Fanning*, who kicked 18 goals against St Kilda in 1947.

Originally from Diamond Creek, Coventry kicked 100 goals against every team in the League, except Footscray. He was most successful against South Melbourne (141 goals) and Fitzroy (137). His 500th goal in League football came against South and his 1000th against the Lions.

Coventry's career average of 4.25 goals a game is surpassed by only one contemporary, South Melbourne's *Bob Pratt* (4.34), who played half as many games.

Coventry and his goalkicking hero, *Dick Lee*, kicked more than 2000 goals between them. They headed the League goalkicking in 16 of the first 41 years of the VFL.

Known by his family nickname of 'Nuts', Coventry had to work hard to cement his place. Slow and awkward in the beginning, he became a more consistent goalkicker after he abandoned the placekick.

He learned to judge his leads to enable him to kick from in front of goal as much as possible. However, when forced into the pockets his ability to 'banana' the ball was superb.

He topped the League goalkicking five years in a row and was the first to kick 100 goals in a season.

According to Collingwood historian Richard Stremski: 'Nuts was a six-footer (just on 183 cm) and weighed only 13 stone (nearly 83 kg) but he had huge hands that swallowed your elbow in a handshake.

'His vice-like grip made it difficult to punch the ball away from him once he had it in his grasp and his broadness and strength drove full-backs mad. Collingwood's biggest and toughest players could neither budge him nor get around him in practice sessions.'

A member of five Collingwood premiership teams, sharpshooting Gordon 'Nuts' Coventry.

The *Australian Footballer* declared: 'Gordon is ... wonderfully well-conditioned and rarely shows distress even after the hardest game. He is one of the few men playing that makes class football look easy.

'He is a very accurate kick, both on short and long distances, and his height and his weight are a great advantage in marking.'

Coventry's year-by-year record its testimony to his greatness and durability:

SEASON	GOALS	GAMES
1920	13	5
1921	19	11
1922	42	18
1923	36	13
1924	18	14
1925	68	18
1926	83	20
1927	97	20
1928	89	20
1929	124	20
1930	118	21
1931	67	18
1932	82	19
1933	108	17
1934	105	19
1935	88	21
1936	60	13
1937	72	19

In addition to his 17-goal blitz against Fitzroy, he also kicked 16 against Hawthorn in 1929, 15 against Essendon in 1933 and 14 against Hawthorn in 1934.

'Coventry was solid and workmanlike,' said Michael Roberts in *A Century of the Best*.

'He was neither fast nor brilliant, but he kept on kicking goals—most of them remarkably, with the one old pair of boots, which he would neither polish nor replace.'

In one his 21 interstate games, against South Australia, he kicked 10 goals and holds the record for most goals by a Victorian in interstate games (100).

He booted nine goals (out of 13) in the 1928 Grand Final, a record not equalled until *Gary Ablett* kicked nine goals for Geelong in the 1989 play-off.

He played in five premiership teams and would have been in six, but for a sensatonal eight-week suspension on the eve of the 1936 finals. He'd been booked for the first time in 17 seasons, for fighting Richmond's Joe Murdoch. The Richmond man had hit Coventry on the back of his neck, where he'd been worried by a mass of boils. Coventry swung wildly in retaliation but barely connected. Both were reported.

According to Stremski, Collingwood pleaded concussion, claiming Coventry went blank and did not know what he was doing—'but the truth might have been a better defence'.

Despite a public outcry which even reached Parliament, the judgement stood and Coventry promptly announced his retirement, only to be talked back for one last season in 1937.

He played in more finals (31) and kicked more goals in finals (112) than any player in League history, until Hawthorn's *Michael Tuck*, the AFL record-holder for the total number of games, eclipsed his mark in 1989.

COVENTRY, Syd (1899–1976)

Captain of Collingwood's four consecutive premiership teams from 1927–30, 180 cm Sydney Alfred Coventry was a much-decorated ruckman and vigorous leader who played a total of 227 games with Collingwood and represented Victoria 24 times. He was State captain in 1930 and 1933.

Coventry joined Collingwood in 1922, having had a season in Tasmania with Queenstown. On his return, he signed with St Kilda but changed his mind, because of his desire to play with his younger brother, *Gordon*, at Collingwood. He was also encouraged by the club's £4 donation for 'new player expenses'.

His natural leadership qualities were soon recognised and in 1926 he was made club vice-captain. He then became Collingwood's longest-serving captain, from 1927–34.

In 1927 he won the Brownlow Medal, the inaugural Copeland Trophy for Collingwood's best and fairest player and was selected by local sportswriters as the 'Champion of the Colony'. In 1932, he again won the club championship.

One of the first to perfect the tactic of dropping back a kick behind the play, he was an inspiration to his team-mates, being fiercely loyal and aggressive when occasion demanded. Once he ran the length of Victoria Park to remonstrate with a Carlton player who had downed his brother.

He coached Footscray in 1936 and 1937, but then returned to Collingwood in an administrative capacity, serving as vice-president from 1939–49 and president from 1950–63. He was a truly great servant of his club.

COWTON, Gary (1952–)

A much-travelled wingman and defender, nicknamed 'Crazy-horse', Cowton played 198 League games from 1971–84 with three clubs. He started and finished his career at North Melbourne, where he played in six Grand Finals in a row from 1974–78. Originally from Benalla, he also represented Footscray and South Melbourne.

CRIMMINS, Peter (1948–76)

Few footballers have been as courageous, inspirational or popular as Hawthorn's jockey-sized rover, Peter 'Meggsie' Crimmins, who captained the club in 1974–75 before tragically dying of cancer just days after the Hawks had won the 1976 premiership. He was 28.

Recruited from Assumption College, he went straight into Hawthorn's senior side in 1966. His father, Bryan, had represented Melbourne in 1944 and taught each of his five sons the rudiments of the game.

At 168 cm and 64 kg, Crimmins was small in stature, but possessed terrier-like qualities. He regularly took on players far bigger than himself without thought of personal injury.

Appointed vice-captain in 1970, he represented Victoria and formed a grand roving combination with a young *Leigh Matthews*. Both were dominant in the 1971 premiership. Even when he learnt, in 1974, that he had contracted cancer, he refused to stop playing. He led the Hawks into the preliminary final and continued playing in 1975. Before the sixth round game against Fitzroy, coach *John Kennedy* told the players it would be Crimmins' last game for at least six weeks. The cancer which had invaded his body had moved into the lungs. Crimmins had 20 kicks in probably his bravest performance.

He returned in the reserves and captained the side to victory in the first semi-final against Essendon, but never played

seniors again. He desperately wanted to lead the Hawks in the Grand Final, but was not selected. Kennedy later admired the decision to leave Crimmins out was the toughest he ever made in football. He had a hunch that Crimmins' presence may have inspired the team, but he and the match committee agreed it was too great a risk to take.

The Hawks were humbled and just over 12 months later—three days after the '76 Grand Final—Crimmins died.

Hawthorn's 'Captain Courageous' Peter Crimmins, with Richmond defender Kevin Sheedy.

He was too ill to attend the match. In a telegram to the players, which Kennedy ready out before the game, he said: 'Good luck to you and all the boys. It will be a long, hard 100 minutes but I am sure you will be there at the end. Regards. Peter Crimmins.'

After his final tactical talk, Kennedy told the team: 'There are a lot of reasons why you have to win today. Most of all, though, win it for the little feller.'

The Hawks duly did, defeating North Melbourne by five goals. That night, some of Crimmins' closest team-mates visited him in hospital with the premiership cup and described the match to him kick by kick. His body was wasted but his grin was as cheeky as ever and he was still talking about beating the cancer.

More than 2000 people attended his

funeral. A cancer research fund was established and more than $325,000 was raised. Hawthorn 'retired' his famous No. 5 guernsey, in the hope that one of his young sports-minded sons, Ben or Sam, might one day play for the Hawks. Ben played at under 19 level.

The club also named its elite under 17 training squad in Crimmins' memory.

From 1966–75, Crimmins played 167 day games and 19 night games with the Hawks, kicking 230 goals.

CRIPPLING INJURIES

Champion boxer and Footscray stalwart, Ambrose Palmer suffered a sickening knock in the opening round of the 1939 season. Sandwiched by two Essendon opponents, he sustained multiple jaw, cheekbone and skull fractures. For some time his life was threatened.

Carlton high-flier Keith Warburton received severe internal injuries in a semi-final against Fitzroy in 1952. Doctors

Footscray's Neil Sachse at training shortly before the collision which left him a quadriplegic.

feared for his life. He recovered in time to play the following season.

North Melbourne's Brian Johnson lost the sight of his right eye after being struck accidentally against St Kilda on 30 April, 1956. An appeal run on his behalf by a Melbourne newspaper raised £10,000.

Footscray's Stephen Boyle was blinded in one eye after an accident against St Kilda on 15 July, 1972. Playing only his sixth match, he was poked in the right eye at the Western Oval. He remained in hospital for three weeks.

Collingwood half-forward John Greening was in a semi-coma for several days after being struck behind play early in the 1972 season. After a long convalescence he represented the Magpies again, without recapturing his best form.*

Footscray's star sporting all-rounder Robert Rose, son of the great *Bob Rose*, was rendered a quadriplegic after the car in which he was driving overturned at Ballan on 14 February 1974, just eight days after his 22nd birthday.

In only his second VFL match in 1975, South Australian Neil Sachse accidentally collided with Fitzroy's Kevin O'Keefe. He received a broken neck which left him a quadraplegic.

On 7 May, 1987, Carlton's star South Australian import Peter Motley was driving home after a team dinner on the eve of a game against Geelong when he was involved in a three-car smash at Clifton Hill. He sustained severe head injuries, a severely bruised lung and a broken leg. He never played again.

CROFTS, Archie (d. 1942)

One of football's first major patrons, grocery magnate Crofts helped lift South Melbourne to the 1933 premiership by ensuring jobs for players during the Depression. Almost a dozen stars were lured from interstate by South's recruiting officer Jack Bohan who promised them regular work with Crofts.

At one stage Crofts employed more than two-thirds of South's senior players in his

* see 'FIVE FAMOUS INCIDENTS'

chain of grocery shops. South Australian Ossie Bertram worked as an accountant for Crofts while other prominent players Norman Reid, Roy Moore and another interstate star, Bill Faull, all became grocers.

Crofts was president of South from 1933–37. He was a member of the Legislative Council and South Melbourne's mayor in its centenary year, 1935.

He was also a very keen and successful racehorse owner. Valiant Chief won him more than £7000 in stake money. El Golea's Newmarket victory was the most famous of Crofts' 57½ wins in eight seasons.

CROSSWELL, Brent (1950–)

One of the most colourful and gifted footballers of the 1970s, Brent 'Tiger' Crosswell had a distinguished 222-game career from 1968–82. He played with three clubs and in four premierships, two with Carlton and two at North Melbourne, where his ability as a 'big-match' player became legend.

At 21, he was stricken with the bone disease, osteomyelitis, and forced out of football for a brief period. The following year he represented Victoria for the first time.

Making his debut as a 17-year-old, he played in the centre in Carlton's 1968 premiership in his first year, and in another in 1970.

His explosive leaping and marking allowed him to play successfully in key positions at both ends of the ground,

despite often conceding height to his opponents.

The 185 cm utility had seven seasons and 96 games at Carlton, before he played in North Melbourne's premierships in 1975 and 1977, where he was noted for his stormy relationship with coach *Ron Barassi*.

Yet he finished his career at Melbourne under Barassi, where he was leading goalkicker in 1980 and runner-up in the best and fairest in 1981.

CUNNINGHAM, Geoff (1959–)

A fiery and determined 183 cm wingman who played 224 games with St Kilda from 1977–89, 'Joffa' was recruited from Golden Point. He never played in a final but represented Victoria seven times. Acting captain in 20 games, he played 99 consecutive matches from 1982–86 before being dropped.

His brother, Darryl, also played League football.

CURCIO, Frank (1913–)

A stalwart Fitzroy ruckman who amassed 251 games from 1932–48, Curcio held the Lions' club record for most games played until 1970. A great leader, elected deputy captain in only his second season, Curcio led Fitzroy from 1938–41 and was vice-captain in his final year.

Known as a 'rough diamond' on the field, he played the violin for a living. He represented Victoria three times.

DAICOS, Peter (1961–)

Magnificently gifted, and noted for his freakish goalkicking ability near goal, 'The Macedonian Marvel' kicked 97 goals in Collingwood's 1990 premiership year.

It was the highest return by a forward pocket player in League annals. Before the play-off, Daicos needed five goals to kick 100, but scored only two in a low-scoring game.

The gifted Peter Daicos with another noted goalkicker, coach of Collingwood's 1990 premiership team, Leigh Matthews.

Twice best and fairest, in 1982 and 1988, the Magpie vice-captain from 1990–92, the 184 cm Daicos kicked a personal best of 13 goals against the Brisbane Bears at Carrara in round 20, 1991. He booted 75 goals for the year to head Collingwood's goalkicking charts for a fourth time. He led the charts again in 1992, but retired after continual leg problems in 1993, having reached 250 games.

Few players in history have possessed his balance of kicking ability. He remains one of the few forwards capable of consistently drilling torpedo-punt goals.

Coach *Leigh Matthews* says he's never seen a player capable of 'doing the impossible' as regularly as Daicos. In the foreword to Daicos' book, *Collingwood and Me*, Matthews admits: 'Watching Peter from the coach's box for the last five years has convinced me that his grubbed kick— bouncing erratically, then breaking at right angles through the open goals—happens far too often for it to be dismissed as pure luck.'

No matter how tough the angle, Daicos always seems able to thread the ball uncannily through the goals to the delight of his adoring army of fans. His black and white No. 35 guernsey is one of the best known of his or any era.

In 1979, Daicos broke through for six senior matches, as a 17-year-old.

Initially playing as a half-forward, he kicked nine goals in one game against Richmond in 1981. In the exciting preliminary final, he booted a crucial goal close to time-on in the final quarter by running around Geelong veteran *Ian Nankervis* to put Collingwood in front and into the Grand Final.

Daicos first represented Victoria in 1982, kicking eight goals on debut against Tasmania. In that year he won his first Copeland Trophy as a centreman, ensuring his star status.

Former Essendon star *John Birt* said Daicos' ballhandling abilities are the equal of two of the game's most outstanding players, *Darrel Baldock* and *Alex Jesaulenko*. 'What Peter can do with the ball at times is unbelievable,' he said.

Daicos says he acquired much of his kicking ability as a child from booting paper footballs, bound up tightly with tape and rubber bands. 'My friends and I used to do torpedoes, drop punts, everything,' he said.

In 1990, Daicos passed 200 League games, twice kicking seven goals in a game and five times booting six.

His skipper *Tony Shaw* said: 'I've never seen another footballer who can consistently produce his magical brand of play. I really think he should have been black because his skills are so similar to Aboriginals'.'

DANIHER, Anthony (1963–)

One of the full-backs who reintroduced the torpedo punt as a telling field-kick, Daniher began his senior career, aged 18, in Sydney in 1981 before joining his brothers, *Terry*, Neale and Chris at Essendon in 1987.

Daniher had six seasons and 115 games with Sydney before being off-loaded because of the club's salary cap restrictions. He'd tired of his jack-of-all-trades role and became Essendon's full-back.

Originally from his family's wheat farm at Ungarie in southern NSW—the Swans' recruiting territory—Daniher says his prodigious kicking was a result of daily competition between his brothers. 'We had plenty of practice back home trying to kick it over the old tin silos,' he said.

A member of Essendon's losing 1990 Grand Final side, Daniher is the tallest of the brothers at 191 cm—and the heaviest at 90 kg. He was admitted to the League's 200-club in 1991, retiring at the end of the 1994 season having played 233 games in 14 seasons.

Terry Daniher with a Gaelic football. In addition to captaining Essendon, he led Australia against Ireland at international Gaelic level.

DANIHER, Terry (1957–)

The eldest and most successful of the four Daniher brothers, renowned for his unbending commitment and courage, Terry captained Essendon, Victoria, New South Wales and Australia and played 313 League games in 17 seasons before his retirement at the end of 1992.

His success was a major embarrassment to South Melbourne which unloaded him—along with his schoolboy brother, Neale—in exchange for Essendon centreman *Neville Fields* at the end of the 1977 season after Terry had played just 19 games.

The 188 cm Daniher was captain when Essendon won back-to-back premierships in 1984–85. Becoming one of the game's most reliable and versatile key-position players, he also led Victoria in 1985 and 1986— playing 10 Big V games. In 1990, he led NSW, and captained Australia in the 1987 Gaelic football series.

Popular and unassuming, with a laconic sense of humour, Daniher has always shown great endeavour and on-field leadership. Best and fairest in 1982, he captained Essendon from 1983–88 and was twice the leading club goalkicker.

Suspended for 11 weeks on striking charges after Essendon lost the 1990 Grand Final—one of the toughest tribunal penalties of modern times—he refused to retire. His professionalism, fitness and running ability remained great assets.

He played his 21st final in 1991, after becoming a member of the elite band of players who have played 300 League games. In 1992, he kicked six goals in his final game in Essendon's VSFL premiership.

Asked what he'd most like to be remembered for, the three-time All Australian said: 'As someone who was honest, week-in and week-out. When my time comes, as long as I've given it my best shot then I'll be happy.'

Learning his football at Ungarie, he used to play two football codes as a teenager— Australian Rules on Saturdays and Rugby

League on Sundays. 'I was able to adapt skills from both codes in helping me to develop,' he said. 'In league you have to put your body in, so I learnt to tackle and also to protect myself. There's a lot of contact, more than football down here. You become used to hard physical knocks and that's very important.'

Daniher said sport was a priority with everyone in his family (he has three brothers and seven sisters) as it opened new friendships. 'To be a sportsman in the country is one of the only ways you've got to meet people and get into towns,' he said.

His first senior game for South Melbourne was in 1976. He was shocked, upon returning from a trip overseas, to be told by his father, Jim, of his premature dismissal. He resolved to fight back.

In his early days at Essendon, he seemed capable of becoming a great full-forward before, in 1979, breaking his jaw. A broken thumb further restricted his progress. But on return he became the team's 'trouble-shooter', playing at both ends of the ground with great determination.

'His terrific courage is probably his outstanding quality,' said former team-mate *Gary Foulds*.

'He has this unbelievable capacity to keep going full-bore all the time,' said veteran *Simon Madden*.

Coach *Keven Sheedy* said it has 'been a privilege' to coach all four Daniher brothers. 'They are a family of great character.'

Terry's brother, Neale, was also elected captain of Essendon, at the start of 1982, but never played a game because of the first of a series of crippling knee operations which severely restricted his career. Before his injury, he was regarded as one of the League's brightest young players and had represented Victoria before he was 21. He made a comeback late in the 1980s. One of his proudest moments came in mid 1990 when he and his three brothers represented NSW in an unexpected victory against Victoria. In 1992, he became Essendon's assistant-coach before switching to Fremantle in 1995.

See: 'BROTHERS, Famous'

DAVIS, Allan (1949–)

At 17, the red-headed forward from champion junior club East Sandringham played in St Kilda's one and only premiership, in 1966. An elusive and highly-gifted player, he had been included for the preliminary final, kicked three goals, and retained his place in the Grand Final.

Amassing 174 games and 307 goals in a decade with the Saints, he played with three clubs in his final five years of League football: Melbourne, Essendon and Collingwood.

His most prolific goalkicking year was in 1971, when he booted 70 goals including 10 against Collingwood and played in another Grand Final. He was equal leading goalkicker, with John Stephens, in 1972 and top again in 1973.

Known for his fiery temperament, the 180 cm Davis was suspended three times on striking charges. As a 19-year-old he was reported for allegedly striking Carlton's aggressive full-back Wes Lofts, an incident which shocked team-mates, many of whom had been bluffed by Lofts' vigour.

A fine mark for his size, Davis had the uncanny ability of being able to side-step opponents and take a shot at goal. He was also brilliant in the mud.

He played a total of 251 League games from 1966–80. He also coached St Kilda in the absence of the ill *Darrel Baldock*.

DAVIS, Barry (1943–)

North Melbourne's first premiership captain, the 185 cm Davis was one of the three big names lured to the Roos at the end of the 1972 season under the short-lived '10 year rule'. (The others were Geelong's *Doug Wade* and South Melbourne's *John Rantall*.)

He'd had an illustrious career at Essendon and played in defence in two premierships, before ruck-roving in North's historic 1975 flag, the club's first in 50 years in the VFL.

A magnificent kick and fine leader, he tallied 291 games in his 15-year career. He also played 11 State games from 1967–73,

Brownlow Medal counts, in 1969 and 1971. He finished just one vote behind Fitzroy's *Kevin Murray* in the thrilling conclusion to the '69 count.

Davis was back at Essendon as assistant coach in 1976 and became senior coach from 1978–80, lifting a young team into the finals in 1979.

DAVIS, Bob (1928–)

Coach of Geelong's 1963 premiership team and a front-line member of the club's back-to-back flags in 1951–52, Davis was known as 'The Geelong Flyer' for his dazzling speed which was likened to the express train from Geelong to Melbourne.

Known for his love of sports cars and for wearing crocodile shoes, he was a boy from the bush who could outrun the hard men from the city.

He played 189 games with Geelong and represented Victoria 13 times. He captained the Cats in 65 matches from 1955–58 and was best and fairest in his second-last season, in 1957.

'His powerful build and long-striding speed helped him to buffet his way through

Barry Davis: 291 games in 15 years.

10 with Essendon and one, as Victorian captain, after transferring to North.

In 1965, he suffered a fractured cheekbone against St Kilda. After missing nine weeks and making a rare appearance in the reserves, he returned for the finals, part of a brilliant half-back line with first-year star Geoff Pryor and rugged centre half-back Ian 'Bluey' Shelton. By defeating St Kilda in the Grand Final, Essendon became only the third team to win a premiership from fourth spot since the Page finals system was introduced in 1931.

Club champion three times in four years, Davis was Essendon's vice-captain in 1969 before succeeding ruckman *Don McKenzie* as skipper in 1970 and 1971.

He twice dead-heated for second in

'The Geelong Flyer', Bob Davis.

the packs,' said arch rival and Collingwood premiership captain *Lou Richards*. 'He played havoc with opposition back-lines. Quite often I've seen him quiet for half a game but suddenly he would come to life and in five or six minutes he would run riot and cut a defence to shreds. Nobody could hold him in these bursts and it usually resulted in Geelong winning the game.'

Davis retired at 30 while still at his peak. Known mainly as a half-forward, he also played in defence and as a ruck-rover late in his career. He was named Victorian and All Australian captain in 1958.

He coached Geelong teams into the finals in four of his six seasons as coach from 1960–65—including the 1963 premiership—but is best remembered for being coach of the Victorian team which lost to South Australia at the MCG for the first time in 37 years and only the fourth time this century. 'No official ever blamed me to my face but it was my first and last year as State coach,' Davis said.

DEACON, Bert (1922–73)

Carlton's first Brownlow Medalist in 1947, when he won in only his second full season, aged 23, Deacon was a centre half-back renowned for his marking—and his sportsmanship. He was recruited from Preston and wished initially to play with *Jack Dyer*'s Richmond.

'He should have been a Tiger,' said Dyer. 'We had it all arranged for him to sign with Richmond; his father turned up, but not Bert. Carlton kidnapped him from work and locked him in the committee room and didn't let him out until they had brow-beaten him into signing. If we'd picked him up at work, he would have been our player.'

The 183 cm Deacon had three debut matches with Carlton in 1942, as an 18-year-old on leave from A.I.F. service duties in the Northern Territory. He played only two games in 1943 and three in 1944, before being a member of Carlton's winning team in the 'Bloodbath' Grand Final against South Melbourne in 1945. He was one of the few players who did not resort to fighting.

Carlton centre half-back and 1947 Brownlow Medallist, Bert Deacon.

DEAN, Roger (1940–   )

Still blamed as the man who cost Melbourne the 1963 premiership, Richmond's State player Roger Dean was at the centre of one of the game's most famous incidents when dynamic ruck-rover *Ron Barassi* was reported for striking him in the second-last home-and-away round that season. Barassi said he never threw a punch and that Dean was only play-acting, but the tribunal suspended him for four weeks. He missed the rest of the season, including Melbourne's two finals. Barassi maintains his innocence even now.

In *Wildmen of Football*, *Jack Dyer* remarked: 'Even Richmond players who viewed the Dean incident agreed Barassi threw a bolo punch, downwards at the ball. He might have grazed Dean's chest but they were convinced that Dean had performed an acrobatic back flip to stage for a free-kick and at no time did he lose possession of the ball. He was left without a mark on his face to indicate a blow of any force.'

Dean started his career as a half-forward and rover, but finished as an attacking back-pocket player. He captained the Tigers from 1968–71, and figured in the 1967 and 1969 premierships. He retired, aged 33, in 1973, having played 244 games.

DEMPSEY, Gary (1948–)

Renowned for the consistency and quality of his high marking, Dempsey had an illustrious career which included 332 games in the VFL. He continued to play until he was nearly 40, in the Queensland league, with Southport, where he finally secured a premiership in 1987, and was runner-up for the 'Brisbane Brownlow', the J. A. Grogan medal.

Badly burnt while helping to fight a New Year bushfire at his parents' farm at Lara, near Geelong, he was forced out of all but two games in 1969. Doctors initially said the severity of the burns—to 75 per cent of his body—would not allow him to play again. But he kicked seven goals in his two return matches and, after 1970, established himself as one of the best followers in the game.

He admitted the fight for his life gave him 'a bit of purpose . . . I realised I had to make something out of my life rather than just cruise along and let it happen. I had a second chance even though the doctors said I wouldn't play football again.'

His habit of dropping a kick behind play became fashionable, but few did it as well as the 197 cm Dempsey, whose superb marking ability was one of the few bright lights in a mediocre team.

He won six best and fairest awards in the next nine years, including five in a row from 1973–77, but only twice played in the finals.

He captained the Bulldogs in 1971–72 and again from 1976–78. In 1975, he won the Brownlow Medal by a vote from Melbourne's *Stan Alves*.

His brilliant play ensured his regular Victorian selection from 1970. In 1972, he was State captain for a match, the year he won All Australian honours. He repre-

Gary Dempsey, Victorian captain in 1972, with stalwart administrator and former Magpie Bruce Andrew after a State match in Perth.

sented Victoria 12 times from 1970–78 and another five times in his six years at North Melbourne.

His transfer to North at the start of the 1979 season made him one of the highest paid players in the game. He said his major motivation was wanting to play in finals regularly. In 1979, he won North's best and fairest, but his wish to play in a Grand Final was never fulfilled.

In the 1979 preliminary final he wrestled persistently with Collingwood's top ruckman *Peter Moore*. This led the VFL, in 1980, to introduce a dividing-line across the centre-circle which forced ruckmen to run in for the tap from opposing sides.

'Collingwood set out to take me out of the game that day,' Dempsey said. '(Umpire) Bill Deller should have free-kicked one or the other of us, each time.'

Dempsey played a total of 337 VFL games from 1967–84—215 in 12 seasons with Footscray and 122 at North.

His field-kicking was only moderate, as

was his speed, but his experience and judgement made him a difficult opponent well into his 30s.

Among his numerous injuries were jaw fractures, cracked ribs, broken teeth, broken nose (11 times) and a permanently croaky voice, the legacy of continual whacks across the throat which weakened his vocal chords.

Footscray's 1992 Brownlow Medallist *Scott Wynd* acknowledged Dempsey's assistance as a rucks tutor after his narrow victory from Hawthorn's *Jason Dunstall*.

DENCH, David (1951–)

The most innovative and aggressive full-back of his and probably any era, Dench became famous for his exhilarating dashes downfield in the mid-1970s when North Melbourne was at its peak.

Recruited from West Coburg in 1969, he was the youngest-ever captain of the Roos at 20. He won four best and fairest

North Melbourne's aggressive defender David Dench spoils Hawk Michael Moncrieff during the 1976 Grand Final.

awards and played in five consecutive Grand Finals (including two premierships) before retiring, having amassed 276 games.

The 188 cm Dench was at least the equal of fellow champion full-backs, Carlton's *Geoff Southby* and Hawthorn's *Kelvin Moore*.

He was acting captain in North's 1977 premiership victory. He was thought to be the most valuable player in the game, bar Hawthorn's *Leigh Matthews*.

Dench said North Melbourne coach *Ron Barassi* helped him immeasurably. 'I wasn't over-endowed with natural skills and he spent a lot of time with me and other players working on that area,' he said.

He overcame crippling knee injuries late in his career, and continued to serve North with zest and energy. Often his daring dashes would take him 80–90 metres downfield. Not only would he start a chain of hand-passes but would be on the end of it, before he roosted the ball deep into attack. Dench remained closely involved with North in his first years of retirement, as coaching assistant to *John Kennedy*.

DIBBS, Charlie (1905–60)

Collingwood's full-back in six Grand Finals, the 175 cm Dibbs played 216 games from 1924–35, including the Magpies' four consecutive premierships from 1927–30. In 1936, he crossed to Geelong as captain-coach but played only the first seven games before retiring and being replaced by *Reg Hickey*.

DIPIERDOMENICO, Robert (1958–)

An irresistible, flamboyant personality who gave new prestige to the term 'battler', DiPierdomenico was the first Hawthorn player to win the Brownlow Medal, in 1986, when he tied with Sydney's *Greg Williams*. But he's renowned even more for his courage in the 1989 Grand Final when he figured in the club's historic back-to-back premiership win, despite a broken rib and a punctured lung, which he ignored until collapsing after the final siren.

It was the most famous of his five pre-

Robert DiPierdomenico: best afield in the '78 Grand Final.

mierships and 25 finals appearances. He was in hospital for a week and later admitted that he might have been endangering his life by playing on. Hawthorn doctor Terry Gay said: 'It's unbelievable that Dipper would haul that big body of his around in such an intense sporting contest while carrying injuries like that. We'll never understand how he kept going.'

Born into a hard-working Italian migrant family, with no background in Australian football, 'Dipper' was nicknamed 'Alphabet' on his arrival at Hawthorn from North Kew in 1975. His first senior coach, *John Kennedy*, told him he had to run straight at the ball, hitting it at top pace. 'He knew that I was never going to be a star player. He just taught me that if the ball was there I'm the one that's going to get it.'

Dipper's sheer strength and courage, combined with loyalty and enthusiasm, turned him from a fringe player who played 99 games at reserves level into one of Hawthorn's first-chosen players in the club's most skilful and successful era.

A last-minute inclusion in the 18 in the 1978 Grand Final, he was best afield. There was no Norm Smith medal then, just a dozen bottles of beer he won courtesy of *The Sun*'s football writers.

Initially renowned for his barn-storming

play in defence, he became an even more valuable player on a wing. Legendary team-mate *Leigh Matthews* declared that Dipper's priceless ability to motivate and enthuse players, especially before a game, guaranteed him a place in his side every time.

He received lengthy suspensions several times, including a five week sentence after the '89 Grand Final. Team-mates walked taller when he was around and there were few more intimidating or exhilarating sights—depending on your affections—when Dipper raced downfield, ball tucked securely under one arm, ready to confront opponents without consideration of personal risk.

His unquenchable spirit and toughness was on show for 240 games and 17 seasons with Hawthorn. Of his Brownlow year he said: 'I felt like I could take on the whole world.' He was a surprise winner and his tally of 17 votes was the lowest winning score since the 3-2-1 voting system was introduced in 1931.

Triple Brownlow Medallist *Bob Skilton* said of the co-winners (DiPierdomenico and Williams): 'It's a great result for the guys who go in and get the ball. It's a long time since a really tough player has won it. Now we have two of them in the one year.'

Later that memorable week, DiPierdomenico played in Hawthorn's premiership side, emulating the feat of St Kilda great *Ian Stewart*, the last man to win a Brownlow and play in a winning Grand Final side in the same year, in 1966.

DITTERICH, Carl (1945–   )

Few have made a more dramatic entry into League football than athletic blond bombshell Carl Ditterich in the opening round of the 1963 season. The exuberant 17-year-old was one of the best afield. A drama-filled career which has few parallels was under way.

Powerfully built at 193 cm and 90kg, he played 285 games from 1963–80: 203 in 13 years at St Kilda and 82 in five at Melbourne. He would have reached 300, but missed 30 weeks through suspension. Reported 19 times—a 'record' surpassed by only one other player, *David Rhys-Jones*—he was found guilty on 11 occasions. His on-field aggression and role of 'protector' impressed team-mates, but not umpires.

Late in 1966, he was suspended for six matches on a charge of striking Fitzroy's Darryl Peoples and missed St Kilda's historic first premiership.

He admitted he often lacked discipline and tended to retaliate too quickly. 'I had an even-up mentality,' he said in a 1991 interview. 'I believed it was an eye-for-an-eye situation.'

His critics said he tended to flail his arms and elbows around too much. Letters of criticism flooded into St Kilda and into newspaper offices. He became the biggest name in the game and a target for opposing sides, who would deliberately try to test his temper, hoping to force him into indiscretions.

Recruited to St Kilda from East Brighton, he was a highjumping champion at Brighton High School, quite an achievement considering he was knock-kneed as a child and wore leg-irons from the age of two to five.

His fairytale beginning earnt him two

Days after his near best afield debut, 17-year-old Carl Ditterich in 1963.

votes in the Brownlow Medal from experienced field-umpire Jeff Crouch. His leaping, stamina and enthusiasm were inspirational as St Kilda won by 18 points. During the game he advised the great *Ron Barassi*: 'Step aside, Granddad.'

Recalling the game, *Jack Dyer* said: 'The ball was bounced and the Saints roared as the long-haired kid sprang into the air with a mighty leap and with a mighty punch sent the ball sailing to his rover. It wasn't scientific, it was even a shade crude, but there was something electrifying about that moment. As the game progressed he continued to leap and bound about the field and give one of the greatest displays of stamina any of the supporters had seen.'

Later that season, after being best afield in the first semi-final, his coach *Allan Jeans* said: 'Carl is a fine boy. He will do anything you ask. He has tremendous stamina and is a great inspiration to the side. *Darrel Baldock* once told me that he had been dead on his feet when Carl burst past him as though the game had been going only five minutes. His energy and enthusiasm lifted Baldock and the rest of the side, too.'

In 1967, he matured as a player, but suffered on-going leg problems. In 1969, he had major surgery to both his ankles, but he won St Kilda's best and fairest award in 1968 and continued to be a regular State representative.

In the summer of 1972–73, like many of the game's leading players, he transferred clubs in the wake of the 10-year rule. He joined Melbourne as the highest paid player in the game and received $60,000 for three years.

'When Ditterich came to Melbourne from St Kilda, he was a really tough, mean footballer who offered a huge amount of protection to the players around him,' said Melbourne great *Robert Flower*.

'He was a productive player, too. He did an enormous amount of work on the ball and could be relied upon to get the knockouts from the centre and to mark around the ground. He shepherded the small men superbly and was there for advice wherever the ball was.'

Ditterich immediately won Melbourne's club championship. He played 53 games in three years before returning to St Kilda from 1976–78 where he formed an aggressive and envied following division with big-name West Australian Garry Sidebottom and *Jeff Sarau*.

After a controversial match against Essendon at Moorabbin in 1978, in which Ditterich was one of three Saints booked, Essendon officials described St Kilda players as 'animals'.

But Ditterich did not compromise his style. Team-mates called him 'The Shadow'. Jack Dyer named him at the top of his 'Terrifying 10'. 'He didn't know his own strength,' Dyer said. 'He loved running and colliding.'

Ditterich returned to Melbourne as playing-coach in 1979–80 before being replaced by Ron Barassi.

DIXON, Brian (1936–)

A decorated and durable winger, renowned for his ball-winning ability, the 176 cm Dixon played in five Melbourne premierships during his 259 game career from 1954–68. A brilliant mark for his size, he often outpointed opposing ruckmen. He was best afield in the Demons' 1960 premiership and winner of the Tassie Medal after dominating the 1961 national championships.

A very fair, fit and intelligent player, he retired as Melbourne's games record holder to concentrate on his political career. He played briefly at Prahran, and in 1971–72 coached North Melbourne.

Renowned for having his socks down and for his ungainly left-foot kicking-style, Dixon regularly averaged more than 20 kicks a game. He represented Victoria 10 times from 1959–63, and played more than 100 games in succession for his club. He was best and fairest in 1960.

Dixon's father was an invalid and young Brian took many after-school jobs to help his family. At eight, he was carting wood, and worked as a newsboy and a grocer's boy.

Schooled at Melbourne High—a classmate of famous Olympian Ron Clarke—he won an Alexander Rushall scholarship at 13. He went on to Melbourne University,

and became head of the Economics Department at Melbourne Grammar and an economics lecturer at his old university. He was elected into State Parliament for the Liberal Party while still playing football at League level.

Later he was Minister for Youth, Sport and Recreation before losing his seat at the 1982 election when the Cain Labor Party swept into power. Within months he'd become executive director of the Sydney Swans.

A single-minded high achiever, noted for his courage and commitment, he was an integral part of Melbourne's 'golden' era of the 1950s.

DONALD, Wally (1927–)

A dashing, hard-hitting defender who played in Footscray's historic 1954 premiership team, Donald had 207 games in 13 seasons with the Bulldogs from 1946–58. He had a great understanding with full-back Herbie Henderson.

He won the best and fairest in 1949, and represented Victoria three times.

DOULL, Bruce (1950–)

An extremely quiet and reserved champion who played in four Carlton premierships and was four times best and fairest, Doull was extraordinary for his durability. He had 18 seasons of League football and on his retirement after the 1986 Grand Final had amassed 359 games, a record surpassed by only four players, Richmond's *Kevin Bartlett*, Fitzroy's *Bernie Quinlan*, Essendon's *Simon Madden* and Hawthorn's *Michael Tuck*.

He shied away from all publicity but is one of the most-loved Carlton players of all time. His long flowing hair and headband became a trademark, along with his unruffled temperament and ice-cool brain.

Dubbed 'The Flying Doormat' because of his long hair which flew out behind him as he ran, he had beautiful disposal, and lightning anticipation and recovery. He also possessed the rare ability of being able to punch the ball in packs with pinpoint precision to team-mates further afield. He

Bruce Doull (right), with Robert Walls, after Carlton's 1972 premiership.

was rarely beaten in one-on-one duels.

From 1971–77, he played 139 games in a row, a feat bettered by only six players in history.

Hawthorn champion *Dermott Brereton* said he found it 'an unforgettable and humbling experience' being opposed to Doull during a final in 1984. 'He made me look ordinary,' said Brereton, then in his third season. 'I had plenty of zip and did a lot of running. Bruce stayed with me but you could tell he was straining.

'At one stage I thought: "Gee, this bloke is going to pass out." Bruce was really huffing and puffing so I went for a run— about 100 metres or so—to see if I could shake him off. As I ran, I could hear him right behind me, gasping for air— exhausted but he wouldn't stop ... talk about willpower! No wonder he was such a highly-rated player.'

His first coach, the great *Ron Barassi*, was one of Doull's greatest admirers: 'He may look like Rasputin the mad monk, but as far as Carlton is concerned he is a knight in shining armour.'

Carlton's legendary ruckman *John Nicholls* said the 185 cm Doull was underestimated for his versatility, especially early in his career. 'He's a magnificent kick and handballer,' Nicholls said, in an interview in 1975. 'He kicks long distances and he

kicks and handballs very accurately, seemingly without effort.

'He's like a cat because he has such great recovery, both on the ground and in the air ... he is unselfish and has tremendous concentration.'

Recruited from Jacana in 1969, Doull believed the more publicity a player received, the greater a target he'd become.

Initially he was an ultra-defensive player, before winning the first of his best and fairests in 1974 in his fifth year, having settled into the centre half-back position.

Previously he'd played on the ball, at half-forward and even full-forward.

'Doully just loved the game, enjoyed the contact and played with an enormous amount of pride,' said former team-mate *Robert Walls*. 'He never missed a training session, never looked for preferential treatment and maintained to the end a consistently high level of performance.'

He represented Victoria 11 times from 1976–81 and again in 1984 when he was recalled, aged 33, for the State-of-Origin game in South Australia which Victoria won by four points.

DROP PUNT, The

Richmond's toughman *Jack Dyer* is generally regarded as being the originator of the kick, but he says he learnt it from Collingwood's *Collier* brothers, '*Leeta*' and *Harry*.

'The Colliers used it solely as a 10-yard pass (rather than handballing),' he said. 'It was a clumsy kick, but I realised its potential because of its accuracy and I set to work modifying the kick and developing it for distance.'

Collingwood's *Peter McKenna* was one of the most successful exponents of the kick. In today's football, Sydney's *Tony Lockett* also uses it with great success.

Dyer says he developed the drop punt late in his career out of desperation after missing so many angle shots at goal with punt kicks. Critics initially called it Dyer's 'crazy kick'—'the silliest looking kick in football history'.

At first Dyer reserved the kick for set-shots at goals, but realised it could become just as valuable around the field. The drop punt is now the most-used kick in the game.

Drop kicks are rarely seen even at training and when boom goalkicker *Peter Hudson* stab-passed two of his four goals on debut for Hawthorn in 1967, he was told in no uncertain terms never to use the kick again!

Place kicks disappeared years ago. Fitzroy full-forward Tony Ongarello, who played in the '50s, was the last player to use them consistently.

The stab pass, as invented by Collingwood's Dick Condon at the turn of the century, and made famous in the '50s and '60s by Collingwood's Thorold Merrett and Geelong's *Bill Goggin*, is also seldom used.

Even torpedo punts, brilliantly used by master goalkickers *Doug Wade* and *Bernie Quinlan*, are rarely seen, except for long shots at goal or by full-backs such as Geelong's Ben Graham.

DUAL SPORTSMEN

Keith Miller, one of the most gifted sportsmen Australia has produced, was not only a champion post-war all-rounder for the Australian Test team—he was a VFL footballer of note. He played 50 games for St Kilda and represented two States.

Possessing style, flair and charm, he played at full-back and full-forward, and was renowned for his long kicking.

Once he kept the great *Bob Pratt* to two goals, but downplayed the effort, saying Pratt—then in the twilight of his career—wasn't serious.

Test contemporary Sam Loxton also played League football for St Kilda, while SA's Gil Langley was a member of Essendon's teams of 1942–43.

Many early Australian Test cricketers also played League football with South Melbourne: Tom Horan, John Barrett, Jas Slight, Frank Allan, George Palmer, Warwick Armstrong and *Laurie Nash*.

Armstrong, 'The Big Ship', had 13 games with South, and was a member of the 1899 team which lost the Grand Final to Fitzroy. His cricketing contemporary *Jack Worrall* played with Fitzroy. So did Ted McDonald, one of Australia's finest fast bowlers.

Among the best-known modern-day cricketers to play League football are: Jamie Siddons (Sydney Swans), Simon O'Donnell (St Kilda), Geoff Parker (Essendon) and *Craig Bradley* (Carlton). Test batting trio Geoff Marsh, David Boon and Mark Taylor also played senior football in their respective States, WA, Tasmania and NSW.

Tasmanian-born Max Walker had almost 100 games at Melbourne and played in the Demons' 1968 night premiership before concentrating on his cricketing career.

Another Test medium-pacer, Neil Hawke, was a brilliant footballer in two States and kicked 110 goals with East Perth in 1959. Contemporary Eric Freeman kicked 81 with Port Adelaide in 1966.

Successfully combining football and cricket has become almost impossible in recent times. The first practice football matches are now played in late January. Overseas exhibition games are often played in October.

Young St Kilda star Robert Harvey, a former Victorian under 19s representative, opened the bowling for Fitzroy before being told by coach *Ken Sheldon* that he should make football his priority and not endanger his fitness by bowling long spells.

Leading footballers to excel at other sports include:

ANGLING—*Rex Hunt* (Richmond/ Geelong/St Kilda), an Australian champion.

ATHLETICS—George Stuckey (Essendon), Norman Clark (Carlton), Bill Twomey snr (Collingwood/Hawthorn), Lance Mann (Essendon/Geelong) and Trevor McGregor (Fitzroy), who all won the Stawell Gift; Austin Robertson snr (South Melbourne) was a three-time world professional sprint champion. *Frank 'Bluey' Adams* (Melbourne) was Australian professional sprint champion.

BALLROOM DANCING—Ron Hillis (South Melbourne) was a ballroom dancing champion of Australia in the 1930s; *Laurie Dwyer* (North Melbourne) also won championships in the early 1960s.

BASEBALL—Justin Charles (Footscray).

BOXING—Ambrose Palmer (Footscray), Bill Lang (Richmond), *Bob Rose* (Collingwood) and Maurice Rioli (Richmond), who was WA amateur welter and light-middleweight champion.

BASKETBALL—Mark Lisle (North Melbourne).

CYCLING—Alan Eade (Collingwood), who competed in the final of the famous Austral Wheel Race.

GOLF—Nick Ryan (South Melbourne), Rick Kennedy (Footscray), Cory McKernan (North Melbourne).

HANDBALL—Bill Serong (Collingwood/North Melbourne) was twice Australian Masters doubles champion.

LAWN BOWLS—Keith Warburton (Carlton), the Victorian State pairs winner in 1972.

MOTOR RACING—Paul Feltham (North Melbourne).

ROWING—Gordon Abbott (Geelong/Essendon), Mark Shea (Essendon) and Alex Sloan (Fitzroy).

RUGBY—Ray Smith (Essendon/Melbourne).

SHOOTING—*Percy Bentley* (Richmond).

SQUASH—Brian Beers (Collingwood).

SURF LIFESAVING—Peter Bennett (St Kilda) and Hugh Strachan (Geelong).

SWIMMING—Vin Coutie (Melbourne), a Victorian champion.

TABLE TENNIS—Jim Thomas (Footscray) and Hec Oakley (St Kilda). Oakley's son, Ross, became the AFL's chief commissioner in 1987.

TENNIS—Sir Norman Brooks (St Kilda), John Bonney (St Kilda) and Todd Viney (Melbourne), who played Linton Cup for SA. Brooks, one of Australia's greatest tennis players, was also twice an Australian foursome golf champion.

WEIGHTLIFTING—Robert Edmond (Carlton).

DUGDALE, John (1937–)

An adaptable, high-leaping key-position specialist who played 248 games with North Melbourne from 1955–70—including one stretch of 100 games in a row—Dugdale spent the first 10 years of his career as a full-forward or centre half-forward. Later he played at full-back.

Recruited from Kensington, he was the club's leading goalkicker on seven occasions, his best year being in 1958 when he booted 57 goals, and the club played in its only finals series of his career. The same year he won an All Australian blazer as a full-forward, a star of the centenary carnival with 18 goals.

He replaced *Noel Teasdale* as club captain after Teasdale was cleared interstate at the end of the 1967 season. Midway through 1968—playing as a centreman—he broke *Allen Aylett's* club record of 220 games. He was best and fairest that year, a mighty feat in his 14th season.

His sons, Dean and Glenn, also played League football.

DUNNE, Ross (1948–)

Famous for booting a goal for Collingwood in the last seconds of the 1977 Grand Final to force a tie against North Melbourne, Dunne was a magnificent kick and fine mark. Nicknamed 'Twiggy' after the super-slim fashion model, Dunne was 194 cm and just 86 kg. In 12 seasons of League football, from 1967–78, he played 213 games, almost all of them in the forward line.

In the 1977 play-off Collingwood trailed by six points with just 50 seconds to go when Dunne marked strongly ahead of North defenders Frank Gumbleton and *Brent Crosswell*. He calmly kicked a torpedo-punt goal from 25 metres and forced a rematch.

DUNSTALL, Jason (1964–)

Queensland's most noted footballer, a remarkable goalkicker with a vice-like marking grip, Jason Hadfield Dunstall topped Hawthorn's goalkicking lists for a ninth consecutive year in 1994, on his way to 1000 career goals, a feat achieved by only two others.

He kicked almost 300 goals in a glorious run of 50 matches in 1988–89, and won back-to-back club best and fairests. He also finished in the first three in each of the 1988–89 Brownlow Medal counts, was the leading VFL goalkicker, and the John Coleman Medallist.

A fractured skull in 1990 and an achilles operation in 1991 reduced his effectiveness, yet he still kicked 83 and 82 goals, including six in Hawthorn's 1991 premiership.

In 1991, when he figured in his fifth Grand Final since joining the Hawks in 1985, he passed 600 goals and maintained his goal average at more than four and a half. In 1992, he was runner-up in the Brownlow, won selection as the All Australian full-forward and became the first permanent full-forward in League history to win a club best and fairest three times.

Team-mate *Dermott Brereton* said Dunstall's body-strength and reflexes make him a formidable opponent in 'one-out' marking duels. 'He is also very consistent, having started his career as primarily a mark-and-kick man. Now he's more of an all-rounder and likely to do just as well in wet conditions as he does on dry days.'

At 188 cm, Dunstall is not tall for a modern-day key-position forward, but his speed in leading and acrobatic marking make him—with Sydney's *Tony Lockett*—the most formidable of modern full-forwards.

As a teenager at Brisbane's Church of England Grammar School, Dunstall played cricket, rugby union and soccer. He also represented Coorparoo in its under-age Australian football teams. He was a Carlton supporter—*Alex Jesaulenko* his hero. But when Hawthorn contacted him after he'd represented Queensland and kicked more than 70 goals in Coorparoo's premiership year, he was glad to come to Glenferrie.

He chose Hawthorn ahead of another interested club, Fitzroy, as the Hawks appeared to be more stable. The opportunity to play regularly in finals had an instant appeal.

'Money didn't come into it (the choice),' he said. 'I was an unrecognised player coming from a non-football state.'

His first contract was for $5000. Now he earns upwards of $200,000 a year.

Fellow Hawthorn goalkicking great *Peter Hudson* says Dunstall's vision in being able to anticipate the fall of the ball and generally convert his set shots was an uncanny and crucial part of Hawthorn's power teams in the late 1980s.

The sturdily-built import played in a forward pocket alongside *Leigh Matthews* in his maiden season before assuming responsibility at full-forward in 1986.

He improved his fitness by training virtually every night of the week and was an immediate success, kicking 77 goals in 1986 and 94 in 1987.

Pitted against Carlton's *Bruce Doull* in the 1986 Grand Final, he kicked six goals, one of his proudest achievements, in Hawthorn's fighting 23 point win. Two weeks previously, he'd been kept goalless by the legendary Carlton backman.

His personal-best tally in 20 finals to the start of '95 is seven goals, kicked in the 1988 play-off against Melbourne when Hawthorn won by a record margin.

He has kicked 12 goals four times at home-and-away level. His best-ever effort is 17 in the seventh round of the 1992 season against Richmond. In the return game against the Tigers he kicked 12. In one quarter, the last, against Geelong in 1990, he kicked seven goals.

While Dunstall is not as accurate a kick as Lockett, his agility allows him to kick more soccer goals and win the ball for snap shots more often than his famed Sydney counterpart. He is also faster and a superior tackler.

When Dunstall and Lockett played together in the Victoria-South Australia State-of-Origin match at the MCG in mid-1989, they kicked nine goals (Lockett five, Dunstall four). SA was beaten by 14 goals.

DURABLE PLAYERS

No senior Australian footballer has emulated the feats of Henry 'Harry' McDonald, the 'grand old man' of Tasmanian coastal football, who was a follower and defender in 346 games in a row from 1903–15 and 1921–28.

Born at Castra, near Ulverstone, he was never reported, and never left the field or missed a game through injury. He was 41 when he played his last games in 1928— he started the year as an umpire, but returned to the Ulverstone side as a forward, where he kicked 47 goals in 10 matches.

His 346 matches in a row comprised 274 roster matches with Ulverstone, 18 finals and 54 representative games. He was vice-captain to the great *Ivor Warne-Smith* in a Union side which played in Hobart, and Ulverstone's vice-captain under legendary coach *'Checker' Hughes* from 1924–26.

McDonald was the first patron of the NWFU's '200 club', formed in 1969. He died in 1974, aged 87.

The great *Kevin Murray* played 323 matches consecutively from the beginning of 1959 until the last match of 1974 (representing Fitzroy in 1959–64 and 1967–74 and East Perth 1965–66).

PLAYERS WHO HAVE BEEN SELECTED IN 100 OR MORE CONSECUTIVE MATCHES (The Top Ten)

PLAYER	CLUB/S SEASONS PLAYED	TOTAL MATCHES	SEASONS ACHIEVED	I.S.S.O.M.D.	CONSEC. MATCHES
Jack Titus	R 1926–43	294	1926–43	0	204
'Jock' McHale	Coll. 1903–18, 1920	261	1903–18	0	191
Jim Stynes	M 1987–94	178	1987–94	0	174
Kevin Bartlett	R 1965–83	403	1975–82	1	173
John Schultz	FO 1958 68	186	1959–68	8	169
Kevin Murray	FI 1955–64, 1967–74	333	1967–74	1	168
John Murphy	FI 1967–77; SM 1978–79; N 1979–80	248	1967–74	2	158
Kevin Bartlett	R 1965–83	403	1966–72	1	150
Alan Ruthven	FI 1940–41, 1943–54	222	1944–52	5	147
Andrew Collins	H 1987–94	168	1988–94	0	145
Don Cordner	M 1941–50	166	1942–50	0	144
Jim Francis	H 1929–33; CA 1934–43	223	1935–42	0	142
CURRENT PLAYERS					
Jim Stynes	Melb 1987–94	178	1987–94	0	174
Andrew Collins	Haw 1987–94	168	1988–94	0	145
Matthew Knights	Rich 1988–94	129	1988–94	0	129
Brett Lovett	Melb 1986–94	185	1987–92	0	117
Steven Wallis	Foots 1983–94	228	1983–87	0	113
Simon Atkins	Foots 1987–94	127	1989–94	0	104

KEY: I.S.S.O.M.D. = Interstate Match Selection on Club Match Day.

Only three other senior-grade footballers have played more than 200 games in a row—South Fremantle pair Stephen Michael (210 from 1975–83) and Gary Scott (205 from 1959–69), and Richmond's *Jack 'Skinny' Titus* (204 from 1933–43).

The much-decorated Michael, an Aboriginal, played 243 games in all. He won two Sandover Medals and All Australian status. Scott played 255 games, captained his club and was best and fairest in 1964.

Titus is one of eight League players to figure in 150 or more consecutive games, the others including *Jock McHale* (Collingwood) 192; *Kevin Bartlett* (Richmond) 173 and 150; *John Schultz* (Footscray) 169; Murray 168; and John Murphy (Fitzroy) 158.

To the start of the 1995 season, Melbourne's *Jim Stynes* had played in 174 consecutive games.

In round 5, 1995, Hawthorn's Andy Collins played his 150th game in a row.

The Melbourne club has had the most 'durable' types—12 players with 100 or more games in succession, including Brownlow Medallist *Dr Don Cordner*, who played 144 matches in a row from 1942–50.

DWYER, Laurie (1938–)

Known as 'Twinkletoes' after he won an Australian Ballroom Dancing Championship, Dwyer was a North Melbourne stalward over 201 games and 15 years. Later he served in many assistant and skill-coaching roles. He was coach of the North reserves in the late 1980s and early 1990s.

Recruited from Murchison, he played with North fourths as a 15-year-old. At the start of 1956, he was appointed captain of the under 19s. He happened to be in the clubrooms prior to a senior practice match when he was asked to fill in for Kevin McMahon who was injured. His father, Leo, a former player and then chairman of selectors, told him to slip home and get his gear. He celebrated senior career was beginning.

Dwyer played wing and centre with great balance and evasive abilities. Twice

runner-up for the Brownlow Medal, in 1961 and 1967, he represented Victoria seven times and went on two international tours, with Harry Beitzel's Galahs.

His courage and skill shone out as North Melbourne struggled through the 1960s. A bout of glandular fever restricted him to just six games in 1970, his final season. Later, he became the senior runner.

Leo Dwyer played 71 games in seven seasons with North, from 1925 to 1935. He was third in the 1928 Brownlow count. Two more sons, Kevin and Cliff, also played with North reserves, while Laurie's sons, David and Anthony, also represented the Roos.

DYER, Jack (1913–)

A bruising follower/forward who reigned for almost 20 years, 'Captain Blood' is the most revered Richmond player of them all, a member of two premiership sides and a legend in his own lifetime.

Playing 'straight-line football', he developed an iron-man image. But he was also a highly talented player, good enough to kick nine goals in a preliminary final and represent Victoria 16 times, including two years as captain-coach (1941 and 1949).

His feat of playing 312 club games for Richmond has been surpassed by only one man, *Kevin Bartlett*. Like the gifted 'KB', Dyer coached his beloved club—for 11 years from 1941–51, including the glorious 1943 Grand Final victory, which became known as 'Dyer's Premiership' when he kicked the goal that put Richmond in front in the last quarter.

Often he took the law into his own hands. It was said he broke more collarbones than a jumps-jockey and put out more lights than the SEC.

'Anything goes,' he'd say, 'as long as you can get away with it.'

Once, after a wild game at Princes Park, he caught the train home and found himself sitting opposite a loyal band of Carlton supporters, none of them too pleased with Jack's treatment of their favourite team that day. 'You must have eaten your babies,' one snarled. 'Me? I'm gentle,' Dyer replied. 'I go to church on Sundays.'

Jack Dyer developed an iron-man image with his 'straight-line football' tactics.

Dyer was taught from a very young age that if you hit somebody, they shouldn't get up. One of his coaches, Br. Peter, a former Sydney rugby union player, told young Jack after a school game that the player whose collarbone he had just broken should not have got in his way. 'If it (shirt-fronting an opponent) was good enough for a Christian Brother, it was good enough for me,' said Dyer.

'Humanitarians can weep, wail and condemn the brutality and dangers of Australian Rules football,' he remarked, 'but they'll never change it. Men are men and this is a game for men.'

He dedicated his book, *Captain Blood*, 'To my mother, who at the beginning of my career started worrying that I would be hurt and finished worrying whom I would hurt.'

Famous adversary *Norm Smith* said Dyer was the game's toughest and most colour-ful player. 'But don't get me wrong, Dyer was not a cowardly football basher,' Smith said. 'He was one of the three greatest foot-ballers the game has produced, probably the greatest. I feel he would have undoubt-edly stamped himself as the most brilliant footballer in the game had he played as an individual rather than for his team.'

Noted writer Alf Brown of *The Herald* said: 'Dyer rose to football on his great ability and cold-blooded, ruthless, relent-less vigour in a football era of rough, tough strongmen . . . It was breath-taking to see Dyer measure up an opponent, crash into him with an iron shoulder. Few could withstand this powerful broadside from Captain Blood. His timing was perfect and remained so to the last. Strangely, I have never met an opponent who resented Dyer's vigour.'

Amazingly, Dyer received only one sus-pension from his five visits to the tribunal. There was only one umpire and no video replay of incidents. Opponents claimed that umpires were frightened of Dyer.

His nickname, Captain Blood, was first penned by hard-hitting *Sporting Globe* writer Hec de Lacy. Hollywood hearthrob Errol Flynn was starring in the popular film *Captain Blood* which was playing at local cinema houses and de Lacy felt the name was perfect for Dyer's tough, blood-spilling image.

Cheeked by Collingwood's *Lou Richards* before the start of a game at Punt Road, Dyer said: 'See that flagpole on top of the grandstand? If you're not careful and get in my way today, I'll sit your head right on top of it.'

Born at Oakleigh on 11 November, 1913 and schooled at St Ignatius and later De La Salle College, he made his debut for Richmond at 16, having been recruited from the Richmond Hill Old Boys. Stand-ing 183 cm tall, he had pace, agility, deter-mination—and a mean streak.

Dyer initially roved for Richmond before playing as a follower, a position in which Smith said 'he had no peer'. In the twilight of his career he played at full-forward.

He was a six-time winner of Richmond's best and fairest award, including four times in a row from 1937–40. He also finished fourth in the 1939 Brownlow count and was still getting votes in his final years after the war. In 1947, he kicked 46 goals and did even better in 1948, with 64.

In his last game, against Geelong in 1949, he booted six goals, including one from his last kick in League football. Richmond won easily.

According to football writer Brian Hansen, 'Richmond and Geelong players started to chair their champion from the field and emotional Richmond and Geelong supporters joined in, singing and cheering in a unique gesture that showed the high regard that all lovers of the game had for this remarkable man ... In the dressing room, there was scarcely a dry eye in a list that boasted some of the wildest and toughest men in football and an equally emotional Jack Dyer declared to his men: "It isn't considered manly for one man to kiss another, but I love you guys so much, I could kiss you all".'

De Lacy wrote: 'It has taken a ton of bismuth powder and bullocks in beef steaks to get old Captain Blood safely through his 312 League games. The great adventure ended today when Jack Dyer, Richmond captain-coach, played his last game.'

There were no comebacks. Dyer continued as non-playing coach in 1950–51 and continued to appear on television and on radio. In 1990, approaching his 77th birthday, he celebrated his 60th year in football, still one of the most-loved figures in the game. Thousands tuned in every week to hear his commentaries on Melbourne radio station 3KZ, before the station dropped football for the 1992 season.

He continued to attend games in his capacity as a football columnist for *Truth Sport*, taking a keen interest in the game, especially the tougher players 'prepared to dish it out'.

See: 'DROP PUNT, The'

EADE, Rodney (1958–)

A member of three Hawthorn premierships, he was one of the best afield in the 1986 victory. He successfully blanketed Carlton champion and playmaker *Craig Bradley*, with 26 possessions to eight.

Recruited from Glenorchy at the recommendation of Hawk champion *Peter Hudson*—he was given Hudson's famous No. 26—Eade played 229 League games and 21 night matches with the Hawks from 1976–87 before joining the Brisbane Bears where he played 30 games in three years. He also had four Victorian games, and represented Tasmania. He'd been made deaf in one ear after a collision in a game as a teenager, but his balance was unaffected.

EASON, Bill

The first Geelong footballer to play 200 games, Eason played 207 matches and kicked 186 goals from 1902–15. He captained Geelong in 68 matches and Victoria in 1912.

Recruited from Barwon, he was a brilliant, attacking player who alternated from centre to half-forward. His quick turns and long-kicking were features of his game.

EDMOND, Jim (1958–)

A strong-marking half-forward best known for his feats at Footscray where he captained the club from 1983–85 and was equal leading goalkicker in 1981, Edmond played a total of 188 League games in 12 seasons from 1977–88.

In 1986, after 154 games at Footscray, he received a too-good-to-refuse offer of $100,000 a year from the Swans, on a three-year contract. But he had just one year in Sydney and two in Brisbane, playing 17 games at each club.

Recruited from Bairnsdale, he also represented Victoria.

Edmond's brother, Robert, played at Carlton and later became a weightlifter of note.

EICKE, Wells (1893–1980)

One of the youngest-ever VFL players when he began at 15, Wellesley Hastings Eicke was a superb leader, who tallied 197 games with St Kilda and 21 with North Melbourne from 1909–26. He played eight State games and captained Victoria against NSW in 1921. At 175 cm, he played centre half-back and was renowned for his marking skill.

He was playing coach of St Kilda in 1919 and 1924. His transfer to North Melbourne for the Shinboners' first year of VFL football in 1925 caused a sensation. His wage of £12 a week was four times the average wage.

But he returned to St Kilda mid-way through 1926, after North won only five games in 1925 and none in 1926.

ELLIOTT, Fred (1883–1960)

A frontline member of Carlton's power teams of the 1900s, 'Pompey' Elliott played in the 1906 and 1908 premierships but missed out on the 1907 premiership through suspension.

Elliott was a quality rover who captained Carlton in 1908—the team lost only once all season—and was playing coach from 1909–11. He tallied 211 games in 13 seasons, after starting in 1899.

ENGLAND v CARLTON

On Saturday, 16 June, 1888, the first international Australian football match was played at the MCG in front of 29,355 excited fans who paid £723 for the privilege. To capitalise on the codes of football played in each colony, the touring Englishmen, mostly rugby union players from northern England, agreed to play rugby in New South Wales (and New Zealand), and Australian football in Victoria and South Australia.

Immaculately attired in red, white and blue, the Englishmen made a great impression. But they preferred not to mark the ball and Carlton, the reigning VFL premiers, won easily, 14.17 (101) to England 2.7 (19).

The Englishmen were commended for their enthusiasm and endeavour—and for their appearance. Writing in *The Australian*, Markwell said, 'The formidable appearance of the visitors, their splendid physique, the neatness of their costume and the appropriateness of their colours (the red, white and blue of old England) formed themes of favourable comment on every side, and indeed, it must be admitted that our men suffered by comparison, for they were neither so massive in stature, nor generally equipped in the matter of attire.'

The tour had been initiated by the enthusiastic *Henry Harrison,* who, on a visit to England four years previously with the 1884 Australian cricket team, attempted to stir up interest in what he considered 'the universal game'.

Sponsored by the well-known cricketing entrepreneurs, Lillywhite and Shewsbury, the Englishmen played a total of 25 games of Australian football, winning 14 and losing 11. One of the most memorable games was in Ballarat when the locals lost in a fierce snow-storm.

EPIS, Alec (1937–)

Alexander Angelo Epis was one of the Western Australia's finest exports to Victorian football.

Born in Boulder, near Kalgoorlie, he played at Nines Rovers before joining Essendon after a two-year clearance dispute.

Recruited as a rover and centreman, 'The Kookaburra' became a great half-back flanker and played in Essendon's 1962 and 1965 premierships.

The 1962 premiership half-back line of Epis, Ian 'Bluey' Shelton and *Barry Davis* is one of post-war football's finest combinations.

A butcher by trade, the 179 cm and 89 kg utility was one of the game's happiest characters, renowned for his non-stop, on-field banter.

ESSENDON

Co-founded in 1873 by well-to-do members of the Royal Agricultural Society, the Melbourne Hunt Club, the Victorian Woolbrokers and the Moonee Valley Club, Essendon's early links were with Melbourne's 'establishment'.

PREMIERS 1897

Essendon, winners of the first VFL premiership, in 1897.

The side originally played at Flemington. Essendon was a foundation and most-powerful member of the VFA, winning four consecutive flags from 1891–94. Between 9 July, 1892 and 1 September, 1894, Essendon played 57 games without loss.

In 1879, it became the first team to kick 10 goals in a game (against Hawthorn) and in the same year played Melbourne in one of the first games under 'electric light'.

Among its early stars was Charlie Pearson, said to be the originator of the high mark. He was named 'Champion of the Colony' in 1886.

Albert Thurgood was another prominent player, renowned for his wonderful field-kicking. In 1899, he place-kicked the ball 98 metres. 'It is seldom such pace, strength, activity and skill are blended in one individual. As a footballer he was a superman,' said *The Argus.*

Thurgood continued his exploits when Essendon became a foundation member of the VFL in 1897.

Big crowds followed the club, known originally as the 'Same Olds', from the very earliest days. On a trip to Geelong in 1880, so many supporters wanted to see the game that the railway authorities organised extra trains, the first 'football specials' from Melbourne to Geelong.

Between 1882 and 1921, the club's home base was in Jolimont, land now taken by luxury apartments.

Essendon won the first League premiership in 1897 under the captaincy of Stawell Gift winner, George Stuckey. Its president Alex McCracken was also the first VFL president. He was one of the founders of the club in 1873, and its first secretary, as a 17-year-old.

Essendon was the first club to wear white knicks in a premiership match (1893) and in finals (1902). This was because some felt its uniform too closely resembled Melbourne colours. Not until 1924 did the League rule that the home team wear black shorts and the visitors white.

Becoming known as the Bombers after their shift in 1922 to the Essendon Recreation Reserve (Windy Hill), close to the Essendon airport, the team won back-to-back premierships in 1923–24 and four in a decade from 1942–53, when it fielded some of the game's mightiest players.

Legendary *Dick Reynolds* played a record 320 games, while the feats of star full-forward *John Coleman* triggered the biggest crowds in history.

In 1950, Essendon lost only one game all year, and was the first side to win premierships in seniors, reserves and the under 19s all in the same season.

Essendon greats *Billy Hutchison, Jack Clarke* and *John Birt* were among the leading small men in the game in the 1950s and 1960s.

The Bombers have been coached by four-time Richmond premiership player *Kevin Sheedy* since 1980. Its premiership teams of 1984–85 are regarded as among the best in League history.

Tim Watson, Simon Madden and *Terry Daniher* were champions of these teams, renowned for their toughness and flexibility.

In 1992, the Bombers became the fourth co-tenants of the Melbourne Cricket Ground. They maintained their adminstrative base at Windy Hill. The tenancy agreement with the AFL and the Melbourne Cricket Club is for a minimum of 30 years with the option of an additional 10 years.

ESSENDON: THE STATISTICS

FORMED: 1872

JOINED LEAGUE: 1897
HOME VENUES: East Melbourne C.G. (1897–1921), Windy Hill(1922–91), MCG (1992–   )
CURRENT HOME VENUE DIMENSIONS: 161 metres × 140 metres
COLOURS: Black guernsey with red sash.
TOTAL FINALS MATCHES: 106 (58 wins, 46 losses, 2 ties)
FINALS RECORD: Premiers: 15 (1897, 1901, 1911–12, 1923–24, 1942, 1946, 1949–50, 1962, 1965, 1984–85, 1993)
Runners up: 13 (1898, 1902, 1908, 1941, 1943, 1947–48, 1951, 1957, 1959, 1968, 1983, 1990)
PREMIERSHIP COACHES: George Stuckey (2), Jack Worrall (2), Syd Barker (2), Dick Reynolds (4), John Coleman (2), Kevin Sheedy (3).
NIGHT SERIES PREMIERSHIPS: 5 (1981, 1984, 1990, 1993, 1994)
YOUNGEST PLAYER: Tim Watson, 15 years 305 days (1977)
OLDEST PLAYER: Charlie Hardy, 38 years (1925)
HIGHEST SCORE: 32.16 (208) v Footscray, R.22, 1982, Western Oval
LOWEST SCORE: 0.9 (9) v Fitzroy, R.1, 1899, Brunswick St Oval
LONGEST WINNING SEQUENCE: 16 (1949–50); 16 (1950–51)
LONGEST LOSING SEQUENCE: 14 (1933)
MOST FINALS: Bill Hutchison 28, Dick Reynolds 27, Tim Watson 23, Harold Lambert 21, Terry Daniher 20, Simon Madden 20.
MOST SEASONS AS COACH: Dick Reynolds 22 (1939–60)
MOST SEASONS AS CAPTAIN: Dick Reynolds 12 (1939–50)

ESSENDON: THE STATISTICS (cont)

MOST GAMES		MOST GOALS	
Simon Madden	378	Simon Madden	575
Dick Reynolds	320	John Coleman	537
Tim Watson	307	Bill Hutchison	496
Gary Foulds	300	Paul Salmon	470*
Terry Daniher	294	Terry Daniher	448
Bill Hutchison	290	Dick Reynolds	443
Don McKenzie	266	Alan Noonan	420
Ken Fletcher	264	Keith Forbes	415
Jack Clarke	263	Ted Freyer	372
Hugh Mitchell	224	Tom Reynolds	361
Barry Davis	218	Tim Watson	337
Paul Van der Haar	201	Hugh Mitchell	306
Glenn Hawker	200	John Birt	303
		Paul Van der Haar	278
		Gordon Lane	256
		Robin Close	233
		Geoff Blethyn	216
		Darren Bewick	215*
		Ted Fordham	214
		Ron Evans	209
		Alan Ezard	200

* current player.

MOST GOALS IN A MATCH: John Coleman 14 v Fitzroy, R.7, 1954, Windy Hill.
John Coleman 13 v Geelong, R.8, 1952, Brisbane E.G.
John Coleman 13 v Hawthorn, R.18, 1952, Windy Hill.
Ted Freyer 12 v Melbourne, R.1, 1935, MCG.
John Coleman 12 v Hawthorn, R.1, 1949, Windy Hill.
Fred Gallagher 12 v Geelong, R.8, 1957, Windy Hill.

BROWNLOW MEDALLISTS: Dick Reynolds 1934, 1937, 1938; Bill Hutchison 1952, 1953; Graham Moss 1976; Gavin Wanganeen 1993.

LEAGUE LEADING GOALSCORERS: Albert Thurgood 26 (1900), Fred Hiskins 34 (1901), Greg Stockdale 68 (1923), Bill Brittingham 66 (1946), John Coleman 100 (1949), John Coleman 120 (1950), John Coleman 103 (1952), John Coleman 97 (1953).

RECORD HOME VENUE ATTENDANCE: 35,791 v Collingwood, R.15, 1909, East Melbourne C.G.
43,487 v Collingwood, R.3, 1966, Windy Hill.
87,638 v Collingwood, R.3, 1993, MCG.

RECORD ATTENDANCE IN ANY MATCH: 116,828 v Carlton, GF, 1968, MCG.

MOST RECENT PREMIERSHIP TEAM: 1993 Essendon 20.13 (133) d. Carlton 13.11 (89).
B: G. Wanganeen, D. Fletcher, D. Wallis. H.B: D. Grenvold, M. Harvey, M. Thompson (c). C: R. Olarenshaw, S. Denham, P. Hills. H.F: M. Mercuri, J. Hird, J. Misiti. F: T. Watson, P. Salmon, M. Long. R: P. Somerville, G. O'Donnell. R: D. Bewick. Interchange: C. Daniher, D. Calthorpe.

EVANS, Bernie (1957–   )

After eight years with South Melbourne, Evans spent his last three seasons at Carlton, defying Sydney owner Dr Geoffrey Edelsten's ultimatum for all Swans players to live in Sydney by 1986.

Evans played 148 of his 185 League games at South from 1978–85. He was best and fairest in 1984.

He didn't play in a final with the Swans and was bitterly disappointed in 1987 when a one-match suspension kept him out of Carlton's 1987 premiership team. He did, however, play in the 1986 Grand Final.

Originally from Port Melbourne, where he had three senior seasons as a teenager, and played in the 1977 premiership side, Evans represented Victoria in 1984. He was a quality rover with great courage.

FANNING, Fred (1922–)

When Western Districts club, Hamilton, offered star Melbourne goalkicker Fred Fanning £30 a week—10 times his wage at Melbourne—the boom 25-year-old said he had no choice but to accept.

Fanning's transfer caused a sensation. He was the League's leading goalkicker in three of the previous four years. His goal sprees—he booted 97 goals in 1947—included a record 18.1 against St Kilda in the final match of the home-and-away season.

Norm Smith's presence at full-forward kept him out of the seniors in the late thirties, despite tallies of 109 and 111 with Melbourne reserves in 1938–39. In mid-season, 1940, he applied for a clearance to Carlton after the Blues guaranteed him six senior games. Melbourne secretary Percy Page told him to be patient and promptly tore up the application: 'You're staying with us,' he said.

Later that year, Fanning played in Melbourne's premiership side. He lined up in a forward pocket next to the legendary Smith, kicking the first goal of the game.

A knee injury, which required an operation, sidelined him in 1941, but he was to lead Melbourne's goalkicking five times in the next six years. In 1945, he was best and fairest and in 1947 made the Victorian team for the Australian carnival.

Opponents found it almost impossible to outmark him, especially when he manoeuvred his huge body into the front of the pack. His grip was vice-like and he rarely juggled marks.

But he sometimes struggled in adverse weather. Representing Victoria against Western Australia in Hobart during the '47 carnival, he had a late chance to win the game for the Vics as he lined up from 40 metres. 'The bell had rung. The ball was like a big greasy pork chop,' he said. 'It wasn't the accuracy I was worried about. It was the distance. I kicked a point and we lost the match.'

Fanning's 18 goal effort in his final League game, at the Junction Oval on 30 August, 1947, included his first 13 goals straight.

At full-back for St Kilda that memorable day was Maj. Gen. Alan Stretton, who was to head the massive relief operation after Darwin had been smashed to bits by Cyclone Tracy on Christmas Day, 1974. Fanning remembers that after he'd kicked his first 13 straight, Stretton said to him: 'Ease up, you're making a fool of me.'

Fanning's brief League career included 411 goals in 104 games. He kicked 11 on three occasions and 10 twice.

He's also the holder of another record, acknowledged in *The Guinness Book of Sporting Records* for kicking a drop kick 105.5 metres during the reserves grand final at the MCG in 1939.

'I was standing right in the centre circle when I made contact,' he said. 'When the ball hit the boot, I knew it was going through (the goals). It bounced on top of the perimeter fence. They measured it later. It was exactly 117 yards.'

FARMER, Graham (1935–)

The game's most-decorated ruckman, the best footballer ever from Western Australia, Graham Vivian 'Polly' Farmer was a superstar in two States from 1953–71. He overcame a serious knee injury to play 392 games: 176 with East Perth, 79 West Perth, 31 Western Australia, 101 Geelong and five Victoria.

He agreed to play at Geelong for £1000 in 1962. His release cost £1500, an unprecedented sum, which was funded by a generous Geelong supporter Frank Moore.

Geelong had finished sixth in 1961 and won the night premiership. Coach *Bob Davis* reckoned the absence of a top ruckman was the only factor stopping the Cats from competing with Hawthorn, the '61 VFL premiers.

Restricted to just six games in his first season because of his famous knee injury—suffered in his maiden appearance—the 191 cm Farmer was supreme in Geelong's 1963 premiership. His revolutionary combination work with star rover *Billy Goggin* started countless attacks.

At the centre bounces and the boundary throw-ins, the coffee-skinned champion

Graham Farmer, football's most decorated ruckman, in his adopted Geelong colours.

He was awarded an MBE for his services to football in 1971. His distinctions at Geelong included a VFL premiership in his second season, when he also finished second for the Brownlow Medal. In 1967, he played in another Grand Final and was captain in his final three seasons.

'Polly is a great champion,' said team-mate Denis Marshall. 'He could play well, anywhere, anytime.'

Another noted ex-Cat, *John Newman*, said: 'Polly Farmer had everything. He had superb control of both sides of his body, mental and physical. He was never flurried, always had plenty of time and was rarely beaten.

'I first saw Polly in a practice game. I walked into the Geelong ground after the head-of-the-river. A big man jumped high over a pack for a boundary throw-in, grabbed the ball in one palm, brought it down to his chest, turned and handballed 30 metres to a team-mate. It was fantastic.'

Geelong coach Davis believes the Cats would have won another flag in 1967 if Farmer had not cramped three times in the torrid last quarter. Each time Farmer went down Richmond scored. 'It was the difference between winning and losing,' Davis claimed.

From the age of three he was raised in an orphanage, Sister Kate's Home for Boys in Perth. Farmer's deep love of football and great skill was soon evident as a young boy. From nine, he started playing competitively at Greenbushes. For five years he played in bare feet, because he couldn't afford boots.

In 1953, at the age of 18, he had his first senior game for East Perth, having been encouraged to join the club by George Sweetapple.

His left leg was slightly shorter than his right, probably from his days of kicking with one shoe on. It cost him a lot of speed and some people thought he'd had an accident, but he was consistently outstanding in his maiden displays. He was a beautiful left-foot drop kick.

In 1956, he won the first of his three Sandover Medals, collected a Simpson Medal for being best afield in East Perth's winning grand final side and snared his

would often grab the ball and then handball 30 metres to waiting team-mates.

He was famous for those precise, creative and spearing handballs. He practised for hours, handballing through his half-opened car window. He became so proficient that he could handball almost as far as he could kick—and with greater accuracy.

'Farmer stands alone in that he used his style and skills to make an original contribution to Australian football,' said his first VFL coach, Davis.

Farmer's fabulous record includes six premierships—three with East Perth, one with Geelong and two with West Perth—and rivals that of any of the game's elite champions. A three-time All Australian, he won:

- The Sandover Medal twice, in 1956 and 1960 and was runner-up in 1957.
- Four Simpson Medals—1956 (v SA), 1958 (v Victoria), 1959 (WA Grand Final v Subiaco) and 1969 (Australian Football Championships).
- The Tassie Medal in 1956.
- Ten club best and fairests in 16 years: seven with East Perth, two with Geelong and one with West Perth.

third consecutive best and fairest.

He made his first attempt to cross to Melbourne, but was told he wouldn't be cleared.

From 1954–61, he won East Perth's best and fairest each year, except 1958 when he missed one-third of the season with a shoulder injury.

After he was best afield against Victoria, Davis asked him to play with the Cats. St Kilda was also keen, but he opted for Geelong, having attended the club's end of season trip to the Gold Coast.

As his record transfer fee was being negotiated in early 1962, Farmer's appearances in Geelong's practice matches caused unprecedented interest. The crowds doubled and then quadrupled to see his magic.

But in the opening minutes of his very first game, against Carlton at Princes Park, the 'Big Cat' badly injured his knee in a clash with Carlton followers Graham Donaldson and Maurie Sankey. Farmer limped away in a daze, his left knee numb, wondering if his VFL career was over before it had started.

He courageously tried to play with the injury, but was carried off the field in three of his five games that season. He had a cartilage removed and missed Geelong's final series.

In 1963, his ruckplay was devastating. The Cats won nine of their last 10 games, including the Grand Final. Farmer's habit of jumping a little earlier than his opponents in ruck contests helped him to use their bodies to gain a 'ride'.

The only player of his era who used his body to the same extent was Carlton great *John Nicholls* and the pair had some wonderful duels. But Nicholls conceded the West Australian's superiority.

'Polly was a magnificent mark and kick and a master of ruck play,' said Nicholls. 'Young players should watch films of Polly and copy his style—it was as close to perfect as you will ever see.

'He was probably the better player, but because of my knowledge of how to use my body and because I was prepared to give him a bit of a biff now and again, particularly with floating arms in the ruck, I found myself nullifying him in most games.'

Many opponents tried to upset him with aggression, but few succeeded. He was reported only once, against Hawthorn in mid-1966, and received a reprimand for striking Hawk toughman 'Delicate' Des Dickson.

Farmer says he used to think about football '24 hours a day'. 'When I arrived home from work at night, I would pick up a football that I would leave lying about the house. When I sat down to watch television it was in my hands.

'I used to throw it into the air—one hand or two. I handled the ball all the time, just like you pick up a knife and fork without really thinking about it. Each morning, I would do 20–25 minutes exercise in the lounge room strengthening my stomach muscles. It was the sort of exercise you did not get when training at the club.'

He returned to Perth in 1968 and lifted West Perth to two premierships in three years. In 1969 he won another Simpson Medal for his performances in the Australian championships.

He was Geelong's non-playing coach from 1973–75, and worked as rucking-coach for the Eagles. He astonished the players with his ability to handball as far as some of them could kick.

FIELDS, Neville (1951–)

Starting and finishing his career at Essendon, Fields played 199 League games from 1969–82. He had 11 seasons at Windy Hill and three with South, after he was traded for young Swan *Terry Daniher*.

A skilled centreman and brilliant left-foot pass who could kick the ball 50 metres without it rising above head-high, Fields was originally recruited from Essendon High School. He won the Bombers' best and fairest award in 1972, a season in which he was Brownlow Medal favourite but polled poorly.

He represented Victoria three times.

FITZROY

Formed in 1884 during an economic boom in Victoria when the population almost doubled, Fitzroy became the seventh senior club in the colony. It emerged from initiatives taken by Fitzroy Cricket Club and the Normandy Junior Football Club. Adopting Normandy's maroon and blue colours, Fitzroy was one of the VFA's most successful clubs. Its notable early players included its first captain, Paddy McShane, champion rover *Jack Worrall*—twice named 'Champion of the Colony'—and Tom Banks, captain of the 1895 premiership team.

One of the eight foundation members of the VFL in 1897, the Maroons won seven premierships and reached the finals on 12 other occasions in their first 27 years—a record equalled by only one other League club, Collingwood.

It won 14 VFL games in a row against both Carlton and St Kilda.

Crowds often in excess of 20,000 witnessed its home matches at the Brunswick Street ground, which from the mid 1880s

Fitzroy president Ern Joseph introduces the Queen to the Fitzroy players, 5 April, 1970.
It was the first time the VFL had played a Sunday football match.

was easily accessible by cable cars.

Three of its between-the-wars stars *Haydn Bunton, Wilfred 'Chicken' Smallhorn* and *Dinny Ryan* won Brownlow Medals. Another legendary figure was goalkicker *Jack Moriarty*, who kicked a record 663 goals in 185 matches from 1922 to 1933. In 1924, he tallied 82 goals, at that time the most ever scored in a VFL season. His 12 goals against North Melbourne at Arden Street in 1928 remains a ground record that will never be beaten, as North now play home games at the MCG.

Fitzroy won its eighth premiership in 1944, under captain-coach Fred Hughson, one of the game's true gentlemen. The temperature that day soared into the high 20s. Many in the crowd of 43,000 had walked miles to the Junction Oval, because of a strike by trams and buses.

Fitzroy defeated *Jack Dyer*'s Richmond by 15 points. One of the Lions' Grand Final 19, winger Noel Jarvis, had two days earlier helped Fitzroy reserves to the premiership.

In the next 35 years, the Maroons made the play-offs only three times.

In 1957, the club became known as the Lions, rather than the Maroons. In the late 1930s, Fitzroy were called the Gorillas.

But the club's on-field fortunes continued to stagnate. Its dismal playing record in the 1960s and 1970s included three wooden spoons in four years, and 11 'last-three' finishes.

In 1967, Fitzroy transferred its home games from Brunswick Street to Carlton's Princes Park. In 1970 it moved again, this time to the Junction Oval, St Kilda, where its fortunes revived. In 1984, it spent its 101st season at Collingwood, and now plays home matches at the Western Oval.

Stalwart players like *John Murphy* had the distinction of playing in the first day game at VFL Park—against Geelong—in April 1970—and in the same month, the first VFL Sunday game, against Richmond. That match was played before a crowd of 38,617 which included Queen Elizabeth and other members of the royal family. Murphy also figured in the first night game at Waverley, when Fitzroy played North Melbourne, in May, 1977.

101

Fitzroy, VFL premiers 1922
  Back row (left to right): W. Hamilton (trainer), J. O'Donnell (trainer), A. Sharp (boot custodian), E. Melling (head trainer), R. Fletcher (trainer), E. Dredge (door keeper), R. King (timekeeper).
  Fifth row: W. G. Cant (committee), S. Laver (committee), H. Trevena (committee), W. Johnson (committee), V. Belcher (coach), A. M. Wood (committee), M. Archdeacon (committee), G. Hamill (trainer).
  Fourth row: A. Stephens (trainer), J. Gough (hon. dentist), M. E. Green (hon. secretary), J. Loveless (vice president), M. Clota (vice president), Cr. D. J. Chandler (president), J. Gray (vice president), W. J. McSpeerin (hon. treasurer), Dr P.A. Parer (hon. medical officer), P. Nelson (trainer).
  Third row: E. G. Elliott, L. Warren, N. Cockram, J. Hamilton, J. Tarbottom, H. Lennie, H. McNeil, H. Jenkin, S. Donnellan, L. Wigraft, G. Collins.
  Second row: G. McCracken, R. Miller, J. Atkinson, S. Nolan, J. Scales, C. Lethbridge (captain), G. Rattray (vice captain), G. Taylor, C. Sherry, R. Merrick.
  Front row: T. Corrigan, C. Keller, H. Carter, L. Gale, J. Freake, C. Fergie, P. Parratt, F. Williams.

In 1979, the club kicked a League record 36.22 (238) against Melbourne.

The club's best finish in recent times came in 1986 when it courageously made the preliminary final, despite many on-field injuries, in a year in which it was so troubled financially that there was talk of extinction.

Writing in *The Sun*, Richmond great *Kevin Bartlett* said should Fitzroy fold, it would mean Victoria 'losing one of its 11 Michelangelos'.

The club has suffered from not having a central base for playing, training, administration and social actitivies.

In late 1989, club directors agreed Fitzroy should amalgamate with Footscray and become known as the Fitzroy Bulldogs. But the merge did not eventuate after a groundswell of disapproval—and donations—from Footscray supporters. Earlier in the '80s the club had nearly combined with Melbourne. Others favoured a relocation to Brisbane.

In 1991, Fitzroy embarked on an extensive fund-raising campaign aimed at wiping-off its accumulated debt of about $1,000,000 and ensuring its long-term future. As part of the activities a 'Legends' match between Fitzroy's team of 1979—which holds the VFL record for highest score—played the '79 Carlton premiership team, and won by several points.

More than $800,000 was raised, halving the club's deficit. As an experiment, four of the club's home matches in 1991–92 were played in Tasmania, but the attendances were mediocre, the club losing almost $100,000 on the venture.

Choosing an all-Melbourne base, the Lions shifted home matches to Footscray's Western Oval in 1994. Some off-shore sponsorhip, via the Nauru Government, ensured its immediate financial future.

FITZROY: THE STATISTICS

FORMED: October, 1883

JOINED LEAGUE: 1897
HOME VENUES: Brunswick St. Oval (1897–1966), Princes Park (1967–69, 1987–93), Junction Oval (1970–84), Victoria Park (1985–86), Western Oval (1994–   )
CURRENT HOME VENUE DIMENSIONS: 176 metres × 123 metres
COLOURS: Light maroon guernsey with royal blue yoke and trimmings with gold monogram and lion emblem.
TOTAL FINALS MATCHES: 59 (34 wins, 25 losses)
FINALS RECORD: Premiers: 8 (1898–99, 1904–05, 1913, 1916, 1922, 1944)
              Runners up: 5 (1900, 1903, 1906, 1917, 1923)
PREMIERSHIP COACHES: Alex Sloan (2), Gerald Brosnan (2), Percy Parratt (1), George Holden (1), Vic Belcher (1), Fred Hughson (1)
NIGHT SERIES PREMIERSHIPS: 2 (1959, 1978)
YOUNGEST PLAYER: Andrew Kuka, 16 years 46 days (1967)
OLDEST PLAYER: Percy Parratt, 38 years (1923)
HIGHEST SCORE: 36.22 (238) v Melbourne, R.17, 1979, VFL Park
LOWEST SCORE: 1.0 (6) v Footscray, R.5, 1953, Western Oval
LONGEST WINNING SEQUENCE: 14 (1898–99)
LONGEST LOSING SEQUENCE: 27 (1963–65)
MOST FINALS: Percy Parratt 19
MOST SEASONS AS COACH: Bill Stephen 11 (1955–57, 1965–70, 1979–80)
MOST SEASONS AS CAPTAIN: Kevin Murray 8 (1963–64, 1967–72)

MOST GAMES		MOST GOALS	
Kevin Murray	333	Jack Moriarty	626
Paul Roos	269	Bernie Quinlan	576
Gary Wilson	268	Gary Wilson	451
Frank Curcio	249	Jimmy Freake	442
Norm Johnstone	228	Alan Ruthven	442
Alan Ruthven	222	Richard Osborne	411
David McMahon	218	Michael Conlan	394
John Murphy	216	John Murphy	326
Warwick Irwin	215	Eddie Hart	323
Alan Gale	213	Bob Beecroft	291
Michael Conlan	210	Paul Roos	270
		Claude Curtin	269
		Tony Ongarello	246
		David McMahon	236
		Owen Abrahams	230
		Warwick Irwin	227
		Haydn Bunton	209
		Gary Lazarus	206
		Keith Stackpole	203
		Percy Parratt	202

MOST GOALS IN A MATCH: Bob Merrick 12 v Melbourne, R.16, 1919, Brunswick St Oval.
                       Jack Moriarty 12 v North Melb., R.11, 1928, Arden St Oval.
                       Bernie Quinlan 11 v North Melb., R.21, 1984, MCG.
                       Richard Osborne 11 v Melbourne, R.18, 1989, Princes Park.

BROWNLOW MEDALLISTS: Haydn Bunton 1931, 1932, 1935; 'Chicken' Smallhorn 1933; Dinny Ryan 1936; Alan Ruthven 1950; Kevin Murray 1969; Bernie Quinlan 1981.

COLEMAN MEDALLISTS: Bernie Quinlan 1983, 1984.

LEAGUE LEADING GOALSCORERS: Jimmy Freake 56 (1913), Jimmy Freake 66 (1915), Jack Moriarty 82 (1924), Bernie Quinlan 116 (1983), Bernie Quinlan 105 (1984).

RECORD HOME VENUE ATTENDANCE: 34,765 v Essendon, R.14, 1923, Brunswick St Oval.

26,173 v Collingwood, R.11, 1992, Princes Park.

28,471 v Collingwood, R.4, 1974, Junction Oval.

17,141 v Sydney, R.22, 1986, Victoria Park.

15,394 v Collingwood, R.16, 1994, Western Oval.

RECORD ATTENDANCE IN ANY MATCH: 87,217 v Collingwood, FS, 1979, MCG.

MOST RECENT PREMIERSHIP TEAM: 1944 Fitzroy 9.12 (66) d Richmond 7.9 (51).

B: C. Denning, F. Hughson (c), A. Fields. H.B: L. Bickerton, N. Hillard, A. O'Bryan. C: B. Calverley, G. Hoskins, N. Jarvis. H.F: S. Dawson, S. Wright, N. Price. F: M. Hearn, K Sier, K. Stackpole. R: S. Clay, J. Symons. R: A. Ruthven. Reserve: D. Murray.

FIVE FAMOUS INCIDENTS

• *Ted Whitten's first-game knock-out, 1951, Punt Road*

Within a minute of booting a goal with his first kick in his first game, 17-year-old *Ted Whitten* was confronted by a wild-eyed Don 'Mopsy' Fraser, the Richmond tough-man, who snarled: 'That's the biggest mistake you ever made, son. You won't see the game out.'

He didn't. Late in the third quarter Whitten was running the same way as the ball. Just before he was flattened he heard a voice saying: 'This is it kid.'

'I saw Mopsy, teeth bared, charging at me like an express train,' Whitten said in *The Wild Men of Football*.

'In horror, I knew I couldn't get out of the way. A wave of agony and next I recall was being carried from the ground on a stretcher.'

Whitten said Fraser had also 'ankle-tapped' him before the start of the game, a charge Fraser admitted to. 'The little niggle I gave him before the start of that match might have stopped him from being a first-game wonder and causing me embarrassment,' he said. 'He was there, in the man's game. You don't give a raw kid any more latitude than you would give an experienced campaigner.'

Whitten became the VFL's glamour player but Fraser received more than 50 weeks' suspension in a career which took him from Richmond, into the VFA and Tasmania. 'I'm not proud of that record,' he once said. 'But I'm not ashamed of it either. It was my way of playing football— hard.'

• *The Bluey Adams–Des Healey collision, 1955 Grand Final, MCG*

For his fifth consecutive finals game in two years, young Demon *Frank 'Bluey' Adams* was warming the reserves bench, itching for a chance on-field.

With only three minutes to go to the final siren, Melbourne were leading Collingwood easily. Geoff Case was taken off on the member's side of the ground. Out rushed Adams from his bench in front of bay four. Propelled by legs which later won him the Australian professional sprint title, he sped onto the arena and spied Collingwood's Des Healey running with the ball in the clear.

'I could see Des but he couldn't see me,' said Adams. 'If he had, he would have swerved and I would have shot straight across the ground into the members' pickets. All I could think was that I had to stop him. Five yards from him I shaped to give him a shoulder and then everything went wrong. I crashed into his face with my head.'

Both men were knocked out. When the dust settled, they lay 10 yards apart. Healey's skull was fractured and his nose broken in five places.

Forty-five minutes later when Adams came-to in the Melbourne dressing rooms, he thought he had been injured in a game against Essendon. He was right, but that had happened nearly two months earlier.

Looking around, he became even more confused. His team-mates had changed into Collingwood jumpers as part of the traditional Grand Final guernsey swap.

Adams had lasted only 10 seconds for the first of his six winning Grand Finals.

Healey, 27, never played again. 'I made up my mind to get out of League football,' he said. 'I couldn't take another blow like that one.'

He could remember little of League football's most violent collision: 'Neil Mann had booted the ball; the pack went for it and it came off their hands. I grabbed it, saw that I was surrounded by wide open spaces so I went for a bounce. I can tell you nothing from then on except I thought the end of the world had come. I never saw Adams. I never saw anyone.'

Healey later coached successfully in the country, at Wodonga and Junee, after his 149 games in eight seasons at Collingwood.

• *The sensational Ken Boyd–John Nicholls clash, Princes Park, 1961*

In two matches against Carlton in 1961, volatile South Melbourne ruckman Ken Boyd was suspended for a total of 20 matches: eight on striking charges against Carlton ruckman *John Nicholls* and rover John Heathcote, and 12 after a League investigation into a behind-play punch which downed Nicholls in the return game at Princes Park.

Boyd claimed Nicholls had deliberately kicked him in the groin at a centre bounce, and admitted running after him and king-hitting him.

'Nicholls had earlier told me what he would do if I bothered him,' Boyd said. 'I told Nicholls: "If you do that I'll knock your head off."'

'He did and I went straight back and hit him as hard as I could.'

His frank admissions sparked a major controversy which caused the VFL to act.

In his book, *Big Nick*, Nicholls denied kicking Boyd. 'I have a clear conscience on the matter,' he said. 'In the 328 games I played, I never used my legs or knees in general ruck play or at centre bounces for anything else but protection.'

Boyd never played in the VFL again—his career ended after just 60 games, missing 30 matches through suspension.

• *The John Greening knockout, 8 July 1972, Moorabbin*

Just as he was being touted as a potential Brownlow Medallist, John Greening's 1972 season came to an abrupt end when he was knocked out behind play in the opening two minutes of the mid-winter game between Collingwood and St Kilda at Moorabbin.

He failed to regain consciousness for 24 hours and it was several days before he came out of a semi-coma. At one stage doctors feared for his life.

Collingwood considered instigating police action against St Kilda player Jim O'Dea, before lodging an official complaint. After a League investigation, a striking charge was laid against O'Dea and he was suspended for 10 weeks.

Greening played again for Collingwood, with nine games between 1974–76, but never again reproduced his scintillating best. He coached in the VFA and in Tasmania: his League career finished prematurely after 107 games in eight seasons, including 94 in a row by the time he was 21.

He polled 14 votes in half a season in the '72 Brownlow to finish seventh. The Medal was won by team-mate *Len Thompson*, with 25.

Almost 18,000 fans attended Greening's benefit match between Collingwood and St Kilda the following March, which raised $20,000 as part of an appeal that netted $50,000.

• *The Dermott Brereton/Mark Yeates pay-back, 1989 Grand Final, MCG*

As *Gary Ablett* was kicking the first of his record-equalling nine goals seconds into the sensational 1989 Grand Final, Hawthorn's *Dermott Brereton* was flat on his back in the centre. His lungs had shut down after a premeditated opening bounce collision with Geelong's Mark Yeates.

In a pay-back for an incident earlier in the year, Yeates spread-eagled Brereton at the bounce, causing rib and spleen damage.

The Hawthorn champion's game looked over before it had even started.

But, showing remarkable courage, he was helped into a forward pocket, refusing orders to leave the ground. His legs were like jelly, and his complexion a sickly yellow. Soon afterwards he goaled from a fine mark, sparking the Hawks to an eight goal first quarter which was crucial to the side winning consecutive flags.

'I thought my ribs were gone and that I'd be useless for the rest of the day,' said Brereton of the incident. 'I told myself to stay on my feet. Then I said "Jesus!" and put one knee on the ground and tried to get a bit of air into my lungs. I couldn't so went onto my back. My lungs shut down for half a minute or so. It was a bit frightening.'

Brereton's barn-storming tactics at the centre bounces had been the centre of much discussion in the lead-up to the final.

At Geelong's Grand Final eve strategy meeting, some 'protection' tactics were planned. 'We didn't want any of our players hurt at the start of the Grand Final,' said centreman *Paul Couch*. 'We discussed many things about our game-plan and tactics and one of them was about stopping opposition players from crashing into our on-ball players at the centre bounce.'

Couch said Michael Schulze would attempt to block Brereton's path. If he got past, Yeates would be there as a back-up.

Brereton dashed into the centre only to be immediately cleaned up by the charging Yeates, who admitted later the pair were 'square'.

Most believed that 'trial-by-video' charges should have been laid against Yeates, who played one more season in the League and then went coaching in Tasmania.

In the Grand Final replay at the start of the '90 season, Yeates and Brereton lined-up on each other. The pair shook hands at the end of the game. 'I certainly respect Dermott and I think he respects me, too,' said Yeates.

FLETCHER, Ken (1948–)

A wingman in the 1968 Grand Final in only his second season, Fletcher played 269 games with Essendon from 1967–80.

He captained the Bombers from 1977–79 and was best and fairest in 1978. Recruited from Essendon High, he represented Victoria eight times.

His son, Dustin, played in Essendon's 1993 premiership in his debut season.

FLOWER, Robert (1955–)

Idolised by thousands, Robert Alan 'Robbie' Flower never realised his ambition of playing in a Grand Final—but he was a sporting genius, a modest hero who was one of the greats of his era.

In a 274-game career stretching 15 years from 1973–87, Flower was accorded almost every accolade, except the Brownlow Medal. He captained Melbourne for seven years and was best and fairest (in 1977). He won the goalkicking four times, represented Victoria on 15 occasions— three times as captain—and was twice All Australian.

In his final season, Melbourne made a bold run at the Grand Final, only to be beaten in the gripping preliminary final by a goal after the siren from Hawthorn's *Gary Buckenara*.

It was 32-year-old Flower's last match. Melbourne had led for most of the day. First into the rooms, Flower hurled a can of Coke at the wall in his frustration. 'The feeling of emptiness was indescribable,' he said. 'We had the game, now we'd lost.'

He'd played 20 of Melbourne's 25 matches of the year. He kicked five goals in the elimination final and four in the first semi. It was a cruel way to finish, especially since he'd missed Melbourne's night premiership earlier in the season.

He'd suffered many injuries during his

For 14 years Melbourne's Robert Flower was an onlooker come the finals action, before Melbourne's bold run at the Grand Final in his farewell season, in 1987.

career, including a broken thumb and a broken collarbone in 1985. He also was worried by persistent shoulder and back problems in his final years.

He originally retired at the end of 1986, but was talked back into playing. Melbourne based a player acquisition fund around the slogan: 'Please Give Robbie Flower One Last Chance To Play In A Final.'

When the fast-improving Demons defeated Footscray and Hawthorn came from behind to win at Geelong in the final home-and-away round, Melbourne clinched its first finals berth since 1964. Flower's September dreams had become a reality, before Buckenara's kick turned them into a nightmare.

The Demons made the Grand Final in 1988, but without Flower, who had retired for good, even though he continued to assist as a skills coach.

Later he became an AFL Rules Committee member and radio commentator, before returning to the Demons in 1992 as match committee chairman.

Flower made his debut against Geelong in the 10th round of the '73 season.

Flower didn't even have a ticket to get into the MCG, and paid at the gate. Despite his nerves, he made a prominent beginning, kicking one goal in his club's 10 goal victory. Wearing guernsey No. 2 from the outset, he was never to be dropped.

Flower played in thick-rimmed glasses and looked even younger than his 17 years. His exciting skills were highly developed, however, and he quickly became Melbourne's first-choice wingman. His acrobatic leaping, speed and baulking ability were features of his game.

Within three years he was playing for Victoria and, at 22, had won his club's best and fairest. In 1978, he was best afield for Victoria against Western Australia, one of the highlights of his career, which included many distinguished displays at state and national level.

Melbourne football journalist Michael Davis said Flower looked more like a contestant from Mastermind than a champion athlete. But few could play at the same dazzling standard.

He twice finished in the Brownlow Medal 'top three', in 1979 and 1984. Many thought a mid-career change of position from wing to a half-back-flank denied him a genuine chance of winning football's most prestigious individual award.

He continued to serve Melbourne loyally—despite some rich offers to lure him away—and happily accepted team-orientated roles designed to make his struggling club more competitive.

North Melbourne legend *Wayne Schimmelbusch* said: 'I paid more attention to Robert Flower than any other opponent when I played on the wing because he was such a good player. He was very difficult because of his great skills. You could be in front of him and he'd outmark you; if you were behind you were gone. Robert was head-and-shoulders above everyone else at Melbourne in terms of value to the side.'

Former teammate *Brent Crosswell* said Flower's unusually long arms made him a deceptively good high-mark. 'For years Melbourne attacked only along Flower's wing . . . Beat Flower and you could just about retire from League football because anything else smacked of anti-climax,' he said.

FONTAINE, Fred

The only Fitzroy player to appear in four premiership sides, Fred Fontaine played 109 games in a decade with Lions from 1898–1907, appearing mainly in key positions.

FOOTE, Les (1924–)

North Melbourne's first Grand Final captain, and one of its first champions, stylish Les Foote was the master of the blind turn, and one of the best players never to win a Brownlow Medal. Foote could weave, dodge and baulk, leaving opponents clutching at thin air.

In 132 games with North from 1941–51—his first as a 16-year-old—he won three best and fairests, was captain for four years and an interstate representative for five out of six years from 1946–51. In 1950, he was State vice-captain.

Les Foote, North Melbourne's greatest post-war player.

North diehards regard teenage debutantes Foote and *Allen Aylett* as the club's greatest players in its first 50 years.

Recruited from local Sunday amateur club, the North Melbourne Colts, the 182 cm Foote honed his baulking skills as a teenage worker in the city. He practised daily among the lunchtime crowds in Swanston and Collins Streets.

Playing as a ruck-rover, fair-headed Foote was his team's best player in the 1950 Grand Final, which Essendon won 13.14 (92) to 7.12 (54). He was also magnificent in the second semi-final and was best afield in the preliminary final.

His prime position was centre, where he played some classic matches. He was also used successfully in the forward line. 'Quite often he appeared to have the ball on a string,' said Collingwood skipper *Lou Richards.*

Football historian Hugh Buggy said of him: 'Les Foote, who swept across the football firmament like a flashing meteor just after the war, was the nearest approach to the ideal all-round footballer since *Dick Reynolds* and *Ivor Warne-Smith.*'

At 27, Foote left North to coach Berrigan in country NSW. He was offered £25 a week, a business and a home.

He returned to League ranks as captain-coach of St Kilda, in 1954–55. He played 33 games. In his first year he was best and fairest.

FOOTSCRAY

Formed in 1883 and best known in its early years as the Footscray Imperials—after the Prince Imperial who had just died—Footscray's origins were very English. Its colours derived from the red, white and blue of the Union Jack, and its nickname was the Bulldogs, that most British of British dogs.

Joining the Victorian Football Association soon after its formation, Footscray initially struggled to compete. It failed to make the first three before winning nine of the next 28 premierships after eight clubs had left the VFA to form the Victorian Football League in 1897.

It became the first senior club to win

three flags in a row, from 1898–1900. Early stars included Arch Clark, John Craddock, Jim Crouch, Dave Decoit, Arthur Gregory, Bill Harris and Jack Marmo.

Its most famous early match was in 1924, when Essendon, the 1924 VFL premiership club, was defeated for the 'Championship of Victoria', an end-of-season charity challenge, the brainchild of celebrated singer Dame Nellie Melba.

Footscray's team that season included skipper Con McCarthy, elusive centreman *Allan Hopkins*, George Bayliss, Alex Eason, Norm Ford, Rupert Gibb and Vic Sampson. It won easily, 9.10 (64) to 4.12 (36). It was alleged later that some Essendon players had deliberately played below their best to win side-bets. Afterwards, fighting broke out in the Essendon dressing rooms. Champion defender Tom Fitzmaurice refused to play for the Bombers again.

The next year, Footscray, then known as the Tricolours, was admitted to the VFL, representing Melbourne's western 'blue-collar' suburbs. But, like fellow 'new chums' Hawthorn and North Melbourne, it had a mediocre start and reached the finals only five times between 1925–50. Only Hawthorn was considered more unfashionable.

The mild-mannered Hopkins was one of the team's few star raters, finishing in the first three in consecutive Brownlow counts from 1929–31. Gifted half-forward, dual best and fairest winner *Alby Morrison*, also gave great service, as did long-serving ruckmen *Arthur Olliver* and Brownlow Medallist *Norman Ware*.

Even a massive recruiting program, which saw the club entice Stan Penberthy (Subiaco), Jack Hanson (Broken Hill), Allan Rait (North Hobart), Doug Ayres and John Hayes (NSW) and Tom Waye (Port Adelaide) failed to lift the club in the '30s.

Until the Coronation year, Footscray had appeared in just six final series and lost every match. But in 1953 it defeated Essendon. Two of its stars were third-year captain-coach Charlie Sutton and *Ted Whitten*, just turned 20.

The club won its only premiership the following year and competed in three other final series in six years. It also produced two Brownlow Medallists in five seasons. Its full-forward Jack Collins was the equal of any spearhead in the game.

Whitten, whose career spanned three decades, was particularly dynamic in the 1950s, while Sutton was a tough and unrelenting on-field force. 'He inspired his players and they admired him,' said legendary *Jack Dyer*. 'They would have died for him on the football field and he for them.'

Sutton played his first match for weeks in the '54 Grand Final, kicking three goals from a forward pocket. The Bulldogs won by 51 points, doubling Melbourne's score, 15 goals to seven.

Despite Whitten's dynamic leadership, the club made only one other VFL Grand Final appearance, in 1961, but was well-beaten by Hawthorn. It led at half-time, but appeared tired later in the game, having had a torrid preliminary final victory against glamour team Melbourne, which was going for its sixth premiership in seven years.

Whitten did captain Footscray to three night flags in the 1960s.

In 1978, Footscray kicked a record 33.15 (213) against St Kilda at its home ground, the Western Oval, one of the longest in the competition at 183.7 metres. Full-forward *Kelvin Templeton* amassed 15 of the 33. But the record was soon afterwards broken by Fitzroy.

In recent times Footscray has battled for survival. The club was insolvent at the end of 1989, but won a reprieve after the football public generously answered a financial SOS. The $1 million raised effectively saved the club, in the short-term.

Footscray supporters, buoyed by the club's battling, big-hearted efforts—especially at home—were also disappointed to see Brownlow Medallists Templeton and *Brad Hardie* released, along with *Barry Round, Bernie Quinlan* and *Brian Wilson*, who won Brownlows at other clubs. Richmond's premiership centreman *Geoff Raines* was originally tied to the Bulldogs as a schoolboy, but allowed to go elsewhere. Well-performed Allan Edwards was another.

But the Bulldogs gained 1990 Brownlow Medallist *Tony Liberatore* from North Melbourne and some astute country recruiting saw the side rise to third in 1992, a season which produced another Bulldog Brownlow Medallist, *Scott Wynd*, from Jacana, in the heart of North Melbourne recruiting territory.

FOOTSCRAY: THE STATISTICS

FORMED: 1883

JOINED LEAGUE: 1925
HOME VENUES: Western Oval (1925–41, 1943–   ), Yarraville (1942)
CURRENT HOME VENUE DIMENSIONS: 176 metres × 123 metres
COLOURS: Royal blue guernsey with red and white bands.
TOTAL FINALS MATCHES: 25 (8 wins, 17 losses)
FINALS RECORD: Premiers: 1 (1954)
　　　　　　　Runners-up: 1 (1961)
PREMIERSHIP COACH: Charlie Sutton (1)
NIGHT SERIES PREMIERSHIPS: 4 (1963–64, 1967, 1970)
YOUNGEST PLAYER: Brian Wilson, 16 years 210 days (1978)
OLDEST PLAYER: Alby Morrison, 37 years 221 days (1946)
HIGHEST SCORE: 33.15 (213) v St Kilda, R.13, 1978, Western Oval
LOWEST SCORE: 1.8 (14) v Geelong, R.12, 1965, Western Oval
LONGEST WINNING SEQUENCE: 9 (1946)
LONGEST LOSING SEQUENCE: 14 (1979–80)
MOST FINALS: Ted Whitten 10.
MOST SEASONS AS COACH: Ted Whitten 13 (1957–66, 1969–71)
MOST SEASONS AS CAPTAIN: Ted Whitten 14 (1957–70)

MOST GAMES		MOST GOALS	
Doug Hawkins	329	Simon Beasley	575
Ted Whitten snr.	321	Kelvin Templeton	494
Arthur Olliver	272	Jack Collins	385
Steven Wallis	228*	Alby Morrison	369
Alby Morrison	224	Ted Whitten snr.	362
Gary Dempsey	210	Arthur Olliver	354
Wally Donald	205	Brian Royal	299
Norman Ware	200	Bill Wood	294

* current player.

MOST GOALS IN A MATCH: Kelvin Templeton 15 v St Kilda, R.13, 1978, Western Oval.
　　　　　　　Simon Beasley 12 v Geelong, R.16, 1982, Western Oval.
　　　　　　　Simon Beasley 12 v Melbourne, R.15, 1985, Western Oval.
　　　　　　　Simon Beasley 12 v Richmond, R.18, 1985, VFL Park.
BROWNLOW MEDALLISTS: Allan Hopkins 1930, Norman Ware 1941, Peter Box 1956, John Schultz 1960, Gary Dempsey 1975, Kelvin Templeton 1980, Brad Hardie 1985, Tony Liberatore 1990, Scott Wynd 1992.
COLEMAN MEDALLISTS: Simon Beasley 1985
LEAGUE LEADING GOALSCORERS: Jack Collins 84 (1954), Jack Collins 74 (1957), Kelvin Templeton 118 (1978), Kelvin Templeton 91 (1979); Simon Beasley 105 (1985).

FOOTSCRAY: THE STATISTICS (cont)

RECORD HOME VENUE ATTENDANCE: 42,354 v Collingwood, R.12, 1955, Western Oval.
14,000 v Richmond, R.12, 1942, Yarraville.
RECORD ATTENDANCE IN ANY MATCH: 107,935 v Hawthorn, GF, 1961, MCG.
MOST RECENT PREMIERSHIP TEAM: 1954 Footscray 15.12 (102) d Melbourne 7.9 (51).
B: W. Donald, H. Henderson, D. Bryden. H.B: A. Martin, E. Whitten, J. Gallagher. C: J. McCarthy, D. Ross, D. Reynolds. H.F: R. Duffy, P. Box, R. Stockman. F: B. Gilmore, J. Collins, C. Sutton (c). R: H. Stevens, A. Edwards. R: J. Kerr. Reserves: A. Nuttall, A. Abbey.

FOTHERGILL, Des (1920–   )

A gifted all-round sportsman who represented Victoria at both cricket and football, the elusive Des Fothergill tied for the 1940 Brownlow Medal with South Melbourne's *'Herbie' Matthews*. The pair could not be separated, even on a countback.

He made his debut for Collingwood from Collingwood Technical School at 16. He was a rover and half-forward with superb talents who suffered knee problems late in his career which restricted him to 111 VFL games, in which he kicked 344 goals, including 50 goals or more in five of his six full seasons.

While still a teenager, the thickset 178 cm Fothergill won Collingwood's famed Copeland Trophy three years out of four, before the League disqualified him when he crossed to VFA club Williamstown without a clearance in 1941. The VFL had halved its maximum payment under the controversial *Coulter Law* to one pound, 10 shillings.

Fothergill was too good for the VFA. He kicked 77 goals and won the Recorder Cup (now the J.J. Liston Trophy), the competition's best and fairest, with a record 62 votes in a brilliant season. But he had to stand out of football when the VFA went into a three-year wartime recess.

After the war, when the League granted an amnesty to all those who had crossed to the Association without clearances, he returned to Collingwood. He kicked 125 goals in two seasons in 1945–46 and played four games in 1947 before going to England to play Lancashire League cricket.

His highest first-class score in 28 matches was 102 against South Australia in Adelaide in 1947–48. In all, he tallied 1404 runs, average 39. He also bowled leg breaks.

FOULDS, Gary (1956–   )

Only the third Essendon player to amass 300 games, Foulds figured in the Bombers' famous back-to-back premiership combination of 1984–85. He retired late in season 1989, having played exactly 300 senior matches in 16 seasons.

A versatile player with exceptional kicking skills, Foulds first played with the Bombers in 1974 as a teenage recruit from West Essendon. Known mainly as a defender, he also played successfully in the forward line and represented Victoria.

He wore the No. 10 guernsey immortalised at Essendon by the great *John Coleman*.

FRANCIS, Jim (1910–   )

An all-round sportsman, who represented Hawthorn at football, cricket and baseball, Francis is best known for his 10-year playing association at Carlton, which included five seasons as captain. Later he coached the Blues for three years.

Playing 60 games at Hawthorn from 1929–33 and 162 at Carlton from 1934–43, he was centre half-back in Carlton's 1938 premiership win.

He left the Hawks in controversial circumstances in June 1934, after a disagreement with Hawthorn over his job in the family's sports-store business. Francis wanted Hawthorn to order its uniforms and gear through him and his father,

Harry. When club secretary Sam Ramsay refused, he sought a clearance and gave Carlton long and distinguished service.

FRASER, Ken (1940–   )

A superb, sticky-fingered high mark who was twice runner-up for the Brownlow Medal, centre half-forward Fraser played 198 games with Essendon from 1958–68. He was captain in his final four years.

He played in premiership teams in 1962 and 1965, was twice best and fairest (1963–64), and represented Victoria seven times. He was appointed State captain for the 1966 carnival in Hobart, but injury restricted him to just one match.

Recruited from Essendon Baptists-St Johns, along with fellow rookie, full-forward *Ron Evans*, the quietly-spoken and gentlemanly Fraser became an Essendon stalwart. He once took 13 marks in a semi-final, quite a feat for a key forward. He was also good at ground level and a fine team man.

His son, Mark, debuted with Collingwood in 1992, before switching to Essendon for the 1995 season.

FRAWLEY, Danny (1963–   )

Returning for a farewell year in 1995, his 12th in League ranks and his ninth as captain, Danny Frawley has been one of St Kilda's most stoic defenders, the best since *Trevor Barker*.

Recruited from Bungaree via East Ballarat, Frawley won St Kilda's best and fairest award and was an All Australian in 1988. He played his 200th game late in the 1993 season.

Goalkicking great *Tony Lockett* rates him the player he least likes to oppose.

FREAKE, Jimmy

Amassed an amazing goalkicking record considering his frail physique: 171 cm and 64.5 kg. A member of two Fitzroy premierships, in 1913 and 1922, he led the club goalkicking seven times and the League table twice, in 1913 (with 56 goals) and in 1915 (with 66, when he finished equal first with Collingwood's *Dick Lee*).

Recruited from Fitzroy Juniors, he was keen to play at Collingwood as a youngster. His hero was Magpie goalkicker *Teddy Rowell*, an expert place kick. Freake practised his place-kicking in his backyard, aiming to kick through an open woodshed door.

He told *The Sporting Globe*: 'I was so cocksure of my ability to kick place kicks straight that I used to bet mates marbles or cigarette cards I could goal through a five-foot goal, at 25 yards.

'I wanted to go to Collingwood and be a goalkicker, but was told that my old schoolmate, Dick Lee, would hold the goalkicking job for years.'

Forming a magnificent combination with Maroons half-forward Percy Parratt, Freake kicked 442 goals in 172 games and also coached Fitzroy, in 1929.

Of Parratt's ability to hit him on the chest with short passes, he said: 'My chest was red raw through taking his passes at practice, but in the first game he nearly knocked me over. Perhaps it was excitement that gave me that feeling, but no player ever drove a ball with such accuracy and speed.'

FREMANTLE

Becoming the second Perth-based AFL team from 1995, the Fremantle Dockers

The inaugural captain of the Fremantle Dockers, Ben Allan.

enjoyed immediate and lucrative corporate and membership support, sharing the revamped Subiaco Oval with the West Coast Eagles.

After four premierships in eight years with Claremont, coach Gerard Neesham immediately attracted some of Fremantle's finest footballing sons back from the east, including Hawthorn's Ben Allan, as captain, Sydney's Scott Watters, Geelong's Stephen O'Reilly and North Melbourne's Peter Mann.

The Dockers introduced a large dose of green into their snappy playing guernseys and were immediately competitive.

Ex-Essendon forward Todd Ridley kicked his team's first goal in round one against Richmond.

The historic first Fremantle team also included the tallest man ever to play Australian football at such an elite level, 210 cm Matthew Burton.

Ben Allan, best and fairest in a premiership team at Hawthorn, was appointed Fremantle's first captain in 1995.

FREMANTLE: THE STATISTICS

FORMED: 1994

JOINED LEAGUE: 1995
HOME VENUES: Subiaco (1995–   ), WACA (1995–   )
CURRENT HOME VENUE DIMENSIONS: Subiaco: 173 metres × 129 metres
WACA: 165 metres × 129 metres
COLOURS: Purple guernsey with green and red chest. Panels separated by a white anchor.
YOUNGEST PLAYER: Jeff White, 18 years 53 days (1995)
OLDEST PLAYER: Andrew McGovern, 27 (1995)
INAUGURAL COACH: Gerard Neesham
INAUGURAL CAPTAIN: Ben Allan

GALE, Alan (1930–87)

A superbly fit and able follower, 'Butch' Gale often rucked for all four quarters of a game in his 14-year association with Fitzroy. Captaining the Lions from 1958–61, he played 213 games and represented Victoria 13 times.

Recruited from the Fitzroy Police Boys Club, the 185 cm Gale played his first match in 1948, becoming known for his tireless displays, often against taller opponents. Extremely team-oriented, he palmed the ball beautifully to his rovers and was a skilled handballer.

His testimonial raised £1000, an indication of his popularity.

For years, he formed a great association on television with Michael Williamson, now the AFL's master of ceremonies. Gale's excited calls for the St Kilda defenders to 'hit the boundary' during the cliff-hanging 1966 Grand Final became legend.

On the eve of the 1987 season, he collapsed and died of a heart attack while addressing the Fitzroy players—at the invitation of coach *David Parkin*—before the club's opening match. He was 56.

Lion-hearted ruckman Alan Gale in action against Hawthorn at Glenferrie Oval in the 1950s.

GALLAGHER, Adrian (1946–)

Gallagher figured in Carlton's 1968 premiership win and was opening bat for the Blues in their 1968–69 Victorian Cricket Association First XI pennant team.

Gallagher had a marvellous understanding with No. 1 ruckman *John Nicholls* and ruck-rover *Sergio Silvagni*. He was first rover in three premierships in 1968, 1970 and 1972.

Nicholls regarded him very highly. Writing in *Big Nick* he said that even though Gallagher 'was pig-headed by nature, he proved his determination to do well in big games. "Gags" would always be relied upon to take those courageous marks while running backwards into packs or in front of goal when backmen were bearing down on him. He would know full well that he was going to be flattened but he would still go for the mark and get his kick.'

Gallagher played a total of 220 games from 1964–76. He finished his career with a brief stint at Footscray—where he was runner-up for the best and fairest in his first year—and North Melbourne.

Carlton's club champion in its memorable 1970 premiership year—despite missing the first six games with injury—Gallagher was a most able rover who improved his left-foot kicking through hours of practice.

GEELONG

One of the two oldest football clubs in Australia, Geelong dates back to 1855 when *Tom Wills* organised some winter recreation for the cricketers from Corio Bay. In 1859, the Corio Bay Club became Geelong Football Club. Its first match, against Melbourne, was played on the Argyle Square ground in Aberdeen Street.

The local newspaper, the *Geelong Advertiser*, applauded the venture. 'The game is one of the healthiest and easiest that could be adopted by persons cramped during the week by desk or counter service and standing in need of a little bracing exercise.'

Originally known as the Seagulls, Geelong became better known as the Pivotians in the late 1870s, because of its

The Geelong team for the round six game against Richmond at the Punt Road Oval in 1952. Shortly afterwards it won the first of a record 23 matches on end.

Back row (left to right): Ivor Gibson (sec.), Noel Rayson, Geoff Williams, Norm Sharp, George Goninon, John Hyde, Bruce Morrison, Russell Middlemiss, Russell Renfrey, George Swarbrick, Reg Hickey (coach).

Middle row: Bob Davis, Leo Turner, Bernie Smith, Fred Flanagan (captain), Tom Morrow, Bill McMaster.

Front row: Neil Tresize, Peter West, Doug Palmer, Peter Pianto and Ron Hovey.

central location in the railway and shipping network for Victoria's Western District.

Located 70 km south-west of Melbourne on Port Phillip Bay, Geelong has been a front-line member of the VFL since its inception in 1897, winning six premierships, its last in 1963. Geelong and Essendon were the two instigators of the formation of the VFL in late 1896.

Games have been played at its present ground at Kardinia Park since 1940. Home games had previously been played at Corio Oval from before the turn of the century.

The Geelong club was the first to introduce modern teamwork. From 1878–88, it won six premierships. Coach *Charles Brownlow* and captain David Hickinbotham devised strategies where forward players led into the ball to try and escape their opponents, and rovers and wingmen attempted to play in the open spaces using speed and evasive skills.

Some of the game's finest players have worn Geelong colours, including the first Brownlow Medallist, *'Carji' Greeves*.

The back-to-back premiership sides of 1951–52, coached by legendary ex-player *Reg Hickey*, are considered among the best

and most exciting teams since the war. Hickey's side won a record 23 games in a row. In 1951, the Cats became only the second club to win the flag and produce the Brownlow Medallist (*Bernie Smith*) and leading goalkicker (*George Goninon*) in the same year.

Fast and spectacular, the elite Cat teams of the early 1950s included 'The Geelong Flyer' *Bob Davis*, star forwards Fred Flanagan and Goninon, defender Smith and followers Tom Morrow and *Russ Renfrey*.

Geelong has always played a highly skilled, open brand of football and has generally finished in the top half of the competition, but for lapses in the mid 1940s, the late 1950s and the early 1970s. The club didn't compete in 1942–43 because of wartime restrictions on travel.

Until the 1989 Grand Final, which it lost by a goal, it hadn't appeared in a play-off for more than 20 years, despite possessing some brilliant footballers. It also lost Grand Finals in 1992 and 1994.

Denis Marshall and *Graham 'Polly' Farmer* and *Gary Ablett* are regarded as the team's finest players over the last three decades.

The Cats were the only VFL club not

located in metropolitan Melbourne until South Melbourne moved to Sydney in 1982.

Geelong's once-formidable home ground advantage has diminished with the advent of the interstate sides. But its renowned country hospitality remains unparalleled.

GEELONG: THE STATISTICS

FORMED: July, 1859

JOINED LEAGUE: 1897

HOME VENUES: Corio Oval (1897–1915, 1917–40), Kardinia Park (1941, 1944–   )

CURRENT HOME VENUE DIMENSIONS: 171 metres × 117 metres

COLOURS: Navy blue and white hooped guernsey.

TOTAL FINALS MATCHES: 80 (33 wins, 46 losses, 1 tie)

FINALS RECORD: Premiers: 6 (1925, 1931, 1937, 1951–52, 1963)
               Runners-up: 7 (1897, 1930, 1953, 1967, 1989, 1992, 1994)

PREMIERSHIP COACHES: Cliff Rankin (1), Charlie Clymo (1), Reg Hickey (3), Bob Davis (1)

NIGHT SERIES PREMIERSHIPS: 1 (1961)

YOUNGEST PLAYER: Ken Newland, 16 years 74 days (1965)

OLDEST PLAYER: Teddy Rankin, 38 years 106 days (1910)

HIGHEST SCORE: 37.17 (239) v Brisbane, R.7, 1992, Carrara

LOWEST SCORE: 0.8 (8) v Fitzroy, R.3, 1899, Corio Oval

LONGEST WINNING SEQUENCE: 23 (1952–53). Undefeated in 26 matches (1952–53)

LONGEST LOSING SEQUENCE: 16 (1941–44). Club did not play in 1942–43

MOST FINALS: 'Jocka' Todd 15, Bill Goggin 15, Peter Walker 15.

MOST SEASONS AS COACH: Reg Hickey 17 (1932, 1936–40, 1949–59)

MOST SEASONS AS CAPTAIN: 'Tracker' Young 9 (1901–09), Reg Hickey (1932–40)

MOST GAMES		MOST GOALS	
Ian Nankervis	325	Doug Wade	834
John Newman	300	Gary Ablett	830*
Bruce Nankervis	253	Lindsay White	429
Bill Goggin	248	Cliff Rankin	400
Reg Hickey	245	Lloyd Hagger	389
Michael Turner	245	Bill Brownless	371*
'Jocka' Todd	232	Larry Donohue	339
Neville Bruns	223	Percy Martini	333
Bill Eason	220	Terry Bright	331
Terry Bright	219	George Moloney	303
Doug Wade	208	Michael Turner	285
Paul Couch	208*	Bill Goggin	279
Andrew Bews	207	George Goninon	278
Gary Ablett	203*	Neil Trezise	272
David Clarke	202	Norm Glenister	263
Russell Renfrey	201	Ken Newland	243
Robert Neal	200	Les Hardiman	236
		Fred Wooller	225
		Jack Metherell	221
		Bill Ryan	220
		Noel Rayson	210
		Paul Sarah	204
		David Clarke	202

* current player.

GEELONG: THE STATISTICS (cont)

MOST GOALS IN A MATCH: Gary Ablett 14 v Richmond, R.9, 1989, MCG.
Doug Wade 13 v South Melb., R.17, 1967, Lake Oval.
Doug Wade 13 v North Melb., R.20, 1971, Kardinia Park.
George Moloney 12 v St Kilda, R.2, 1931, Corio Oval.
Gary Ablett 12 v Richmond, R.20, 1990, MCG.

BROWNLOW MEDALLISTS: 'Carji' Greeves 1924, Bernie Smith 1951, Alistair Lord 1962, Paul Couch 1989.

COLEMAN MEDALLISTS: Gary Ablett 1993, 1994.

LEAGUE LEADING GOALSCORERS: Eddie James 27 (1897); Eddie James 31 (1899); Lloyd Hagger 78 (1925); George Moloney 109 (1932); Lindsay White 86 (1948); George Goninon 86 (1951); Noel Rayson 80 (1955); Doug Wade 68 (1962); Doug Wade 96 (1967); Doug Wade 127 (1969); Larry Donohue 105 (1976); Gary Ablett 129 (1994).

RECORD HOME VENUE ATTENDANCE: 26,025 v Collingwood, R.15, 1925, Corio Oval.
49,107 v Carlton, R.19, 1952, Kardinia Park.

RECORD ATTENDANCE IN ANY MATCH: 109,396 v Richmond, GF, 1967, MCG.

MOST RECENT PREMIERSHIP TEAM: 1963 Geelong 15.19 (109) d Hawthorn 8.12 (60). B: I. Scott, R. West, J. Watts H.B: J. Devine, P. Walker, S. Lord. C: H. Routley, A. Lord, J. Brown. H.F: G. Hynes, F. Wooller (c), J. Sharrock. F: J. Yeates, D. Wade, C. Rice. R: G. Farmer, P. Vinar. R: W. Goggin. Interchange: K. Goodland, A. Polinelli.

GILL, Frank (1909–70)

Full-back in Carlton's 1938 premiership team, Gill played 205 games from 1929–42. He also appeared in the 1932 Grand Final. His nephews, John and Barry Gill, also represented Carlton.

GLEESON, Brian (1934–)

St Kilda's second Brownlow Medallist, Gleeson won in 1957. He was appointed captain, but tragically never played again after injuring his knee in a pre-season trial game at the start of the 1958 season. He attempted several comebacks, most notably at the start of the 1959 season, but never got past the practice matches.

Recruited from St Pat's Ballarat, a school renowned for its football prowess, the 189 cm Gleeson started in League football as a forward before developing into a tireless follower.

A brilliant mark and good kick he played four matches with Victoria in 1957 during his eye-catching season in which he won the Medal by four votes from Richmond's *Roy Wright*.

He played 70 games and kicked 52 goals in his five years with the Saints. His brother, Terry, also played in the VFL, with Melbourne.

GLENDINNING, Ross (1956–)

One of the most versatile and skilful interstate imports into VFL ranks, Glendinning was fast, a superb mark and equally proficient on both sides of his body.

A 15-year, 301-game player from 1974–88, he was recruited to East Perth straight from Scotch College, as a 17-year-old.

Second in the Sandover Medal as a teenager, he won the Brownlow Medal in 1983, mid-way through his League career in Melbourne. In 1982, he'd been runner-up.

The 188 cm utility had to stand out of football for six months before winning a release to North Melbourne—but only after he'd played the second half of the 1977 season back at East Perth.

Glendinning says his skills with the left and right foot were carefully honed by his father—who also played at East Perth. 'Dad was always particular, even in the backyard, about how I held and dropped the ball.'

He first played Sunday League as a nine-

117

year-old at Floreat Park, but only after he'd been to Sunday School. 'I'd have to make a mad dash to get to the football before the first ball was bounced,' he said. 'To do that I had to get out of my Sunday best into my football gear as Dad drove to the game!'

Ross Glendinning, captain of the West Coast Eagles in 1987–88.

Hawthorn's champion forward *Dermott Brereton* named him as his toughest opponent: 'When Ross was at his top at North Melbourne, he had everything I had—plus a lot more.' Glendinning represented Western Australia 13 times and Victoria twice.

His first 190 games in nine League seasons were spent at North Melbourne before he returned to Perth to become inaugural captain of the West Coast Eagles. Playing at full-forward, he led his club's goalkicking in consecutive seasons, including 73 goals in 1988, his final year.

At North Melbourne he won back-to-back club championships and in one game against Melbourne, in 1979, he booted 10 goals.

GOALKICKING LEGENDS

The most glittering full-forwards in VFL history both average more than five goals a game: Hawthorn's *Peter Hudson* (5.64) and Essendon's *John Coleman* (5.48).

Collingwood's *Gordon Coventry* remains the greatest goalkicker in League history, having notched 1299 goals in 18 seasons. *Doug Wade*, who played at Geelong and North Melbourne, also amassed more than 1000.

The most prominent modern-day goal-kickers are Hawthorn's *Jason Dunstall* and Sydney's *Tony Lockett*.

Dunstall passed 1000 career goals late in the 1994 season.

Kicking 100 goals in a season remains an illustrious feat and many believe the record of 150 held jointly by South Melbourne's *Bob Pratt* and Hawthorn champion Hudson may last into the 21st century.

Only twice in the first 70 years of League football did two men kick more than 100 goals in the same season: in 1933, Pratt (109) and Coventry (108) and 1934, Pratt (150) and Coventry (108).

Pratt's record of 150 goals is regarded as superior to Hudson's 150, almost 40 years later, as he played in 21 games, compared with Hudson's 24.

In 1992, Dunstall kicked 145 goals and Lockett 132.

In 1969, five forwards in senior football competitions around Australia kicked 100 goals: Doug Wade and Peter Hudson (VFL), Austin Robertson (WA), Fred Phillis (SA) and Steve Taylor (QAFL).

Among the most legendary interstate goalkickers are South Australian Ken Farmer who averaged more than six goals a game in amassing 1419 goals in 224 games with North Adelaide from 1929–41. He topped the SANFL goalkicking 11 years in a row, kicking 100 or more goals every season, including a career-best 23.6 against West Torrens in 1940. In one memorable solo effort in 1940, Farmer kicked 9.6 out of a team score of 9.10 against Glenelg.

Port Adelaide's Tim Evans also kicked more than 1000 SANFL goals—1044 in

248 games from 1975–86, while contemporary Phillis notched 884 in 280 games with Glenelg from 1966–81.

Norwood's 'Bos' Daly was the first to kick 20 goals in a game. He notched 23 against West Adelaide, in 1893.

Austin Robertson jnr, whose father played in South Melbourne's 1933 premiership side, remains Western Australia's most prolific goalscorer, with 1278 in 252 games with Subiaco from 1962–74. His career was interrupted by a year in VFL ranks with South Melbourne in 1966. He kicked 15 goals in a game against East Fremantle in 1968.

West Perth's Teddy Tyson kicked 1203 goals in 227 games from 1930–45 including 17 out of 18 in a losing score against Swan Districts. Contemporaries East Fremantle's George Doig and South Fremantle's Bernie Naylor also scored 1000-goals-plus and have higher goals-per-game averages.

Naylor's feats are particularly freakish. He kicked 100 goals in five of his nine seasons and, in 1953 against Subiaco, kicked a WAFL record 23 goals, including 12 in one quarter. His record of 153 goals in the home-and-away matches in 1953 has been surpassed only once, by Robertson, who kicked 157 in 1968.

Doig, from one of WA's most famous footballing families, kicked 106 goals in his first season of senior football in 1933. He repeated the effort for the next eight years, a WA record. In 1937, he was one of five players in the WA league to kick 100 goals, an Australian 'first'.

Tasmania's goalkicking leader is VFL champion Hudson who, in 159 games with New Norfolk and Glenorchy, amassed 994 goals at an average of 6.08 a game. North Hobart's Allan Rait was also prolific, with 748 goals from 1927–37. He was the first Tasmanian to kick 100 goals in a season, in 1930. He also played VFL football with Footscray in 1933–34. In one game against Carlton he kicked 10 goals.

Queensland rover Owen Backwell has been the QAFL's most prolific goalkicker over a 300-game career, while the NSW league's Melbourne import, Peter Ruscuklic, created an Australian record in 1981, when he kicked 213 goals for East Sydney. The previous record was 188 by Williamstown's *Ron Todd* in 1945.

South Sydney's Bill Wood kicked 28.4 against Sydney Naval in 1943, including 12 goals in the final term.

The ACT's most outstanding recent goalkicking performance came from Ainslie's Paul Angelis, who kicked 29.9 from 40 shots against West Canberra in 1984, on his way to 139 goals in a season.

LEADING LEAGUE GOALKICKERS: 1897–1994
(500 or more goals in league matches)

NAME AND CLUBS	MATCHES	GOALS IN A CAREER	10 IN A MATCH	50 IN A SEASON	100 IN A SEASON
Gordon Coventry (Coll., 1920–37)	306	1299	11	13	4
Doug Wade (Geel./NM, 1961–72)	267	1057	4	11	2
Jason Dunstall (Haw., 1985–94)	208*	1011	14	9	5
Jack Titus (Rich., 1926–43)	294	970	3	10	1
Leigh Matthews (Haw., 1969–85)	332	915	2	10	0
Tony Lockett (St.K., 1983–94)	183*	898	15	10	3
Peter McKenna (Coll., 1965–75)	191	874	13	7	3
Gary Ablett (Haw./Geel., 1982, 1984–94)	209*	839	12	9	2
Bernie Quinlan (Fitz./Foots., 1969–86)	366	815	2	6	2
Kevin Bartlett (Rich., 1965–83)	403	778	0	5	0
Bill Mohr (St. K., 1929–41)	195	736	3	8	1
Peter Hudson (Haw., 1967–74; 1977)	129	727	12	6	5
Harry Vallence (Carl., 1926–38)	204	722	5	7	0

LEADING LEAGUE GOALKICKERS: 1897–1994 (cont)
(500 or more goals in league matches)

NAME AND CLUBS	MATCHES	GOALS IN A CAREER	10 IN A MATCH	50 IN A SEASON	100 IN A SEASON
Dick Lee (Coll., 1906–22)	230	707	1	8	0
Bob Pratt (South Melb., 1930–39; 1946)	158	681	8	6	3
Jack Moriarty (Ess./Fitz., 1922–33)	170	662	2	8	0
Michael Moncrieff (Haw., 1971–83)	224	629	3	5	0
Michael Roach (Rich., 1977–89)	200	607	5	5	1
Stephen Kernahan (Carl., 1986–94)	199*	596	1	9	0
Kelvin Templeton (Foots./Melb., 1974–85)	177	593	1	5	1
Simon Beasley (Foots., 1982–1989)	154	575	5	7	1
Simon Madden (Ess., 1974–92)	378	575	0	0	0
Norm Smith (Melb./Fitz., 1935–50)	228	572	1	4	0
Dick Harris (Rich., 1934–44)	196	550	1	6	0
Peter Daicos (Coll., 1979–93)	250	549	1	5	0
Lindsay White (Geel./SM, 1941–50)	144	542	6	6	0
John Coleman (Ess., 1949–54)	98	537	12	5	3
Brian Taylor (Rich./Coll., 1980–90)	140	527	3	6	1

* current player.

LEADING GOALKICKERS ON A GOALS-PER-MATCH RATIO

PLAYER	CLUBS/SEASONS	MATCHES	GOALS	RATIO
Peter Hudson	Hawth. 1967–74, 1977	129	727	5.64
John Coleman	Ess. 1949–54	98	537	5.48
Tony Lockett	St Kilda 1983–94	183*	898	4.90
Jason Dunstall	Hawthorn 1985–94	208*	1011	4.86
Peter McKenna	Coll. 1965–73; Carlt. 1977	191	874	4.57
Tony Modra	Adelaide 1992–94	50*	220	4.40
Bob Pratt	South 1930–39, 1946	158	681	4.31
Ron Todd	Coll. 1935–39	76	327	4.30
Allen Jakovich	Melbourne 1991–94	47*	201	4.27
Gordon Coventry	Coll. 1920–37	306	1299	4.24
Gary Ablett	Haw. 1982/Geelong 1984–94	209*	839	4.01
Doug Wade	Geel. 1961–72; North 1973–75	267	1057	3.95
Fred Fanning	Melb. 1940, 1942–47	104	411	3.95
Jack Moriarty	Ess. 1922; Fitz. 1924–33	170	662	3.89
Sel Murray	North 1937–44, 1948; Rich. 1945–46	121	459	3.77
Bill Mohr	St Kilda 1929–41	195	736	3.77
Lindsay White	Geel. 1941, 1944–50; South 1942–43	144	542	3.76
Brian Taylor	Rich. 1980–84; Coll. 1985–90	140	527	3.76
Mark Jackson	Melb. 1981–82; St Kilda 1983; Geel. 1984–86	82	308	3.75
Simon Beasley	Foots. 1982–89	154	575	3.73
Noel O'Brien	Carlton 1954–55	32	117	3.65
Peter Sumich	West Coast 1989–94	124*	451	3.63
George Margitich	Melb. 1930–34	75	267	3.56
Harry Vallence	Carlt. 1926–38	204	722	3.53

(Minimum ratio: 3.5)
* current player.

MOST GOALS IN A QUARTER

EIGHT			
PLAYER/TEAM	OPPOSITION	QUARTER	YEAR
Gordon Coventry (Collingwood)	Hawthorn	first quarter	1929
Bob Pratt (South Melbourne)	Carlton	third quarter	1934
Bob Pratt (South Melbourne)	Essendon	fourth quarter	1934
Harry Davie (Melbourne)	Carlton	fourth quarter	1925
SEVEN			
PLAYER/TEAM	OPPOSITION	QUARTER	YEAR
Fred Fanning (Melbourne)	St Kilda	second quarter	1947
Bob Pratt (South Melbourne)	Footscray	fourth quarter	1934
Jim Baird (Carlton)	Fitzroy	third quarter	1942
Doug Wade (North Melbourne)	Collingwood	third quarter	1974
Jason Dunstall (Hawthorn)	Geelong	fourth quarter	1990
SIX*			
PLAYER/TEAM	OPPOSITION	QUARTER	YEAR
Jason Dunstall (Hawthorn)	Richmond	first quarter	1992
Tony Lockett (St Kilda)	Sydney	first quarter	1992
Gary Ablett (Geelong)	Sydney	second quarter	1994

* recent examples shown only.

GOGGIN, Bill (1941–)

One of post-war football's most-decorated rovers who maintained his close association with the game years after his retirement, Goggin captained Geelong and Victoria, famous for his formidable combination-work with the Cats' master ruckman *Graham 'Polly' Farmer*.

Recruited from North Geelong, the 175 cm rover played his first game in the fourth round of the 1958 season and first represented Victoria as a 19-year-old in 1960. He had a total of 14 games with the Big V.

A leading member of Geelong's 1963 premiership side, Goggin is regarded as the finest small man in Geelong's illustrious history. He played 248 games in 14 seasons, was twice best and fairest, club captain for four years and State captain in 1968. One of his proudest moments was in 1971 when he cracked *Reg Hickey*'s Geelong games record.

Renowned for his stab passes, which he chipped with great accuracy, Goggin was

Billy Goggin, 14 years of stalwart service for Geelong. He's pictured with Hugh Stachan after his last game, against Richmond at the MCG.

121

also a very courageous player with speed and rare ball-handling gifts. He finished in the Brownlow Medal top eight on four occasions.

Later he coached Geelong West to a VFA premiership, before joining Footscray as coach from 1976–77. He resigned early in 1978 but returned to senior coaching ranks for the first of his three years at Geelong in 1980. Later he served as a very active committeeman, helping to recruit players such as *Gary Ablett, Greg Williams, Bernard Toohey* and Bruce Lindner.

He coached the Victorian State team from 1987–93.

GOLDSMITH, Fred (1932–   )

The only full-back ever to win the Brownlow Medal, 'Fireman Fred' Goldsmith's win in 1955 was the biggest shock since Richmond's *Stan Judkins* won in 1930. He didn't even win South Melbourne's best and fairest, yet polled 21 votes from the umpires to defeat Essendon rover *Bill Hutchison* by one.

Opponents averaged more than four goals a game against him in 1955, but his exceptional high marking and field-kicking were a highlight in an otherwise mediocre season which saw South Melbourne finish 10th.

Goldsmith started as a forward, having amassed 29 goals in one match with Spotswood in 1950. He had three debut games with South in 1951 and eight in 1952 as a forward flanker before being used at full-back from 1953.

Sometimes he played full-forward and full-back in the same game, depending which way South Melbourne was kicking: with the wind or against it!

He was State full-back in 1956, State full-forward in 1957 and State full-back again in 1958. He played for Victoria 11 times.

He played 119 games and kicked 107 goals with South.

GONINON, George (1927–   )

A much-travelled Tasmanian born goal-sneak who played with seven clubs—including two in the VFL—Goninon led the League goalkicking in 1951, with 86 goals, an outstanding effort in his first full year at Geelong.

He made his debut at Essendon in 1948, but *John Coleman*'s presence restricted his senior appearances to just nine (for eleven goals), including the opening two matches of the 1950 season.

Transferring in time for Geelong's round five game against Collingwood, he immediately established his place and in the second semi-final that season kicked a record 11 goals. A fortnight later, he was a member of Geelong's premiership team.

He appeared in another flag-winning side with the Cats in 1952, altogether playing 87 games and kicking 289 goals from 1948–54.

At 182 cm and 80.5 kg, he relied on his slick, sure groundplay for the majority of his possessions. His drop punting for goal was deadly accurate.

Before coming to the mainland, he kicked more than 100 goals with Burnie in the 1947 season. He also played with NSW club, Newtown.

GOSS, Normie (1952–   )

After a series of successful seasons at VFA stronghold Port Melbourne, where he won the best and fairest with the fourths, thirds, seconds and twice in the seniors, Goss had six years at South Melbourne and five at Hawthorn. He was 19th man in Hawthorn's 1978 premiership side, his first year at the club.

He joined South in 1972, the season after the great *Bob Skilton* retired, and the skilful left-footed rover was best and fairest and leading goalkicker in 1974. A prolific kick-winner, he had 121 games at South and 82 at Hawthorn, amassing a total of 284 goals.

In 1981, he passed 200 League games and represented Victoria against Queensland. He'd first played for Victoria almost a decade previously, in only his second season of League football. His brothers, Paul and Kevin, also played League football.

GRACE, Michael

Played in four premierships, two with Fitzroy (1898–99) and two at Carlton (1906–07) in a 167-game career with three clubs: Fitzroy, Carlton and St Kilda. Later he played in NSW.

A follower and forward, he kicked 214 goals in his career. His best season was in 1906 when he booted 50 goals to head the VFL goalkicking.

GRAHAM, Jack (1917–84)

A tireless follower renowned for his towering marks and raking drop kicks, Graham captained South Melbourne from 1946–48, amassing 227 games and 234 goals in 15 years. He was best and fairest in 1945 and leading goalkicker in 1941 and 1948.

Originally from Red Cliffs, the 191 cm Graham played at centre half-back in South Melbourne's 1936 Grand Final team and in the first ruck in the infamous 1945 'Bloodbath' Grand Final.

His grandson, Ben, first appeared with Geelong in 1993.

GRASSHOPPERS

West Australian Dale Kickett completed a rare footballing trek when he joined the Fremantle Dockers for the 1995 season.

Fremantle was Kickett's sixth senior club in as many years, including five at AFL level.

Previously, he represented Fitzroy (15 games in 1990), West Coast (two, 1991), St Kilda (21, 1992), Essendon (eight, 1993) and his 'home' club Claremont (1994).

His wanderings surpass even those of between-the-wars ruckman Les Hughson, who played senior football at five VFL clubs in 11 years from 1927–37—Collingwood (one game, 1927), Hawthorn (four, 1928), Carlton (12, 1933–34), St Kilda (41, 1934–36) and Fitzroy (15, 1937).

More than a dozen players have played senior football at four League clubs, including, most recently, *Geoff Raines*, Peter Francis, *Mark Jackson*, Brian Wilson and Stuart Wigney.

One of the most renowned 'nomads' was enigmatic 'Bustling Bill' Barrot, centreman in Richmond's 1967–69 premierships.

Coming to Richmond from Jordanville High as a 17-year-old in 1961, his transfer to St Kilda in a swap deal with *Ian Stewart* was one of the major talking points of the 1971 season. Barrot played just two games at St Kilda before finishing the season at Carlton. Stewart won the Brownlow Medal.

Within 12 months, Barrot was appointed captain-coach of West Torrens, after appearing in VFA club Oakleigh's 1972 premiership. But within two years he was back and in 1975 played half a dozen games with North Melbourne reserves.

Renowned goalkicker *Peter McKenna* also had six senior clubs.

Among the most notable of early football nomads are:

* Dan Minogue, one of only three players to captain three clubs, Collingwood, Richmond and Hawthorn for 10 seasons, between 1914–25. A member of Richmond's 1920–21 premiership teams, Minogue also coached Carlton, St Kilda and Fitzroy.

* W. 'Bull' Adams, a member of West Australia's 1921 carnival side, later played with Fitzroy, Northcote, Preston and North Launceston, before returning to the mainland and representing Prahran and Melbourne. Adams also coached South Melbourne.

* 'Jerry' Borthwick also had a remarkable career in Victoria and Western Australia in the early 1900s. He played with Essendon Town (1904), Port Melbourne and Footscray (VFA), Essendon (VFL), Broken Hill, Midland Junction and East Perth (WA) before finishing his career at Prahran in 1919.

* 'Bos' Daly was a leading goalkicker at four South Australian clubs, Norwood, South Adelaide, West Torrens and North Adelaide from 1892–1903. He also played for West Adelaide.

* Jack Wollard and six clubs in Western Australia and South Australia, his most notable times coming in his first three years at Port Adelaide when he led the 1910 team to a premiership.

10 of the best

1937: Geelong 18.14 (122) d Collingwood 12.18 (90)

A match played at a wonderfully high standard. Both sides fielded their strongest teams and both were superbly fit.

Collingwood had defeated the Cats in an exhibition match six weeks earlier in Devonport. After they dashed away early, leading 6.3. to 3.3, a third consecutive premiership seemed within reach of the Magpies. It was a stunningly fast, exciting contest, highlighted by spectacular marking and kicking.

The game was entirely free of malice and featured dazzling bursts of play. It was a textbook demonstration of Australian Rules.

At quarter time, Geelong's champion playing coach *Reg Hickey* made some crucial changes. He sent Les Hardiman from full-back to centre half-back to mind the in-form *Ron Todd*. Defender Joe Sellwood went to centre half-forward, ruckman John Evans to full-forward and Gordon Abbott into the ruck. Hickey shifted himself onto crack Magpie goalkicker *Gordon Coventry*, in his final game.

Playing inspired football, Geelong reduced Collingwood's lead to five points at half time and by three-quarter time had tied the scores at 80 points apiece. Collingwood fought desperately to regain its early ascendancy but could not stop Geelong from adding six goals to one in the final term. Geelong's winning margin was 32 points. It was the Cats' 14th win on end.

Even in defeat, the Magpies were lauded for their fair play and sportsmanship. Players were stopped in the street and praised for their part in the game.

Collingwood officials commented that if they had to be beaten, it was good that Geelong—the most hospitable of clubs—was the victor, rather than an arch rival such as Carlton!

Geelong
B.: Bernie Hore, Reg Hickey (c-c), Allan Everett.
H.B.: Jack Grant, Joe Sellwood, Tom Arklay.
C.: Laurie Slack, Fred Hawking, Angie Muller.
H.F.: Jim Wills, Gordon Abbott, Clive Coles.
F.: Jack Metherell, Les Hardiman, John Evans.
Rucks: 'Peter' Hardiman, George Dougherty.
Rover: Tommy Quinn.
19th: Geoff Mahon.

Collingwood
B.: Harold Rumney, Jack Regan, Bervyn Woods.
H.B.: Fred Froude, Marcus Boyall, Jack Ross.
C.: Jack Carmody, Marcus Whelan, Reg Dowling.
H.F.: Des Fothergill, Ron Todd, Vin Doherty.
F.: Phonse Kyne, Gordon Coventry, Albie Pannam.
Rucks: Albert Collier, Percy Bowyer
Rover: Harry Collier (c).
19th: Len Murphy.

1945: Carlton 15.13 (103) d South Melbourne 10.15 (75)

Known as the 'Bloodbath' Grand Final, it was the most vicious play-off of them all. The on-field brawling convinced many of the record 62,986 crowd that they were attending an 'all-in' boxing match. Players were brutally felled, including several behind play. With tempers raging out of control, police several times had to take the field to help restore order.

Nine players were reported. South's Ted Whitfield was suspended for the entire 1946 season, team-mate Jack 'Basher' Williams for 12 weeks, Carlton's Bob Chitty and Ron Savage for eight, along with South pair 'Gentleman' *Jim Cleary* and Don Grossman, who also received eight.

A 10th player, Carlton wingman Fred Fitzgibbon, who did not play in the match because of suspension, was given another four weeks for jumping the fence and taking part in one of the brawls.

South Melbourne entered the play-off favoured to win, having had a week's break. It was felt South's imposing goal-to-goal line of Cleary, Williams, *Herbie Mat-*

Carlton's 1945 premiership squad.
  Back row (left to right): Charlie McInness, Wally Alexander, Doug Williams, Ken Hopper, Alex Way, Jim Jones, Jim Clark.
  Second row: V. Brown, Ken Baxter, Ron Boys, Don Beauvais, Ken Hands, Jim Baird, Bert Deacon, Clint Wines.
  Sitting: Ron Savage, Jim Mooring, Lance Collins, Bob Chitty (captain), Rod McLean, Arthur Sanger, Jack Bennett.
  Front: Ron Hines, Herb Turner, Mick Price, Fred Fitzgibbon.

thews, *Ron Clegg* and veteran *Laurie Nash* would be decisive, even though the game was at Carlton.

South was leading in the second quarter when vicious fighting erupted after Carlton centre half-forward *Ken Hands* was knocked unconscious before a centre bounce.

As he was being assisted off, '63,000 fans screamed for blood as players converged on each other, throwing fists and boots,' wrote Graeme Atkinson in *The Complete Book of VFL finals*.

Bottles were thrown onto the ground and South Melbourne players were booed and pelted with rubbish as they left the field at half time, with Carlton holding a two point break.

There was more violence to come. Carlton strongman Bob Chitty—a central figure in many of the brawls—was felled behind play, causing police to rush onto the ground.

Afterwards, Cleary accused Chitty of being the villain. He told Chitty: 'Bob, you should have been a dentist. You enjoy hurting people.'

Hands, 18, showed great courage in returning to the field after half time. His example was an inspiration to his teammates. The Blues extended their lead to 23 points at three-quarter time and won by 27. Carlton full-back Vin Brown was best afield, and restricted his formidable opponent Nash to two goals.

It was a huge effort by Carlton, after their tough preliminary final victory against Collingwood just seven days earlier. Skipper Chitty had played the preliminary and Grand Finals with a protective hand guard after he'd sliced off the top of one of his fingers in a work accident.

Carlton half-back Jim Clark said Chitty was upset at seeing the teenage Hands felled. Carlton players blamed South strongman Williams.

'Bob proceeded to put the South forward division out of business with a series of bone-rattling charges into the packs,' said Clark.

'I was mighty glad to finish that game in one piece but there was a lot of bad feeling over what happened on the field—unfortunately it continued off the field (too). . . I have played in many great games over the years, but that one Grand Final is one game I'll never forget. How could I? I still have the scars to remind me!'

In the final term, players, umpires, trainers, spectators and police all became involved after one incident. Goal umpire Whyte chased South's Teddy Whitfield up the ground to take his number. Whitfield responded by taking his jumper off. Two police seized an overcoated man and hurried him off the ground. It was Fitzgibbon who had been outed only the week before in Carlton's fiery preliminary win over Collingwood.

The premiership was one of Carlton's greatest triumphs, in a season it had opened with three successive defeats. Relations between the two sides were strained for years. That night, South players and committeemen were barred from attending the traditional 'after-match', an example of the ill-feeling of that infamous last Saturday in September.

THE TEAMS

Carlton
B.: Arthur Sanger, Vin Brown, Jim Baird.
H.B.: Bob Chitty (c), Bert Deacon, Jim Clark.
C.: Herb Turner, Clinton Wines, Doug Williams.
H.F.: Lance Collins, Ken Hands, Alex Way.
F.: Rod McLean, Ken Baxter, Jim Mooring.
Foll.: Ron Savage, Jack Bennett.
Rov.: Albert Price.
Res.: Charlie McInnes.

South Melbourne
B.: Brian Kelly, Jim Cleary. Don Grossman.
H.B.: Robert Matlock, Jack Williams, Jack Danckert.

C.: Ted Whitfield, Herbie Matthews (c), Billy King.
H.F.: Vic Castles, Ron Clegg, Kevin Smith.
F.: Alan Linden, Laurie Nash, Billy Williams.
Foll.: Jack Graham, Jack Dempsey.
Rov.: Reg Richards.
Res.: Ron Hartridge.

1948: Melbourne 10.9 (69) tied with Essendon 7.27 (69)

Football's first drawn Grand Final remains memorable as the day Essendon threw away a premiership. *Bill Brittingham* kicked 2.8 and several more out of bounds on the full in a nightmarish afternoon which literally turned him to drink. When the match started, the Bomber full-forward had never touched a drop . . . an hour after it finished he was drunk!

The Bombers were clearly the best team all year and easily defeated Melbourne in the second semi-final.

But their amazing inaccuracy in a hard-slogging game, combined with some Melbourne changes, proved crucial. Rover *Bill Hutchison* did not kick his team's first goal until 50 minutes into the match. At half time, Essendon trailed 2.15 (27) to Melbourne's 4.5 (29). Despite a better third quarter, it lapsed again in the last, kicking 1.7 to Melbourne's 4.1.

The Demons were attacking when the siren rang, but Essendon full-back Cec Ruddell swept the ball clear after veteran *Norm Smith* looked like scoring for the Demons in the hectic final seconds.

The Bombers had led by two goals in the final quarter but goals by *Jack Mueller* and Adrian Dullard levelled the scores. Essendon's final score of 7.27 was the most inaccurate display since Collingwood kicked 11.23 (89) to defeat South Melbourne 10.18 (78) in the 1936 play-off.

Melbourne had caused a shock by bringing in Denis Cordner, younger brother of captain Don, for the match. He hadn't played with the club since 1943 but, like another inclusion, Doug Heywood (who'd previously played in 1944), had been starring in the amateurs.

It was the second consecutive year in which poor kicking had cost Essendon the flag. In 1947, the Bombers booted 11.19

(85) to go down to Carlton 13.8 (86) by a point.

The following week, in the Grand Final replay, Melbourne kicked six goals to nil in the first quarter and won by 39 points.

Twenty years later Brittingham said in an interview: 'I will admit I had shots for goal which didn't even score and I can clearly remember booting the ball out of bounds from deliberate shots inside the goal square. Can you blame me for getting into the grog later!'

THE TEAMS

Melbourne
B.: William Deans, Shane McGrath, Stan Rule.
H.B.: Colin McLean, Denis Cordner, Geoff Collins.
C.: Max Spittle, George Bickford, Len Dockett.
H.F.: Doug Heywood, Lance Arnold, Noel McMahen.
F.: Jack Mueller, Norm Smith, Ernest Craddock.
Foll.: Don Cordner (c), Adrian Dullard.
Rov.: Alby Rodda.
Res.: Gordon Bowman, Eddie Jackson.

Essendon
B.: Chris Lambert, Cec Ruddell, Percy Bushby.
H.B.: Harold Lambert, Wally Buttsworth, Norm McDonald.
C.: Robert Bradley, Albert Harper, George Hassell.
H.F.: Dick Reynolds (c-c), Ted Leehane, Jack Jones.
F.: Bob Syme, Bill Brittingham, Keith Rawle.
Foll.: Bob McClure, Doug Bigelow.
Rov.: Bill Hutchison.
Res.: Wally May, Vic Fisher.

1964: Melbourne 8.16 (64) d Collingwood 8.12 (60)

When 17-stone Ray Gabelich ran 45 metres bouncing the ball awkwardly and rammed home a goal to put Collingwood in front 21 minutes into the final term of the gripping '64 Grand Final, Collingwood fans danced in jubilation. Another flag— and at the expense of old enemy Melbourne—or so they thought.

Gabelich, the largest and slowest man on the field, had taken a pass from *Des Tuddenham*. With no one between him and the goal square, he took off. 'I didn't have time to think of anything except keeping a ball that seemed determined to get away from me in control,' he told reporters later.

After four precarious bounces, Gabelich finally reached the square and from point-blank range booted a goal that lifted Collingwood into the lead by three points.

The mountainous roar of delight was heard for miles. Melbourne coach *Norm Smith* said it was 'the most stirring and thrilling effort in football history'.

But Melbourne still had time to come back. Minutes later, *Brian Dixon* kicked to half-forward. The ball was punched off the hands of a pack straight to Demon back-pocket Neil 'Froggie' Crompton, who was almost 100 metres out of position, having followed his resting rover Mick Bone into the forward line.

Crompton hadn't kicked a goal in five years, but his snap shot from 40 metres never looked like missing. 'I saw *Ron Barassi* and Kevin Rose go for the ball,' Crompton said. 'Then it was coming straight for me. I grabbed it, kicked for goal and that was that.'

Bone said he had drifted up beyond the centre. 'I bent to pick up the ball and it bounced over my right shoulder to Neil Crompton who just kicked. I bet you he told you he lined it up!'

Barassi said later: 'It was the sweetest, most glorious kick of the whole darn season.'

A few Collingwood officials wanted to hang Bone afterwards for being so far out of position and forcing an extra Melbourne man (Crompton) into play. 'There weren't a lot of free drinks being bought,' Bone said.

Collingwood attacked again but Ian Graham kicked out of bounds and was unlucky soon afterwards not to be awarded a free kick right in front.

Graeme Wise, who had rucked all day, and Barry Bourke, switched from full-forward into defence, both made timely saves. The siren rang, heralding Melbourne's magnificent win.

It was one of the greatest finishes ever to a Grand Final, an old-fashioned heart-stopper.

THE TEAMS

Melbourne

B.: Neil Crompton, Bernie Massey, Tassie Johnston.
H.B.: Tony Anderson, Brian Roet, Frank Davis.
C.: Brian Dixon, Don Williams, Frank Adams.
H.F.: Brian Kenneally, Graeme Jacobs, Barrie Vagg.
F.: John Lord, Barry Bourke, John Townsend.
Foll.: Graeme Wise, Ron Barassi (c).
Rov.: Hassa Mann.
Res.: Peter McLean, Ken Emselle.

Collingwood

B.: Ron Reeves, Ted Potter, Trevor Steer.
H.B.: Laurie Hill, John Mahon, Duncan Wright.
C.: Ricky Watt, John Henderson, Bert Chapman.

H.F.: Des Tuddenham, Kevin McLean, David Norman.
F.: Terry Waters, Ian Graham, Denis Dalton.
Foll.: Ray Gabelich (c), Kevin Rose.
Rov.: Mick Bone.
Res.: Max Urquhart, Ken Turner.

1966: St Kilda 10.14 (74) d Collingwood 10.13 (73)

Kevin 'Cowboy' Neale's feat of kicking five goals in St Kilda's historic first premiership barely rates a mention when the exciting '66 Grand Final is discussed. *Barry Breen*'s wobbly punt kick which bounced through for the winning point with only minutes to play is *the* highlight of the game.

It was yet another heartbreaking finish for Collingwood, which had courageously levelled the scores coming into time-on

St Kilda's 1966 premiership team.
  Back row (left to right): Jim Read, Rodger Head, Alan Davis, Jeff Moran, Kevin Billing, Ross Smith.
  Middle: Daryl Griffiths, Travis Payze, Bob Murray, Brian Sierakowski, Ian Synman, John Bingley, Allan Morrow, Ian Stewart.
  Sitting: Kevin Neale, Barry Breen, Verdun Howell, Allan Jeans (coach), Darrel Baldock (captain), Brian Mynott, Ian Cooper.

through a long goal from Max Pitt and a point from skipper *Des Tuddenham*.

After Breen's snap shot the Magpies attacked again, only to be repelled by Saint full-back *Bob Murray*. His drop kick to the outer half-back flank was marked by Alan Morrow just as the siren rang again and again, courtesy of the excited St Kilda timekeeper Fred Farrell.

The Saints had led narrowly for much of the day, buoyed by the powerhouse forward play of Neale and spring-heeled jumping-jack Ian Cooper, who claimed a dozen marks between them.

Cooper's wind-assisted, 70-metre spiral punt goal in the third quarter helped his team to regain the ascendancy after Collingwood led by a point at half time.

Brownlow Medallist *Ian Stewart* had 25 kicks in the centre. Brian Sierakowski's safe marking in defence and *Ross Smith*'s courageous roving were further highlights.

Collingwood's rookie rover *Wayne Richardson* had a chance to goal right on time-on, but his shot went out of bounds. Earlier in the game, another youngster, *Len Thompson*, had missed a goal from 10 metres out.

It was a fine comeback by the Saints, who had gone down to Collingwood by 10 points in the second semi.

St Kilda coach *Allan Jeans* thanked his players for their effort and closed his glowing tribute by saying: 'I have never owed anyone the debt I now owe to you boys. Anything you want just ask.'

Defender Ian Synman yelled out: 'Well, what about a loan of fifty quid for a start!'

Cooper, the general choice as best man afield, said afterwards: 'That off-the-cuff remark brought the house down. The loudest and longest burst of laughter I ever heard. A fitting end to a great afternoon in the St Kilda colours.'

THE TEAMS

St Kilda
B.: Roger Head, Bob Murray, Brian Sierakowski.
H.B.: Verdun Howell, Ian Synman, John Bingley.
C.: Jeff Moran, Ian Stewart, Jim Read.

H.F.: Ian Cooper, Darrel Baldock (c), Barry Breen.
F.: Alan Morrow, Kevin Neale, Allan Davis.
Foll.: Brian Mynott, Daryl Griffiths.
Rov.: Ross Smith.
Res.: Travis Payze, Kevin Billing.

Collingwood
B.: Ian Montgomery, Peter Boyne, Terry Waters.
H.B.: Laurie Hill, Ted Potter, Lee Adamson.
C.: Peter Patterson, Colin Tully, Errol Hutchesson.
H.F.: Des Tuddenham (c), Doug Searl, Max Pitt.
F.: Ray Gabelich, Ian Graham, Gary Wallis.
Foll.: Len Thompson, Kevin Rose.
Rov.: Wayne Richardson.
Res.: Trevor Steer, John Henderson.

1970: Carlton 17.9 (111) d Collingwood 14.17 (101)

The greatest finals comeback of them all. The match of the century. The ultimate triumph. Carlton's 1970 come-from-the-clouds Grand Final win was all that and more.

In one of the most lopsided openings to a post-war Grand Final—witnessed by an all-time record crowd of 121,696—Carlton trailed by 44 points at half time.

It could easily have been more. Collingwood missed some sitters, but led 10.13 to 4.5 at the main break. *Des Tuddenham's* goal almost on the half time siren was looked upon by some to be the 'sealer'.

During the interval, Collingwood fans crammed the dressing-rooms, already believing that the 12-year premiership drought was over. According to Richard Stremski in *Kill for Collingwood*: 'The jubilation may have lulled some players into a false sense of security; it may have put undue pressure on others. In retrospect, many resented the intrusion. It was difficult to go back on the ground properly motivated when people and already praised your victory.'

Star full-forward, *Peter McKenna*—who'd averaged nine goals a game against Carlton that season and already had five goals to half time—had been concussed in a collision with team-mate and ex-skipper Tuddenham. Rover *Wayne Richardson* had

Carlton's pacy Ted Hopkins triggered an amazing transformation coming on as 19th man in the 1970 Grand Final.

a corked thigh. But few expected the team to cave in.

Among several crucial positional changes, Carlton coach *Ron Barassi* benched West Australian Bert Thornley for the pacier Ted Hopkins and asked his players to play on at all costs, using handball to break Collingwood's flow. Even the master coach must have been amazed at the transformation in the next hour.

The Collingwood forwards were left floundering as the Carlton backs handballed and ran their opponents around. Hopkins raced in for two goals in as many minutes, Syd Jackson goaled from the boundary and *Brent Crosswell* added another. Four goals in eight minutes and suddenly Carlton was back in the game. By three-quarter time, Collingwood's lead had been slashed to 17 points. Carlton had kicked eight goals straight to 3.3.

The will-o-the-wisp Hopkins hit the post but *Len Thompson* goaled to extend Collingwood's lead to 21 points. It was only a temporary reprieve. Carlton players who

hadn't been sighted in the first half were suddenly in the play. The risky handball tactics, which started from the very last line, were paying enormous dividends.

With two minutes, plus time-on, to play in the final term, Collingwood's lead was just one point. Many spectators became hysterical. Crosswell marked and goaled to put Carlton in front amid scenes of wild excitement. Moments later, *Alex Jesaulenko*'s long left-foot snap shot from the outer half-forward line bounced through an open goal to seal a 10 point victory.

Collingwood had won everywhere but on the scoreboard, having more kicks, marks and scoring shots. Crosswell was best afield, ahead of team-mate *David McKay*.

Carlton full-back Kevin Hall said Barassi had been at his fiery best at half time, demanding that the Carlton players handball 'like the Harlem Globetrotters', and play a keepings-off game to break Collingwood's flow.

'I still don't know if it was a master stroke of coaching or plain desperation that brought about the famous "Operation Handball" tactics,' said Hall in an interview years later.

'Barassi had gambled on the Magpies relaxing with their big lead and getting careless in defence. A look at the video tape shows that six of the eight goals kicked in that sensational third quarter burst were scored by unguarded Carlton forwards . . . even after all those years I still get pleasure from watching a replay film of that amazing game . . . the second half of course.'

THE TEAMS

Carlton

B.: Barry Gill, Kevin Hall, Vin Waite.

H.B.: John Goold, David McKay, Barry Mulcair.

C.: Gary Crane, Ian Robertson, Phil Pinnell.

H.F.: Brent Crosswell, Robert Walls, Syd Jackson.

F.: Peter Jones, Alex Jesaulenko, Bert Thornley.

Foll.: John Nicholls (c), Sergio Silvagni.

Rov.: Adrian Gallagher.

Res.: Ted Hopkins, Neil Chandler.

Collingwood
B.: Colin Tully, Jeff Clifton, Peter Eakins.
H.B.: Denis O'Callaghan, Ted Potter, Lee Adamson.
C.: Robert Dean, Barry Price, John Greening.
H.F.: Max Richardson, Len Thompson, Con Britt.
F.: Ross Dunne, Peter McKenna, Wayne Richardson.
Foll.: Graeme Jenkin, Terry Waters (c).
Rov.: Des Tuddenham.
Res.: Bob Heard, Ricky Watt.

1975: North Melbourne 19.8 (122) d Hawthorn 9.13 (67)

North Melbourne broke its 50-year premiership drought in convincing fashion, and *Ron Barassi*'s coaching genius was again a major factor as the much-fancied Hawthorn combination succumbed by 55 points.

It was an unforgettable day for North supporters. President *Allen Aylett* said: 'For months we received letters and personal visits from people who had been following North for 50 years and even longer. All said it was the greatest day of their lives and they really meant it. That euphoria will never be experienced again.'

Hawthorn had beaten North three times that season, but were without skipper *Peter Crimmins*, who was battling illness and was passed over for selection.

Barassi made several important pre-match moves, relegating the 200 cm Barry Goodingham to the bench and starting versatile Gary Farrant in defence.

Hawthorn appeared top-heavy—and it had some magnificent individual performers such as centre half-back *Peter Knights*, but North proved too desperate and dedicated.

Second-game full-forward Michael Cooke, who had kicked four goals on debut in the second semi-final, was taken off in the second quarter, hardly having touched the ball. Full-back *Kelvin Moore* was injured and limped from the ground in the third term.

Defenders *John Rantall* and *Brent Crosswell* were North's best. Rantall shadowed star Hawk rover *Leigh Matthews* when he rested up forward.

North led by 29 points at three-quarter time. Hawthorn tried desperately hard to stay in the game but could kick only behinds. After reducing the deficit to 24 points, the Hawks conceded a goal to Arnold Briedis and North added five more in an inspired 10-minute spell to seal the result. Briedis kicked four goals for the quarter.

It was a memorable night. Thousands congregated at Arden Street to welcome their returning heroes, who were introduced one by one by television personality and long-time North supporter, Ron Casey.

It was a humbling experience for the Hawks, one players never forgot. Coach *John Kennedy* said the loss made it easier for players to maintain their momentum the following season when they turned the tables on North in the 1976 Grand Final.

THE TEAMS

North Melbourne
B.: Ross Henshaw, David Dench, Frank Gumbleton.
H.B.: Brent Crosswell, Gary Farrant, John Rantall.
C.: Keith Greig, John Burns, Peter Chisnall.
H.F.: Wayne Schimmelbusch, Arnold Briedis, Sam Kekovich.
F.: Malcolm Blight, Doug Wade, Paul Feltham.
Foll.: Mick Nolan, Barry Davis (c).
Rov.: Barry Cable.
Res.: Barry Goodingham, Gary Cowton.

Hawthorn
B.: Peter Welsh, Kelvin Moore, Mike Moncrieff.
H.B.: Bohdan Jaworskyj, Peter Knights, Ian Bremner.
C.: Stuart Trott, Kelvin Matthews, Geoff Ablett.
H.F.: Shane Murphy, Alan Martello, John Hendrie.
F.: Bernie Jones, Michael Cooke, Barry Rowlings.
Foll.: Don Scott (a-c), Michael Tuck.
Rov.: Leigh Matthews.
Res.: Leon Rice, Des Meagher.

1977: Collingwood 10.16 (76) tied with North Melbourne 9.22 (76)

The dramatic finish to the 1977 Grand Final, when Collingwood's *Ross 'Twiggy' Dunne* marked and goaled at the 32-minute mark of the final quarter to level the scores and force a replay, will never be forgotten.

Contesting in the centre of a large pack, Dunne took a strong mark and, from 20 metres, torpedoed the ball straight through. There were just 40 seconds to go. Had the siren sounded at the 30-minute mark, as often happens, North would have been premiers on 24 September—rather than a week later.

The only person who appeared genuinely happy in the North rooms afterwards was marketing manager and ex-player Barry Cheatley. 'Great result, boys,' he said. 'The replay will be worth big dollars to the club—see if you can do it again next week!'

North had appeared nervous and played far below expectations. They trailed by 27 points at the last change, but hit the front coming into time-on, thanks to an inspired five-goal burst. When Phil Baker goaled from a mark at the 25-minute mark, North led by seven points and seemed home.

But Collingwood launched several desperate counter attacks. *Peter Moore* scored a point to reduce the lead to a single kick and then *Billy Picken* kicked the ball high to the front of the goal square. *Brent Crosswell* and Frank Gumbleton unsuccessfully tried to knock the ball away from Dunne.

'There was absolutely no doubt about Dunne's last-second mark,' coach *Ron Barassi* said later. 'The hands of the other players had to be peeled away to reveal the grip of Dunne, firmly on the ball. If there had been any doubt about the mark it would have left an unsavoury taste to the finish.

'When the siren sounded the feeling among the players and coaches was the same as the crowd. Everyone was stunned.

'You go into a match, particularly a Grand Final, for a win, knowing perhaps there could be a loss. You don't even think of a draw.'

When the siren sounded, many players slumped to the ground in exhaustion, hardly believing the 80th VFL Grand Final pennant was still to be won.

North ruckman *Peter Keenan* said: 'The draw was only the second in VFL (Grand Final) history and at the siren the 36 players, dog-tired and emotionally drained, could scarcely believe they had to go through it all again seven days hence.'

North's seasoned recruit from Melbourne, winger *Stan Alves*, was clearly best afield. *Wayne Schimmelbusch* was also gallant.

The North room was silent until Barassi entered. Congratulating his players on their fightback, he said: 'It should have won you the match. It did in fact win us the match . . . then we lost it! But it was still a magnificent quarter . . . bloody magnificent. And I'm grateful that we're still here with another chance next week.

'Whatever happens next Saturday, the team that wins will prove itself the greatest of all in Australian Rules history . . . And that's when we'll win it.'

North did, too, but it was another thriller. Collingwood trailed by just 12 points, nine minutes into the final quarter. But North accelerated again, in a high-standard game, taking their second flag in three years. Many, including Collingwood coach *Tom Hafey*, believed Phil Carman's two-match suspension from the second semi-final had been a crucial factor in the Magpies' failure.

THE TEAMS

North Melbourne
B.: Ross Henshaw, David Dench (a-c), Frank Gumbleton.
H.B.: Gary Cowton, Darryl Sutton, Ken Montgomery.
C.: Stan Alves, Xavier Tanner, Wayne Schimmelbusch.
H.F.: Steven Icke, Malcolm Blight, Arnold Briedis.
F.: Brent Crosswell, Phil Baker, John Cassin.
Foll.: Peter Keenan, John Byrne.
Rov.: Barry Cable.
Res.: Stephen McCann, Bill Nettlefold.

Collingwood

B.: Robert Hyde, Kevin Worthington, Doug Gott.

H.B.: Andrew Ireland, Bill Picken, Phil Manassa.

C.: Rick Barham, Stan Magro, Wayne Gordon.

H.F.: Wayne Richardson, Ross Dunne, Graeme Anderson.

F.: Peter Moore, Rene Kink, Ray Shaw.

Foll.: Len Thompson, Max Richardson (c).

Rov.: Ron Wearmouth.

Res.: Gerald Betts, Shane Bond.

1984: Essendon 14.21 (105) d Hawthorn 12.9 (81)

Essendon completed the 'double' of day and night premierships, and ended Hawthorn's dream of historic back-to-back flags with a record nine-goal final quarter which catapulted the Bombers into the lead after they'd trailed 10.8 to 5.15 at the last break.

The initiative of Essendon coach *Kevin Sheedy* was a telling factor. All year he'd slotted players around from position to position, looking for the most versatile line-up. His foresight paid off, when defenders Paul Weston and Norm Smith Medallist Bill Duckworth were moved into the forward line in the last term with immediate result.

The Bombers were to defeat Hawthorn again in 1985, by a record margin. Coach *Allan Jeans* said: 'In '85 we wouldn't have won if we'd started at nine o'clock in the morning. It was their year. They were a much better side. But '84 was the Grand Final we should never have lost.'

Gary Ayres said: 'It (the '84 Grand Final) is probably my worst memory in football. We had a terrific chance of achieving back-to-back and we let it slip. We should have had that match sealed by half time.'

Both sides had 14 scoring shots by the main break when Hawthorn led 8.6 to 3.11. At one stage it was 32 points up, but few supporters felt comfortable. Essendon's inaccuracy was the only factor stopping it from being closer coming into the final term.

Celebrated ruckman *Simon Madden*, taken from the ground after an unimpres-

sive first half, led the final charge, when he took over at the centre bounces. Within 25 seconds of the start of the last quarter, Leon Baker had goaled, followed quickly by Peter Bradbury. When the running Baker added another in mid quarter, the Bombers led. Hawthorn briefly snatched back the lead when Peter Curran replied, but Essendon, on a roll, added four quick goals, including two to *Tim Watson*, to seal it.

Essendon had inspirational players everywhere. Duckworth's tackling and chasing was exceptional. In the third term, he gave Hawk Ken Judge 20 metres start and almost ran him down.

THE TEAMS

Essendon

B.: Neil Clarke, Paul Weston, Bill Duckworth.

H.B.: Peter Bradbury, Kevin Walsh, Shane Heard.

C.: Merv Neagle, Leon Baker, Gary Foulds.

H.F.: Glenn Hawker, Paul Van der Haar, Terry Daniher (c).

F.: Alan Ezard, Roger Merrett, Frank Dunell.

Foll.: Simon Madden, Tim Watson.

Rov.: Darren Williams.

Int.: Mark Harvey, Mark Thompson.

Hawthorn

B.: Gary Ayres, David O'Halloran, Colin Robertson.

H.B.: Rod Lester-Smith, Chris Mew, Peter Schwab.

C.: Robert DiPierdomenico, Terry Wallace, Peter Russo.

H.F.: Peter Curran, Dermott Brereton, Ken Judge.

F.: Michael McCarthy, Leigh Matthews (c), Richard Loveridge.

Foll.: Michael Byrne, Michael Tuck.

Rov.: Russell Greene.

Int.: Rodney Eade, Ian Paton.

1989: Hawthorn 21.18 (144) d Geelong 21.12 (138)

The closest and most drama-filled Grand Final of the 1980s remains a modern-day classic, from 15 seconds into the first quarter when champion Hawthorn forward *Dermott Brereton* was flattened off the ball,* to the last minutes when ex-Hawk *Gary Ablett* kicked his ninth goal to bring Geelong within reach.

The skill and sheer courage displayed by heroic players from both teams was extraordinary. Brereton, suffering from internal bleeding and damaged ribs, refused to go off. So, too, did Hawk team-mate *Robert DiPierdomenico* who broke a rib and had his lung punctured. *John Platten* was concussed, Scott Maginness ran into a goal post, Darrin Pritchard and *Michael Tuck* were hobbling, but all gave their best, helping the Hawks to capture back-to-back flags for the first time.

The team finished with a dozen fit men. Hawthorn officials later said that if it had been a tie, only a skeleton side would have made it into the replay.

Geelong was as glorious in defeat as any side could be. Overly-aggressive early, which probably cost it the game, it conceded a 40 point quarter time lead. Even with Ablett's brilliance, it could only reduce the deficit to 36 points at the final change.

Hawk coach *Allan Jeans* had urged his players to 'pay the price', telling them the story about a little boy who wanted to buy a pair of shoes and how he regretted the next day buying the cheaper pair. An emotional Jeans asked his players if they were prepared to pay the price, 'now and not tomorrow'. Again and again he demanded: 'Pay the price! Pay the price!'

In *The Hard Way*, the history of Hawthorn, author Harry Gordon says: 'For a time before the match, after all the inspirational talk and the detailed instructions, Jeans left the players alone. "I'm only the navigator," he said. "You're the drivers. You make your pledge to yourselves, make it in the room where it's honest, where you're not showing it to the crowd, where you can be fair dinkum with yourselves alone." And he walked out.'

Ablett's massive contribution deservedly won him the Norm Smith Medal. He was superlative.

Team-mate Darren Flanigan also played brilliantly in the second half to help the

Cats climb back into the contest. Most agreed that if the game had gone another minute or two, Geelong would have won.

THE TEAMS

Hawthorn
B.: Andrew Collins, Chris Langford, Gary Ayres.
H.B.: Scott Maginness, Chris Mew, John Kennedy.
C.: Robert DiPierdomenico, Anthony Condon, Darrin Pritchard.
H.F.: Dean Anderson, Dermott Brereton, Gary Buckenara.
F.: Peter Curran, Jason Dunstall, Chris Wittman.
Foll.: Greg Dear, Michael Tuck.
Rov.: John Platten.
Inter.: James Morrissey, Greg Madigan.

Geelong
B.: Spiro Malakellis, Tim Darcy, Michael Schulze.
H.B.: Mark Yeates, Mark Bos, Steve Hocking.
C.: Neville Bruns, Paul Couch, David Cameron.
H.F.: Garry Hocking, Barry Stoneham, Gary Ablett.
F.: Bruce Lindner, Bill Brownless, Robert Scott.
Foll.: Damian Bourke, Mark Bairstow.
Rov.: Andrew Bews.
Inter.: Darren Flanigan, Shane Hamilton.

GREEN, Michael (1948–)

A strong marking ruckman who figured in four Richmond premiership teams, the 194 cm Green played 146 games in nine full seasons from 1966–75. He took most marks in League football in 1969.

GREENE, Russell (1957–)

One of the Mornington Peninsula's most-decorated sons, Greene played 304 games from 1974–88: 120 in six and a half seasons at St Kilda and 184 in nine at Hawthorn. He spent half of his 300th game, at Geelong, on the bench and retired several weeks later after the 1988 Grand Final.

A superbly fit ruck-rover, whose hand-

---

* see 'FIVE FAMOUS INCIDENTS'

A superb running player in a champion team . . . Hawthorn's Russell Greene.

ball skills and tireless running helped him into three Hawthorn premiership sides, Greene was Victorian captain in 1985, a member of four State teams and an All Australian player, in 1984 and 1985. He also won Hawthorn's best and fairest in 1984. In one match against Sydney, he had almost 40 possessions.

He made his debut with St Kilda at 16, via Frankston thirds, while still at Karingal High. Greene always had enormous ability. He finished third in St Kilda's best and fairest, and was judged the VFL's rookie of the year in his first season in 1974. Brownlow Medallist and former Saint captain *Neil Roberts* forecast: 'Russell Greene is a youngster who could end up in the same star bracket as *Keith Greig, Kevin Bartlett, Royce Hart, Ian Stewart* and Co.'

But the long-haired, 185 cm winger lacked the necessary commitment at his first club. Despite making the State side as a 21-year-old in 1978, he was swapped in May, 1980, for fringe Hawthorn pair Tony King and Mark Scott.

Shocked by his surprise sacking, he immediately worked harder at his game, and became a front-line player in Hawthorn's champion teams of the 1980s.

'The fact that St Kilda was prepared to let me go was a kick in the butt, so I decided then to make the most of my chance at Hawthorn,' he said. 'I wanted to be remembered as a consistent footballer and immediately started training harder and doing extra training on my own because I wanted to make it.'

He overcame knee injuries and his mid-career sacking to become a top-liner. One of his highlights was his near best-afield effort in the 1983 Grand Final, which Hawthorn won by a record margin of 83 points.

Coach *Allan Jeans* said: 'He's a fine example of what can be done if you put your head down and work.'

Greene said Jeans had told him one day he was only the '14th or 15th' player chosen each week at Hawthorn. 'That really stuck in my gut, so I set about working towards being one of the first half dozen selected,' he said.

Greene coached Hawthorn under 19s for three years from 1989–91. His brother, Mark, also played League football, while his father-in-law, Frank Sedgman, is a former Wimbledon tennis champion.

GREEVES, 'Carji' (1903–63)

Winner of the inaugural Brownlow Medal in 1924 as a 20-year-old in only his second season with Geelong and second in 1925–26 and 1928, Warragul-born Edward Goderich 'Carji' Greeves was a superbly fit centreman from Geelong College. He played 137 games from 1923–33, including the 1925 and 1931 premierships.

His magnificent field-kicking was a feature of his game and he was invited to coach students at the University of Southern California on how to kick.

Vice-captain of Geelong in 1930, he represented Victoria in 1925–26 and was renowned for his expertise in other sports including rowing, cricket and tennis.

GREIG, Keith (1951–   )

One of only two players to amass 300 games for North Melbourne, Greig played for 15 years. He was renowned for his balance, breathtaking skill and scrupulously fair approach. St Kilda's *Ian Stewart* is the only other post-war player to emulate his feat of consecutive Brownlow Medal wins.

Greig's long-striding runs, aerial ability and ball control delighted the fans. But few expected him to win a Brownlow. He was a 25–1 chance in 1973 and said he'd come along on the night purely to enjoy himself. He won by two votes from Essendon's *Graham Moss* and four from Hawthorn's *Leigh Matthews*.

In 1974, when North Melbourne made its second ever Grand Final, he won again, this time by four votes from Melbourne's *Gary Hardeman*. He finished eighth in 1975, a season he believed was superior to both his 1973 and 1974 years!

The wingman played in North's historic 1975 premiership, one of the three best afield. Assigned a tagging role against Hawk champion Matthews in the 1976 Grand Final, he was twice knocked out. In 1977, he was restricted to the first eight games of the year before having an operation on an injured knee. He missed both the tied Grand Final and the replay.

After the operation, to repair his medial lateral and cruciate ligaments, it took him a year to re-establish himself as one of the game's champions.

He won North's Syd Barker Medal as a defender in 1980, and captained the club for three years from 1976–78.

In 1978, he captained Victoria. He played 13 State games from 1971–83. Recruited from Brunswick in 1971, he represented Victoria in his first season—after just eight games.

He was second in the best and fairest three times before he broke through to win in 1980.

North Melbourne administrator Ron Joseph recruited Greig just before the Kangaroos were about to lose their zone to Fitzroy. 'It took us right until the deadline

Keith Greig represented Victoria after just eight senior games.

before Keith came to North (in 1970),' he said. 'It became a bit of a battle to make sure he crossed the line, as at that stage he was quite content to just go along and play Association football with Brunswick.'

Awarded an MBE, in 1975, for his services to football, Greig said his longevity was possibly only through sympathetic handling by one of his last coaches, *Barry Cable*, who agreed that he didn't need to train four nights and on Sunday mornings like the younger players.

Greig had been an outstanding schoolboy player. His father played 100 games with Brunswick City and his brother, Ian, represented Brunswick.

After lengthy negotiations, he signed with North in 1970 and was ready for his VFL debut at the start of the 1971 season, though Brunswick battled hard to keep him.

The VFA club took out a Supreme Court writ to prevent Greig from registering and playing with North. But the matter was resolved, and Greig played the first of his 300 games.

His motto to youngsters will stand the test of time: 'You can be up and down in football, but no matter how you are playing, always perform at the best of your ability. Even when you aren't going well in terms of creating play, nullify your opponent.'

In 1992, he re-joined North, having one season as chairman of selectors.

HAFEY, Tom (1931–)

When Tom Hafey was appointed Richmond's coach in 1966, the Tigers hadn't won a flag since 1943 or even made the finals in 20 years. A battling player who had six years and 66 games at Richmond, he'd established a fine country football reputation, having played 104 games with Shepparton including three consecutive premierships as captain-coach.

Hafey lifted the club to fifth in 1966 and won four flags in the next eight seasons: 1967, 1969, 1973 and 1974. Only three other post-war clubs, Essendon, Geelong and Melbourne, had previously won back-to-back flags.

Obsessed by football and renowned as a perfectionist, Hafey had originally been appointed ahead of a more celebrated ex-Tiger Ron Branton. He adopted the play-on tactics of the great Len Smith, Richmond's coach in 1964–65. His athletic young Tigers, many of them mobile six-footers, formed the most vaunted team in the land.

Tom Hafey shares in the joy of Richmond's 1973 premiership along with players Craig McKellar, Brian Roberts and Laurie Fowler.

Hafey wanted his team to play like prize-fighters, go the full distance and end up exhausted.*

Celebrated centre half-forward *Royce Hart* said Hafey was a 'human dynamo' with the rare gift to bring players to their peak at the most important moments.

'He is like a motor mechanic working on an engine,' said Hart. 'He gets it going smoothly and everything runs well by the end of the season. This is borne out by the fact that we won our last eight games before the flag in 1967. The following year we won our last five in succession to finish fifth. In 1969, we took the premiership.'

Hafey's winning ratio at Richmond in 11 seasons and 250 games was almost 70 per cent. He was also a regular choice as Victorian coach from 1971–81.

Joining Collingwood in 1977 after a much-publicised internal bust-up at Richmond, Hafey demanded a professional outlook and piloted the club's rise from the ignominy of its first-ever wooden spoon in 1976, into the '77 Grand Final.

Long-term Collingwood captain *Tony Shaw* said Hafey's loyalty to his players and his ability to mix in any social arena were among his major assets.

'He had a theory that if you were down in a match, he would leave you in the same position and waited until you lifted. This often worked, especially if we were in a winning position late in the game,' Shaw said.

'Because of our fitness, blokes would be able to outrun opposition players and finish the game off as winners.

'Desperation was a key topic for him. A famous quote of Tom's was that no-one ever drowned in their own sweat on the football field.'

In 138 games and five and a half years at Victoria Park, his winning record was 65 per cent. He was sensationally sacked in mid-year 1982, but proved his durability—and negotiating ability—by coaching for three years at Geelong from 1983–85, and three years in Sydney, where he guided the Swans to back-to-back finals appearances. He retired at the end of 1988.

* see 'STRATEGIES'

Hafey remains one of only eight men to coach four or more VFL premiership teams. Fourteen Hafey-coached players have also graduated to senior League coaching levels.

Known as 'T-shirt Tommy' for his habit of wearing T-shirts, whatever the weather, he engendered tremendous loyalty at his clubs. He coached in 10 Grand Finals, for four premierships (all at Richmond), five losses and a draw. His Collingwood teams figured in five Grand Finals in six years but didn't win once.

Magpie insiders believed Hafey had performed miracles to help lift the side into the Grand Final in several of the years. His critics claimed he tended to over-train his players—especially around finals time—and not make enough moves.

In 1982, Collingwood players, led by skipper *Peter Moore*, combined to have Hafey sacked. They held a players' meeting, ostensibly to discuss the side's seven consecutive losses, but the effect was to stir more discontent against Hafey. On 31 May, after an eighth-straight loss on the previous weekend, club president John Hickey sacked him.

A teetotaller and fitness disciple, well known for his daily runs along Mentone beach and beyond, Hafey once told his wife, Maureen, that he was going to run down to Sorrento from his Melbourne bayside suburb of Beaumaris. She picked him up at Dromana. He was exhausted. He'd run almost 50 km.

HAMMOND, Charlie

One of only 20 players to figure in five or more premierships, Hammond was a member of five Carlton flag teams from 1906–15, including the premiership treble in 1906-07-08. He played in the ruck, amassing 136 games, having been recruited from Northcote.

HAMPSHIRE, Ian (1948–)

A powerfully-built follower from Portland who tallied 224 games from 1968–82, 'Bluey' Hampshire's career blossomed after leaving Geelong where he was often

the No. 2 ruckman in his eight years and 113 games. He dominated at Footscray, playing more than 100 games and later coaching the club for part of 1982 and all of 1983.

A strong mark, the 196 cm and 104 kg ruckman was a fine team player, who won Victorian honours for the first time in 1981, aged 33.

The week before his appointment as Footscray coach in mid-1982, he was on the interchange bench for the Bulldogs—a meteoric rise!

HANDS, Ken (1926–)

Centre half-forward in Carlton's 1945 and '47 premierships, Hands became a fine and resolute ruckman, playing 211 games from 1945–57. As a first-year teenager he played in the infamous '45 Grand Final, in which he was severely concussed just before half time. He returned in the second half to kick an invaluable goal.

In 1953, when he won Carlton's best and fairest award, he was also a star per-

Ken Hands: three goals as a teenager in the infamous 1945 'Bloodbath' Grand Final.

former with Victoria at the Australian carnival in Adelaide.

Tough and ruthless, 'Solvol' Hands was an inspirational leader, captaining the Blues from 1952–57 and coaching the club from 1959–64.

Hands was also active in recruiting, and enticed the young rucking giant *John Nicholls* to Carlton.

HARDEMAN, Gary (1950–)

One of the few League footballers to register 200 games without figuring in a final, Hardeman was runner-up in the 1974 Brownlow Medal count and equal third in 1972. A talented and dependable centre half-back, he played 226 games in 12 seasons with Melbourne.

He left the Demons at the end of the 1977 season for Sturt, where he played 46 games, before returning to Melbourne in 1981 for nine more VFL games.

He won Victorian selection in seven of his 12 seasons and also represented SA four times. In 1972, he was an All Australian.

HARDIE, Brad (1962–)

One of the many outstanding players from South Fremantle, the much-travelled Hardie emulated the great *Haydn Bunton*'s feat by winning the Brownlow Medal in his first year of League football, with Footscray in 1985. Before signing with the Bulldogs, he won the Simpson and Tassie Medals in 1984.

Footscray won his services ahead of five other clubs. 'Shane O'Sullivan (Footscray administrator) painted a magnificent picture of the club,' he said. 'I wanted to be part of a team that was starting to become something rather than an established club.'

He was a member of South Fremantle's 1980 premiership team, best and fairest in 1982, runner-up in the Sandover Medal in 1983 and club captain in 1984. He played mainly as a centreman and half-forward in Perth.

Winning his Brownlow as a free-flowing back-pocket player, he helped Footscray

The much travelled Brad Hardie after winning the Simpson Medal for Western Australia against Victoria, 1989.

into the 1985 preliminary final which it lost narrowly to Hawthorn.

Only the third West Australian to win the Brownlow, he was voted best afield five times.

Twelve months later, the controversial red-head quit Footscray, citing a personality clash with coach *Mick Malthouse*. Taken from the ground in a late-season game against Carlton, he crossed the boundary, ripped off his Footscray jumper and waved it angrily at Malthouse, sitting in the coach's box, 60 metres away. Later he said: 'There is no way I could ever play in a team coached by him under any circumstances . . . if he stays I'll have to go.' A fine of $5000 added to his anger.

He was cleared to Brisbane for $270,000, a record fee. He became the first Bear to amass the 100 game-and-goal 'double'. He led the goalkicking in consecutive years in 1989–90, and in 1989 kicked nine against Carlton at Princes Park.

But he did not consistently reproduce his '85 Medal form and was often criticised for being overweight and out of condition. After 101 games, he joined Collingwood, his third senior club in eight years, but was delisted for the start of the 1993 season.

Former Footscray team-mate *Doug Hawkins* said the 181 cm Hardie was 'an amazing player . . . funny thing about him, he only had little chunky legs, but over 10 yards, not too many blokes could beat him.'

His decorated career is all the more merit-worthy considering that he suffered burns to 65 per cent of his body while trying to help a neighbour extinguish a backyard fire. Doctors told him the burns were so severe that his football career was in jeopardy.

HARRIS, Dick (1913–93)

A sharp-shooting rover, Dick 'Hungry' Harris amassed 550 goals in his 196 matches with Richmond from 1934–44, including seven in the 1943 Grand Final against Essendon, the second of his two premierships. Later he played in the VFA for 10 years, notably at Williamstown, before finishing at 42.

His Richmond team-mate *Jack Dyer* said the 167 cm Harris was a 'great footballer and a glorious kick for goal'. He was also fiery, appearing before the tribunal eight times.

'I don't think he ever missed a goal,' Dyer said. 'When he had it, I'd walk back to the centre. I didn't have to wait for the umpires to wave the flags.'

HARRIS, Leon (1958–)

A Fitzroy stalwart through the club's most successful recent era of the 1980s, 'Mork' Harris played 186 games from 1979–89 and represented Victoria in the Australian Bicentenary carnival in 1988.

He was quickly recognised as a most courageous and committed utility player who refused to allow knee injuries to reduce his performance. He had six knee operations during his career, including three in 12 months and developed a habit of walking in icy sea water before a match.

HARRISON, Henry Colden Antill (1836–1926)

One of the pioneers of the game, he was responsible for redrafting the rules in 1866, which were first drawn seven years previously by a group including his cousin, *Thomas Wills*.

He championed the most important amendment which required players to bounce the ball 'every five or six yards'.

He was Richmond's first captain. He also led Melbourne and Geelong and in one game, in 1861, represented both clubs—Melbourne at the start of the match and Geelong at the finish, to help even the balance of the game after Melbourne had broken away to a decisive lead.

His great talent, however, was as an administrator. In 1877, when William Clarke, the largest landowner in the colony, was appointed the Victorian Football Association's first president, Harrison was vice-president.

He'd only retired from the game a few years earlier in 1872, aged 35. He once declared football was 'not suitable for menpoodles and milksops'.

He worked tirelessly to persuade other States and countries to take up the game. It gave him great pleasure to see New Zealand participate at the first Australian championships in 1908, the year in which he became known as the 'father' of the game.

A journalist wrote of him: 'Every groundsman and official and member is a friend of his. He loves to loiter in the dressing rooms, where there is the reek of training oil and perspiration. It is the smell of powder to a war horse. Before the game starts, he has some advice to give both sides. It is to tell them to play the game and remember that football is a game.'

HART, Royce (1948–)

A post-war footballing great, the dynamic centre half-forward played in four Richmond premierships.

Born a farmer's son, in Whiteford in the Tasmanian midlands, Royce Desmond Hart represented Richmond in 190 matches from 1967–77, was twice best and

Richmond's Royce Hart after the Tigers clinched back-to-back premierships in 1974.

fairest and leading goalkicker, captain for four years and All Australian. Later he coached at senior VFL level.

Few have achieved more in football than the superbly balanced and spring-heeled left-footer who marked as well as anyone in the game and could kick goals from 60 metres.

Until a sudden growth spurt in his mid-teens, Hart played all his junior football as a rover.

Spotted by Richmond's local scout Harry Jenkins, his signing-on fee was six shirts and a suit!

He made his debut against Essendon in the opening round of 1967 in front of 80,000 fans at the MCG. Hart kicked 3.7 from full-forward, having 14 kicks and 10 marks in a most auspicious debut.

The Tigers lost only three games all year to storm into the finals. Nineteen-year-old Hart kicked six goals in the second semi to ensure his club's first Grand Final appearance since 1944. In the Grand Final he kicked three goals as the Tigers won a high-standard match against Geelong by just nine points. During the last quarter, the teenager took a remarkable high mark after jumping into opponent Peter Walker from the side. It remains one of the most remembered of Hart's greatest marks.

He was to repeat his premiership triumph two years later in 1969, when he also became only the second player—after WA's Stan 'Pops' Heal—to figure in two Grand Finals in two States within a week of each other. After helping Richmond defeat Carlton in the VFL Grand Final, the following weekend he appeared for Glenelg against Sturt, at a fee of $2000, said to be a record for one game. A national serviceman, he'd been stationed in Adelaide during the year, training with Glenelg during the week and flying to Melbourne for matches. He obtained the necessary permission via the Australian National Football Council, but was knocked out in the first minutes of the game. His team-for-the-day was well beaten.

One of his most remembered finals matches was in the 1973 preliminary final against Collingwood when, coming on from the reserves bench after half time, he inspired a remarkable Richmond comeback, despite carrying leg and groin injuries into the game. After the Tigers had trailed by 34 points, Hart kicked two goals to lead the revival and the following weekend captained the first of back-to-back premierships.

Throughout his illustrious career, he had to combat many injuries and said in his book *The Royce Hart Story* that he expected to be knocked out at least five times each season.

In 1974, full-forward *Doug Wade* declared Hart the best player in the game. 'His brilliance and determination makes him an inspiring player and he'd be the first one I'd try and recruit, if I had the chance.'

Deadly with his precise drop punts, Hart kicked 370 goals at Richmond, including 55 in his first season and 59 in his fourth to head the club goalkicking.

He ignored doctor's advice that he could cripple himself for life and kept playing into his 11th year, before being injured against Melbourne and announcing his retirement.

Hart was a specialist coach at Tigerland in 1968 before coaching the Richmond reserves in 1969 and in 1970–71, crossing as senior coach to Footscray for two full seasons before being replaced in mid-year 1982, by *Ian Hampshire*.

HAWKER, Glenn (1961–)

A gifted, skilful running player who was off-loaded by Essendon after playing exactly 200 games from 1978–88, he finished his career at Carlton, amassing in all 227 games.

He played at half-back in Essendon's back-to-back premiership sides in 1984–85, after being on the wing in the 1983 Grand Final. He was best and fairest in 1986, having rejected a rich offer to join Sydney. Few kicked with his precision on either foot.

He was given *Bruce Doull*'s No. 11 guernsey when he joined Carlton but did not play consistently in any of his three seasons because of injury.

HAWKINS, Doug (1960–)

One of Footscray's favourite sons, Hawkins played a record 329 games in 17 senior seasons before reluctantly switching to Fitzroy in 1995, the Bulldogs having told him to retire.

Originally from Braybrook, Hawkins was Footscray's captain from 1990–93 and best and fairest in 1985. He also represented Victoria five times.

One of the game's great wingmen in the 1980s, his popularity was so immense that the Bulldogs named the outer wing at the Western Oval in his honour.

Kevin Bartlett said: 'Doug Hawkins is more than just a marvellous footballer, he is an inspiration to the hordes of football fans in the western suburbs.'

In the preface to *Hawkins: My Story*, Carlton coach *David Parkin* commented: 'There are no obvious flaws in his football make-up. Capable of marking against the talls, out-manoeuvring the medium strongs, a quickness and agility to go with the athletes, and outstanding ground work to match any small, makes him a terribly

difficult opponent to counter.'

A fearless player, his feats of bravery are well known. Former coach *Mick Malthouse* said: 'Doug is one of the most courageous players I have met in my career. When blood was spurting from a facial injury against Richmond he refused to come off the ground because the ball was in his area and indeed he won two more kicks. The trainers told me afterwards he was bleeding profusely but I guess it was red, white and blue blood because he is all Footscray.'

In mid-1986, he badly damaged knee ligaments against Collingwood after a collision with *Tony Shaw* and was sidelined for 10 months. It remains the most serious of a string of injuries which affected his final seasons.

Rejecting an offer to join the Adelaide Crows in 1991, Hawkins continued to serve Footscray proudly, playing mainly in the forward pocket where his goalkicking was a great asset.

HAWTHORN

Formed in 1874, the combination of several local sides, the club played at Meany's Paddock, adjacent to its present administration and training base at Glenferrie Oval. It was a most insignificant and often-humiliated suburban team, even after moving to Glenferrie in 1903 and joining the VFA.

Its first official colours were red and navy blue, before a predominantly brown guernsey with a gold V was adopted. In 1933, the club reversed its guernsey to one of yellow with a brown V. It triggered a new nickname, the 'Mustard Pots' but the guernsey and the name were not a success. In 1950, the modern brown and gold striped guernseys were first worn.

According to the club's historian, Harry Gordon, Hawthorn has always had to do it 'the hard way', rarely attracting quality players like the other, more fashionable, inner-city clubs.

After being accepted into the VFL in 1925, it took Hawthorn 32 years to make the finals. Even in its 11 VFA years, it played off only once, in 1923. Known as the Mayblooms or Mayflowers, it was a chopping block for almost every team it played.

Big-name coaching imports including Dan Minogue, Bert Chadwick, 'Jiggy' Harris and *Roy Cazaly* could do little to lift their teams from being permanent 'cellar-dwellers'.

The club's first important win didn't come until the 18th round of 1930 when it knocked Melbourne out of the finals with a 12.18 (90) to 10.17 (77) victory at Glenferrie Oval.

So unsuccessful were the Hawks before and after the war, that leading *Sporting Globe* writer Hec De Lacy advocated (in 1953) that the Hawks be expelled from the League and a new club 'in a growing suburb like Coburg' introduced.

It took the Hawks until 1960 to record their first victory against Collngwood at Victoria Park and until 1961 to win a premiership.

Its muddy home ground of Glenferrie—known as the 'Sardine tin'—was just 165 metres by 149 metres, the smallest and slushiest ground in the competition, renowned for restricting even the most skilful sides.

In 1957, the Hawks reached the finals for the first time under coach Jack Hale and made it through to the preliminary final before being outclassed by eventual premiers Melbourne.

Its efforts in the next 35 years of winning seven premierships, the first in 1961, three in the 1970s and three in the 1980s, was equalled by only one other club, Carlton.

For the first time in history in 1988–89, Hawthorn won back-to-back flags, including the last under the VFL banner. It played in a record-equalling seven straight

Graham Arthur, captain of Hawthorn's first premiership team in 1961.

Grand Finals from 1983–89. In 1991, it won another play-off.

The club's skilful running game and close family-like atmosphere became the envy of every other team.

From 1982–94, the Hawks appeared in 13 consecutive final series, a League record.

Off the field, the club became regarded as one of the most financially secure, well served by corporate sponsors, especially since, in 1974, shifting home games away from Glenferrie to Princes Park, Carlton.

Now its home is spacious Waverley, which it shares with St Kilda.

HAWTHORN: THE STATISTICS

FORMED: February, 1873

JOINED LEAGUE: 1925
HOME VENUES: Glenferrie Oval (1925–73), Princes Park (1974–91), Waverley Park (1990–   )
COLOURS: Vertical brown and gold striped guernsey
TOTAL FINALS MATCHES: 54 (34 wins, 20 losses)
FINALS RECORD: Premiers: 9 (1961, 1971, 1976, 1978, 1983, 1986, 1988–89, 1991)
          Runners-up: 5 (1963, 1975, 1984–85, 1987)
PREMIERSHIP COACHES: John Kennedy snr (3), David Parkin (1), Allan Jeans (3), Alan Joyce (2)

143

HAWTHORN: THE STATISTICS (cont)

NIGHT SERIES PREMIERSHIPS: 8 (1968–69, 1977, 1985–86, 1988, 1991–92)

YOUNGEST PLAYER: John Peck, 16 years 255 days (1954)

OLDEST PLAYER: Michael Tuck, 38 years 96 days (1991)

HIGHEST SCORE: 36.15 (231) v Fitzroy, R.6, 1991, North Hobart

LOWEST SCORE: 1.7 (13) v Melbourne, R.9, 1926, MCG

LONGEST WINNING SEQUENCE: 12 (1961)

LONGEST LOSING SEQUENCE: 27 (1927–29)

MOST FINALS: Michael Tuck 29, Leigh Matthews 29, Chris Mew 28, Gary Ayres 28, Dermott Brereton 26, Robert DiPierdomenico 25, Rodney Eade 24, Chris Langford 24, Russell Greene 20, John Kennedy jnr. 20, Peter Schwab 20, Jason Dunstall 20

MOST SEASONS AS COACH: John Kennedy snr 14 (1960–63, 1967–76)

MOST SEASONS AS CAPTAIN: Graham Arthur 9 (1960–68)

MOST GAMES		MOST GOALS	
Michael Tuck	426	Jason Dunstall	1011*
Leigh Matthews	332	Leigh Matthews	915
Don Scott	302	Peter Hudson	727
Kelvin Moore	300	Michael Moncrieff	629
Gary Ayres	269	John Peck	476
Peter Knights	265	Dermott Brereton	427
Chris Langford	256	Alec Albiston	381
John Kennedy jnr	241	Gary Buckenara	293
Robert DiPierdomenico	240	Bert Hyde	268
Graham Arthur	232	Butch Prior	258
Chris Mew	230	John Hendrie	254
Rodney Eade	229	Peter Crimmins	231
Michael Moncrieff	224	Ted Pool	230
Alan Martello	223	John Kennedy jnr	210
John Peck	212	Graham Arthur	201
David Parkin	211	Peter Knights	201
Jason Dunstall	208*	Paul Hudson	200*
Geoff Ablett	203		
Ted Pool	200		
John Platten	200*		

* current player.

MOST GOALS IN A MATCH: Jason Dunstall 17 v Richmond, R.7, 1992, Waverley
Peter Hudson 16 v Melbourne, R.5, 1969, Glenferrie Oval
Peter Hudson 13 v South Melb., R.11, 1969, Glenferrie Oval
Peter Hudson 13 v South Melb., R.8, 1970, Glenferrie Oval

BROWNLOW MEDALLISTS: Col Austen 1949, Robert DiPierdomenico 1986, John Platten 1987

COLEMAN MEDALLISTS: Jason Dunstall 1988, 1989, 1992

LEAGUE LEADING GOALSCORERS: John Peck 75 (1963); John Peck 69 (1964), John Peck 56 (1965), Peter Hudson 125 (1968), Peter Hudson 146 (1970), Peter Hudson 150 (1971), Peter Hudson 110 (1977), Leigh Matthews 68 (1975), Jason Dunstall 132 (1988), Jason Dunstall 138 (1989), Jason Dunstall 145 (1992).

RECORD HOME VENUE ATTENDANCE: 36,000 v Carlton, R.1, 1965, Glenferrie Oval
34,727 v Collingwood, R.9, 1977, Princes Park
72,765 v Collingwood, R.6, 1992, Waverley

RECORD ATTENDANCE IN ANY MATCH: 118,192 v St Kilda, GF, 1971, MCG
MOST RECENT PREMIERSHIP TEAM: 1991 Hawthorn 20.19 (130) d West Coast 13.8 (86)

B: A. Collins, C. Langford, G. Ayres. H.B: M. Tuck (c),
C. Mew, R. Jencke. C: D. Pritchard, B. Allan, A. Gowers.
H.F: P. Hudson, D. Brereton, T. Hall. F: D. Jarman, J. Dunstall,
P. Dear. R: S. Lawrence, A. Condon. R: J. Platten. Interchange:
D. Anderson, J. Morrissey.

HEALY, Gerard (1961–)

After winning the Brownlow Medal in 1988, Healy became the highest paid footballer in the AFL, on a $1.2 million contract over five years.

A serious wrist injury, sustained against Footscray in mid-1990, cruelly ended his career. After two operations failed, he retired, saying his wrist was too sore to even allow him to play golf—another of his favourite sports.

Gerard Healy in Melbourne colours before his switch to the Sydney Swans.

In 12 years of League football with Melbourne and the Sydney Swans, he played 211 games, but was restricted to just 19 mathces in 1989–90. He had six operations in his final 18 months of football: two on his wrist, two on his groin, one on his achilles and one on his mouth.

After winning Melbourne's best and fairest in 1984 and being runner-up in 1985, he won three in a row at Sydney from 1986–88. His '88 season was his best and came up after a summertime ownership blow-up which almost saw him return to Melbourne. Playing consistent, inspired football, he won the Brownlow Medal by four votes from Essendon's *Simon Madden*, despite missing the final week of the season because of a groin injury which had flared mid-year.

He wore a woman's corset to help better support the injury. He found it highly embarrassing walking into the women's section of one shop and asking for the corset in his size. 'One lady asked me if I wanted a matching bra!' Healy said.

His best performance of the year came in the State game in Perth when he gathered 36 possessions and kicked 5.1 to win the Simpson and E. J. Whitten Medals.

Winning All Australian honours in 1986, 1987 and 1988, he also represented Victoria 12 times.

'It's a tragedy he's going out so early,' said his team-mate and close friend *Greg Williams*. 'We (the Swans) couldn't have a bigger loss than Gerard.'

Originally from Edithvale-Aspendale, where he'd played in an open-age premiership as a teenager, two of Healy's six senior seasons at Melbourne were spent in tandem with his younger brother, Greg, a former Morrish Medal winner.

Starting as a winger before a successful forward line shift—he kicked 77 goals in 1982—his career blossomed after coach *Ron Barassi* agreed to allow him to ruck-rove in 1984. He was Melbourne's best player for three weeks in a row, his fitness and ballwinning ability a strongpoint in a mediocre side.

He played 130 games with Melbourne before joining Sydney in 1986. Brother Greg also amassed more than 100, captaining the Demons into the 1988 Grand Final and representing Victoria in 1989. Like Gerard, he won Melbourne's best and fairest. A third Healy brother, Matthew, represented Sandringham. The boys' grandfather, Bill O'Brien, played League football, with South Melbourne.

HEATH, Kevin (1950–)

A superbly built defender who played 218 games at two clubs from 1968–80, Heath had eight years and 141 games at Hawthorn before finishing at Carlton. Recruited from Assumption College, he played for Victoria twice and was a member of Hawthorn's 1971 premiership team.

He left Hawthorn after a falling-out with coach *David Parkin*, who said in Hawthorn's history, *The Hard Way*: 'Kevin had been a wonderful player, but seemed to have lost his way.'

HEAVYWEIGHTS

When Dean Farnham turned 13 he was already a massive 196 cm and a South Australian State schoolboys representative. Ten years later, he was representing Fitzroy, one of the biggest men of his or any other era.

Injuries, including a dislocated knee—which required two operations—restricted him to just 15 matches in his first year (1974) and two in his second before he returned to Adelaide, where he'd been a star at Central Districts.

Other players to weigh in at 110 kg or more included West Australian trio Ray Gabelich, Alex Ishchenko and John Ironmonger, South Australian Richard Lounder and North Melbourne's 'Galloping Gasometer' Mick Nolan.

Big Mick, an endearing character who was virtually immovable at boundary throw-ins, played more than 100 games in North Melbourne's glory era of the mid-to-late 1970s.

Late in his League career, his weight ballooned to around 120 kg—and he was even heftier when he played in Queensland.

The much-travelled hotelier Brian 'Whale' Roberts, the first to represent the three major States—WA, SA and Victoria—was a major asset at Richmond. He played in the Tigers' back-to-back premierships of 1973–74 before surprisingly being transferred to South Melbourne—along with *Graham Teasdale* and Francis Jackson—as part of the clearance arrangement for John Pitura.

Born in Millicent (SA), Roberts played at 111 kg before retiring at the end of the 1975 season. For years he ran the Cricket Club Hotel opposite the old South Melbourne ground.

The heaviest player currently playing is Sydney's *Tony Lockett*, whose weight varies from 103–110 kg. Early in his career at St

HEAVIEST LEAGUE PLAYERS

WEIGHT (kg)	PLAYER	TEAM/SPAN	MATCHES
124	Mick Nolan	North Melbourne 1973–80	107
116	Richard Lounder	Richmond 1989	4
115	Dean Farnham	Fitzroy 1974–75	17
113	Brian Roberts	Richmond 1971–75/Sth Melb 1975	93
110*	Paul Salmon	Essendon 1983–94	196
110	Hugh Moffatt	Richmond 1921–22	9
110	John Ironmonger	Sydney 1985–87/Fitz. 1988, 1990–91	43
110	Ray Gabelich	Coll. 1955–60, 1962–66	160
110*	Tony Lockett	St Kilda 1983–94	183
107*	Saverio Rocca	Collingwood 1992–94	50

* current player.

Kilda, the Saints were so worried by Lockett's expanding waistline—especially during the summer months—that they built bonuses into his contract to encourage him to be a particular weight at a certain stage of his pre-season.

HENDRIE, John (1953–   )

A grandson of Gil Hendrie, who played in Hawthorn's very first team when it joined the VFL, 188 cm 'Bomber' Hendrie was a top half-forward flanker who figured in two premierships, in 1976 and 1978, during his 11-year, 197-match career.

Originally from Moyhu in Fitzroy's zone, Hendrie was considered such an outstanding schoolboy prospect that Hawthorn sat him on the bench, aged 15, in the reserves for a match in 1969 to tie him to the club.

Hendrie's headmaster at Scotch College reluctantly gave his permission, as long as Hendrie sat on the bench throughout.

Hendrie joined the Hawks three years

John Hendrie, a two-time Hawthorn premiership player and equal third in the 1975 Brownlow Medal count.

later, being the only recruit to break into the 1971 premiership side for the first round of 1972.

A glorious mark and long left-foot kick, he was a star in a champion team throughout the 1970s, mixing his football with senior District cricket at Hawthorn-East Melbourne. After playing only eight senior games in 1981, he sought a clearance to Footscray. Hawthorn refused, coach *Allan Jeans* saying he would regret not playing all his football at the same club.

After just one more game in 1982, he retired to NSW where he was prominent in the Sydney league.

See: 'INACCURATE KICKING'

HICKEY, Harry (1917–   )

A three-time winner of Footscray's best and fairest award, Harry Hickey's impressive career was interrupted by the Second World War.

Polling 11 Brownlow votes in his first season, 1938, he finished among the top six players in each of his next three seasons.

A highpoint in his career came during the 1944 season when, with the scores tied in the final home-and-away round against Carlton, he lifted the Bulldogs into the four by scoring a point after the siren from 50 metres.

HICKEY, Reg (1906–73)

A scrupulously fair and brilliant centre half-back, Reg Hickey played 245 games for Geelong, a club record which stood for more than 20 years. A player in two premiership teams, he was also coach of the great 1951–52 flag sides, regarded as Geelong's best ever.

Under his inspiring influence, the Cats went 26 matches without defeat in 1952–53. Hickey's philosophy was to win, as long as you enjoyed the game along the way.

Hickey captained the Cats a record 148 times, polled 98 Brownlow Medal votes, represented Victorian 17 times, including two years as captain (1932 and 1935) and won Geelong's best and fairest in 1928 and 1934.

His No. 18 guernsey number is Geelong's most revered.

According to Geelong historian Col Hutchinson, opponents found Hickey almost impossible to tackle, such was his ability to weave and baulk, quite rare in a man his height (185 cm) and weight (92 kg).

'His clearing dashes were inspirational,' said Hutchinson. 'He was able to adapt to any conditions, was tough and fast and could kick well with either foot.'

His playing career lasted 15 years (including six as playing coach), while he had 11 further years as non-playing coach from 1949–59.

In 1937, his first full year as captain-coach, he led the Cats to a memorable 32-point Grand Final victory against Collingwood.

The Hickey-coached Geelong premiership teams of 1951–52 were among the paciest of any era. The side very nearly won a third flag in a row, in 1953, going down by just 12 points to Collingwood.

HIGH FLIERS

Essendon's turn-of-the-century star, Charlie Pearson, was the father of the high mark, the game's most exciting skill.

Pearson was said 'to take risks with his rocketlike leaps into the air for his marks'. Not everyone liked it. One old-timer commented: 'This new fangled idea in marking will ruin the game. People come to see football, not men leaping into the air.'

Renowned early exponents of the high mark included Jack Monahan, *Albert Thurgood, 'Dick' Lee, Roy Cazaly*, Dave McNamara, Horrie Clover, *Gordon Coventry, Ron Todd* and *Bob Pratt*.

Laurie Nash once quipped that his South Melbourne team-mate Pratt flew so high, he used to come down with splinters on his hands!

Melbourne follower Harold Ball was also a renowned aerialist. Swung into defence in the final quarter of the 1940 preliminary final against Essendon, he took 15 marks in less than 25 minutes in a solo

Adelaide's Tony Modra makes a spectacular leap, courtesy of Footscray's Brad Nicholson at Football Park in 1994.

North Melbourne full-forward Phil Baker's magnificent leap in the 1978 Grand Final, courtesy of Hawthorn pair Kelvin Moore (left) and Ian Paton.

Steve Silvagni's Mark of the Year, Carlton v Collingwood, MCG, 1990.

effort which enabled Melbourne to win by five points.

In the last two decades, Terry Waters, *Alex Jesaulenko*, Billy Picken, Bill Ryan, *Royce Hart* and Phil Baker are renowned for their finger-tip marking exploits.

Among the finest marks in the League currently are Adelaide's Tony Modra, Carlton trio *Stephen Kernahan*, James Cook and Steve Silvagni, St Kilda's *Stewart Loewe*, Richmond's Matthew Richardson and Hawthorn's *Jason Dunstall*. Ex-Lion Alastair Lynch, now with Brisbane, is also spectacular in the air.

Geelong's *Gary Ablett* possesses Pratt-like leaping abilities. He took some of the finest marks of the 1980s, many from a 'standing start'.

St Kilda's Nicky Winmar learnt to leap by jumping off an old tree stump in the front of his parents' WA home. He took the 1992 mark of the year, against Essendon.

HOPKINS, Allan (1904–)

After he finished second in the Brownlow Medal three years in a row from 1929–31, the VFL sent the Footscray centreman with the bandy legs a citation praising his sportsmanship and ability.

When countbacks were outlawed so that more than one player could win the Medal, it was suggested that the seven men who had lost the Medal on countback should be honoured. In 1989, they were awarded retrospective Medals. Hopkins received one for his 1930 season when he tied with Richmond's *Stan Judkins* and Collingwood's *Harry Collier*.

Fast off the mark and possessing clever evasive skills, he first represented Footscray when it was in the VFA and, in a 10-year League career, played 153 games. He was captain in 1926, captain-coach in 1930 and club champion in 1931.

One 1930 profile of him said: 'He has the right football sense ... his sense of anticipation is often uncanny and this bewilders many players.'

HOWELL, Verdun (1936–)

Another of St Kilda's magnificent Tasmanian recruits who helped revitalise the ailing club's fortunes in the 1950s, snowy-headed Howell was an attacking full-back who loved to back his judgement and run at the ball, even if it meant leaving his opponent 30 metres behind.

His spectacular marking and dashes downfield were recognised by the field umpires who, in his very first full year, awarded him 20 Brownlow votes, equal to the winner, South Melbourne's *Bob Skilton*.

Howell lost the Medal on the old countback system, but 30 years later, was awarded one retrospectively.

At a celebratory luncheon to mark Howell's award, Skilton said Howell was one of the greatest players he'd seen.

Recruited from City South, Launceston—but not before a protracted clearance dispute which saw him stand out of the first half of the 1958 season—Howell played the first of his 166 League games at Windy Hill in the 13th round against Essendon.

Selected for the first time at full-back, he restricted crack Essendon goalkicker Ron

Evans to just one goal. Coach Alan Killigrew said: 'At two o'clock we had our fingers crossed. By five, we knew a star was born.' Essendon kicked 17.30 and Howell was so fatigued from kicking off that he strained a hamstring.

Howell represented Victoria nine times from 1959–75 and was vice-captain to fellow Tasmanian *Darrel Baldock*, in the club's historic 1966 premiership.

While playing two-thirds of his career in defence, he also proved a most capable forward and enjoyed immediate success in the mid-1960s when coach *Allan Jeans* swapped Howell with VFA recruit, full-forward *Bob Murray*.

Murray became a tremendous defender, while Howell, in only his second game at full-forward, kicked nine goals.

In one game against North Melbourne at Coburg in 1965, Jeans kept Howell at one end of the ground all day—playing him at full-back when St Kilda kicked against the wind and at full-forward when it went with it.

HUDSON, Peter (1946–)

One of post-war football's most celebrated players, the Tasmanian-born goal-kicking legend topped 100 goals in 11 of his 14 full senior seasons, eight in Tasmania and six with Hawthorn.

In his first five VFL years, before a knee injury cruelly intervened and threatened to end his career prematurely, Hudson kicked 598 goals including a record-equalling 150 in Hawthorn's 1971 premiership year.

Hudson's recruiting was Hawthorn's most important interstate signing since the arrival of Adelaide of beanpole ruckman Clayton 'Candles' Thompson in the 1950s and signified the club's determination to match it with the very best teams.

Hudson topped the VFL goalkicking four times, amassing 100 goals in five seasons. His goal average of 5.64 is unequalled in League football history. Hawthorn rose from 10th place in his first season, 1967, into the finals in 1971 and has remained a power ever since.

Hudson, 190 cm and 91 kg, favoured flat punts when shooting for goal, believing

Peter Hudson goes for goal No. 151 late in the 1971 Grand Final, only to kick into the man on the mark, St Kilda's Barry Lawrence.

he could kick them longer than the drop punt, without losing accuracy. He scored 10 or more goals in a match on 12 occasions. Against St Kilda in 1971, he kicked 12 straight.

'In those days if you kicked the ball out in front of Hudson, his judgement, use of the body and sure hands meant he would get it almost every time,' said *Leigh Matthews*. 'He was a superb mark and extremely accurate kick ... the equal of any player I've seen in the years before he severely damaged a knee.'

Hawthorn, under the astute coaching of *John Kennedy*, developed an open forward line system which often saw Hudson and his opponent 50–60 metres from any other player on the ground.

Hudson kicked 16.1 against Melbourne in 1969. In a sensational start to the opening round of 1972 at Glenferrie Oval, he kicked eight goals in the first 50 minutes against the Demons before tearing a cruciate ligament in his right knee after a collision with Melbourne's Barry Bourke.

He'd marked within close range and almost certainly would have had his ninth goal before half time—but was unable to take the kick. He was carried from the ground on a stretcher. He believed he was on course that day to surpass *Fred Fanning's* record of 18 goals in a game and later blamed the condition of Glenferrie Oval for the injury. 'If it had been a muddy day I wouldn't even have hurt my knee,' he said. 'But the ground had become rock hard during the summer and for that first match there had been no rain to soften it. My foot just hit the ground, my body turned, the knee had nowhere to go. It just stopped still and down I went.'

The condition of Hudson's knee was headline news for weeks. A report in the Melbourne *Herald* said: '. . . Hudson's knee has replaced Ron Barassi's groin as Australia's longest running sporting story . . . Almost daily bulletins are released on the Hudson knee and these are relayed to a breathless public.'

In an extraordinary comeback against Collingwood in the second-last round of 1973, he kicked eight goals despite being overweight. He jarred his bad knee early in the match yet beat four opponents, who appeared almost mesmerised by his presence.

Kept goalless in only three of his 129 VFL games and in just five during his 333-match senior career, 'Huddo' began his schoolboy sporting career as a soccer goal-keeper. When he was 12 and in his first year at high school in New Norfolk, he switched to Australian Rules.

On arrival at Hawthorn in 1967, when he became the club's highest-paid player, Hudson said it was 'like coming into a family'. He finished with 57 for the season, and was second on the VFL goalkicking charts.

Proving virtually unstoppable in the next four years, he kicked 125, 120, 146 and 150 goals, averaging more than six a game with a succession of deadly performances. His century effort in 1968 was the first time in 16 years a VFL goalkicker had amassed three figures.

Selected as an All Australian in 1966 and 1969, he won six club best and fairests, including Hawthorn's club championship in 1968 and 1970 and the Tasmanian Football League's William Leitch Medal in 1978 and 1979.

Representing Glenorchy in 1978, he established a new Australian goalkicking high of 191 goals (breaking *Ron Todd*'s 188 set with VFA club Williamstown in 1945) and the following year became the first man to kick 200 goals in a senior season. He finished with 209 including 18.2 and

15.6 against Hobart. He also kicked 16 goals against North Hobart.

He finished with six goals in his last match, aged 35, in the 1981 Tasmanian Football League preliminary final.

His senior career spanned two full decades and broke into a third. In all, he netted 2191 goals.

He also holds the record of kicking the most goals in a final, 14, for Glenorchy against Hobart in the TFL second semi-final in 1981. He started the game on the reserves bench, not coming onto the ground until the 17 minute mark of the first quarter.

One of Hudson's few regrets in football is being concussed in the 1971 Grand Final and not remembering as much about Hawthorn's narrow victory as he would have liked. He kicked three goals in the game to equal *Bob Pratt*'s long-standing League milestone of 150 and had several opportunities in the final term to break the record, only to kick out of bounds on the full and into man-on-the-mark Barry Lawrence both times from close range. He said he was 'in a fog' for much of the game and kept seeing 'extra' goalposts. He later had 11 stitches inserted in a cut ear after being collected by St Kilda's *Kevin Neale* before half time.

Asked if he was disappointed in not breaking Bob Pratt's record, he said: 'I played a premiership and equalled the record of a very great footballer, all in the one match . . . it wouldn't have been a true record anyway. Pratt kicked his 150 in fewer matches than I did. I'm happy enough to have my name bracketed with his.'

Paul Hudson has blossomed into a top-liner. Like his bigger and stronger father, he is uncanny around goal. In 1991, when he played in Hawthorn's day and night premierships, he kicked 60 goals, finishing second in the goalkicking to *Jason Dunstall*.

HUGHES, Frank (1894–1978)

Francis Vane 'Checker' Hughes was a coaching mastermind who followed up dual premiership success as a player at Richmond with five premierships as a coach, one with the Tigers and four with Melbourne—all in a remarkable 20-year period which also featured five other Grand Final appearances.

A wonderful football psychologist and orator, he coached Victorian teams with distinction, the last in 1953 when the Vics won the Australian championships in Adelaide. He was almost 60.

His playing career at Tigerland spanned 10 years from 1914 to 1923. He was the team's centreman in the 1920 premiership and roved in the 1921 flag. He was vice-captain to Dan Minogue in 1922, but lost form and half-way through the season was asked to coach Richmond seconds, a job he maintained, as playing coach, the following year.

He coached Tasmanian coastal club Ulverstone into three successive grand finals from 1924–26, and then returned to the mainland at the invitation of noted secretary Percy Page to become Richmond's senior coach. The Tigers lost three consecutive play-offs, but won the flag in 1932. When Page joined Melbourne, Hughes followed.

It took time to instil some toughness and quality into the side. Melbourne had won only one premiership in more than 30 years and were regarded in some quarters as being 'soft'.

Hughes and Page sacked the no-hopers and has-beens, weeded out many of the college kids who weren't fully committed and, in each of their first two seasons, introduced 13 newcomers.

The vigorous recruiting attracted players such as Wally Lock, *Jack Mueller*, *Norm Smith*, Ron Barassi snr, Alan la Fontaine, Alby Rodda, *Percy Beames* and Maurie Gibb. Hughes also changed the team's nickname from the Fuchsias to the Demons.

Lifting the team into the preliminary final in 1936–37 and narrowly missing the finals in 1938, the stern, business-like Hughes knew he was on the verge of something special.

Melbourne won three premierships in a row from 1939–41, rivalling the Collingwood teams of the late 1920s as the VFL's best in the first 50 years of competition.

The side's memorable 1940 victory against Richmond was an example of Hughes' leadership skills.

Hughes used versatile Jack O'Keefe to successfully shadow Richmond champion *Jack Dyer* in Melbourne's upset win. 'I told O'Keefe that I wanted him to follow Dyer everywhere, even if he became full-forward or centre half-forward,' Hughes said. 'I had noticed that Dyer was never as effective against a player who stood shoulder to shoulder with him.'

Returning as Melbourne's coach from 1945–48, Hughes led the team into three Grand Finals (two in one year), the '48 triumph, after the first play-off was tied, being a fabulous way to end his career.

Asked to explain the secrets of success, Hughes said: 'The personal touch. When I became coach of Richmond my chief aim was to teach the players to play with determination. I told them little or nothing about guile, but I soon found there was more in football than the strong determined type of game and I concentrated more on theory.

'It is important to study the strength and weaknesses of opposing sides and plan accordingly.'

He said many of the best coaches were not necessarily champion players, but were invariably keen students of the game and, in effect, psychologists.

He was a great believer in taking time to help individual players and discuss their weaknesses. He introduced variety into his training sessions and liked the players to be involved, where necessary, in match-day planning.

Hughes' son, Frank jnr, also played League football, with Richmond in 1944.

HUGHES, Les (1884–1962)

A three-time Collingwood premiership player, 'Flapper' or 'Lofty' Hughes was named at centre half-forward in the 1910 victory and rucked in the 1917–19 wins in his 209 match career from 1908–20. He was 38 in his final season.

In the acrimonious 1910 final against Carlton, he was decked before the first bounce and king-hit in the final quarter.

Les Hughes, one of football's most durable champions.

Four players, two from each side, were suspended for a season to a season-and-a-half.

The 188 cm follower was renowned for being a big-match specialist. *The Australasian* commented: 'Jogging tirelessly from start to finish, Hughes is a constant battler who indulges no relaxing of effort and yields no weariness.' He played three State games.

HUNT, Rex (1949–)

A burly, strong-marking forward, who also played successfully in defence in mid-career, 193 cm Hunt was a member of two Richmond premierships before having two seasons at Geelong and three at St Kilda. Representing Victoria in his final season, he played 202 games from 1968–78 and was also a great success in the VFA with Sandringham, despite his weight ballooning above 100 kg.

A long, often erratic, left-foot kick, he led Richmond's goalkicking in 1969 and 1970, even though his third season was interrupted by national service. He recovered from a bout of hepatitis in early 1972, to win back his place in mid-year and play in another Grand Final.

He switched to Geelong in 1974. His senior debut was delayed until the eighth round, but he made an immediate impression, several times taking 15 marks in a game and dominating in two seasons at centre half-forward.

He served St Kilda manfully and the Saints finished sixth in his final season in 1978. Retiring from League football at 29, he had two further seniors seasons at Sandringham in 1980–81, when he booted 203 goals, including 110 to be the VFA's leading goalkicker for the 1981 season. In his final game, he kicked 10 goals in a losing side against Preston in the preliminary final.

He later attracted a cult following as a football and fishing commentator, being named the 1992 Media Personality of the Year by the AFL Media Association.

HUTCHISON, Bill (1923–82)

One of the game's most distinguished rovers, Hutchison won the 1953 Brownlow Medal at the age of 30. He'd lost on a countback in 1952, but years later his feat in dead-heating was recognised when he was awarded another posthumously.

Essendon's Billy Hutchinson made 10 Grand Final appearances, a record surpassed by only one player, Hawthorn's Michael Tuck.

His extraordinary record includes 10 Grand Final appearances for four wins, five losses and a draw. He played 295 games in 16 seasons from 1942–57, figuring in Grand Finals in his first and last seasons.

Hutchison's early years were spent on a wing or at half-forward. Lightly-built, his amazing skill helped him stay out of trouble.

He was a star in Essendon's much-feted 1949–50 premiership teams and in 1951 was appointed captain for the first of seven seasons.

Twice an All Australian, he represented Victoria in four carnivals, 1947, 1950, 1953 and 1956. In all, he played 30 games with Victoria, a record surpassed by only one other player, Carlton's *John Nicholls*, who played 31 times.

He won the Bombers' best and fairest seven times, equalling *Dick Reynolds'* great record.

Hutchison's delivery to champion full-forward *John Coleman* was impeccable. His speed allowed him to break clear of packs and he could kick long and accurately even when running at top pace. His stab-passing was a delight.

Hutchison kicked 457 goals in his career, twice kicking seven in a match.

He coached Essendon under 19s on his retirement as well as being assistant-coach for several years to John Coleman. He helped in recruiting and was a Victorian selector from 1978–80, just two years before his death at the relatively young age of 59.

ICKE, Steven (1956–)

Highly skilled and mobile, Icke played successfully at both centre half-forward and centre half-back. He was a member of North Melbourne's 1977 premiership team and enjoyed immediate success at Melbourne, winning the Demons' 1982 best and fairest after being sold—along with *Brian Wilson*—to help finance North's purchase of the Krakouer brothers from WA. Icke knew nothing of the negotiations and claimed afterwards he'd been treated 'like a piece of cattle'.

Recruited from Noble Park, he played 198 games from 175–87 (120 with North and 78 with Melbourne) and represented Victoria. His career was shortened by a snapped achilles tendon in 1983—courtesy of an exposed sprinkler box at VFL Park—and a knee reconstruction three years later.

INACCURATE KICKING

Even the game's most elite players have sometimes 'choked' when kicking for goal. The VFL's greatest goalkicker, Collingwood's *Gordon Coventry* once kicked 1.13 in a club game against St Kilda in 1930.

Footscray's 'Mr Football', *Ted Whitten*—normally a magnificent field kick—kicked 2.13 against South Melbourne in 1956.

In 1948, *Bill Brittingham* kicked 2.8 in football's first drawn Grand Final.*

Colourful North Melbourne forward Arnold Briedis had one of the most nightmarish days on record in the 1977 drawn Grand Final against Collingwood when he kicked 0.7, in a team score of 9.22 (76).

Hawthorn's *John Hendrie* kicked 2.8 in the 1976 Grand Final.

In the very first VFL final series in 1897, Geelong's Arch Thompson kicked 0.8 against Melbourne. Two years later, giant team-mate *Eddie James* kicked 1.9 against Fitzroy and 5.16 against St Kilda.

One of the most recent examples of poor conversion was in the fourth round, 1995, when Hawthorn's Paul Hudson converted

* see 'GREAT GRAND FINALS'

just two of his 12 shots on goal against St Kilda. He finished with 2.4, four other shots going out of bounds and two other snap shots failing to make the distance.

MOST BEHINDS IN A GAME:

Goals/behinds

5.16 Eddie James (Geelong) v St Kilda, 1899

1.13 Dave McNamara (St Kilda) v Richmond, 1922

1.13 Gordon Coventry (Coll.) v St Kilda, 1930

2.13 Ted Whitten (Foots.) v South Melbourne, 1956

6.12 Alex Jesaulenko (Carlton) v Hawthorn, 1969

7.12 Ron Todd (Coll.) v Richmond, 1938 (he also kicked five out of bounds).

0.11 Tom Allen (Richmond) v Nth Melbourne, 1949

0.11 Stuart Spencer (Melbourne) v Geelong, 1956.

INTERSTATE FOOTBALL

See: 'NATIONAL AUSTRALIA FOOTBALL COUNCIL'.

IRWIN, Warwick (1952–)

A finely skilled ruck-rover, he started and finished his 14-season senior League career at Fitzroy, having 231 games including 16 in two seasons at Collingwood in 1981–82.

Recruited from Surrey Hills, he was an excellent mark and a fine on-field leader. He first represented Victoria as a 20-year-old.

In 1981, he transferred to Collingwood for $60,000 plus three players, the most notable being Leigh Carlson. He didn't win a release until mid-season after threatening court action. After playing on a wing in Collingwood's losing 1981 Grand Final, operations on both his knees forced him to miss the entire 1982 season.

In 1983, he was swapped back again after being told that Collingwood wanted to encourage younger players.

JAMES, Edward (1874–*)

The VFL's leading goalkicker in each of the first three years of competition, Eddie James was a giant of a man at 193 cm.

Alternating between full-forward and ruck, he led Geelong's goalkicking for three years from 1897–99 before a knee injury, in 1900, forced his retirement.

Recruited from Geelong Grammar, he first represented Geelong as an 18-year-old in 1892 and in 46 League games kicked 85 goals. He also represented Victoria and was considered such a formidable player that opposing backmen often used unfair tactics to unsettle him.

JAMES, John (1934–   )

Another forward-line player who successfully reverted to defence, Carlton's Johnny James won the 1961, Brownlow Medal from a back pocket. His skill, rare

Attacking defence, Carlton's Johnny James.

judgement, coolness and ball-winning ability were features of his game.

Renowned for wearing his socks down, James had been a schoolboy goalkicking

star at St Pat's College, Ballarat. In one match he kicked 34 goals.

He joined Carlton as a 19-year-old, but within several seasons had settled into defence, playing first as a back-flanker and then in a back pocket, where he quickly built a reputation as one of the safest and most consistent defenders in the game.

He won three Carlton best and fairests, in 1955, 1960 and 1961, and represented Victoria 15 times, including the 1953, 1956 and 1961 carnivals.

Team-mate *John Nicholls* said: 'Often his actions reminded me of a cat because he could take freakish marks, twisting his body in the air. In his ground play, he twisted and weaved, sometimes running backwards out of packs. And he was hard to tackle because his strength was unreal.'

He played 195 games with Carlton from 1953–63 and almost 400 in two decades of city and country football.

His son, Michael played 12 games with Carlton in 1991–92.

JEANS, Allan (1933–   )

League football's longest-serving and most successful modern-day coach, Allan 'Yabbie' Jeans coached 575 games spanning four decades and three clubs. Jeans coached St Kilda to its only premiership in 1966, led Hawthorn to three flags in 1983, 1986 and 1989, and in 1992 replaced *Kevin Bartlett* as Richmond coach. His record is unequalled by any living coach.

He's one of only three coaches, the others being *Jock McHale* and *Tom Hafey*, to have coached more than 500 games. Only McHale (eight premierships at Collingwood), *Norm Smith* (six at Melbourne) and *Jack Worrall* (five at Carlton and Essendon) have had more Grand Final success.

After his speech during the long interval in the '89 Grand Final, several players had tears in their eyes as they re-entered the oval. Vice-captain *Gary Ayres* compared it to Jeans' 1983 Grand Final address, when he got everyone to link hands and make a pledge: 'No matter what happens, we'll win today.'

In Hawthorn's history, *A Hard Way*,

Allan Jeans' greatest triumph: Hawthorn's 1989 premiership. The master coach is lifted into the air by Peter Curran and John Kennedy jnr after Hawthorn's six point win.

Jeans told Harry Gordon how he likes to tell his players stories: 'I like to keep it simple. That's why I talk about football being like cooking sausages ... that you can fry them, curry them, put apple sauce with them. They're still sausages, all you are doing is dressing them up. The basics are still the basics and part of coaching is presenting them differently, so that they don't become monotonous.'

A great reader, Jeans used to search for motivating stories which he could apply to football.

He lifted the Hawks into five consecutive Grand Finals before being forced to stand down as coach in 1988 because of a brain haemorrhage suffered in October, 1987.

He was given only a 60/40 chance of living and his future coaching prospects looked bleak. But he returned in 1989. The much-remembered victory on Grand Final day was a fitting reward for one of football's most outstanding figures.

Born in Finley, NSW, he was just 27 when he first coached St Kilda. He'd played 77 games from 1955–59 mainly as a flanker with the Saints—plus one match, as 19th man, with Victoria 'B' in 1959.

Initially rejected by Carlton, he was invited to St Kilda by new coach *Les Foote*, who had been playing in the Tocumwal–Finley area.

Tough and ferocious at the ball—if not overly quick or skilful—Jeans was a fine team-man before a chest injury forced him to stop.

In 1960, he coached St Kilda reserves for a short period before taking over from Jim Francis as senior coach in 1961. It was the beginning of more than three decades of coaching: 16 years at St Kilda, nine at Hawthorn, one at Richmond and several years in coaching and selection capacities with Victoria and NSW.

Under his firm, no-nonsense rule, the Saints made the finals nine times, including three Grand Finals. The historic '66 flag is a golden memory.

'A premiership was something which had eluded our club for 92 years,' he said. 'It was an enjoyable moment but I hadn't realised the full impact of it until I started to receive numerous letters of appreciation from people who had followed the club for years. It brought them tremendous elation.'

For more than 25 years, Jeans combined his work in the police force with football. It wasn't until 1987 that he followed the trend to take on coaching full-time.

One of his greatest honours was having legendary coaching rival *John Kennedy snr* ask him to coach Hawthorn, in 1981. In his discussions with Kennedy and club president Ron Cook, Jeans asked why Hawthorn wanted an outsider. 'They just said they felt it was time and that I was the right person,' he said.

'They made an offer and I said I'd go home and talk it over with my wife. I was only home half an hour when Cookie was on the phone ... "What did your wife say?"

'I said I'd take the job.'

Jeans' simple philosophy to football is that there are three basic situations in a match: 'Either we've got the ball, they've got the ball, or the ball is in dispute.'

One of his star pupils, St Kilda's George Young, once said of him: 'Allan demanded discipline and no-one was allowed to break the rules. He had a personal interest in all his players and everyone respected him.'

In his younger years, Jeans used to like to wrestle with the Hawthorn players. He'd take on five and six in a row, but always after training when most were exhausted. He stopped after *Gary Buckenara* threw him onto his forehead one Sunday morning. Much to the amusement of the Hawthorn players, he appeared on 'World of Sport' later that morning with a huge bandage on his head.

Before accepting the Richmond coaching job for 1992, he discussed the opportunity with his friends at Hawthorn. He'd worked in recruiting areas for the club in 1991 and was again itching for the ultimate challenge. However, after just one season, he stood down, on health advice.

JESAULENKO, Alex (1945–)

One of the greatest players ever, Austrian-born Alex Jesaulenko possessed freakish ball-skills and an extraordinary leap which ensured headlines from his very first year when he finished third in the Brownlow Medal.

A member of four Carlton premiership sides, the last as captain-coach, the magnificently-balanced Jesaulenko played 283 games from 1967–81, amassing 260 games (and 424 goals) at Carlton and 23 matches (and 19 goals) in his final seasons at St Kilda.

Representing Victoria 15 times from 1967–76, he was twice State captain and All Australian, twice Carlton's best and fairest and the first Blue forward to kick 100 goals in a season. Later he coached two League clubs. In 1993 he coached VFA club Coburg.

Born in a refugee camp in Salzburg in 1945, during the last months of the war in Europe, he migrated with his Ukrainian father and Russian mother when he was three. Growing up in Canberra, the young 'Jezza' was keen on soccer and didn't play Australian football until he was 14.

Alex Jesaulenko's classic leap, over Collingwood ruckman Graeme Jenkin, during the 1970 Grand Final.

When he moved to Melbourne as a clerk for the Navy, Carlton signed him.

In his first sensational year of League football, the 21-year-old catapulted high over taller opponents, hanging in the air for spectacular marks. He proved just as effective at ground level.

His coach, *Ron Barassi*, was so moved by his introduction that he said: 'Alex Jesaulenko is Carlton's football freak. Personally I don't envy any player who is given the job of minding him for a full 100 minutes.

'He does not rely on any one facet of football to get kicks. He has been compared to *Darrel Baldock* but I believe he is better because he is a higher mark, is much faster and kicks more accurately. His marking from the front-on position is unbelievable.'

Leading Carlton's goalkicking in four consecutive years, he had a key involvement in Carlton amassing a new VFL record of 30.30 (210) in the second round of the 1969 season, booting 6.9 in the 128-point devastation of Hawthorn. In the 1972 Grand Final against Richmond, he kicked seven goals to equal the League record.

One of his proudest feats was in May 1973, when he kicked 10 goals in Victoria's four point win against South Australia in Adelaide. Later that night, his first child was born. 'I was the happiest man in the world that night,' he said. 'It was one of those days when everything went right.'

In an interview in 1974, former Collingwood skipper *Des Tuddenham* said Jesaulenko was the player he'd most like in his side: 'He can do just about anything,' he said. 'He's a tremendous ball-getter, at times he appears to have it on a string. He can inspire a whole team because of his ability to leave the opposition standing through his sheer brilliance.'

At 182 cm, he invariably conceded height to his opponents, but his uncanny anticipation and extraordinary high marking expertise made him virtually unstoppable. His mark on the shoulders of Collingwood ruckman, Graeme Jenkin, during the 1970 Grand Final is regarded as a modern-day classic.

The best of Jesaulenko captivated fans for years. While his most breathtaking games were in attack, later in his career he successfully adapted to a half-back flank.

His final game at Carlton was the 1979 Grand Final, which the Blues won in a fantastic finish by just five points. Captain-coach Jezza broke a bone in his ankle during the game, but hobbled out for the final moments, to be carried around the MCG in a memorable lap-of-honour. It was the crowning point of his career.

He was to leave Carlton over the summer after political in-fighting split the club. Joining St Kilda, he became playing coach after the opening two rounds of the 1980 season and remained until the end of 1982 when he severed his VFL links and shifted back interstate.

He made a dramatic return to League football in mid-1989, replacing *Robert Walls* as Carlton's coach. Just over a year later, he, too, was replaced, having failed to lift Carlton into the finals. Jesaulenko was bitterly disappointed. It was a tragic way to end one of the most spectacular League football careers of them all.

JESS, Jim (1955–   )

A long-kicking, key-position player who was dominant in Richmond's 1980 premiership, the 189 cm Jess had 223 games and represented Victoria four times in his 13 years at Tigerland.

A magnificent high mark, he played at centre half-back in Richmond's losing 1982 Grand Final side.

He rejected rich offers from Carlton and Collingwood in mid-career to continue at Richmond, where he was one of the club's most popular players. A great character, he was renowned for his practical jokes. He put a young wild pig in team-mate *Michael Roach*'s locker one night.

Injuries forced him to leave League ranks in 1988. 'If I hadn't played football I'd still be shearing sheep,' he said on his retirement.

He and former Richmond team-mate *Mark Lee* played in a premiership with the Burnie Hawks, before Jess rejoined his original country club, Avoca. In one game, in 1993, he kicked 20.1 as Avoca defeated Landsborough 55.16 to 4.4.

See: 'LONGEST KICKS'

JOHNSON, Bob jnr (1929–   )

A member of five Melbourne premiership sides and chosen nine times for Victoria from 1957–60, 'Big Bob' Johnson was a double-decker ruckman with uncanny goal sense whose career spanned more than 25 years and seven clubs.

At 198 cm and 102 kg, he was one of the biggest players in the game and virtually unstoppable at his best. He played in 11 Grand Finals—seven with Melbourne and four with East Fremantle.

He was also a wonderful character who, on his return from Western Australia, became a magnetic drawcard in the VFA in the early 1970s. Once when answering a tribunal charge after a rough-house game against Port Melbourne, he told the Association commissioners: 'You can't suspend me. People come to see me play. If I don't play, no-one will show up.' He was exonerated.

On another occasion, when addressing his players before an important match, he cleared the rooms, allowing no-one to stay but two journalists. Mid-way through his speech, he pointed at the reporters. Raising his voice, he thundered: 'And those blokes, the people who write about you, don't think you can win today! Go out there and show them and everyone else just how good you are. Stick it right up 'em!' With that he walked out. Winking at the embarrassed reporters, he said: 'Thanks boys. See you after the match.'

Ron Barassi said of his old Demon teammate: 'Bob Johnson had a great football brain and was one of the best forward-pocket ruckmen I have seen. If Bob had been able to stay happy with football in Melbourne, he would have been ranked with *John Nicholls* and *'Polly' Farmer.'*

Opposing supporters couldn't believe the stream of free kicks Johnson received. Noted football writer Alf Brown dubbed him the greatest football dramatist of all time. If caught out of position in a marking duel, he'd invariably end up on his hands and knees, appealing to the umpire for a 'push' or alleged rough treatment in a pack. Quite often, he'd fool them, too.

Among the best players afield in Melbourne's '57–'59–'60 premierships, the giant left-footer kicked 267 goals in 144 games with the Demons from 1954–61, before switching to East Fremantle where he played 110 games from 1962–66. In 1965, a premiership season, he kicked 107 goals including 13 against East Perth.

His father, 190 cm Bob snr, played 108 games with the Demons, including the 1926 premiership, in which he kicked 6.7 from centre half-forward.

JOHNSON, Robert 'Tassie' (1937–   )

Another talented Apple Islander who played top-class football in Melbourne, Robert Edward Johnson played 209 games from 1959–69, appearing in the 1959, 1960 and 1964 premiership teams.

Originally from North Launceston, he was known as 'Tassie', so there could be no confusion between him and established senior pair *'Big Bob' Johnson* and *Trevor Johnson*.

A strong, no-nonsense player, 189 cm Tassie won Victorian selection in his second season. He represented the Vics almost every year, until 1967.

He was Melbourne's captain in 1969, his final season.

JOHNSON, Trevor (1935–   )

A versatile 195 cm follower who played in four Melbourne premierships, Johnson had 117 games from 1955–62, including flags in each of his first three seasons. In the 1960 Grand Final, he was one of three Johnsons in Melbourne's starting 18, along with *'Big Bob'* and *'Tassie' Johnson* (no relation).

JOHNSTON, Wayne (1957–   )

One of the acknowledged big-match 'superstars' of the 1980s, Wayne Johnston played in four Carlton premierships, represented Victoria five times in State-of-Origin games and was twice the Blues' club champion. In 209 games from 1979–90, he kicked 283 goals, was leading goalkicker (with 51) in 1980 and club captain in 1984–85.

He suffered a run of major injuries from mid-career. In 1991, he played briefly at Sturt in the SANFL.

Invited to Carlton as a teenager, his first attempts to play League football were unsuccessful. He was even rejected by VFA club Oakleigh before settling in at Prahran, where he had four seasons, including the 1978 premiership year in which he kicked 73 goals.

Friends suggested he should try out at Melbourne but new Carlton coach *Alex Jesaulenko* refused to consider a clearance until Johnston, 21, had completed a full pre-season and played in the practice matches. He missed initial selection in the first major trial, but a senior player withdrew giving him a chance. He kicked five goals to become one of Carlton's most important recruits.

Wayne Johnston, the 'ultimate' big match player.

He was one of the outstanding players afield in the 1979 Grand Final. *The Herald*'s Alf Brown commented: 'First year player Wayne Johnston ... was irrepressible on a half-forward flank. He showed great pace and anticipation and carried Carlton into attack repeatedly in the muddy conditions.'

Becoming known as 'The Dominator', he played in 10 consecutive finals series. No Carlton player had a bigger influence in the games which mattered most.

Dual premiership coach *David Parkin* said Johnston needed the extra challenge of a big game to perform at his best. 'If it was a non-event game with nothing hanging on it, he was likely to be a poor player,' he said. 'But put him into a big game with a personal opponent he respected and he'd be one of your best players every time. He had an enormous capacity to pump himself up and get the best out of himself when it mattered. He had a fire in his belly, a passion for a contest like very few other players.'

When Parkin left the Blues to coach Fitzroy, Johnston would invariably star in matches against him. Parkin would assign two and sometimes three taggers a game. Few moves worked and when the Fitzroy runner came back to the bench after completing the shifts, he'd invariably have a

message from Johnston to Parkin: 'You'll have to do better than that, Parkin!'

He played only 19 games in his final two seasons with the Blues, suffering severe internal injuries after colliding with Geelong's *Gary Ablett* in the third round of 1989. He wanted to continue with the Blues in 1991, but Carlton felt he had become too injury-prone and didn't want to subject him to any further pain.

JOHNSTONE, Norm (1927–)

A rugged follower and forward known as one of Fitzroy's toughest post-war players, the tank-like Johnstone played in 228 games and kicked 185 goals from 1944–57. He was best and fairest in 1947 and headed Fitzroy's goalkicking in 1955. His drop-kicking was a feature of his game. He represented Victoria in 1948.

JONES, Peter (1946–)

A happy-go-lucky ruckman known for his exuberance on and off the field, 'Percy' Jones played 249 games with Carlton, including four premierships from 1966–79

Peter Jones, one of Carlton's most popular post-war ruckmen.

and was held in such high esteem that he coached the club in 1980.

For many years, he was rucking understudy to legendary *John Nicholls*—and then to West Australian Mike Fitzpatrick.

At 198 cm and 105 kg, he was rarely out-marked once he parked his huge frame in front of the pack. His ruck play improved with regular on-ball responsibility and he became one of the best followers in the competition. In 1973, he was best and fairest in a star-studded team which made the Grand Final, only to be beaten by Richmond. In 1977, he represented Victoria.

JUDKINS, Stan (1907–86)

The likeable 166 cm winger and centre-man known as 'The Tin Hare', Judkins won the 1930 Brownlow Medal with just four (best afield) votes, the lowest tally of any winner in history. He tied with Footscray's *Allan Hopkins* and Collingwood's *Harry Collier* and was awarded the Medal, amid much controversy, as he'd played the least number of matches (just 12) and been left out of the Richmond side for the last month of the home-and-away season. Almost 50 years later, shortly after Judkins' death, Hopkins and Collier were awarded retrospective Medals.

'I remember I was out of work and in bed one morning when my dear old Dad came in with the morning's *Age* and said: "Congratulations son, you've won the Medal!" I said: "What's that?"

' "You've won the Brownlow Medal," he said. In those days we didn't have any razzamatazz. The League wrote me a letter asking me to come in and accept the

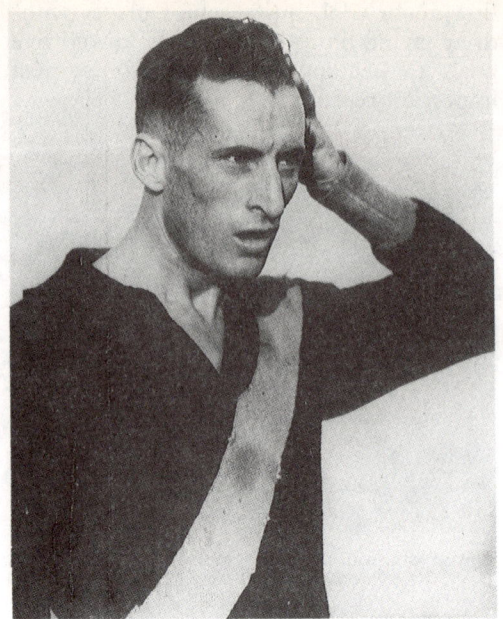

Initially told he was too small for senior football, Richmond's Stan Judkins won the 1930 Brownlow Medal with the lowest number of votes (four) on record.

Medal. I got the train in from Greensborough—which was really the country then—and they gave me a framed certificate and the medal.

'The ceremony was over by 8.30 p.m. and I had to wait until 9.20 p.m. for the next train home. They didn't run as often then.'

His speed and slick ball-handling were his major attributes. He played 133 games from 1928–36 with the Tigers, including two premierships in 1932 and 1934.

His son, Noel, became one of football's most renowned recruiting officers with Essendon in the 1980s and 1990s.

KEANE, Merv (1953–   )

A polished and determined running player from Wycheproof who figured in three Richmond premierships, two as a half-back in 1973–74, Keane played 238 games from 1972–84 and represented Victoria against Queensland in 1980.

His skills were generally underrated, certainly by the umpires who took 11 years before granting him his first votes in the Brownlow Medal.

Later he coached in Adelaide.

KEENAN, Peter (1952–   )

One of the most-travelled and colourful members of the League's '200-club', Peter Patrick Pius Paul Keenan—known universally as 'Crackers'—played 213 games from 1970–82. He started and finished his career at Melbourne, where he played 131 games and kicked 107 goals in eight seasons.

A member of North Melbourne's 1977 premiership team, he also played at Essendon.

Legendary for his on-field humour and antics, he was also a very skilful player, who overcame a lack of speed with his stamina and anticipation. He used to try and intimidate opposing ruckmen—but never Carlton's *John Nicholls*. 'He was too big and he just used to laugh at me anyway!' said Keenan.

Before an opening bounce, he'd ask Carlton's *Peter Jones* if he'd taken his ugly pill, or Collingwood's *Peter Moore* if he had any life insurance.

His nickname came from a schoolboy incident at Assumption College, when he received a free kick after being felled behind play. He deliberately bombed his kick straight into the head of his assailant, who'd made the mistake of standing on the mark. He was flattened. A team-mate told Keenan: 'You're just crackers!'

He made his debut for Melbourne in the opening round of the 1970 season against South Melbourne. In his second game he kicked four goals against Hawthorn, but was suspended after his third—the first of several offences, which cost many matches, including the 1978 Grand Final after he was found guilty of striking Hawthorn's *Don Scott* in the second semi.

'Scott sucked me in on that occasion and I fell for it,' Keenan said. 'Over the years the sight of each other has been like a red rag to a bull and there's never been any love lost between us.'

One of his proudest moments came in his ninth year when he was selected for the *Ron Barassi*-coached Victorian team, in 1978. 'I feel like one of Barassi's chosen apostles,' he said.

Asked to relate his most embarrassing moment in football, Keenan said it was in his early years at Melbourne, when journalist Claudia Wright visited the rooms. 'I saw her coming towards me and tried to pull my jumper down as I had nothing else on. She saw my action and said: "Don't worry—I've seen better on boy scouts." '

KEKOVICH, Sam (1950–   )

The son of a Yugoslav migrant who had represented his country at soccer, 'Slamming Sam' Kekovich was a lead member of North Melbourne's historic 1975 premiership before weight and communication problems saw him cleared to Collingwood.

Kekovich had 124 games with North from 1968–76. After his explosive debut seasons as a ruck-rover, he was dubbed the 'new Barassi' but lacked consistency and was headstrong.

When fit, he could be unstoppable and was best suited to a free, on-the-ball role where he used his natural strength and aggression to advantage.

Originally from Gunbower, near Echuca, Kekovich joined North from Myrtleford as a teenager. At 15, when he first played open-age football, his body was as developed as most of the men. He played alongside his older brother, Brian, who soon afterwards joined Carlton and played in the 1968 Grand Final.

Kekovich, 189 cm and 98 kg, was the youngest winner, at 19, of North's Syd Barker Medal. In one match, against Richmond, that season, he had 25 kicks, eight marks and kicked six goals.

But his weight ballooned and he had trouble dealing with coach *Ron Barassi*'s discipline.

After a younger team-mate *David Dench* was preferred as North's captain in 1972, Kekovich's interest declined and he suffered the first of frequent fines and suspensions. One time he missed training after being stranded in Wagga having attended a race meeting. He also appeared nude in a newspaper centrefold.

Kekovich had four matches at Collingwood in 1977 before playing in Prahran's 1978 premiership side, one of the finest all-time Association teams.

KENNEDY, John jnr (1959–)

A member of Hawthorn's four premierships in the 1980s, 'Roo' Kennedy was a more adaptable player than his famous father—and just as strong and determined. He could well have played more than his 241 games in 13 senior seasons, but for knee and achilles injuries.

In the 1983 Grand Final, he nullified Essendon's highly rated import Rene Kink and in 1984 won Victorian selection.

A popular character and great teamman, Kennedy's resolve to play at the highest level for as long as he could was highlighted in 1988, when he showed great courage to return to the senior team and play in his fifth Grand Final after having to miss the first half of the season with a heart ailment. He'd suffered from dizziness, shortness of breath and an irregular heartbeat.

Late in the season, he played his 200th game, against North Melbourne, then coached by his father. He said in an interview to mark his milestone: 'I was surrounded by it (football) as a child … I've never felt my father was a burden to me. I'm proud and privileged to be a Kennedy—if only I could contribute half as well as he had.'

KENNEDY, John snr (1928–)

Coach of Hawthorn's historic 1961 premiership team and one of the game's most inspirational leaders, 'Kanga' Kennedy's

playing and coaching career spanned two clubs and four decades. A wonderful orator, his pre-game addresses were highly motivational.

After a 30-year association with Hawthorn, including 10 as a player and 14 as coach, he coached North Melbourne for five years, being the VFL's first 60-year-old coach since Collingwood's '*Jock*' *McHale*.

John Kennedy, three premierships in 14 years as Hawthorn's coach.

A fine, competitive ruckman, he won four best and fairests in 164 games, being captain from 1955–59 and a four-time Victorian representative.

Melbourne great *Bob Johnson* said of Kennedy: 'He was the most difficult ruckman to win a kick against. You could never get a run at the ball. He would stand so close you could not make a move at the ball. He would lean on you, stand on your toes. And he was tremendously strong.'

Kennedy was captain-coach of Victoria in the 1957 state game with Tasmania.

Immediately after retiring as a player in

1959, Kennedy was appointed Hawthorn coach. His early teams of the '60s were dubbed 'Kennedy's Commandos'. Their severe pre-season fitness routines at the infamous Bulleen 'torture camp' included players running with huge sand-bags on their backs and clawing their way via ropes from one side of the Yarra River to the other.

His own fitness and stamina levels were truly amazing and, at 47, he registered as a professional runner.

Many admitted to being intimidated by him. He called players by their surnames and some didn't like it. Young star *Leigh Matthews* said he used to have nightmares about Kennedy. '... (But) he was God-like,' said Matthews.

His strength of purpose and character and his humility seemed to rub off on his players which is probably one of the key reasons why people seem to say that Hawthorn players don't generally get too carried away with their performances.

His trademark old brown raincoat and booming voice remain an unforgettable part of Hawthorn's transformation from an easybeat into a genuine power.

Becoming a 'father figure' at Glenferrie Oval, Kennedy was inspiring, innovative and thorough.* His coaching successor at Hawthorn, *David Parkin*, said of him: 'He's the single most special person I've met in my life and a magnificent speaker. He could quote Marx and the Bible and Churchill, roll them into one address that was relevant to the task of playing football.'

In 1985, at Hawthorn's 'Mayblooms to Hawks' dinner, he was asked to compare Hawthorn's first two premiership teams. The 1971 team had a definite edge in skill, he said. 'They had a marvellous record that year and there were some wonderfully gifted individuals in the team. Having said that ... if the two teams ran out onto the field against each other, I don't think the 1971 team would ever have got the ball to use the great skill they possessed! With the 1961 team, fierceness and aggression were developed to almost frightening proportions.'

Innovative and unbending, Kennedy helped launch football into the era of grinding training and fitness schedules.

He believed the lessons to be learnt from the game could be successfully applied in life. 'It takes two minutes to discover a friend on the football field and up to two years in the ordinary world,' he once said.

Perhaps his toughest decision was to omit club captain *Peter Crimmins* from Hawthorn's 1975 Grand Final team.

Crimmins was ill with cancer and hadn't played since round six. However, he had returned for five matches at reserves' level, including a final. Kennedy had a hunch that the Hawks would have been lifted by Crimmins' presence. After an even first three quarters, North ran away with the game in the last term, winning by 55 points.

Hawthorn played in the Grand Final again in 1976, this time defeating North Melbourne for the flag and Kennedy immediately took leave of absence. He was never to return as coach, although he continued to serve the Hawks during the next six years as a committeeman, chairman of selectors and, for two years, as vice-president.

In his eight years in between coaching jobs, Kennedy had many offers from other clubs—Carlton, Melbourne, Collingwood (the team he followed as a child) and St Kilda among them—but they were all rejected.

In November, 1984, when he announced he would coach North Melbourne, he said: 'It's pretty close to the biggest decision I've ever had to make in football. I'm back for the same reason I gave it up—a family reason.'

He showed in 1985 he still had a flair and drive for football, lifting North Melbourne from 11th to fourth. The Roos made the finals again in 1987.

Making way at the end of 1989 for Roo legend *Wayne Schimmelbusch*, he said: 'I'd be lying if I said I was feeling anything other than sadness at not being coach. We all have dreams. You dream of a premiership and being the coach. But that's a little bit sentimental and there's no room for sentiment in football ... I owe a great debt

* see 'STRATEGIES'

to North Melbourne. It's been a great thing for me and my family to be associated with North Melbourne football club.'

After several years as a member of North's board of directors, Kennedy became one of those most responsible for running the game as chairman of the AFL's commission.

KEOGH, Trevor (1949–)

A livewire and skilled rover from Sandhurst who was twice best and fairest at Carlton, Keogh played 208 games from 1970–81. He figured in the 1972 and 1979 premierships.

At 177 cm and 67 kg he was one of the speediest players in the game and helped form Carlton's notable 'mosquito squadron' in the late 1970s.

KERNAHAN, Stephen (1963–)

One of the most-decorated players of them all, the strong-marking Kernahan reached his 200 game AFL milestone at the start of the 1995 season.

While awards such as the Brownlow Medal have eluded him, there have been few finer League imports from South Australia.

A five-time All Australian, the 196 cm Kernahan won three Carlton best and fairests after earlier winning three with Glenelg.

He headed Carlton's goalkicking in each of his first nine AFL seasons and in 1995, captained the Blues for the ninth consecutive year. In his first year as skipper in 1987, Carlton won the premiership. He is the only footballer to captain his team, win the goalkicking, and the best and fairest in the same year.

In 1993, when the Blues lost the Grand Final, Kernahan kicked 7.4.

Few have been as inspirational—or as modest about their achievements.

Like SA team-mate *Craig Bradley*, Kernahan has been a regular State representative, invariably as captain. In 1984, before crossing to Melbourne, he kicked 10 goals in a classic performance for SA against Victoria at Football Park.

He also kicked 10 at club level, against St Kilda at Princes Park in 1989 and against Footscray at the MCG in 1995.

His achievements would have included a Magarey Medal, but for a one-match suspension which made him ineligible.

His father, Harry, was also a leading player at SANFL level, captaining Glenelg for several seasons in the mid-1960s.

KNIGHTS, Peter (1952–)

For a footballer who was afraid of heights, Peter Knights' dare-devil football acrobatics were truly extraordinary. Twice second in the Brownlow Medal, Knights was a great entertainer, one of premiership-specialist Hawthorn's most elite post-war performers.

In 267 games with Hawthorn from 1969–85, the long-kicking blond won the best and fairest, was leading goalkicker, represented Victoria nine times and played in three premierships.

Best afield in the 1976 Grand Final, his athleticism and marking at centre half-back

Hawthorn's acrobatic Peter Knights after receiving his 1983 Grand Final medallion from the Governor of Victoria, Sir Brian Murray.

166

was a matchwinning factor in Hawthorn's five goal win against North Melbourne.

He was judged the VFL Personality of the Year by the Melbourne football writers and if it hadn't been for injury—which sidelined him for seven matches—would almost certainly have won the Brownlow. He polled 45 votes, to finish second behind Essendon's *Graham Moss*, with 48. In his victory speech, Moss said: 'Peter would probably be standing up here instead of me if he hadn't been injured.'

He represented Victoria for the first time in his third season, winning the Simpson Medal for being best afield in the game against Western Australia.

At his best in the most important games, his solo effort at centre half-back in the 1975 Grand Final was one of the few highlights for the Hawks. He produced a brand of football magnificence which touched the hearts of thousands.

The 1975 season was his only uninterrupted year and he won the best and fairest ahead of *Leigh Matthews*, his flair and dash winning him the nickname of 'Peter Perfect'.

'Not only was his football of such a high standard, but so was his personal image,' said Carlton great *Wayne Johnston*. 'He was the clean-living, good-looking all-Australian boy who didn't smoke, rarely drank and enjoyed an impeccable reputation in his personal life.'

His extraordinary leaping continued to be a highlight. 'I don't say to myself, "I'm going to jump on someone's shoulders," ' Knights said. 'I never realise I'm up in the air until I'm coming down.'

He conceded he was terrified of heights: 'Getting up a ladder or a tall building frightens the daylights out of me,' he said. 'Even as a kid I couldn't bear to climb high trees—I'd stick around the lower branches.'

In 1983, he had one of his most satisfying seasons, despite a stress fracture in the lower back which required daily physiotherapy, an hour and half each day, six days a week.

In 1985, the last of 17 seasons, one of his most miraculous efforts came against Carlton in the 10th round. Playing in a forward pocket, he kicked nine goals, a career-best effort.

He became a skills coach at Hawthorn before coaching AFL newcomer, Brisbane, in its opening three seasons. He was dramatically replaced late in 1989 by Paul Feltham.

Later he coached Devonport, before becoming Hawthorn's fulltime senior coach, in 1994.

KYNE, 'Phonse' (1915–85)

Centre half-forward in Collingwood's back-to-back premierships in 1935–36, Alponsus Edward Kyne played 245 games and coached 271 games in a 30-year Victoria Park association. He became one of the Magpies' greatest coaches, being in charge of the 1953 and 1958 premiership sides.

In his 13 full seasons as coach, Collingwood contested the finals eight times, making the Grand Final on six occasions. He won 60 per cent of his matches as coach and hated to lose. 'If we got beat, I used to stamp on the (Saturday night) *Sporting Globe*,' he remembered.

In an inspirational speech before the 1958 Grand Final—in which Collingwood's opponent Melbourne was going for a fourth consecutive premiership to equal Collingwood's record—he told his players to 'bleed' for the club.

He told them, as coach, he would be out there with the team in spirit. So would all Collingwood's past players, particularly those from the golden era of the late 1920s, whose record was in jeopardy.

'They'll be feeling every bump, every mark and every kick with you,' he said. 'There will be times when you are exhausted, when you can hardly breathe.

'That is when I want you to go harder, as hard and harder than any other Collingwood player before you. If Melbourne win today, they equal our record; don't let them get away with it.'

Collingwood historian Richard Stremski said when Kyne finished his speech, the players 'felt invincible'.

'They were ready to kill for Collingwood.'

Kyne's key strategic move was the inclusion of Barry 'Hooker' Harrison as a shadow for Demon champion *Ron Barassi*. Instructed to stay with Barassi all day no matter what, Harrison obliged, but Melbourne charged to an early lead.

Acting captain Murray Weideman went to Harrison at quarter time and said: 'Let's see who we can collect.'

Barassi was whacked above the eye where full-back Harry Sullivan had already opened a wound. He and other Melbourne players retaliated, lost concentration and Collingwood reversed a three-goal quarter-time deficit to lead by two points.

At half time the great Melbourne coach *Norm Smith* begged every Melbourne player to once again concentrate only on the ball, but after *Ian Ridley* had his nose broken, the head-hunting resumed. Collingwood went on to win a memorable game, a result many termed 'the upset of the century'. It was Kyne's finest hour.

Recruited from Old Paradians and rejected by Melbourne, his 'first-choice' club, the 188 cm forward/follower played eight games for Victoria. In 1960, he was State coach.

LAIDLAW, Clyde (1933–)

Until the domination of Hawthorn's *Dermott Brereton* in the 1980s and early 1990s, no post-war centre half-forward had ever figured in four premierships, as Portland's 184 cm Clyde Laidlaw did from 1955–60 during his 124 game career which spanned a total of nine seasons. In 1957, when business commitments restricted him to just six games, a thigh injury sidelined him from the final series.

LANGFORD, Chris (1963–)

The pain of being left out of a Grand Final helped re-launch Chris Langford's career, and in 1991, the superbly built defender figured in his fourth Hawthorn premiership team, as well as representing Victoria at full-back against South Australia and Western Australia.

Twenty-one-year-old Langford was bitterly disappointed to miss selection in Hawthorn's 1984 Grand Final 20. 'You can't go much lower than that,' he said. 'I resented myself rather than anyone else. I brought the situation on myself and I don't want to go through that again.'

Langford had played virtually every game in 1984, including the early finals, before his omission. He dedicated himself to a new level of consistency and early in 1992 joined the League's illustrious '200-club', captaining the side in the absence of injured pair *Gary Ayres* and *Dermott Brereton*.

An All Australian player in 1987, he has twice won the E. J. Whitten Medal for being best afield at State level. In 1994, he captained Hawthorn before standing down with work commitments which took him interstate.

LAW, John (1959–)

A dependable, big-hearted clubman denied the opportunity of playing in a Grand Final or representing Victoria in a 12-year career, Law played 219 games from 1978–89. He captained North Melbourne in his final two and a half seasons.

Recruited from Strathbogie, the 185 cm half-back was renowned for his courage, consistency and durability.

LEE, Mark (1959–)

A decorated, formidable ruckman who helped lift Richmond to the 1980 premiership as a 21-year-old, the 199 cm Lee had 15 years at Tigerland, playing 233 games from 1977–91. Elected an All Australian three times, he played six State matches, was best and fairest in 1984 and captained the club from 1985–87.

While not overly strong in the air, his aggressive ruckplay at centre bounces intimidated many opponents.

He later played with Tasmanian team Burnie with success.

LEE, Walter 'Dick' (1889–1968)

The first of the great VFL full-forwards, Walter Henry 'Dick' Lee was so loved by Collingwood that he was made captain in 1920–21, a rare distinction for a goalkicker.

He was a dashing, colourful and courageous player, who scored many of his goals through the place kick.

Known as football's great stuntman, he was such an accurate kick that amusement

One of football's most famous early photographs, Collingwood's Dick Lee marking against Carlton at Victoria Park in 1914.

parks banned him from competing in straight-kicking competitions, saying he'd send them broke!

Sporting his famous No. 13 guernsey throughout most of his 16-year, 230-match career (from 1906–22) he kicked 707 goals, at an average of 3.06 goals a game. With scoring rates having doubled, his average would be worth five or six goals, making his feats comparable to the greatest modern-day goalkickers such as *Hudson*, *Dunstall* and *Lockett*.

Just 175 cm, he played in three Collingwood premierships (1910–17–19), was judged 'Champion of the Colony' twice (1910, 1915) and represented Victoria in four carnivals (1908, 1911, 1914, 1921). He headed the VFL goalkicking a record 10 times—eight times being outright first—and was regarded as the greatest Collingwood player of the era spanning World War One.

His record would have been even more impressive but for injury. After playing only one game in 1912, he underwent the first successful cartilage operation on an Australian footballer. Lee also served Collingwood loyally off the field, serving 16 years as Collingwood vice-president. His father, Wal, a former playing member of the Britannia club in the 1880s, was Collingwood's head trainer for more than 40 years.

Writing in the *Sporting Globe* in the 1940s, Richmond's *Vic Thorp*, one of the greatest early full-backs, said of Lee: 'He was more than just a good footballer. He was above everything else a really quick thinker. An opponent had to be on the watch not only for his dazzling leads but for the dozen and one tricks he was likely to spring . . . as a footballer he was just outstanding—he might have played anywhere on the field, for his anticipation and sense of the game was uncanny.

'He was an amazing mark. It did not seem to matter how he was herded off a mark, let him get a spring at the ball and he'd get his hands on it. He also had a trick of flying high into the air as if miles too early for marks. But he would stiffen himself and hang there as if suspended and down he'd bring the ball.'

LEEK, Geoff (1932–)

After failing to make the list at Collingwood, Leek became one of Essendon's finest post-war ruckmen. In 12 years, the 193 cm prematurely balding follower amassed 190 games and was vice-captain for six years. He played in three Grand Finals, including the 1962 premiership.

LEVER, Harry

Captain and full-back in St Kilda's first Grand Final side in 1913, Lever played 217 games from 1905–22. He also represented Victoria and was one of the last players to wear a cap during matches.

LIBBIS, Billy (1903–86)

One of 11 Collingwood players to figure in all four of the club's consecutive premierships from 1927–30, William Edward 'Pickles' Libbis roved in 138 games from 1925–33, before crossing to Melbourne after refusing a 10 shilling pay cut. He played 37 games in three years with his adopted club, before serving Northcote usefully.

Best afield in the 1929 Grand Final, Libbis was recruited from Fairfield and developed so quickly under *Jock McHale* that he was his team's first-choice rover ahead of the great *Harry Collier*, in his club's glory reign.

Team-mate *Gordon Coventry* rated him the most dashing rover he saw in his illustrious League career.

At 173 cm and 70.5 kg, he was not a robust player but his play was strong and determined, his understanding with ruckman *Syd Coventry* a feature. He represented Victoria seven times.

LIBERATORE, Tony (1966–)

One of the smallest players to win the Brownlow Medal, Liberatore's one vote triumph in 1990 was one of the most popular wins in modern times.

He defeated Collingwood's Graham Wright by one vote and Carlton's Stephen Silvagni by two, completing a unique

170

treble, having previously won the reserves' Gardiner Medal (twice) and the Morrish Medal (best and fairest in the under 19s).

The 164 cm 'Libba' had played only 18 senior games in his first four senior years. Coach *Mick Malthouse* believed he was too small and didn't kick the ball long enough to be of value.

But when Malthouse went to Perth, his successor Terry Wheeler gave the hard-working Liberatore the opportunity he needed and he immediately became a front-liner.

LIGHT BRIGADE, The

One of the most successful and best-known 'midget' footballers was Kevin Coghlan, who played more than 90 games with Collingwood and Hawthorn from 1949–56. Nicknamed 'Skeeter', he had exceptional goal sense.

At 55 kg, he was post-war football's lightest player.

The lightest player in League history is Essendon's 'Tich' Shorten, who was just 47.2 kg when he played in the mid-1920s.

Former Melbourne and St Kilda rover Paul Callery was also tiny at 163 cm and 67 kg. As a youngster he'd swing from the rafters in his garage to help stretch his body, but always remained at a jockey's height.

LOCKETT, Tony (1966–)

One of the most talented and controversial footballers of the modern age, Anthony Howard 'Plugger' Lockett's shift to Sydney for the start of the 1995 season stunned St Kilda fans, who regarded the goalkicking colossus as integral to the club's planned 1995 revival.

A three-year contract, reputed to be worth a record $1.6 million, was negotiated, Lockett telling his friends that it was simply too big an offer to ignore. Five clubs had made offers, St Kilda being hamstrung in the bidding by its own financial problems.

Despite a run of injuries and suspension which restricted his appearances to only two in every three games, Lockett's goalkicking record at St Kilda was enormous—898 goals in 183 games at just fractionally below five a game.

After kicking a club record 117 goals in 1987 and becoming the first full-forward to win the Brownlow Medal, Lockett's next six seasons were severely interrupted by either injury or suspension.

In 1991, he won the John Coleman Medal, despite missing the first third of the season because of a badly bruised back. In 16 home-and-away games, he averaged more than seven goals a game, and for the year topped 120 goals, including 13 against Carlton in round 21.

LIGHTEST LEAGUE PLAYERS

WEIGHT (kg)	PLAYER	CLUBS/SPAN	GAMES
47.2	George 'Tich' Shorten	Essendon 1923–26	53
52.2	James 'Nipper' Bradford	Collingwood 1943/North 1949	16
54	Jack Carney	Geelong 1930–34/Carl. 1936–41	163
54	Charlie Hardy	Essendon 1921–25	36
55	Kevin 'Skeeter' Coghlan	Collingwood 1949–52/Hawthorn 1953–56	90
60	Bruce McMaster-Smith	Fitzroy 1960–61/Carl. 1962–64/St K. 1965	54
61	Rowland Watt	Essendon 1922–31	140
65	Barcley Bailes	Fitzroy 1905–09	79
66	Danny Craven	St Kilda 1989–92/Brisb. 1993–94	53*
66	Matthew Lappin	St Kilda 1994	9*

* current player.

Tony Lockett's brilliant marking and goalkicking deeds threaten the records of the game's most renowned goalsharps.

In consecutive comeback matches from round seven to round nine, he kicked 12, 10 and 12 goals; 34 in three weeks, equalling one of legendary *Bob Pratt*'s longstanding records. In the first of these comebacks, against the Adelaide Crows at Moorabbin, he kicked nine goals in the opening hour and had a 10th before half time, but it was disallowed.

In 1992, he kicked 132 goals, a new personal high, including 15 against Sydney and 12 against Brisbane, his popularity reaching a new high.

Taller and heavier than all the other champion full-forwards, he was recruited from North Ballarat in 1983, soon after his 17th birthday. His coach, Tony Jewell, had him in defence for a brief period before he took over at full-forward.

His enormous potential was confirmed in the opening match of the 1984 season when he kicked seven goals against Essendon.

He tallied 77 for the year, St Kilda's next best goalkicker being rover Silvio Foschini with just 27.

In mid-career, Lockett increased his

bulk and already-considerable physical power.

His weight ballooned past 110 kg and he suffered several crucial leg injuries which cruelly denied him further opportunities to kick the ton. However, when he did play, he was awesome. In 1989, he kicked 70 goals in the first nine games, including 12 against West Coast Eagles, only to be suspended for a month for striking Eagle Guy McKenna.

His quick leading, sticky-fingered marking and pinpoint drop punts resulted in him heading St Kilda goalkicking in eight of his first nine seasons. *Peter Hudson* commented: 'Tony's capable of doing anything and he's only going to get better.'

In 1994, when Lockett kicked 11 goals against Sydney in round 7, he became the first League full-forward to kick double figure tallies in 15 matches. His last three goals came in the final three minutes, including the matchwinner after the siren. In the most spectacular finishing burst in League history, St Kilda won the match by a point, having trailed by 48 points, seven minutes into the final quarter. The Saints kicked seven goals to nil in the final 12 minutes.

However, in a controversial aftermath, Lockett was suspended for eight weeks after being found guilty of striking Sydney's Peter Caven during the game. It was the heftiest penalty of his career, bringing his total suspensions to 21 in 12 years with the Saints.

Lockett's father, Howard, played more than 500 games of country football.

See: 'HEAVYWEIGHTS'

LOEWE, Stewart (1968–   )

A big-marking forward who regularly took more marks than anybody else in the AFL in the early 1990s, Loewe replaced *Tony Lockett* as St Kilda's full-forward from the 1995 season.

A St Kilda best and fairest, two-time All Australian and regular State representative, the 195 cm Loewe combined superb fitness with his aerial strength.

Originally from Mt Eliza, he was tied to

Hawthorn as a schoolboy, but the Hawks relinquished their hold and he was a star with St Kilda virtually from his first season, as a teenager in 1986.

LONGEST KICKS

Termed 'boomers' or 'ball-bursters', the most prodigious kicks in modern football remain mainly unmeasured. Despite advances in fitness and equipment, today's players, while generally more precise and versatile with their kicks, do not roost the ball any greater distances than their predecessors.

One of the biggest recent kicks was by 24-year-old St Kilda ruckman Jeff Fehring against Collingwood on 11 April, 1981. Winning a free kick behind the centre circle at Moorabbin, his booming spiral punt, assisted by a slight breeze, bounced two metres inside the goal before bouncing through for a goal. It travelled 86 metres (94 yards), before bouncing.

The kick was described as 'freakish' and was only the fourth goal of his career, but Fehring insisted his shot was deliberate and that he had been practising his torpedoes at training.

On Easter Monday, 1983, Richmond's *Jim Jess* spiralled the ball from the goal-square past the centre of the Melbourne Cricket Ground. Observers believed it flew more than 80 metres.

Bernie Quinlan regularly punted the ball 70 metres, and was known in his years at Fitzroy as 'Superboot'. With his first club Footscray, he drop-kicked the ball 77.72 metres (85 yards) in 1966.

Quinlan was one of the last players to consistently drop-kick the ball huge distances. Now players are forbidden to practise drop kicks even in the warm-ups at training. Coaches say the kick is too inconsistent. Quinlan says lower-cut boots and softer toes make big kicks more difficult. The key to kicking large distances consistently, he says, is in the timing, not in the power.

Geelong's Bill Brownless once kicked a ball straight up over a 50 metre silo in country NSW with his bare feet to win a side bet, a free round of drinks.

North Melbourne pair *Ross Glendinning* and *Malcolm Blight* were also big kicks. Blight was famous for his after-the-siren goal against Carlton in 1976 which travelled 70 metres.

Footscray great *Ted Whitten* is said to have drop-kicked the ball 82.3 metres (90 yards) against Melbourne at the Western Oval in 1958.

West Australian Darren Bennett, who played League football with West Coast and Melbourne, was so renowned for his punt kicking that he went to America and was a reserve when the San Diego Chargers made the 1994 American NFL Superbowl.

The very longest kicks the game have seen were Essendon's *Albert Thurgood* and St Kilda's 193 cm left-footer Dave McNamara, who both were spectacular place kicks. Essendon's field-kicking champion Thurgood had a dozen kicks of 75-plus metres recorded. In 1899, he place-kicked the ball 98.48 metres (107 yards, two feet and one inch). In 1893 he drop-kicked the ball 82.3 metres and the following year punted it 80.47 metres.

Dave McNamara is said to have place-kicked the ball 96.52 metres (105 yards, one foot) with a slight following wind at the St Kilda Cricket Ground in July 1914, a record which is disputed, however, by St Kilda's historian Russell Holmesby, who says McNamara's best was 97 yards. Recruited from Benalla, he represented Victoria in the 1908 and 1914 carnivals, having his last game at St Kilda, aged 36. He captained the Saints in 1908, before turning 21. He was judged the player of the carnival in the inaugural championships in 1908.

A member of Essendon's VFA premierships in 1911–12, he kicked 107 goals in 1912, the first player in Australian football to kick 100 goals in a season.

In 122 senior games, he kicked 622 goals, his field-kicking the cornerstone of his game.

LONGMIRE, John (1970–)

At 19, Longmire won the John Coleman medal for topping the League goalkicking.

But for a bad case of the jitters in the final home-and-away match of the year against Collingwood, when he kicked 2.8, Longmire would have been the first teenager since *John Coleman* to kick 100 goals in a season. He finished with 98.

Despite a knee reconstruction which sidelined him from the 1993 final series, Longmire again headed North's goalkicking in 1994, for the fifth year in a row, equalling *John Dugdale*'s post-war club record.

Recruited from Balldale in NSW, Longmire kicked 82 goals as a 16-year-old with Corowa–Rutherglen before coming to North Melbourne. He had previously been tied to South Melbourne but was cleared, sight unseen, for $15,000.

In 1990, when he won the best and fairest, he created a new club goalkicking record when he booted 14 goals against Melbourne, lifting North to a mammoth 31.14 (200). Earlier in the year, against Richmond, he kicked 12 as North reached a club record of 32.17 (209). Representing NSW against Victoria in the State-of-Origin match, he kicked eight in wet conditions as NSW clinched its first win against the Big V in 55 years.

LORD, Alistair (1940–)

A runaway winner of the 1962 Brownlow Medal with 28 votes, one of the highest tallies recorded, the handsome centreman—recruited, with his identical twin brother, Stewart, from Cobden in 1959—had a dream year, averaging 30 kicks a game and helping Geclong into the '62 preliminary final.

There was a sensation early in the season after boundary umpire L. J. Sullivan reported Alistair on a charge of striking in a game against Richmond. Geelong claimed Sullivan had mistaken Alistair (No. 4) for Stewart (No. 6). The case was abandoned. The tribunal's acting chairman Tom Hammond said it would help if one of the twins grew a moustache to assist in identification!

Some cynics claimed Alistair had mistakenly been given some of his brother's votes, but he won by such a huge margin

that it didn't matter anyway!

The 180 cm Lord had initially played as a forward flanker, making his debut against Richmond in round three, 1959. Stewart was first selected for the opening round of 1960.

Playing his best football as a free-running centreman, who often became a seventh forward, Lord kicked 89 goals in his 122-match career. He also represented Victoria five times in 1962–63, joining Stewart in the 1963 premiership team.

LORD, John jnr (1937–)

A big-hearted, prematurely balding follower/forward, Lord played in four Melbourne premierships from 1957–64 in his 132 match, 80 goal, nine year career. Recruited from Echuca in 1957, the 188 cm ruckman retired at the end of the 1965 season. His father, John snr, also played League football, at Melbourne and St Kilda.

LUKE, Sir Kenneth (1898–1971)

One of football's most influential administrators, his foresight and enthusiasm was instrumental in the building of Waverley Park, which many believed should have been named in his honour.

Founder of the provident fund and a fervent believer in the Coulter Law as being the saviour of the less affluent clubs, Luke was a distinguished and much-decorated man who possessed the 'common

Influential administrator Sir Kenneth Luke (centre) is flanked by Sir Henry Winneke (left) and Sir Rohan Delacombe (right) at the 1967 Grand Final.

174

touch'. He was one of the prime movers in Melbourne winning the right to stage the 1956 Olympics.

Ken Luke started work as a 14-year-old on wages of two shillings and sixpence a week. President of the VFL from 1956–71, he was also president at Carlton for nearly 20 years.

LYON, Garry (1967–   )

A graceful, versatile forward with superb kicking skills, 192 cm Lyon replaced Greg Healy as Melbourne's captain in 1991 and, after initial injury problems, won All Australian selection in 1993 and 1994.

Replacing the injured Allen Jakovich at full-forward, Lyon kicked 79 goals in 1994, including 10 in the first semi-final against Footscray. He also captained Victoria for the first time.

Originally from Kyabram, Lyon was Melbourne's best and fairest in 1990 and 1994. He also played in Melbourne's Foster's Cup pre-season victories in 1987 and 1989.

His father, Peter, played two senior seasons with Hawthorn in 1963–64, including the 1963 Grand Final.

Garry Lyon: 10 goals in a final.

MACLURE, Mark (1955–)

One of the best-performed footballers to be recruited from the Sydney metropolitan area, Perth-born Maclure was centre half-forward in three Carlton premierships, before retiring after the 1986 (losing) Grand Final, having played 243 games in 13 seasons.

A reliable kick at goal, he headed Carlton's goalkicking, in 1977—one of only two times in his career the Blues failed to make the finals.

Captain in his final year, he represented Victoria three times. He fought back from a serious back injury in 1983 to continue to give Carlton sterling service.

Mark Maclure fought back from a serious back injury to be a consistent performer at centre half-forward for Carlton. He's pictured marking against Melbourne at the MCG in the early 1980s.

MADDEN, Justin (1961–)

Younger than his much-decorated brother, *Simon*, 207 cm Justin Madden is one of the tallest men ever to play League football. At the start of the 1995 season, he was within range of 300 games, the majority at Carlton where he'd spent all

but three of his 15 senior seasons.

He'd left Essendon before the start of the 1983 season, having played 45 matches as well as representing Victoria. He disputed his ranking of No. 13 among Essendon's senior-list players. Citing 'considerable personal difficulty' with coach *Kevin Sheedy*, he said he'd have a better chance of becoming a regular No. 1 ruckman elsewhere.

After his initial nervous beginnings, Justin was rucking regularly ahead of his brother at Windy Hill before his shift, where he immediately became an understudy again, this time to Carlton skipper Mike Fitzpatrick.

On Fitzpatrick's retirement, Madden's career blossomed. He finished second to *Brad Hardie* in the 1985 Brownlow Medal count and won Carlton's best and fairest in the same year. He also won in 1991.

A member of Carlton's 1987 premiership team, he played in another Grand Final, in 1993.

Up until the start of the 1995 season, no set of brothers had played more senior games than the Maddens' proud aggregate of 664.

MADDEN, Simon (1957–)

Retiring at the end of the 1992 season after 378 games and a record 575 goals, the decorated Essendon follower's feats rival those of the game's very best big men. A four-time best and fairest, two-time leading goalkicker, dual premiership ruckman and successful captain of Victoria, Madden's loyalty to Essendon was rivalled only by his enduring popularity.

In 1985, he won the Norm Smith Medal for being best player afield in the Grand Final. In 1989 he surpassed *Dick Reynolds'* long-standing club record of 320 games and in 1991, broke legendary goalkicker *John Coleman's* mark of 537 goals.

In 1974, in his fourth game, against North Melbourne, the athletic schoolboy with the shoulder-length hair kicked six goals.

After winning Essendon's best and fairest twice in three years, the 22-year-old with the extraordinary leap and marking

Decorated Essendon and Victorian follower Simon Madden after a State match in WA.

prowess was appointed Essendon captain, leading the Bombers in 1980 and 1981.

In April 1982, the year he forfeited the leadership to Neale Daniher, Madden spent time in the reserves and on arriving just 35 minutes before the game start, was relegated to the interchange bench. A week later, he was elevated to the acting captaincy of the Bombers in a night football match. Casting aside his personal disappointments, he vowed to resurrect his career.

Madden's effort in the 1985 Grand Final was extraordinary. He controlled the air like a colossus, taking 14 marks and having 12 kicks and 10 handballs. Essendon blitzed Hawthorn, prompting veteran Hawk captain *Leigh Matthews* to declare the Bombers the best team of all time. From the mid-1980s, Madden was regarded as the most devastating centre bounce ruckman in the competition. He developed different angles, learning to ward the opposing ruckman off with his right arm while hitting the ball with his left.

In the summer of 1985–86, the 198 cm follower had been offered more money than any footballer before him—$500,000-plus to cross to the privately-owned Sydney Swans. Most saw it as a too-good-to-refuse offer, except for Madden, who declared: 'You can take the boy out of Essendon, but you can't take Essendon out of the boy.' Instead he signed an agreement tying him to the Bombers for five years.

He played his 19th State match, when captaining Victoria against Western Australia in Perth in 1991.

A back injury restricted him to just seven senior games in 1992. He and close friend *Terry Daniher* played their last games together in the final home-and-away round of 1992.

MAGEE, Stuart (1943–)

A determined centreman who played 94 games at South Melbourne, and 122 at Footscray, Magee represented Victoria twice and was captain of Footscray in 1970 after the great *Ted Whitten's* mid-season retirement.

Born in Ireland and recruited to League ranks via Altona, he played 216 games from 1962–75.

He later coached in Perth.

MAKEHAM, Bob (c. 1901–1974)

Centre half-forward in Collingwoods' 1927 premiership team and best afield in the 1930 success, Makeham played in the club's four consecutive premierships from 1927–30, amassing 157 games from 1923–32.

MALTHOUSE, Mick (1953–)

Tasted his finest moments in football in 1992 as coach of the West Coast Eagles when the West Australian-based AFL team became the first from interstate to win the premiership.

After near misses in his first two seasons as coach, and an unsteady start in 1992, Malthouse's professionalism and preparation was paramount in his team's comfortable Grand Final victory, against Geelong.

On the siren, delighted members of his team raced 100 metres across the ground to embrace Malthouse, who was in tears at the culmination of his dream.

In 1994, the Eagles triumphed again, giving Malthouse, a 200-game coach, his second flag in three years.

As a no-nonsense defender for St Kilda and Richmond, he played 53 games in five years with the Saints from 1972–76 and 121 in eight seasons with Richmond from 1976–83, having been told by St Kilda coach *Allan Jeans* that he'd struggle for a senior game had he remained at Moorabbin.

He was a member of Richmond's 1980 premiership team, being renowned for his aggression at the centre bounces.

Joining Footscray as senior coach in 1984, he lifted the Bulldogs into the preliminary final in 1985 and won more games than he lost in 135 matches before becoming the first non-West Australian to coach the Eagles, from 1990.

An intense and sometimes fiery coach, he worked hard to develop the defensive side of the Eagles' play, constantly reminding his players of the 'one per centers'— the little things—which can mean the difference between winning and losing.

MARTELLO, Alan (1952–)

An athletic centre half-forward whose thumping torpedo punt kicks often travelled 70–75 metres, Martello spent 11 seasons and 224 games at Hawthorn before finishing at Richmond where he had 32 games in two and a half years. Knee injuries finished his career, but not before he'd played in five Grand Finals, four at Hawthorn and one, at full-back, for Richmond.

The youngest player, at 25 years eight months, to play 200 games, a milestone he reached in 1978, Martello was also centre of another 'first'—in 1978 he was suspended for one match after not playing for Victoria in an end-of-season State-of-Origin game in Perth.

MATTHEWS, Herbie (1913–90)

Tied with Collingwood's *Des Fothergill* for the 1940 Brownlow Medal, polling not only the same votes in the same number of games, but in an identical 3-2-1 split. Both Matthews and Fothergill received a replica of the Medal. The VFL retained the original.

Recruited from Fairfield in 1932, Matthews, immediately made an impression with his eagerness to 'play-on'. While most players stopped after a mark for a free kick, he'd race off, using his pace and evasion skills to full advantage. Sturdily built and a good mark, his initial games were as a winger. Later he played centre, his stab-passing a delight.

He retired after the 1945 season, being upset by a 'guilty' verdict (he was severely reprimanded) received after the infamous 'Bloodbath' Grand Final between South and Carlton. He'd been reported on a charge of throwing the ball away after a free kick had gone against him. He'd captained the side for eight seasons, a record later broken by another champion small man, *Bob Skilton*.

After stints at Oakleigh and Ringwood, he returned to South Melbourne as non-playing coach from 1954–57. In all, he played 188 games with South and represented Victoria on six occasions.

MATTHEWS, Leigh (1952–)

Few players in the history of football have achieved as much as the powerhouse Hawthorn rover, who ranks with Footscray's *Ted Whitten* as post-war football's most formidable figure.

When he retired after the 1985 Grand Final, he'd played 332 club games; won Hawthorn's best and fairest eight times; kicked 915 goals, a record for a rover; been involved in four premierships—his last as captain—and represented Victoria on 14 occasions.

Captain of the Hawks for five years, an All Australian in 1972 and State skipper in 1980, he polled 202 Brownlow votes, his best finishes being third in 1973 and equal third in 1983.

Leigh Matthews addresses Collingwood pair Nathan Buckley (left) and Paul Williams, during the 1994 season.

His astonishing ball-handling skills, disposal, strength and toughness made him an outstanding player in a champion team. His aggression often displeased umpires— he conceded later he often stretched the rules to the absolute limit—but he was revered at Hawthorn and insiders hope he'll one day return to Glenferrie, as senior coach.

At his best, Matthews was a human cannonball, steaming fearlessly into packs and knocking over anything in his way. He was ruthless and, with his chunky frame and treetrunk legs, was responsible for flattening dozens of opposing players.

He intimidated many of his opponents. 'If someone knocked me down I was very happy to get up and look at them as if to say: "You're not going to hurt me." When I was young, I really didn't feel I could be hurt.'

In his second State match, in Perth, in 1971, he cannoned into WA's roving star *Barry Cable*, who had to be helped from the field. It was the first of many aggressive incidents involving Matthews, which scarred his career.

During the last of his 17 League seasons in 1985, he was deregistered for four weeks after Geelong's *Neville Bruns* had his jaw broken in a behind-the-play incident. He was also convicted for assault. He success-

fully appealed and was placed on a 12-month good behaviour bond.

Recruited from Chelsea on Melbourne's Mornington Peninsula, he joined the Hawks in 1969.

Seeing him split packs as a 17-year-old in a reserves game against Essendon, champion team-mate *Peter Hudson* nicknamed him 'Barney' after Barney Rubble in 'The Flintstones'.

The more notorious nickname of 'Lethal Leigh' was invented by *Lou Richards*.

Coach *John Kennedy* knew Matthews had extraordinary talent and a capacity to work. Under his stern tutelage, Matthews first represented Victoria as a 19-year-old, in 1971—the year Hawthorn won its second premiership.

So hard did Kennedy work him that Matthews admitted he used to have nightmares about the great coach. 'You held him in awe,' Matthews said. 'He was great for young players because he always made sure you kept your head on your shoulders . . . (But) he really got to me for a couple of years.'

Matthews shared the champion's quality of performing in big matches. The tougher the situation the better he seemed to play. Possessing the ability to outmark the tallest players afield, he was rarely beaten in the ground-level duels. In the 1978 Grand Final—the year before the Norm Smith Medal was introduced—he was clearly best afield, having 24 kicks, four handpasses and booting four goals.

A deadly kick, he could weave, spin and baulk and find enough space to have a snap shot at goal, even when he appeared hopelessly surrounded.

In 1975, he headed the League goalkicking with 68 goals and topped Hawthorn's goalscoring charts on six occasions, his best return in a season being 91, in 1977.

He twice kicked 11 goals in a game, against Essendon in 1973—when he played his greatest match, having 42 possessions—and against Melbourne in 1981.

Hawthorn recognised his worth in the summer of '79, after he'd won his sixth best and fairest, by agreeing to increase his salary to $40,000 a year, an unprecedented amount—and almost double the next-best-paid Hawk, skipper *Don Scott*.

In 1986, he was offered $680,000—plus bonuses—for five years to coach Sydney. He agreed, in principle, providing the first year salary of $100,000 was paid in advance. He never heard back from the northern club. Days later, *Tom Hafey* was appointed coach and Matthews went to Collingwood, first as assistant to *Bob Rose*, before taking over as senior coach after three games of the 1986 season.

After lifting the Magpies into the five in 1988–89, Collingwood won the 1990 flag, its first for 32 years. Matthews' Midas touch was working again. He was appointed for a further five years after the 1992 season.

In 1994, his ninth season, he passed 200 games as a League coach.

Matthews' brother, Kelvin, played 156 games and kicked 169 goals in 11 years of League football from 1972–83. He had six years at Hawthorn and five at Geelong, representing Victoria (alongside his brother) in 1974.

McCANN, Steve (1958–)

Made a 'Boy's Own Annual' entry into League ranks, playing in three Grand Finals in his first two years and amassing 226 games in 12 seasons with North Melbourne from 1977–88. A member of four State teams—his first at 22—he was recruited from St Pat's College, Geraldton, as an untried 16-year-old.

He was best-known for his athleticism and marking ability at centre half-forward, but could also successfully play in defence. He was named an All Australian in 1983.

McCONVILLE, Peter (1958–)

Extremely versatile and a fine overhead mark for his size, McConville played in three premierships in his first five years at Carlton and, in a 12-year League career which finished prematurely because of injury at St Kilda, amassed 194 games.

He represented Victoria in 1983.

McCORMACK, Basil (1904–73)

Half-back flank in six Richmond Grand Finals, including two premierships in 1932 and 1934 after being recruited from Rochester in 1925, the 180 cm McCormack played 199 games in 12 seasons with the Tigers.

McGREGOR, Rod (1882–1962)

One of the finest pivots in the early years of VFL football, 'Wee' McGregor—so-named because of his light build—played in four premierships with Carlton and missed a fifth, in 1907, because of injury. Amassing 236 games from 1905–20, he also represented Victoria three times.

Part of the first great centreline in League history—in combination with wingers George Bruce and Ted Kennedy—he was Carlton vice-captain in 1916–17 and club captain in 1918.

A tireless performer, he was awarded a

Rod McGregor formed one of the finest early centrelines with fellow Carlton players George Bruce and Ted Kennedy.

special prize in 1919 for not missing a single training session.

McGUINNESS, Tony (1964–)

One of the premier rovers in the early years of the AFL, McGuinness was on the verge of 200 club games at the start of the 1995 season, his 10th in League ranks.

Originally from Glenelg, where he won the Magarey Medal (in 1982), McGuinness played 109 games in six seasons with Footscray, winning the best and fairest in 1987, before returning to South Australia to represent the Adelaide Crows.

Tony McGuinness: a great in two States.

Superbly fit and with tremendous pace, McGuinness finished in the top two places in the Crows' best and fairest in each of his first three seasons. He won the award in the club's inaugural year and was captain in 1995.

He also continued to represent SA at State of Origin level with distinction.

McHALE, James 'Jock' (1882–1953)

One of the game's finest and most durable coaches, James Francis 'Jock' McHale's uninterrupted reign from 1913–50 is unequalled in League football annals. He coached Collingwood to eight flags, as well as playing in another.

His 16 year/261 game playing span at Collingwood included a club record of 191 consecutive games which still stands today; only Richmond's *Jack Titus* (202) played more games in a row.

Born at Botany Bay, McHale played schoolboy football with Christian Brothers, East Melbourne, having moved to Melbourne with his parents at the age of five. As a junior, he represented Coburg for three seasons from 1900–02.

Late in 1902, he unsuccessfully sought a trial at Collingwood, the team he followed. However, returning to Victoria Park the following year, he was accepted and played in a premiership, the first of three as a player over a 17-year period. For 11 years, he was playing coach, his powerful, well-disciplined teams becoming known as 'The Machine'.

In his 38 years as coach, McHale lifted the Magpies into the finals on 25 occasions. His most glittering achievement was when the Magpies won a record for premierships on end from 1927–30.

McHale's tenacity and anticipation as a centreman and in defence contributed to many Magpie victories. He also represented Victoria three times. At 180 cm and 78 kg, he was tireless and a great leader, captaining Collingwood in 1912–13 and again for part of 1917.

As coach, he ruled with an iron hand, demanding his Collingwood teams play with ferocity and feeling. For much of his career he coached for £3 a match—the same figure as the players were receiving.

While not renowned as a great 'teaching' coach in the mould of the finest modern-day leaders, McHale fearlessly moved players around, especially if they were being beaten in their usual spots.

Another of McHale's great strengths was his uncanny ability to know when players were fit. He was a great believer in fitness

181

Jock McHale coaches Collingwood against arch rival Carlton during the 1947 season. Syd Coventry (left) and Bob Rush look on.

rowly to Fitzroy, a young *Jack Regan*, who'd missed a crucial shot late in the game, approached McHale to apologise and was told: 'Go and throw yourself in the bloody Yarra!'

The day after Collingwood won the exciting 1953 Grand Final, he had a heart attack and died a week later. Doctors said the strain of the last quarter, when Geelong looked like bridging Collingwood's 29-point three-quarter time lead, had been too much for him.

McHale's son, Jock jnr, played 33 games with the Magpies from 1941–44.

McKAY, David (1949–)

A versatile key-position player renowned for his aerial acrobatics and marking, 'Swan' McKay played in four Carlton premierships, three as a defender, in his 263 game career from 1969–81.

His sky-scraping, defensive mark in the 1972 Grand Final against Richmond was one of the marks of the year. Few players

and warned his players against drinking, other than on weekends.

In the 1917 Grand Final against much-fancied Fitzroy, he was convinced that the Maroon forwards were too light to withstand heavy buffeting and instructed his defenders to hit as hard as they could. On a sodden Melbourne Cricket Ground surface, Collingwood had 29 scoring shots to 14, winning the Grand Final by 35 points in a game which enhanced the Magpies' reputation as one of the most physical sides to play the game.

'McHale's half time addresses were inspirational,' said Collingwood historian Richard Stremski. 'Generally, he did not rehash the first half, but "got inside" the players by instilling the club spirit into them. He gave them "fire in their bellies".'

He was a happy man when Collingwood teams won and would often sponsor the players who he thought went well that day up to the local brewery where he worked as a foreman, produce the keys to the bar and 'shout'.

But he could be inconsolable and was a man to be avoided if Collingwood lost. One day after the Magpies went down nar-

High-flying David McKay, one of the game's noted post-war aerialists, taking this one ahead of Richmond trio Royce Hart, Neil Balme and Ricky McLean.

rivalled his consistent ability to hover in mid-air and pluck the ball out of the sky. When in the mood, he could be unbeatable.

McKay represented Victoria four times.

McKENNA, Peter (1946–   )

One of the most famous full-forwards of the post-war era, McKenna kicked 873 goals in 193 League games. His prowess with the drop-punt was unrivalled. He averaged 4.52 goals a game.

A soccer convert who became a dead-eye-dick around goals, Collingwood's Peter McKenna with Bob Rose (left), Neil Mann and Collingwood teammates Denis O'Callaghan and Lee Adamson after a big home win in the late 1960s.

He tallied 180 games and 838 goals with Collingwood from 1965–75 before he was badly hurt in one of his rare reserves appearances.

He played his early matches at centre half-forward and was shifted to full-forward by chance during a Victorian match in Tasmania in 1967.

'For more than a half, I barely had a touch, before *Norm Smith* (the Victorian coach) shifted me to full-forward,' he said. 'Suddenly it all clicked. I kicked five goals on Paul Vinar in the third quarter before going over on my ankle and being carried off on a stretcher. Smith came up to me afterwards and said: "Listen son, when you get back to Melbourne, see what you can do ... I reckon you're a natural full-forward."'

At 191 cm and 86.5 kg, McKenna was able to mark with the biggest players, but was best known for his quick leads and safe hands which provided a safe target for Collingwood's brilliant small players including Barry Price and *Wayne Richardson*.

He three times kicked 100 goals in a season, topping the League lists in 1972 (with 130 goals) and 1973 (84). His best effort was in 1970 when he kicked 143, to finish second to Hawthorn's *Peter Hudson*, with 146.

'A real rivalry developed between us,' he said. 'It was only human nature. Hudson was so good. He was always up the top of the goalkicking and I loved to beat him, not that it happened too often until he broke down with his knee injury.'

Topping the Magpies' goalkicking eight times, McKenna's best efforts were 16 goals against South Melbourne in 1969, 13 against Richmond in 1972 and 12 goals on four other occasions, including the opening game of 1966 against Hawthorn.

In 11 games with Carlton at the end of his career he kicked 35 goals.

McKENZIE, Don (1939–   )

Recruited from St John's Baptists, McKenzie was first ruckman in Essendon's

Don McKenzie: three Grand Finals with Essendon.

183

1965 premiership win and played in two other Grand Finals in an illustrious 266-game career from 1960–74.

At 188 cm, he conceded height to most of his opponents but had a big leap, stamina and great spirit. A fine overhead mark, he represented Victoria in 1967, was Essendon best and fairest (1966) and skipper (1969).

McLEISH, David (1950–)

A skilled, well-balanced half-back from Kerang who had 12 seasons of League football, McLeish totalled 214 games with South Melbourne from 1969–80 and represented Victoria.

McMAHON, David (1951–)

A versatile half-forward from Preston who played 219 matches from 1973–84, McMahon was renowned for his risk-taking and aggression at the ball. He several times fell into dispute with the Lions over his contract but remained loyal throughout 12 years of League football. He represented Victoria three times.

MEAGHER, Des (1944–)

A member of Hawthorn's 1971 premiership team, Mcagher played 198 games from 1966–76 and represented Victoria three times, including twice during his second season in 1967.

Meagher was a great ball-winner, who bumped the ball down forward as quickly as he could, without the pinpoint precision of his modern-day team-mates.

He remained faithful to Hawthorn and coached the reserves for more than 15 years.

MELBOURNE

Founded in 1858 by one of the 'fathers of football,' *Thomas Wentworth Wills*, Melbourne is the oldest established football club in Australia. The first rules of the Australian code were drafted in May, 1859 by Melbourne officials including Wills, *H.C.A. Harrison*, G. Bruce, T.S. Marshall and the Rev. A. Brown.

In the first seasons of the Challenge Cup competition, Melbourne players wore long white trousers, shirts and caps and were known as the 'Invincible Whites'.

A maroon stripe was added in 1862 and the cap changed to royal blue in 1864. Four years later, it became red, but as some players continued to wear their old blue caps, it was decided to combine the red and blue colours, as worn today.

Initially the Melbourne footballers were not allowed to play on the famed Melbourne Cricket Ground, but when gate-takings for a game against Carlton in 1879 exceeded £500, permission was given for the footballers to use the ground for half the year.

The club was a foundation member of the VFA, playing all its home matches at the MCG.

Joining the VFL in its opening year, 1897, Melbourne soon won a premiership, in 1900, but it wasn't until the 1930s that it became a genuine power, despite fielding some champions including *Ivor Warne-Smith* and 'Bert' Chadwick.

Until the arrival of famed coach 'Checker' Hughes in 1933, the club languished, renowned for playing a 'pretty' brand of football, not overly physical—or successful. Most of its players were college kids who played for the fun of it.

The club won three premierships in a row from 1939–41. It was Melbourne's first golden era. Among the team's many champions were goalkickers *Norm Smith*, *Jack Mueller*, Alan La Fontaine, 'Bluey' Truscott, *Percy Beames* and the *Cordner* brothers.

La Fontaine, who had a brilliant amateur football record, was known as 'Little Lollies'—he kicked goals in 100s and 1000s. He became a star-rating VFL centreman, with the fast-leading Smith and strong-marking Mueller forming a formidable two-pronged goalkicking combination.

The 1950s proved to be an even more successful era for Melbourne. The club figured in seven consecutive Grand Finals from 1954–60 for five flags, including three in a row from 1955–57. The Demons won 109 of 128 games under the coaching of *Smith*, one of the game's greatest and most ruthless leaders and the astute administration of secretary Jim Cardwell.

Smith had a direct hand in 10 of Melbourne's 12 VFL premierships, four as a player and six as coach.

Ron Barassi jnr, Frank 'Bluey' Adams, Laurie Mithen, Noel McMahen, Stuart Spencer and *Bob Johnson* were among Melbourne's champions in the 1950s.

Barassi's dynamic leadership and ruck-roving was a feature of Melbourne's great years. After he left the club to coach Carlton in 1965, Melbourne crumbled and it took the club more than two decades to again make the finals and 25 years before it appeared in another Grand Final.

Among the team's modern-day heroes are *Robert Flower*, Hassa Mann, *Stan Alves* and *Greg Wells*. Brownlow Medallist *Gerard Healy* also spent his first seven years at Melbourne before transferring to Sydney, in 1986.

Former Richmond half-forward John Northey coached the team into five final series in a row from 1987–91. His successor, Neil Balme, made the finals in his second year, 1994.

MELBOURNE: THE STATISTICS

FORMED: 1858

JOINED LEAGUE: 1897

HOME VENUES: MCG (1897–1915, 1919–41, 1946–   ), Motordrome (1932), Punt Rd. Oval (1942–46, 1956)

CURRENT HOME VENUE DIMENSIONS: 161 metres × 140 metres

COLOURS: Navy blue guernsey with red yoke.

TOTAL FINALS MATCHES: 72 (43 wins, 27 losses, 2 ties)

FINALS RECORD: Premiers: 12 (1900, 1926, 1939–40–41, 1948, 1955–56–57, 1959–60, 1964)
Runners-up: 4 (1946, 1954, 1958, 1988)

PREMIERSHIP COACHES: Robert Wardill (1), 'Bert' Chadwick (1), 'Checker' Hughes (4), Norm Smith (6).

NIGHT SERIES PREMIERSHIPS: 3 (1971, 1987, 1989)

YOUNGEST PLAYER: Sid Catlin, 16 years 230 days (1966)

OLDEST PLAYER: Jack Mueller, 35 years (1950)

HIGHEST SCORE: 28.14 (182) v North Melb., R.21, 1986, MCG
28.14 (182) v North Melb., R.5, 1991, MCG

LOWEST SCORE: 0.2 (2) v Fitzroy, R.16, 1899, Brunswick St Oval

LONGEST WINNING SEQUENCE: 19 (1955–56)

LONGEST LOSING SEQUENCE: 20 (1981–82)

MOST FINALS: Frank Adams 22, Ron Barassi jnr 21

MOST SEASONS AS COACH: Norm Smith 16 (1952–67)

MOST SEASONS AS CAPTAIN: Robert Flower 7 (1981–87)

MOST GAMES		MOST GOALS	
Robert Flower	272	Norm Smith	546
Brian Dixon	252	Fred Fanning	411
Stan Alves	226	Jack Mueller	379
Greg Wells	224	Percy Beames	327
Garry Hardeman	221	Robert Flower	315
Jack Mueller	217	Ron Baggott	308
Percy Beames	213	Bob Johnson snr	302
Norm Smith	211	Ron Barassi jnr	295
Don Williams	206	Garry Lyon	284*
Ron Barassi jnr	204	George Margitich	267

MOST GAMES		MOST GOALS	
'Tassie' Johnson	203	Bob Johnson jnr	267
Stephen Smith	203	Bob McKenzie	255
		Greg Wells	250
		Ian Ridley	228
		Vin Coutie	212
		Darren Bennett	211
		Brian Wilson	208

* current player.

MOST GOALS IN A MATCH: Fred Fanning 18 v St Kilda, R.19, 1947, Junction Oval.
Harry Davie 13 v Carlton, R.14, 1925, Princes Park.
George Margitich 12 v North Melb., R.17, 1931, MCG.
Bob Johnson snr 12 v Hawthorn, R.11, 1933, MCG.
Norm Smith 12 v Footscray, R.17, 1941, MCG.

BROWNLOW MEDALLISTS: Ivor Warne-Smith 1926, 1928; Don Cordner 1946; Brian Wilson 1982; Peter Moore 1984; Jim Stynes 1991.

LEAGUE LEADING GOALSCORERS: Vin Coutie 39 (1904), Harry Brereton 56 (1912), Norm Smith 88 (1941), Fred Fanning 62 (1943), Fred Fanning 87 (1944), Fred Fanning 67 (1945), Fred Fanning 97 (1947).

RECORD HOME VENUE ATTENDANCE: 99,346 v Collingwood, R.10, 1958, MCG.
13,000 v Richmond, R.2, 1932, Motordrome.
30,000 v Essendon, R.14, 1946, Punt Rd Oval.

RECORD ATTENDANCE IN ANY MATCH: 115,802 v Collingwood, GF, 1956, MCG.

MOST RECENT PREMIERSHIP TEAM: 1964 Melbourne 8.16 (64) d Collingwood 8.12 (60).
B: N. Crompton, B. Massey, R. (Tas.) Johnson. H.B: A. Anderson, B. Roet, F. Davis. C: B. Dixon, D. Williams, F. Adams. H.F: B. Kenneally, G. Jacobs, B. Vagg. F: J. Lord, B. Bourke, J. Townsend. R: G. Wise. R. Barassi (c). R: H. Mann. Reserves: P. McLean, K. Emselle.

MERRETT, Roger (1960–)

An aggressive ruckman/forward who was a late developer, Merrett played in back-to-back premierships at Essendon before joining the Brisbane Bears for his final seasons.

His hard-at-the-ball aggression—especially in the mid-1980s—upset many opponents. Some referred to him as a 'hitman', saying he used vigour unnecessarily and on occasions, unfairly.

He was twice suspended in 1983, including a two-week penalty for striking Hawthorn captain *Leigh Matthews*.

Making no apology for his on-field ruthlessness, he said: 'I just play the ball hard and whoever is in the way, well that's just too bad.'

Named an All Australian in 1985, he captained Victoria in 1986, before leaving the Bombers after 149 games in 1988, to join Brisbane. He showed grand on-field leadership at the fledging club and in 1990 replaced Mark Mickan as captain. He also played his 200th League match.

To the start of the 1995 season, his sometimes turbulent 277-match career had included four State matches.

MERRIGAN, Harvey (1949–)

Originally from Gippsland and recruited to Fitzroy from Hampton Park, the 189 cm full-back played 198 VFL games from 1969–81 and was a Victorian representative in 1973, 1974 and 1978. Best and fairest in 1974, he captained the Lions in 1978.

MEW, Chris (1961–)

A key defensive member in Hawthorn's golden Grand Final run in the 1980s, Mew figured in five premierships and three other Grand Finals from 1983–92, having begun his career as a 19-year-old in 1980.

Playing his early football at full-back, he became one of the dominant centre half-backs in the competition. He represented Victoria five times and, in 1990, passed 200 games.

MILLANE, Darren (1965–91)

Just one year after he'd jubilantly held the ball aloft signalling Collingwood's first premiership in 32 years, Darren Millane was tragically killed in a car accident in South Melbourne.

The 26-year-old's death prompted the biggest funeral in Melbourne for years, more than 5000 people cramming inside and outside the Dandenong Town Hall to pay their last respects.

Civil celebrant Dally Messenger quoted one of former U.S. President John F. Kennedy's famous lines: 'There is no greater tragedy than the death of a young man in the prime of his life.'

Collingwood 'retired' Millane's famous No. 42 guernsey and announced the Darren Millane Perpetual Memorial Shield would be awarded each year to the player selected by his team-mates for the most inspirational acts during matches. Gavin Brown was the first winner.

Joining Collingwood from Dandenong—where he'd been captain while still a teenager—the 185 cm Millane played 147 games with Collingwood from 1984–91, represented Victoria and won the Copeland Trophy. His courage in playing the 1990 final series with a broken thumb was inspirational.

Collingwood coach *Leigh Matthews* liked to play him on the wing, but with his athletic build and marking prowess, he could also successfully adapt to key forward positions.

Millane protected team-mates with his aggression and fire, being renowned for kicking uplifting goals when needed.

MILLS, Bert (1910–)

One of Hawthorn's foremost players in its early years, Bert Mills amassed 196 games from 1930–42, won Hawthorn's best and fairest three times, and represented Victoria 11 times.

MITCHELL, Barry (1965–)

A heady rover who played his 200th game late in the 1994 season, Mitchell had nine years with Sydney before crossing to Collingwood for a year and on to Carlton where he immediately achieved his ambition of playing in finals.

Barry Mitchell, during his days with Sydney.

Recruited from Mulgrave, Mitchell was one of South Melbourne's Melbourne-based players who was happy to shift when the ailing club was directed to Sydney.

Winner of Sydney's best and fairest award in 1991, a season in which he also won All Australian honors and the E. J. Whitten Medal, Mitchell's courage, stamina and ballwinning abilities were a constant feature in a poorly-performed team.

Dubbed 'the million dollar man' in 1993 after being drafted by Collingwood, he struggled for recognition and was far more settled playing alongside his old Sydney team-mate, Greg Williams, at Carlton.

MITCHELL, Hugh (1934–)

A prominent Essendon ruck-rover, who also filled-in successfully at full-forward on *John Coleman's* enforced retirement, the 183 cm Mitchell played 225 games from 1953–67, representing Victoria on six occasions.

Best and fairest in 1959, he figured in four Grand Finals, being prominent in the 1962 and 1965 premierships.

MITHEN, Laurie (1934–)

A champion centreman and Melbourne's best and fairest player in consecutive seasons in 1958–59, Mithen played 154 games from 1954–62.

Publicity-shy off the field, he was an aggressive, direct player, who once kicked six goals in a quarter, against Fitzroy at the old Brunswick Street Oval in 1959.

Recruited from Ormond where he'd won the amateur's 'A' Grade best and fairest, he played in a Grand Final in his first year, 1954, the first of his involvement in seven play-offs in a row.

MOHR, Bill (c. 1910–1971)

Wilbur T. 'Billy' Mohr headed St Kilda's goalkicking for 12 straight seasons from 1929–40, amassing 736 goals in 195 games, at an average of 3.77. In 1936, he topped the League goalkicking with 101 goals, an exceptional effort considering the champion full-forwards of the era and St Kilda's chequered season which saw it win only half its matches.

Lithe and nimble, Mohr regularly won State selection from his second season, when he finished second in the goalkicking to his long-time rival, Collingwood's *Gordon Coventry*.

An exceptional ground player, he represented Victoria 18 times, a St Kilda record. In the 1930 Australian carnival in Adelaide, he kicked 16 goals against Queensland and 35 for the series.

Twice kicking 11 goals in a game, his

St Kilda's finest between-the-wars goalkicker and the first to the 100 goal milestone, Billy Mohr.

best performance came at the Junction Oval in 1931, when St Kilda defeated Collingwood late in the season in an extraordinarily high-scoring match, 21.16 (142) to 20.8 (128).

Both Mohr and Coventry kicked 11 goals. Mohr's high marking and general display were described as the best exhibition ever seen on the ground. Aged 21 and playing only his 52nd game, he kicked four goals in the first quarter, as the Saints shocked with their strong display.

MOLONEY, George (1909–)

The celebrated centreman and full-forward started and ended his career in Western Australia, where he was among Claremont-Cottesloe's most-decorated players, winning the 1936 Sandover Medal and a prime force behind his team playing in five WA grand finals in a row from 1936–40.

In five years at Geelong, he also had a remarkable record, amassing 303 goals in 88 games, including 109 in 1932 to head the League goalkicking.

He was also equal second in the 1932 Brownlow, a performance equalled by only two other modern-day full-forwards, Hawthorn pair *Peter Hudson* (1971) and *Jason Dunstall* (1988 and 1992) and surpassed by only one other, *Tony Lockett*, who won the Medal in 1987.

Kicking 19 goals in his first two games—seven against Collingwood and 12 against St Kilda, 21-year-old Moloney played in a premiership in his maiden year in the VFL in 1931.

Fast, clever and a good mark for his size—he was just 174 cm and 72.5 kg—he won Geelong's best and fairest in 1932, was leading goalkicker from 1931–33 and a Victorian representative in 1932.

His snap shooting at goal was uncanny. Many of his majors came from shots over his head or shoulder as he ran away from goals to find space.

In rounds 15–16, 1932, he became the first player in League history to score 10 goals or more in successive matches.

MONCRIEFF, Michael (1952–)

A versatile key-position player, renowned for his goal-sense, the 192 cm Moncrieff played in Hawthorn's 1976–78 premiership teams and headed the Hawks' goalkicking five times in a 225-game career from 1971–83. After missing selection in the '83 premiership side, he crossed to St Kilda in an attempt to continue in League football but suffered a serious knee injury in his first 1984 practice match. Normally a prodigious kick, he said he found he could kick only 40–45 metres and retired.

He amassed 628 goals at an average approaching three a game. He three times kicked 10 goals in a match, but was always regarded as *Peter Hudson*'s 'understudy'—an unfortunate label considering his own considerable talents.

For most of his career, 'Mongoose' Moncrieff suffered from poor eyesight. He saw the ball much later than opponents. He could not read scoreboards. One day against Richmond he kicked 1.8. The days he wore 'soft' contact lenses he did much better. The next week, against St Kilda, he kicked 8.2!

Moncrieff represented Victoria three times.

His father, Alan, played 90 games with Footscray.

MONTGOMERY, Ken (1951–)

A dedicated half-back, Montgomery played 189 games from 1968–81, represented Victoria and won North's best and fairest, in 1972. His grandfather, William, played with North when it was in the VFA, while his father, William jnr, also played with the club. His uncle Alan and cousin Ron also represented North.

Recruited from Pascoe Vale, Montgomery debuted as a 17-year-old and played in four Grand Finals, for one win, a tie and two losses. He returned to North Melbourne from 1990–94 as chief executive.

MOORE, Kelvin (1950–)

Cool, calculating and consistent, Kelvin Moore rates as one of the champion post-war full-backs. His aerial judgement and high marking were as sharp as his off-field humour.

Not only did he play 301 games with Hawthorn from 1970–84, he represented Victoria 13 times, won All Australian honours and later served as a State selector.

He missed just one game in nine years and had amassed 128 matches in a row before suffering a ruptured testicle in a late-season match against Essendon which led to his omission from the '83 premiership side.

In the 21st round of 1984, he became the third Hawthorn player to reach 300 games, leading the side for the only time in his career with skipper *Leigh Matthews*, vice-captain *Peter Knights* and deputy-vice *Michael Tuck* all sidelined with injury. 'The boys might have responded to my leadership,' he quipped after Hawthorn's defeat of Collingwood.

Originally recruited as a full-forward from Frankston Peninsula, the 188 cm defender was rarely beaten and played in three premierships, being one of the best afield in the 1971 Grand Final, when he held in form St Kilda full-forward *Allan Davis* to one goal. Returning exceptional statistics for a full-back, he had 18 kicks and took six marks to be one of the best three players afield.

MOORE, Peter (1957–)

A dual Brownlow Medallist, winning one with Collingwood (1979) and another with Melbourne (1984), 198 cm Moore was a gifted athlete renowned for his speed, ballhandling and all-round skills. The big blond twice won Collingwood's best and fairest, was leading goalkicker in 1977–78 and captained the club in 1981–82.

He made his debut in late 1974 and played 161 games in nine years at Collingwood, becoming renowned as the best 'running ruckman' in the game.

Used at centre half-back in 1975 and 1976, he tired of being *Len Thompson*'s rucking understudy and considered transferring to South Fremantle for the 1977 season.

But he agreed to stay under first-year coach *Tom Hafey*. Given a new role, he kicked 76 goals from full-forward.

From 1979, with Thompson's transfer to South Melbourne, he became Collingwood's No. 1 ruckman. His mobility and enthusiasm won him the first of consecutive Copeland Trophies. He also won the Brownlow Medal, by a vote from Fitzroy's *Gary Wilson*.

Collingwood gambled on his fitness in the 1981 Grand Final but Moore, nursing a hamstring injury, was a mediocre performer.

It was a bitter day for the Magpies, the club failing to win its eighth play-off in a row. A first-year captain, Moore was devastated and later argued with coach Hafey. According to Collingwood historian Richard Stremski, the pair almost came to blows.

Within 12 months, after a year of acrimony which saw Hafey sensationally sacked in mid-season, Moore was recruited to Melbourne—along with another Brownlow Medallist, Footscray's *Kelvin Templeton*—in a five-year contractual deal which

Peter Moore, two Brownlows, 249 games and the State captaincy.

cost Melbourne amost $1 million.

He broke his jaw in his first year and was written off by some as a poor investment, but he returned in career-best form in 1984, relishing his usual on-ball position and winning the Brownlow by three votes from Collingwood's *David Cloke*.

Team-mate *Tony Shaw* said Moore 'had everything.'

'He could run like a hare and could kick the ball a mile.'

Essendon champion *Simon Madden* said Moore was the fastest big man he ever had to combat. 'He's the sort of player who if you give him a yard he'd take five. But his pace was not his only strength because he was a strong mark and had a big spring which made him hard to counter in rucking duels.'

Moore retired at the end of 1987, aged 30, having played 249 games. One of his most memorable achievements was being named Victorian captain, against Tasmania, in 1981, one of 11 State appearances.

MORIARTY, Jack (c. 1901–1980)

One of the most prolific between-the-wars full-forwards, the 175 cm Moriarty became Fitzroy's No. 1 goalkicker after being discarded by his original League club, Essendon.

He kicked 626 goals in 157 games in his 10 years with the Maroons from 1924–33. His yearly tallies included 83, 82, 81, 70 and 68. His average of 3.58 goals a match was one of the best of his era.

Recruited from Essendon 'A' in 1921, he had one senior season with the Bombers, in 1922, heading the goalkicking with 36 goals in 13 matches before controversially being omitted from the preliminary final side. His replacement, Greg Stockdale, kicked five of Essendon's six goals in the Grand Final and did so well in 1923 that Moriarty was not recalled from the reserves.

On transferring to Fitzroy in 1924, Moriarty broke Stockdale's League record for the most goals in a season, heading the VFL charts with 82 goals.

In 1927, he kicked a personal-best 12 goals against North Melbourne, a League high which was to stand for only two years.

His feat of kicking 83 goals in 1927 remained a Fitzroy record until 1979, when Bob Beecroft booted 87.

MORRIS, Bill (1922–60)

Known as 'Paleface' or 'Trophies' Morris, the decorated ruckman won the 1948 Brownlow Medal, was equal second in 1946 and equal third in 1950. Only one other Richmond player of the period, the immortal *Jack Dyer*, had a more distinguished record. Morris won Richmond's best and fairest on three occasions and represented Victoria 13 times, twice as captain.

Born in Culcairn in the NSW Riverina, Morris spent time in Tasmania before settling with his family in Melbourne where he became a prominent member of the Scotch College senior cricket and football teams.

Tall and angular, he represented Old Scotch in the amateurs and in 1940 played

A gentleman in an era of rough and tough players, Richmond's gifted follower Bill Morris.

one match for Melbourne reserves. In 1942, he transferred to Richmond as part of a swap for youngster Colin Galbraith.

After serving in the Armoured Division during the war, Morris partnered Dyer in the Richmond ruck from 1944. His agility and amazing spring helped to give his rovers an armchair ride. He also developed great stamina, being able to run on the ball for long periods.

'Morris was known as "Paleface" to the players because of his handsome, pallid complexion,' said football writer Brian Hansen. 'He was an unforgettable footballer. The umpires loved him, the crowds idolised him and the players fought for him. He was so scrupulously fair that when a confused umpire threatened to report him over an incident in which he played no part, Morris retorted: "Do that and I will retire instantly. I will not tolerate that slur."

'The umpire realised Morris meant what he said and that his own life would not be worth living. There was no report.'

Morris played 140 games at Richmond,

being a gentleman in an era of rough and tough players.

'If he knocked somebody down he would stop and pick him up,' said Dyer. 'You could not get him to play tough football and I didn't try; his value was in his artistry. I was the protector. He was the craftsman.'

The 186 cm Morris captained Richmond in his final two years, in 1950 and 1951, before crossing to Box Hill in 1952.

He took his own life, aged 38, in May 1960, by inhaling gas.

MORRISON, Alby (1908–   )

Beautifully balanced, with great speed off the mark, Morrison built his reputation as a forward but also did well when used on the ball. He played 224 games and kicked 369 goals in 14 seasons with Footscray.

Captain-coach in 1934 and captain in 1935 and 1937, he twice won Footscray's best and fairest award and represented Victoria 15 times in his career which spanned 1928–46.

In only his second season, in 1929, he kicked 10 goals in a game against Hawthorn and five times led Footscray's goalkicking, including 50 goals as a first-year rookie.

MORWOOD, Shane (1961–   )

A highly-skilled half-back flanker, who started his career as a forward, 191 cm Shane Morwood played 212 League games from 1981–93, including Collingwood's 1990 premiership.

Originally from Noble Park, he debuted as a teenager at South Melbourne, playing in the club's last premiership, a night flag in 1982.

In 1988, he joined brothers, Tony and Paul, in playing 100 VFL games, a unique achievement.

He also represented Victoria four times.

MORWOOD, Tony (1960–   )

A gifted half-forward with superb marking skills, Morwood amassed 229 games with South Melbourne and the Swans from 1978–89.

The second eldest of six brothers, all of whom played football, 186 cm Tony twice represented Victoria and twice topped South's goalkicking.

MOSS, Graham (1950–   )

Weeks after winning the 1976 Brownlow Medal, Essendon's import ruckman Graham Moss announced his return to his original West Australian club, Claremont. His contract allowed him to be cleared back to his old WA club whenever he wished. The Bombers made a huge counter offer, guaranteeing to pay him more per season than any player in their proud history. But the 195 cm and 102 kg Moss was adamant. His great League career was over, at 26.

The relaxed ruckman whose apparent nonchalance became a trademark had just four seasons and 89 games with the

A star ruckman in two States and winner of the 1976 Brownlow Medal, Claremont's Graham Moss shared the ball expertly with his running players.

Bombers. He was the first Essendon player since legendary *Dick Reynolds* to win three consecutive best and fairest awards.

Rarely beaten for knock-outs, he was a great 'body' player who protected his rovers and, like Geelong champion *Graham 'Polly' Farmer*, was renowned for his effective handball. He had courage, was a magnificent mark and invaluable when resting in a forward pocket. He averaged 14 marks, 15 handballs and 10 kicks a match while at Essendon.

A gentle giant and an inspiring figure wherever he played, Moss had almost 370 games in his 16 senior seasons—254 with Claremont, 89 at Essendon, 21 with Western Australia and five with Victoria.

Recruited from Dalkeith, where he first represented Cobbers as a 12-year-old in the Dalkeith-Nedlands juniors, Moss debuted in senior WA ranks as an 18-year-old in 1969, going on to win four consecutive club championships at Claremont from 1977–80.

His run of seven consecutive best and fairests—including his Essendon treble—has rarely been equalled in senior Australian football.

An All Australian and WA captain, he also captain-coached Claremont from 1977–83 including three grand finals in a row, for one win and two losses, and continued as non-playing coach until the end of the 1986 season. Later he served as general manager of the West Coast Eagles.

MUELLER, Jack (1915–   )

Strong-marking and spring-heeled Jack 'Melba' Mueller rates as one of the game's finest follower/forwards. Best-remembered for his remarkable senior comeback in 1948, he played a major role in Melbourne's premiership, kicking 20 goals in three finals matches.

Mueller, 33, kicked eight goals in the preliminary final, six in the drawn Grand Final and six in the Grand Final replay. He'd spent the whole season as reserves' captain.

Two years later, the Demons tried it again, but Mueller kicked only two of Melbourne's six goals, the Demons being eliminated in the first week of the finals.

Mueller's feats were all the more remarkable considering he lost two fingers above the knuckles in a factory accident after he'd played just one season of League football. He was working for a Carlton box manufacturer when he caught his right hand in a machine that punched holes through cardboard boxes. Doctors said he could never play again.

Wearing a protective black glove on his right hand (in the first eight matches of 1935), Mueller's marking remained unimpaired. His 'eight-finger grip' was famous. In the last quarter against Carlton in 1936, he took 14 marks.

At 191 cm and 90 kg, the burly Mueller was a formidable opponent who had the ability to dominate no matter his position. He became renowned as the greatest big-match footballer of his era.

Figuring in four premierships with the Demons, including the treble from 1939–41, Mueller's superb fitness was as important an attribute as his marking.

Noted football writer Alf Brown said Mueller won premierships for Melbourne 'off his own boot'.

'He was always fit,' said Brown. 'Even as a non-playing coach he trained hard. He was an adherent of the *Checker Hughes* football axiom: "You play as you train."'

When he retired in 1950, he'd played 216 games in a career spanning 17 seasons, represented Victoria five times, won Melbourne's best and fairest three times and been leading goalkicker twice.

Celebrated Demon Alan La Fontaine said: 'I have seen many players, but none as great as Mueller.'

In *Football's 50 Greatest*, Greg Hobbs rated Mueller as the seventh-best player of all time, saying he 'had the ability to inject life into seemingly beaten Melbourne teams with his sheer explosiveness . . . his presence in the thirties and forties was something football will never forget.'

Mueller regularly flew his drop kicks and torpedo punts 60–65 metres, forming a fine combination with the more agile *Norm Smith*, who would lead for the ball from full-forward, leaving sticky-fingered Mueller one-out with his opponent in the goalsquare.

Mueller's final game with Melbourne was in 1954 when he filled-in with the reserves. It was the last of his many come-back games.

MURPHY, Frank (1905–)

Joining his brother, Len, in Collingwood's 1928–30 premiership teams, noted centre half-forward Frank Murphy also played in the Magpies' 1927 flag, having 145 games from 1925–34 and Len, a forward/follower, 173 from 1928–37. Len Murphy missed the 1936 premiership side after receiving an eight week suspension for striking during the second semi-final.

Recruited from Thornbury CYMS via Mernda, 180 cm Frank Murphy was pacy, agile and a fine mark for his size, teammate *Gordon Coventry* describing him as 'a champion' in his position. He wrote in *The Sporting Globe* in 1938: 'For 10 years he played in front of me and could take credit for 100s of the goals I scored. Murphy helped me in all the games when I scored a big bag of goals.' He twice represented Victoria. Len Murphy played once for his state.

MURPHY, John (1949–)

While the decorated rover/centreman never achieved his ambition of playing in a Grand Final, Murphy's career included his first 158 matches in succession, five Fitzroy best and fairests and nine Victorian games.

The 181 cm redhead had 216 games with the Lions from 1967–77 before shifting to South Melbourne for 23 games in 1978–79 and North Melbourne for nine games in 1979–80. He kicked 373 goals.

Captain of Fitzroy for five years from 1973–77, he hoped by transferring that he would play in a side good enough to make the finals.

He had to go the VFL appeals board to win a release.

MURRAY, Bob (1942–)

Renowned for taking the last mark of the titanic 1966 Grand Final which stopped a last-gasp Collingwood thrust and ensured St Kilda its first ever premiership, Launceston-born Murray played 153 games with the Saints in 12 seasons.

Recruited from Sandringham where he played in the 1962 premiership as a forward, 185 cm Murray became one of the most noted full-backs of his era. He won St Kilda's best and fairest in 1969 and represented Victoria from 1967–70.

MURRAY, Kevin (1938–)

One of Australian football's grandest players who recorded a massive 424 games in 20 seasons, the celebrated Fitzroy stalwart is the oldest winner of the Brownlow Medal (in 1969, aged 31). He twice came second, in 1960 and 1962.

His ability to continue playing, despite injury, was remarkable.

Kevin Murray: his Brownlow came at the age of 31. He finished in the Brownlow top 10 eight times, winning 10 best and fairests, nine at Fitzroy and one at East Perth.

He was forced out of Fitzroy's first semi-final side of 1958, but it was the last game he was to miss—except for interstate contests and a two-year stay in Perth—in almost 275 matches with the Lions.

Ted Whitten christened him 'Bulldog'. Fitzroy supporters called him 'Miracle Man'—not only for his ability to play with injury, but his success rate against taller and stronger opponents.

He played 106 club games in succession before leaving to captain-coach East Perth in 1965–66 and another 167 consecutively on his return before his retirement at the end of 1974, when he became only the fourth Australian Rules footballer to receive an MBE.

Starting with Fitzroy in 1955 as a 16-year-old, he won the club's best and fairest eight times, tied for a ninth club championship, was captain of the Lions for six seasons and captain-coach for two.

Graduating from Fitzroy thirds under coach Len Smith, 16-year-old Murray was the youngest to don Fitzroy's maroon and blue colours.

He played 15 games in his first year and was never to play less than 15 in a season, despite some painful injuries which would have daunted players of less courage and resulted in him wearing a back brace for many years.

Tragically he played in only two finals in a record 333 matches with Fitzroy and never appeared in a VFL Grand Final. In 1966, when he was interstate, East Perth made the grand final, only to lose to Perth.

Murray loved State matches and represented Victoria each year from 1957–64. He played for WA in 1965 and 1966 as captain-coach, one of his greatest thrills in football. He reappeared for Victoria in 1969, his Brownlow year, and in all played 30 State games, 24 with Victoria and six with WA. Twice named an All Australian, in 1958 (with Victoria) and 1966 (for WA), he was Victoria's captain in 1964.

His remarkable playing career continued at VFA club Sandringham in 1975–76 where he was captain-coach. He continued playing into his early 50s, in Super-rules and 'Legends' matches.

His senior aggregate of 448 games has been surpassed by only one other senior level player, Glenelg's Peter Carey, who played 467 matches.

Murray's proud record consists of:
- 333 day games with Fitzroy
- 17 night games
- 44 games with East Perth (WAFL)
- 24 Victorian representative games
- six West Australian State games
- 24 with Sandringham (VFA)

If his practice matches are also included, his tally approaches 500 matches, a stunning performance for a player once considered too skinny and frail to get a game at under-age level.

Murray had speed, strength, skill and determination. Although he was only 180 cm, he had a very long reach and could compete with far taller players.

Generally regarded as the greatest half-back flanker the game has seen, he was also a star at centre half-back or on the ball. He protected his younger players. Many opponents were intimidated by his tough looks.

Fitzroy's stand at the Junction Oval is named in his honour.

His father, Dan, was a reserve in Fitzroy's 1944 premiership team.

See: 'DURABLE PLAYERS'

MYNOTT, Brian (1944–)

Born in Southhampton, England, the 193 cm first ruckman played 211 games with St Kilda from 1964–75, including the Saints' historic 1966 premiership.

He was an extremely fair player who rarely ruffled tempers in the fashion of his exuberant contemporary *Carl Ditterich*. He played in St Kilda's 1971 Grand Final side and was a member of two Victorian teams.

NANKERVIS, Bruce (1950–)

The younger brother of another Geelong stalwart, *Ian Nankervis*, Bruce Nankervis blossomed from a forward flanker into a creative, attacking half-back, playing 256 games from 1970–83. He represented Victoria 11 times.

Bruce Nankervis (left) with brother, Ian, and nephews, Andrew and Wayne.

NANKERVIS, Ian (1948–)

A three-time winner of Geelong's best and fairest award, Nankervis first won senior selection in 1967 as a 19-year-old, when he shared the roving duties with veteran *Billy Goggin*.

Rangier than his brother *Bruce*, he roved for his first eight seasons before switching to the back pocket where he was so successful that he found himself being tagged, opposing coaches having tired of his constant running and rebounding style from the last line of defence.

In 17 years and a club record 326 games

of League football, he captained Geelong 110 times (from 1978–81), kicked more than 200 goals and was a Big V regular, twice leading his State. In 1975, he was equal leading goalkicker with Larry Donohue and in 1980 was accorded All Australian status.

NASH, Laurie (1909–86)

'Who was the greatest player ever?' the cub reporter asked the great Laurie Nash.

'Son,' replied a straight-faced L.J.: 'I look at him every morning when I shave!'

It was one of Nash's most-loved one-liners.

No-one ever took any offence. Laurence John Nash *was* one of *the* greats. He could take spectacular marks, kick 70 metres with either foot and entertain for hours with his tall stories and true.

He once kicked 18.2 for Victoria in just three quarters against South Australia in 1934, having been moved from defence after *Billy Mohr* was injured. Nash said he could have kicked 27 that day, 'but for the selfishness of the rovers' (*Percy Beames* and *Haydn Bunton*).

An Australian Test cricketer as well, Nash was a legend at South Melbourne. With full forward *Bob Pratt*, he formed a superlative combination which was the envy of opposing clubs during the mid-1930s.

Nash's reign was spectacular and brief. After six years and 99 League games, he joined VFA club Camberwell and became an even bigger star. Returning to South for one final season after the war, he figured in the infamous 'Bloodbath' Grand Final against Carlton.

The Tasmanian-born Nash first represented the Australian XI during the 1931–32 summer and his arrival on the mainland was greeted with jubilation by both cricket and football supporters. But he played only one more Test, against 'Gubby' Allen's Englishmen in 1936–37, and never represented Victoria at Sheffield Shield level. His highest score was 241 not out for Tamar in 1930–31.

On Grand Final day, 1933, in front of a record crowd of 75,754, Nash took five telling marks in the first term, as South kept Richmond goalless. *Jack Dyer* was shifted onto Nash to try and restrict his influence, but it was too late—'L.J.' was having a day out and was unquestionably the best player afield, having 29 kicks, two handballs and 13 marks.

'It was the proudest moment of my life when the bell rang and I knew I was a member of the premier Victorian team,' Nash said. 'And what a great band of fellows and officials. It was a pleasure to play and work with them. The team spirit was wonderful and every player was a personal friend of the other.'

Nash played in four consecutive Grand Finals at South, including three in a row at centre half-forward, his most-renowned position, where he kicked most of his 246 career goals.

In one match against Collingwood after the war, Nash, then 36, had kicked five goals against a teenage Len Fitzgerald when he took another mark and lined up for his sixth goal. As he deliberated, he asked Fitzgerald: 'What foot do you want me to use to kick this goal?'

Fitzgerald didn't know what to say, so Nash said: 'I'll kick it with my left foot.' He did, too, from 50 metres out!

In his final year, in 1945, he kicked 56 goals to head South's goalkicking, including two in the Grand Final, a torrid game in which 10 players were reported.

See: 'BROTHERS, Famous'

NATIONAL AUSTRALIAN FOOTBALL COUNCIL

Known previously as the Australian National Football Council, the Australian Football Council and the National Football League of Australia, the NAFC formulates and controls the laws of the game.

It was originally formed in 1906, just prior to the first national championships held in 1908 in Melbourne. Each State is represented on the NAFC which also does much to champion the game outside Australia, in New Zealand and Papua-New Guinea.

The number of affiliated bodies increased to nine when the Victorian Football Association and the All Australian Amateur Council were admitted in 1950.

Initially the Australian Championships involved seven States, plus New Zealand, before becoming a four-State 'first division' competition after the 1961 titles held in Brisbane (except in 1966 when the VFA competed in Hobart).

A two-division system remains, the last truly national titles having been held in Adelaide in 1988.

Victoria dominated the early Australian championships, winning 15 of the first 18 titles, but State-of-Origin football has lessened the Big V influence.

From 1937, a best and fairest player was named at each carnival, to perpetuate the memory of Eric Tassie, a former president of the national body.

Three players have each played in five carnivals:
- W. J. Truscott, who represented Western Australia as a rover in 1908, 1911, 1914, 1921 and 1924;
- Fos Williams who roved for South Australia in 1947, 1950, 1953, 1956 and 1958;
- Arthur Hodgson, who represented Tasmania in 1947, 1953, 1956, 1958 and Victoria in 1950 as a centreman/half forward.

The first player to represent multiple States in interstate carnivals was Bill Mayman, who played 315 senior games in 28 interstate matches in three States, represented SA (in 1914, as captain), WA (1921) and Tasmania (in 1924, as captain).

Others to have played for three States at carnival level include Brian Roberts (WA, SA, Victoria). Most recently, Brett Allison represented ACT, NSW and Victoria at State-of-Origin level.

More recently, among the most successful sate players have been *Garry Lyon*, *Gary Ablett* and *Paul Roos* (Victoria), *Stephen Kernahan*, Andrew and Darren Jarman (South Australia), and Guy McKenna, Peter Matera, and Don Pyke (Western Australia).

INTERSTATE MATCH RECORDS:
1897–1994

MOST MATCHES FOR VICTORIA

John Nicholls	31
Bill Hutchison	30
Ted Whitten	29
Jack Clarke	27
Syd Coventry	26
Bob Skilton	25
Kevin Murray	24*
John Schultz	24
Gordon Coventry	23
Fred Flanagan	21
Kevin Bartlett	20
Dale Weightman	20

* also played 6 matches for WA (1965–66).

MOST MATCHES FOR WESTERN AUSTRALIA

Graham Farmer	31 + (5 Vic)
Jack Clarke	26
Jack Sheedy	23
Merv McIntosh	23

MOST MATCHES FOR WESTERN AUSTRALIA (cont)

Barry Cable	22 + (1 Vic)
Brian Peake	22
Derek Chadwick	21
Denis Marshall	20 + (8 Vic)
Graham Moss	20 + (5 Vic)
Bill Walker	20
Ray Schofield	20
Les McClements	16 + (5 Tas)
Haydn Bunton jnr	11 + (11 SA)

MOST MATCHES FOR SOUTH AUSTRALIA

Walter Scott	39
Lindsay Head	37
Fos Williams	34
Neil Kerley	32
Jack Tredrea	31
Russell Ebert	29
John Cahill	29
Geof Motley	28
Frank Golding	28
Bob Hank	27

A champion Victorian team from 1964 which defeated Western Australia in Melbourne, 24.21 (165) to 7.11 (53).

Back row (left to right): John Schultz, Graham Farmer, Tassie Johnson, John Nicholls, Gordon Collis, B. Doolan (head trainer).

Centre row: J. Parker (selector), Laurie Hill, Graham Arthur, Doug Wade, Ted Whitten, Alan Morrow, John Ibrahim, Neil Crompton, Bill Goggin, A. L. Price (selector).

Front row: Dr C. Marshall (medical officer), Bill Brown, Russell Blew, Hassa Mann, Norm Smith (coach), Kevin Murray (captain), A. Trainor (manager), Bob Skilton (vice-captain), Ian Law, John Waddington, H. Okey (selector), K. Connal (property steward).

The Jarman brothers, Darren (left) and Andrew—two of South Australia's best-performed State-of-Origin players in recent times.

INTERSTATE MATCH RECORDS:
1897–1994 (cont)

MOST MATCHES FOR TASMANIA

Michael Hunnibell	27
Neil Conlan	26
Colin Moore	25
Scott Wade	24
Des James	23
Trevor Leo	23
Danny Ling	23
Rex Garwood	20
Robbie Dykes	20
Wayne Fox	20

NEAGLE, Merv (1958–)

Runner-up in the 1980 Brownlow Medal count, he was a member of Essendon's 1984 premiership side and would have played again in the 1985 triumph but for injury. A volatile, skilful wingman, he had 148 games in nine years before accepting a $135,000-a-year offer to play in Sydney, along with fellow big-name Victorian imports *Greg Williams*, *Gerard Healy* and *Bernard Toohey*.

Neagle played his finest football at Essendon, despite an undisciplined streak which led to several run-ins with coach Kevin Sheedy. In 1980 and 1981, he was runner-up in Essendon's best and fairest and in 1983—when the Bombers qualified for their first Grand Final in 15 years—he was their best player in the finals. In 1981 and 1984 he played in night flags with the Bombers.

Injuries restricted him to just 56 games in five years with Sydney.

He represented Victoria five times.

NEAL, Robert (1956—)

The red-headed son of a Wynyard potato farmer, 'Scratcher' Neal first represented Geelong in 1974 as a 17-year-old. In an illustrious 15 year career, he tallied 220 games, including 200 with the Cats and 20 in his final two seasons with St Kilda.

At 22, he became one of the youngest ever to play 100 games.

His pace, tackling and chasing were features of his game. He generally played on the wing.

NEALE, Kevin (1945–)

An imposing and colourful key-position player, 'Cowboy' Neale played 236 games with St Kilda from 1965–77, including

'The Cowboy', St Kilda's colourful key position specialist Kevin Neale.

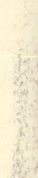

three Grand Finals in 1965, 1966 and 1971. He also represented Victoria.

Recruited from South Warrnambool as a back-pocket ruckman, his first seasons were spent at full-forward before he finished in defence. A huge man, he regularly played at weights in excess of 105 kg, but was surprisingly agile for his size and in 1983 won St Kilda's best and fairest award.

St Kilda's leading goalkicker from 1966–69, his best effort was in 1966 when he kicked 55 goals.

See also: 'AUSTRALIAN CAPITAL TERRITORY'

NEWLAND, Ken (1949–)

Geelong's youngest-ever player at 16 years and two months, Newland was a brilliant ruck-rover, renowned for his spectacular marking and polished disposal. In a 14-year career from 1965–78, he played 216 games, including 198 with Geelong. He also represented Footscray.

NEWMAN, John (1945–)

One of only two Geelong players to figure in more than 300 VFL games, John Noel William 'Sam' Newman played 303 matches from 1964–80. Recruited from Geelong Grammar where he was an outstanding schoolboy, Newman's natural athleticism soon lifted him into senior ranks, for the third round of 1964.

A rucking protege of the great *'Polly' Farmer*, the 189 cm Newman's expertise at centre bounces and boundary throw-ins is legend.

His longevity was all the more remarkable considering the serious kidney injury he suffered in the first semi-final against Collingwood in 1967. Part of his kidney was removed in a three-hour operation, but he bounced back in 1968, available from the opening match—against his surgeon's advice—and winning the first of his two best and fairest awards. Learning to protect his right side from injury, his pinpoint left-hand palming became a feature of his game.

Newman won All Australian honours in 1969 and represented Victoria eight times. Late in his career he played in white cricket boots, mainly to help protect his ankles, which had been a constant problem throughout his 17 seasons.

He estimated he missed almost 140 games, or six seasons, because of injury. Apart from his kidney injury, he had six operations on his ankles—including one in which he had an artificial ligament inserted—his nose was broken four times, his jaw once and his toes three times.

NEW SOUTH WALES

Competition matches were first held in Sydney in 1880. The first interstate game played under 'Victorian Rules' was between NSW and a Bendigo representative side, in Bendigo in 1881. NSW won by four goals to one goal.

Philip Sheridan was the first president of

The promotional poster released for the NSW-Victoria game at the Sydney Cricket Ground in 1990. Gerard Healy (NSW) and Dermott Brereton (Vic.) are featured. NSW scored a shock win.

the NSW Football Association, a position he held for 11 years from 1880–90, before passing key responsibility to Albert Nash, one of the keenest early supporters of the game.

The Waratah rugby club was one of the pioneers of the game. Many club members favoured it, as fewer injuries occurred than in rugby union games.

The first challenge matches played for the Flanagan Cup were popular, and the Carlton club from Melbourne visited, playing a rugby game and a Rules match against Waratahs, losing the first but winning the second. Among the several thousand spectators present were the Colonial Governor and his wife.

Competition continued until 1893, but the administrative base was weak and interstate rivalry overwhelming. The competition failed to restart in 1894. Many players drifted to other codes.

A base of supporters remained loyal and a group, including Newtown secretary, Bendigo-born Jim Phelan, contacted the Victorian Football League, urging a League game be played in Sydney to help re-establish the game in the NSW capital. Early in the 1903 season, Collingwood played Fitzroy on a ground which is now the Sydney Cricket Ground, attracting a crowd of 15,000, including the Governor-General of Australia. The players wore numbers on the backs of their guernseys while another 'first' was the use of boundary umpires.

The NSW football league was established from 1903. Eleven clubs competed for the premiershp: Alexandria, Ashfield, Balmain, East Sydney—one of the original clubs from the 1880s—Newtown, North Shore, Paddington, Redfern, Sydney, West Sydney and YMCA.

Interest in the game mushroomed to areas including Lithgow, Newcastle and the Riverina. In 1911, the NSWFL purchased land in Alexandria where a magnificent ground and grandstand was established. It hosted the 1914 Australian carnival, but it was a financial disaster and eventually the League forfeited the ground.

Reserve grade teams dropped out of the competition in 1916. By 1920, only five senior sides remained.

The NSW league was at its strongest in the years 1939–45 when many servicemen from around the country were stationed in Sydney and played for local sides, attracting the largest crowds in history.

But it wasn't until 1970, when the VFL match of the day was televised live each Saturday, that the game became truly accepted. The arrival of South Melbourne in 1982 increased the momentum. Millions of dollars were spent promoting the game, especially in its stronghold, the Riverina.

However, crowds disappointed, especially after the Sydney Swans struggled for survival, its private owners threatening to withdraw support unless they received AFL assistance.

Ron Barassi's arrival in mid-year 1993 and the revamping of Sydney's administration to a more traditional football structure helped to give NSW football fresh impetus. The arrival of big name Victorians *Tony Lockett* and *Paul Roos* for the start of the 1995 season fuelled expectations that the Swans could finally rise from the bottom of the ladder, increasing interest in the game at all levels.

MOST VFL/AFL MATCHES BY PLAYERS FROM NEW SOUTH WALES
(150 matches or more)

PLAYER	MATCHES	TEAMS	SPAN	RECRUITED FROM
Terry Daniher	313	South Melbourne/Ess.	1976–92	Ungarie
Bernard Toohey	263	Geelong/Sydney/Foots.	1981–93	Barooga
Mark Maclure	243	Carlton	1974–86	East Sydney
Anthony Daniher	233	Sydney/Essendon	1981–94	Ungarie
Dennis Carroll	219	Sydney	1981–93	Albury

MOST VFL/AFL MATCHES BY PLAYERS FROM NEW SOUTH WALES (cont)
(150 matches or more)

PLAYER	MATCHES	TEAMS	SPAN	RECRUITED FROM
Bill Mohr	195	St Kilda	1929–41	Wagga
Glenn Coleman	190	Fitzroy/Sydney/Foots.	1980–84, 1986–92	Southern Districts
Jack Hawkins	182	Geelong	1973–81	Finley
Greg Lambert	168	South Melbourne	1966–79	Corowa
Michael Byrne	167	Melbourne/Hawthorn	1977–89	North Shore
Ross Henshaw	167	North Melbourne	1971–83	North Albury
Ricky Quade	164	South Melbourne	1970–80	Ariah Park
Russell Morris	159	Hawthorn/St Kilda	1984–94	North Shore
Bert Clay	157	Fitzroy	1940–51	Henty
David Murphy	156	Sydney	1984–93	Turvey Park
Bill Brownless	155*	Geelong	1986–94	Jerilderie

* current player.

NEW ZEALAND CONNECTION, The

New Zealand competed in the first Australian championships under the captaincy of Mr T. J. Wright in 1908, winning two and losing two of its matches.

The NZ team startled the Governor of Victoria, Sir Thomas Carmichael, during the team's march past when they let fly with a Maori war cry.

As far back as 1882, 36 clubs were playing 'Australian Rules' in NZ.

While the rugby codes have dominated, football is still played on the islands at the major centres of Auckland, Christchurch and Wellington.

At the end of the 1991 season, St Kilda played Geelong in an end-of-season game in Auckland.

Several notable League footballers are NZ born including current North Melbourne and State centreline player Wayne Schwass.

NICHOLLS, John (1939–)

Captain in three Carlton premierships and one of the game's finest followers, the imposing big man with the treetrunk thighs was synonymous with Carlton's rise in the mid-1960s. Although relatively short for a ruckman (just 189 cm), Nicholls was capable of destroying the opposition with his dynamic ruck skills and sharp football brain.

His tally of 328 games was a record at the time of his retirement. His 31 State matches is unsurpassed.

Expert in tapping or palming the ball to team-mates, Nicholls formed a legendary combination with Carlton's first rover *Adrian Gallagher*.

In the high-scoring '72 Grand Final, Nicholls played as a forward-pocket ruckman and kicked six goals.

Feared by rival players, he acted as his team's protector and was renowned for having a long memory. Sensationally knocked out by Richmond's Laurie Fowler in the fiery opening minutes of the 1973 Grand Final, Nicholls goaled from the free kick, but his side lost. Nicholls remembered little of the game. 'It was the nearest I'd been to being KO'd in my career,' he said later.

It was to be the sixth and last Grand Final of Nicholls' illustrious career, which included 24 finals.

On his arrival with his much-feted older brother, Don, at Princes Park, Nicholls was a fresh-faced novice with skinny arms and powerful legs. he said it took him years to successfully compete against more experienced opponents. His first captain, *Ken Hands*, was as major ally in helping to arch his big physique between his opponent and the ball, often to the frustration of opponents. In 1961, South Melbourne's Ken Boyd king-hit Nicholls from behind, and was suspended for 12 weeks.*

Nicholls won Carlton's best and fairest award five times, including the first at 18.

His battles with Geelong champion *Graham 'Polly' Farmer* were marvellous. They both possessed quick and astute football brains, natural ability, height, weight and physical strength. They were also master of ruck play, being unmatched for their consistency.

Nicholls played with tremendous authority and revelled in the challenge of playing for Victoria. He figured in four carnivals, being selected as an All Australian in 1966 and All Australian captain in 1969. He captained Victoria in 1969 and 1970.

Nicholls became playing coach of Carlton from 1972–74 and non-playing coach in 1975.

Nicholls' brother, Don, played 77 matches with Carlton from 1956–61.

NIGHT FOOTBALL

The old Lakeside Oval in South Melbourne was the long-time venue for the first years of the night football competition, originally played at the end of season involving the teams who had missed the day finals.

The only exception was in 1957 when all teams competed. South Melbourne won three of the first five premierships. Footscray and North Melbourne were also prominent before the competition ended in 1971.

The first 15 years of the competition were characterised by fighting, on and off the field. There were several ill-lit spots on the field, especially in front of the old bowling green, prompting many brawls and reports.

'The night games were some of the toughest I played,' said Footscray's *Ted Whitten*. 'At that little dark corner at the lake end, you had to have eyes in the back of your head. There was a lot of evening

up. I was no Robinson Crusoe. I was letting them go too.'

North Melbourne legend *John Dugdale* said: 'The games were pretty fiery. There were a lot of reports, more so than in the day football. Every game had a blue. The games were taken very seriously by the lower sides, perhaps more so than by the teams which had just missed out on the four.'

In the first year, 1956, the games were keenly supported for their 'novelty' value. An average crowd of 20,000 saw the seven games, including 33,120 for the final, in which South defeated Carlton for the K.G. Luke trophy. Clubs split a handsome dividend of £800 after the inaugural year. Players received up to £10 a game, at least double their Saturday home-and-away wage.

Following the initial vibrant years of competition, the crowds and receipts waned. Players preferred to rest after the season.

After a five year lay-off, the competition was revived in 1977, with direct television and the involvement of some interstate clubs.

Waverley hosted most of the games, which were played mid-season, featuring even bigger prizemoney than on offer for the day competition.

From the 1990s, the competition was changed to a pre-season format, Essendon winning three premierships and Hawthorn two.

NOONAN, Alan (1947–)

Essendon's leading goalkicker in seven of his 11 seasons at Windy Hill, strong-marking Noonan played 192 games from 1966–77, finishing his career with a season at Richmond.

The gifted forward from Warragul wore *John Coleman*'s famous No. 10 guernsey and enjoyed his best seasons in 1973–74 when he kicked 140 goals.

His best individual effort was eight against Fitzroy in 1969. On his transfer, only three Essendon players had kicked more than his career mark of 420, in 182 games.

* see 'FIVE FAMOUS INCIDENTS'

Alan Noonan wearing Essendon's famous No. 10 guernsey.

Noonan first represented Victoria as a 19-year-old in 1967. He played seven State matches.

NORTH MELBOURNE

The North Melbourne football club has had a long and colourful career, highlighted by the golden era of the 1970s, when the club played off in six Grand Finals in a row, winning two, losing three and tying once.

Some of the game's mightiest players have worn the famous Blue and White from post-war goalkicking great John 'Jock' Spencer and canny blond *Les Foote* through to modern-day champions such as *Keith Greig, Wayne Schimmelbusch, David Dench, Malcolm Blight* and *Ross Glendinning.*

While the club had to wait 50 years for its first premiership, it rarely went through a season without causing at least one upset. Its strength of character was always evident.

The old Arden Street oval has been North's training and administrative base since 1882. Home matches are now played at the Melbourne Cricket Ground.

In the 1970s and 1980s, the club qualified for the finals on 11 occasions, including seven times in eight years under the great *Ron Barassi.*

For some years, North Melbourne (established 1869) played its home matches at Royal Park, before moving to the Macauley Road oval in 1879. The ground was a gluepot, a virtual swamp, before it was totally overhauled and became a fine wet weather venue used to host all the Victorian Football Association finals.

North had been a co-founder of the VFA in 1877 and won six premierships from 1903–19. It created a milestone of 58 games without loss frm 25 July, 1914 to September 1919.

North unsuccessfully attempted to enter League ranks several times before finally being invited (with Hawthorn and Footscray) to join in 1925.

The club's first game was against Geelong at Corio Oval on 2 May, 1925 and, thanks to two goals in time-on, it won

North Melbourne's post-war goalkicking great, Jock Spencer.

204

9.13 (67) to Geelong's 8.11 (59), quite a feat as Geelong lost only one other home-and-away game on the way to the premiership.

It took 25 years before the Northerners (or Shinboners) had a strong enough combination to play off for a flag and a further 25 years before they actually won a premiership.

Now the Roos are being billed as one of the likely teams of the '90s, having qualified for consecutive final series under the astute coaching of Denis Pagan in 1993–94.

NORTH MELBOURNE: THE STATISTICS

FORMED: 1869

JOINED LEAGUE: 1925
HOME VENUES: Arden St. Oval (1925–64, 1966–85), Coburg (1965), MCG (1984–)
CURRENT HOME VENUE DIMENSIONS: 161 metres × 140 metres
COLOURS: Vertical royal blue and white striped guernsey
TOTAL FINALS MATCHES: 43 (17 wins, 25 losses, 1 tie)
FINALS RECORD: Premiers: 2 (1975, 1977)
                  Runners-up: 4 (1950, 1974, 1976, 1978)
PREMIERSHIP COACHES: Ron Barassi (2)
NIGHT SERIES PREMIERSHIPS: 3 (1965, 1966, 1980)
YOUNGEST PLAYER: Robert Peterson, 16 years 45 days (1968)
OLDEST PLAYER: Syd Barker, 37 years (1927)
HIGHEST SCORE: 35.19 (229) v Sydney, R.6, 1993, Princes Park
LOWEST SCORE: 2.7 (19) v Geelong, R.1, 1930, Corio Oval
LONGEST WINNING SEQUENCE: 9 (1977–78). Undefeated in 12 matches (1977–78)
LONGEST LOSING SEQUENCE: 35 (1933–35)
MOST FINALS: Wayne Schimmelbusch 29, Keith Greig 23, David Dench 23, Malcolm Blight 22, Gary Cowton 22
MOST SEASONS AS COACH: Wally Carter 11 (1948–53, 1958–62)
MOST SEASONS AS CAPTAIN: Wayne Schimmelbusch 9 (1979–87)

MOST GAMES		MOST GOALS	
Wayne Schimmelbusch	306	Jock Spencer	475
Keith Greig	297	Malcolm Blight	445
David Dench	275	John Longmire	436*
John Dugdale	248	Sel Murray	407
Steve McCann	226	John Dugdale	358
Allen Aylett	220	Wayne Schimmelbusch	354
John Law	219	Bill Findlay	350
Laurie Dwyer	200	Syd Dyer	323
		Allen Aylett	312

* current player.

MOST GOALS IN A MATCH: John Longmire 14 v Melbourne, R.14, 1990, MCG
                       John Longmire 12 v Richmond, R.2, 1990, MCG
                       Jock Spencer 11 v South Melb., R.16, 1950, Lake Oval
                       Malcolm Blight 11 v Footscray, R.17, 1981, Western Oval
BROWNLOW MEDALLISTS: Noel Teasdale 1965; Keith Greig 1973, 1974; Malcolm Blight 1987; Ross Glendinning 1983
COLEMAN MEDALLISTS: Malcolm Blight 1982, John Longmire 1990

NORTH MELBOURNE: THE STATISTICS (cont)

LEAGUE LEADING GOALSCORERS: Doug Wade 103 (1974), Malcolm Blight 103 (1982), John Longmire 98 (1990)

RECORD HOME GROUND ATTENDANCE: 35,116 v Carlton, R.19, 1949, Arden St Oval

21,626 v Collingwood, R.10, 1965, Coburg

72,216 v Collingwood, R.9, 1994, MCG

RECORD ATTENDANCE IN ANY MATCH: 113,839 v Richmond, GF, 1974, MCG

MOST RECENT PREMIERSHIP TEAM: 1977 North Melb. 21.25 (151) d Collingwood 19.10 (124)

B: R. Henshaw, D. Dench (c), F. Gumbleton. H.B: G. Cowton,
D. Sutton, K. Montgomery. C: S. Alves, X. Tanner,
W. Schimmelbusch. H.F: S. Icke, M. Blight, A. Briedis.
F: B. Crosswell, P. Baker, J. Cassin. R: P. Keenan, J. Byrne.
R: B. Cable. Reserves: S. McCann, W. Nettlefold.

NORTHERN TERRITORY

Founded in 1917, the Northern Territory Football League has developed and
encouraged football to elite status in
Darwin. The NT seasons stretch from
October to April when most sportsminded Australians are revelling in
cricket.

In 1992, a $7 million stadium was
opened at the league's new headquarters
at Marrara.

Until the 1960s, when David Kintilla
went to South Adelaide, the first full-

MOST VFL/AFL MATCHES BY PLAYERS FROM THE NORTHERN TERRITORY
(100 matches or more)

PLAYER	MATCHES	TEAMS	SPAN	RECRUITED FROM
Michael McLean	157*	Footscray/Brisbane	1983–94	Nightcliff
Maurice Rioli	118	Richmond	1982–87	Sth Fremantle via Melville Island
Michael Long	102*	Essendon	1989–93	St. Mary's

* current player.

Two of the Territory's finest football products, Maurice Rioli and Michael Long.

blood Aboriginal to represent South Australia, the game in Darwin had stagnated.

Subsequently, an array of Territory stars from Melville Islander Maurice Rioli, to Michael Long, Michael McLean and Gilbert McAdam (from Alice Springs) have made an impression in Victorian football.

Rioli originally played senior football with South Fremantle before joining Richmond.

NORTHEY, John (1943–   )

Having helped end Melbourne's finals drought when in only his second season as coach, in 1987, he lifted the Demons into the finals for the first time in 23 years. Had it not been for a goal after the siren by Hawthorn's *Gary Buckenara*, Melbourne would have played off in the Grand Final in a fairytale ending to a season in which it charged from 11th into the last three.

A fine communicator and tough when he had to be, Northey returned to his original club, Richmond, as coach in 1993.

He had previously played 117 games and kicked 192 goals as a half-forward for the Tigers from 1963–70.

Known as 'Swooper', he played in Richmond's 1967 and 1969 premiership teams before crossing to Western Suburbs in Sydney where he won two more flags (1971 and 1973) and on to Redan in the Ballarat league where he again was a success.

Northey coached Sydney in 1985 and Melbourne for seven years before coaching his 200th game, with Richmond in 1993.

OLDEST PLAYERS

Harold Vivian 'Vic' Cumberland, the oldest player, at 43, to appear in a VFL game, was a dynamic ruckman with superb stamina, who played for 22 seasons. He was aged 43 years and 48 days for his last game, for St Kilda against South Melbourne at the Lake Oval, in 1920.

The much-travelled Cumberland and Carlton's Jim Flynn, who was 40 when he came out of retirement to play for the Blues in the 1910 finals, are the only 40-year-olds to play League football.

Horrie Clover (Carlton), *Les Hughes* (Collingwood), Charlie Hardy (Essendon), Harry Lever (St Kilda), *Alby Morrison* (Footscray), Percy Parratt (Fitzroy) and *Michael Tuck* (Hawthorn) were all 38.

It appears Cumberland's remarkable record of endurance, which has already stood for more than 70 years, may never be broken.

Born in Toorak on 4 July, 1877, and renowned as being strong, vigorous and fair, Cumberland's career took him all over Australasia. The first great interstate import into the VFL, he amassed an estimated 400-plus games, involving:
- Tasmania: 1894–98 (113 games);
- Melbourne (VFL): 1898–1901 (50 games, 18 goals), including Melbourne's 1900 premiership;
- Western Australia: 1902 (19 games);
- St Kilda (VFL): 1903–04, 1907–08, 1912–15, 1920 (126 games, 72 goals);
- Auckland, NZ: 1905–06 (32 games);
- Sturt, South Australia: 1909–11 (44 games);
- Interstate: (27 games);
- Overseas: with the Australian Forces in World War One.

Winner of SA's Magarey Medal in 1911 and the star ruckman of the 1911 Australian carnival, Cumberland was 180 cm and 86 kg. Newspapers of the time called him a 'Human Atlas', admiring his fitness, quick-thinking and team play.

He died, aged 50, in a car accident.

Other stalwarts:

* The much-travelled Joe Littler was 50 when he captained Wynyard in 1932, his final season. A member of Launceston's 1897 premiership side, Littler also played in Western Australia and in Victoria with South Melbourne (in 1903). In all, he participated in 14 premierships and almost 500 senior games. On his retirement, the president of the Northern Tasmanian Football Association, Mr R. Tyson, described Littler as 'the best footballer in Tasmania in the last 40 years'.

* Dick Condon was 44 in his final season with VFA club Williamstown, in 1922. A champion rover at Collingwood, where he played 149 games in nine seasons, he also played with Richmond and North Melbourne (VFA). He roved in two Collingwood premierships in 1902–03.

* Harry Coventry, a noted all-sports-

Vic Cumberland (extreme left) pictured in Melbourne colours playing against Geelong in 1899. Others pictured are: Fred McGinis, Jack Parkin, Fred Elliott, Jack Conway and Jack Leith.

man, was another 400-game player, having his first game with Latrobe, aged 13, and his last, in 1927, at 43. A chemist, he played all his football in Tasmania, being a noted ballhandler. He also assisted in the development of the young *Ivor Warne-Smith*.

* Jack Moroney was 42 when he captained the Australian Capital Territory at the 1933 Australian carnival. He appeared with St Kilda in 1909 and had 15 years at VFA club Prahran before shifting to Canberra.

* Jack Gardiner was 42 on his retirement in 1925. After beginning at Carlton (16 games, 1901–02) and Melbourne (53 from 1903–08), he became the Tasmanian Football League's coach and umpire for the 1908 Australian titles. Returning to football as a player, Gardiner figured in three consecutive premierships with Canamore from 1909–11. Later, he played with City and North Hobart. He was captain–coach in his final playing season, 1925, when he won his sixth flag.

* George 'Tony' Tyson was 42 on his final appearance for the Kalgoorlie Railways in the strong WA Goldfields competition in 1929. He represented Western Australia in three carnivals, being a leading member of one of WA's most famous footballing families.

* Gordon Bowman, a member of Melbourne's 1948 premiership side, was 42 when he played his last game for Newtown in the 1969 NSW League grand final. He had 52 games at Melbourne and 29 at Hawthorn before coaching in Tasmania, Queensland and NSW, where he played in back-to-back flags in 1967–68, the last as a 41-year-old.

OLLIVER, Arthur (1917–88)

Renowned for his durability, despite a pencil-thin 189 cm figure which won him a nickname 'Lolly Legs', Olliver was a fine high mark who played in the ruck or in key positions with commitment and consistency.

He remains one of Footscray's greatest stalwarts, having amassed 271 games from 1935–50. Captain-coach for six of his last seven seasons, he was best and fairest in 1944 and equal best and fairest, with *Norman Ware*, in 1941—the year Ware won the Brownlow.

A two-time Victorian representative, Olliver started his career at centre half-back before developing into a follower. He also kicked 355 goals, topping Footscray's goalkicking in successive years in 1936–37.

O'NEILL, Kevin (1908–85)

Figuring in five Richmond Grand Final sides, including four in a row from 1931–34, the 175 cm O'Neill was a member of the football's most-feted pre-war full-back line, in combination with full-back Maurie Sheahan and fellow back-pocket player, Martin Bolger.

Renowned for bustling taller opponents off their game, he played 209 games from 1930–41 and represented Victoria 10

OLDEST VFL/AFL PLAYERS

PLAYER/CLUB	AGE	FINAL SEASON
Vic Cumberland (Melbourne/St Kilda)	43	1920
Jim Flynn (Geelong/Carlton)	40	1910
Horrie Clover (Carlton)	38	1931
Charlie Hardy (Essendon)	38	1925
Les Hughes (Collingwood)	38	1920
Harry Lever (St Kilda)	38	1922
Alby Morrison (Footscray)	38	1946
Percy Parratt (Fitzroy)	38	1923
Ted Rankin (Geelong)	38	1910
Michael Tuck (Hawthorn)	38	1991

Post-war football's most-feted full-back line: Martin Bolger (left), Maurie Sheahan and Kevin O'Neill.

times. He was among Richmond's best three players in each of the Tigers' two flags, in 1932 and 1934.

OSBORNE, Richard (1964–)

A dashing defender-turned-forward who reached 200 games with his second League club, Sydney, in 1993, Osborne was another of Fitzroy's recent elite to quit the club in mid-career.

Fitzroy's leading goalkicker for five seasons, including four in a row from 1986–89, the 182 cm Osborne captained the Lions in 1991, capping a fine comeback after having his knee reconstructed late in 1989.

Osborne averaged more than two goals a match at Fitzroy, despite starting his career as a running half-back. While he had only one season with Sydney before switching to Footscray, his 10.2 for the Swans against Melbourne in round 13, 1993, was an exceptional effort and lifted his adopted side to its only win of the season.

Osborne represented Victoria seven times.

OVERSEAS-BORN PLAYERS

Australian football's recruiting net widened in the 1980s with Melbourne's signing of leading Irish teenagers, Paul Earley and *Jim Stynes* and young Scot, Sean Wight.

More than 30 League footballers have been born outside Australia, the most successful being Carlton legend *Alex Jesaulenko*, who was born in Salzburg, Austria, in the last months of World War Two.

More recently, Hawthorn's Stephen Lawrence, one of the best afield in the 1991 Grand Final, was born in Zimbabwe. His father, Godfrey, represented South Africa at Test cricket.

Fitzroy's John McCarthy comes from Wales, North Melbourne's Wayne Schwass from New Zealand and Carlton's Mil Hanna from Lebanon.

Among the ranks of overseas-born League footballers are:

210

OVERSEAS-BORN VFL/AFL PLAYERS

PLAYER	COUNTRY OF BIRTH	AFL TEAMS AND SPAN	MATCHES	GOALS
Colin Alexander	England	Collingwood 1989–91/Brisbane 1992–93	29	31
Mark Bayliss	England	Collingwood 1989	4	6
Peter Bennett	New Zealand	Hawthorn 1976–77/Essendon 1978–81	79	27
Lawrence Bingham	England	Hawthorn 1988–90/St Kilda 1992–93	25	0
Wayne Blackwell	England	Carlton 1984–90	110	80
Chris Burton	England	Footscray 1980–84/Richmond 1985–88	116	35
Ian Dargie	England	St Kilda 1989–90/West Coast 1991	11	1
Paul Earley	Ireland	Melbourne 1984	1	1
Fred Fairweather	England	North Melbourne 1944–46	54	14
Harry Frei	West Germany	Footscray 1973	6	0
Andy Goodwin	England	Richmond 1987–91/Melbourne 1992–93	73	9
Milham Hanna	Lebanon	Carlton 1986–94	151*	64
Paul Harding	England	Hawthorn 1987–88/St Kilda 1989–91/West Coast 1992–94	116*	14
Alex Jesaulenko	Austria	Carlton 1967–79/St Kilda 1980–81	280	444
Stephen Lawrence	Zimbabwe	Hawthorn 1988–94	101*	22
Johnny Leonard	England	South Melbourne 1932	12	17
Stuart Magee	Ireland	South Melbourne 1962–68/ Footscray 1969–75	217	149
John McCarthy	Wales	North Melbourne 1986–93/ Fitzroy 1994	129	156
Marty McDonnell	New Zealand	Footscray 1939–50	90	1
Dermott McNichol	Ireland	St Kilda 1990	3	1
Ian Muller	South Africa	Carlton 1984–85/St Kilda 1988–91	27	2
Brian Mynott	England	St Kilda 1964–75	209	73
Richard Nixon	England	Richmond 1987–90	37	3
Tom O'Halloran	New Zealand	South Melbourne 1918–21	52	12
Polly Perkins	England	Richmond 1940–49	148	0
Don Pyke	USA	West Coast 1989–94	103*	45
Jose Romero	Chile	North Melbourne 1988–94	89*	98
Wayne Schwass	New Zealand	North Melbourne 1988–94	122*	68
Joe Sellwood	New Zealand	Geelong 1930–45	180	97
Ben Sexton	New Guinea	Footscray 1991–94	30*	26
Jim Stynes	Ireland	Melbourne 1987–94	178*	109
Sandford Wheeler	USA	Sydney 1989–94	43	7
Sean Wight	Scotland	Melbourne 1985–94	129*	63

* current player.

PANNAM, Charles snr (1874–1952)

The founding member of one of football's greatest families, Charlie Pannam snr was a celebrated rover who had 170 games and kicked 111 goals with Collingwood from 1897–1907. A member of Collingwood's 1902–03 premiership teams, he was captain in 1905, the year he topped the VFL goalkicking with 38. In 1902, he was the first VFL player to reach 100 games.

He coached Richmond in 1912.

His younger brother, Alby, also played with Collingwood. One of his five sons, Charles jnr, was a great centreman after the First World War, playing with Collingwood, South Melbourne and Brunswick.

A six-time State representative and founding member of a great football dynasty, Collingwood's Charles Pannam snr.

Sixteen years after Charlie jnr's debut, his younger brother, Albert, appeared, becoming one of Collingwood's great rovers in a career from 1933–45. He was a regular Victorian player and, in 181 club games, kicked 455 goals.

Charlie snr's grandsons, *Lou* and *Ron Richards* also represented Collingwood with distinction.

The Pannams originated from Greece. Their family name was Pannamopoulos.

PARKIN, David (1942–)

One of a select few to captain and, later, coach a premiership team, Parkin has been one of post-war football's most outstanding contributors, his 30-year involvement produced four flags: one as a player and three as coach.

He represented Victoria five times and coached the State on nine occasions, including the 1979 National Football League championships.

Tallying 211 games with Hawthorn from 1961–74, he passed 300 VFL matches as coach in 1991, having begun with the Hawks in 1977. Later he coached at Carlton and Fitzroy, maintaining his meticulous match preparations, including his exhaustive dossiers on opposing teams and players.

'He was totally organised, thorough, intense, enthusiastic and a good communicator with players,' said former teammate *Leigh Matthews*.

The 180 cm Parkin debuted with the Hawks as an 18-year-old in 1961, playing initially as a utility. Finding himself best suited to defence, he played in the back pocket in the 1963 Grand Final side and again in the 1971 team which came from behind to defeat St Kilda for the flag. In 1965, he was Hawthorn's best and fairest. From 1969–73, he was captain.

His courage was one of his major assets but also resulted in him receiving many concussions. He estimated he was knocked out 10 times in his career.

In 1975, he coached Subiaco. In 1977, he took over as senior coach of Hawthorn for the first of four seasons.

The Hawks lost the preliminary final in his first year, but made the Grand Final in his second, easily defeating North Melbourne. After successive poor seasons when the club failed to make the finals,

Parkin resigned, having learnt that members of the senior executive were considering their coaching options.

David Parkin with the 1971 premiership cup.

Parkin went to Carlton to coach where he enjoyed considerable success, helping Carlton to back-to-back premierships in 1981–82.

Parkin's strategies revolved around the lessons he'd first learnt under *John Kennedy* at Hawthorn. His Carlton sides ran straight at the ball and, if they wavered, they paid for it at training the following week. The fierce man-on-man duels at training sometimes resulted in serious mid-week injuries.*

In 1986, Parkin lifted Fitzroy into a preliminary final—its first in more than 25 years. In 1991, he returned to Carlton, the Blues making the 1993 Grand Final.

To the start of the 1995 season he had won 218 of his 374 matches as senior coach, a winning ratio of 58 per cent.

* see 'STRATEGIES'

PECK, John (1937–93)

Hawthorn's youngest-ever player and one of its greatest goalkickers, Peck is the only post-war full-forward to head the VFL goalkicking charts three years in a row, from 1963–65.

Recruited as a follower/forward from Canterbury, he played 233 games and kicked 475 goals from 1954–66 before crossing to Port Melbourne where he had his final two senior seasons, including the infamous '67 VFA grand final.

He topped Hawthorn's goalkicking eight times, and also represented Victoria seven times, from 1960–64.

A strong, physical player who used his strength to good effect, he's best-remembered for knocking out South Australian Brian Sawley during a State game in 1963, after claiming he'd been deliberately kicked.

The incident so enraged the SA fans that many jumped the fence and ran at Peck, only to be stopped by a human barrier of Victorian players and policemen.

Describing the KO punch in *Wild Men of Football*, *Jack Dyer* said: 'Peck hurtled from the ground swinging a ferocious uppercut which was the perfection of timing. It landed so squarely and firmly on Sawley's jaw that it lifted him off the ground. Sawley crashed flat on his back without a muscle twitching. He lay prostrate with his feet upturned.'

Amid great controversy which at one stage threatened the friendly football relations between the two States, the South Australian tribunal found Peck guilty of striking and passed on the case to the VFL to decide a penalty. League tribunal chiefs agreed Peck had been acting under extreme provocation, but still outed him for two weeks. It was the first time he had been suspended in 10 years of big-time football.

Peck's career was all the more notable because he was a chronic asthma sufferer. He also played for several seasons with a painful abscess on the ball of one foot which forced him to wear a slipper during the week and severely restricted his training.

PEKIN, Tim (1965–)

Versatile defender who was among the fittest players in the AFL in the early 1990s, Pekin had 107 games with Fitzroy before crossing to St Kilda and playing another 100.

Originally from Colac–Coragulac, Pekin was runner-up in St Kilda's best and fairest in 1990.

PERT, Gary (1965–)

One of Fitzroy's most loyal players until having his payments slashed by half after a knee reconstruction, Pert joined Collingwood and finished runner-up in the Copeland Trophy in his first year, 1992.

A dependable, long-kicking full-back, who was one of the game's genuine champions before a run of injuries, Pert passed 200 games in the 1993 season.

Recruited from Bulleen, the 187 cm Pert debuted with Fitzroy aged 16 and first represented Victoria at 18, being the youngest since *Carl Ditterich*, two decades earlier.

He was an All Australian in 1985 and Fitzroy's best and fairest in 1989.

His father, Brian, also played more than 100 games at Fitzroy.

PICKEN, Bill (1956–)

One of post-war football's great characters, big-marking Billy Picken played 11 of his 13 League seasons at Collingwood, winning the 1983 best and fairest. He played 212 of his 240 games at Victoria Park and represented the Swans in 1984–85 before returning to Collingwood for his final season in 1986.

A Victorian representative on seven occasions, 185 cm Picken was renowned for his ability to perform in the most important games. He played in five Collingwood Grand Finals, including the famous tie of 1977.

When flying for marks, he often would yell: 'Yours Billy.' His non-stop chatter amused team-mates and sometimes aggravated opponents.

Bill Picken: one of football's greatest characters.

PINNELL, Phil (1951–)

Had a dream start to his League career, playing in three Carlton Grand Finals in his first six years and missing a fourth only through a chronic knee problem.

A determined half-back who was also successful on the wing, Pinnell played 173 games at Carlton from 1968–79, before having his final two seasons at Melbourne. In all, he played 201 games.

PLATTEN, John (1963–)

One of the few players to win both the Magarey and Brownlow Medals, the pint-sized, scrupulously fair rover with the mop-top hair and No. 44 guernsey was the premier rover in Australia throughout the 1980s.

He played in Grand Finals in each of his first four seasons at Hawthorn, for three wins and a loss. In 1991, he played in another, when Hawthorn defeated the Eagles.

Hawk fans compare his courage and spirit to the great *Peter Crimmins*.

Diminutive John Platten flies for a spectacular mark against Carlton pair Des English and David Rhys-Jones.

No other Brownlow winner has worn a jumper with a bigger number than Platten's 44. He was often asked to take a lower number in his early days at Hawthorn, but preferred to stay with the No. 44 he'd first worn at Central Districts. In 1990, Platten passed 100 League games, but had a poor year by his own remarkably high standards, being restricted by a wrist injury which required summertime surgery. In 1991, when he started to again play with his old zest, Hawthorn clinched the double chance, in a formidable late-season burst.

'I have a lot of pride to do well,' he said. 'I love the game, love the club. You only play 10 or 12 years and you've got to get as much out of it as possible.'

He again won All Australian honours in 1992 and in 1994 reached 200 AFL games.

POOL, Ted

Arrived in Melbourne in 1926 to seek his footballing fortune, having played successfully in WA with Kalgoorlie City.

Several clubs were interested and he chose Hawthorn, amassing 200 games from 1926–38 and representing Victoria seven times. The Hawks did not have a finer between-the-wars rover.

PRATT, Bob (1912–)

Taking some of the most sensational, sky-scraping marks in League history, Bob Pratt became one of the most legendary footballers of them all. He broke the 100-goal barrier in three consecutive seasons as South Melbourne enjoyed its halcyon years. He played in four consecutive Grand Finals, from 1933–36.

In 1934, the 180 cm Pratt kicked 150 goals, a VFL record which was never surpassed. In 1971, Hawthorn's *Peter Hudson* equalled it, but played 24 games, compared with Pratt's 21.

In 157 games from 1930–39, Pratt kicked 678 goals at more than four goals a match. He had one comeback game after the war, in 1946, kicking two goals.

His old team-mate *Laurie Nash* once said of Pratt's leaping: 'He was the greatest

Bob Pratt with his son Bob jnr, who also played League football.

high mark I have ever seen. How he didn't kill himself in some of his marking efforts I will never know.'

Essendon legend *Dick Reynolds* said Pratt's leaping was uncanny. 'One day I saw his boot going past my head and couldn't believe how he could get there. When he hit the ground, he rolled like a cat and never seemed to get hurt.'

Pratt also liked to lead, making him an extremely tough player to counter.

His best day at League level was 15 against Essendon, in 1934.

He took just 13 matches to reach 100 goals that season, a record which has been challenged but never broken.

Pratt was only of average height but his acrobatic spring and strong hands made him the most exciting player of his era. Sometimes he leapt so high that he'd go straight over the top of packs.

Surprisingly, he never won South's best and fairest and even in his golden year of 1934—when he smashed *Gordon Coventry*'s League record of 124—polled only 13 votes in the Brownlow to finish eighth, behind Essendon's *Dick Reynolds*.

In 1991, he conceded that Hudson and Essendon legend *John Coleman* were 'not bad'.

'But Coleman played in two premiership sides and they try to say he was as good a forward as me. He had all the opportunities, so why couldn't he kick 150?'

See also: 'HIGH FLIERS'

QUEENSLAND

In 1991, Queensland enjoyed a historic win against Victoria, its first victory against the Big V in matches since 1924. The Queenslanders won the State-of-Origin contest 23.14 (152) to Victoria's 15.18 (108). The side included a dozen players from the Brisbane Bears and was captained by *Roger Merrett*.

The State also had regular interstate competition with NSW, ACT and Tasmania. Matches with NSW date back to 1884.

Queensland was one of seven teams to contest the first Australian national football championships, in Melbourne in 1908, but didn't win any of its three games. It wasn't until 1933, in Sydney, that it broke through, defeating Canberra 20.16 (136) to 14.10 (94).

It has not contested a national title,

Sandgate's Dan Brennan, one of the few to play more than 300 QAFL senior games.

other than in 'B' division, since the war.

While Australian football still trails in popularity behind the rugby codes and basketball, its influence is considerable throughout Queensland with competitions, junior development and coaching activity in areas including Brisbane, Bundaberg, Cairns, Townsville, Mackay, Central Highlands, Rockhampton, the Sunshine Coast, the Gold Coast and Mt Isa.

Ipswich was one of the State's first footballing strongholds, in 1885 recording a victory against Essendon.

The first Queensland club, the Brisbane Australian football club was formed in 1866.

In 1879, a controlling body—the forerunner of the present Queensland Australian Football League—was entrusted to oversee the running of the game in Queensland and in 1883, Queensland sent delegates to the Intercolonial football conference. More than 300 clubs emerged in the first 30 years.

One of Queensland football's most prominent administrators was Mayne secretary, J. A. 'Joe' Grogan, whose memory has been annually honoured, since 1946, with the presentation of the Grogan Medal for the best and fairest player in the Queensland competition.

The QAFL grand finals are played at the 'Gabba, famous for being one of Australian Test cricket's major venues and home of the Brisbane Bears.

Noted former VFL players to play in the QAFL in recent times include post-war greats *Gary Dempsey*, *Carl Ditterich*, *John Rantall* and *Alex Jesaulenko*, who was captain-coach of Sandgate in 1983–84.

Among the most prominent Queenslanders at VFL/AFL level are *Jason Dunstall* (Hawthorn), Scott McIvor (Brisbane Bears) and Gavin Crosisca (Collingwood). Frank Dunell is one of the few Queenslanders to play in a Grand Final. He appeared in Essendon's 1984 premiership team. Four QAFL players had amassed 300 or more games to the start of 1992: Syd Guildford 333 (Wilston Grange), Owen Backwell 323 (Western Districts), Dan Brennan 319 (Sandgate) and Don Smith 300 (Sandgate).

MOST VFL/AFL MATCHES BY PLAYERS FROM QUEENSLAND
(100 matches or more)

PLAYER	MATCHES	TEAMS	SPAN	RECRUITED FROM
Jason Dunstall	208*	Hawthorn	1985–94	Coorparoo
Scott McIvor	165*	Fitzroy/Brisbane	1985–94	Wilston–Grange
Gavin Crosisca	140*	Collingwood	1987–94	Western District
Dean McRae	117*	North Melb./Sydney	1987–94	Sandgate
Ray Smith	116	Essendon/Melbourne	1971–75	Western Dist.
Frank Dunell	115	Essendon/Brisbane	1979–88	Windsor-Zillmere
Richard Murrie	111	Footscray/Geelong/Rich.	1975–83	Mayne
Marcus Ashcroft	104*	Brisbane	1989–94	Southport
Keith Schaffer	102	South Melbourne	1947–53	South Surfers
Stephen Lawrence	101*	Hawthorn	1988–94	Morningside

* current player.

Brisbane's Scott McIvor: one of the most successful Queenslanders at AFL level.

Bernie Quinlan with his first League club, Footscray.

QUINLAN, Bernie (1951–)

One of post-war football's finest players, the first man to play 300 games, win a Brownlow Medal and kick 100 goals in a season, the athletic Quinlan (193 cm and 93 kg) played 367 games and kicked 815 goals in a magnificent 18-season career, from 1969–86.

He spent his first decade at Footscray, having a reputation as a brilliant but inconsistent player before blossoming at Fitzroy, winning the 1981 Brownlow Medal (along with South Melbourne's *Barry Round*) at the age of 30 and twice kicking 100 goals in a season—in 1983 (116) and in 1984 (105).

Robert Walls, a playing great at two clubs, said Quinlan was the greatest player (with Carlton's *John Nicholls*) that he'd ever seen.

'Quinlan played better football in his early 30s than he did a decade earlier,' Walls said. 'It didn't just happen, he did lots of upper body work, became really strong and kept the legs fresh with cycling and swimming. He looked after himself, didn't smoke, rarely drank and ate sensibly.

'The young Fitzroy players were like pups as they followed Quinlan around, such was their admiration for him.'

Renowned for his thumping field kicks, using a fluid, economic action, Quinlan became known as 'Superboot'. One of his drop kicks in 1966 was measured at 85 yards.

His best years were at centre half-forward, but he could also play at centre half-back and in the ruck. He topped Fitzroy's goal-kicking charts, playing at full-forward, in five of his last six years. His highest goal tally in any game was 11.

In 1995, he returned to the Lions, as senior coach.

RAINES, Geoff (1956–)

A strong-willed and supremely gifted centreman, Raines had 254 League games, spread over 14 years and four clubs. Best known for his successes at Richmond—where he spent his first seven senior seasons—the 180 cm Raines was one of the three best players afield in the Tigers' 1980 premiership side, won three best and fairests and All Australian selection.

Rated one of modern day football's most complete players, he possessed immaculate skills, superb long-kicking ability and the aggression and class to take on bigger players in marking, tackling and shepherding duels.

Geoff Raines, soon after debuting with Richmond in 1976.

He made his senior debut in 1976 as a wingman and in 1977 began a distinguished reign as Richmond's centreman, amassing his best and fairest 'treble', including two in a row in 1980–81, as well as finishing second on another occasion.

Gifted Aboriginal Maurice Rioli's arrival forced him back onto the wing for periods in 1982 and after the Tigers lost the Grand Final, Raines swapped to Collingwood, saying he needed fresh challenges. He'd played 134 games with the Tigers. His transfer was one of the costliest ever. In return for his release, the Tigers received $200,000 cash as well as three Collingwood players: Neil Peart, Wally Lovett and Terry Domburg. It was the major play in a costly poaching war which erupted between the two clubs, sending both to the brink of financial ruin.

At Collingwood he had a horror year in 1983, and was forced to have an ankle operation. Within three years, he had transferred to Essendon, where he played only briefly before joining Brisbane.

One of the Bears' biggest-name imports, he rewarded the faith of coach *Peter Knights* by finishing in the top two in the best and fairest two years in a row, in 1987–88.

Representing Victoria 11 times, he was twice an All Australian. He quit on the eve of his 15th season in 1990, saying he wanted to do 'other things in life'.

RANTALL, John (1943–)

An accomplished and durable half-back, who for a short time held the VFL record for the most games ever played, dark-haired Robert John 'Mopsy' Rantall amassed 336 matches in an illustrious 18-season career at three clubs, South Melbourne, North Melbourne and Fitzroy.

Few rivalled his coolness, skill or consistency in blanketing big-name forwards. He also played with success in the centre, and was a member of North Melbourne's historic 1975 premiership team.

He returned to South Melbourne the following year for four more seasons, creeping to within just three games of *Kevin Murray*'s VFL games record.

At 36, he felt he was still good enough for one last season, but South disagreed and he was forced to transfer to Fitzroy for his farewell matches. While he played only six games, it was enough to give him the record.

Held in the highest esteem by his peers, Rantall was recruited from Cobden in 1963 and won interstate selection after just eight games. He represented Victoria five times, was South Melbourne captain in 1972 and runner-up in South's best and fairest in 1971.

John Rantall: one of the big names to change clubs through the VFL's controversial 10-year service rule in 1973.

REGAN, Jack (1912–88)

Known as 'The Prince of Full-Backs', the 185 cm Regan played in five consecutive Collingwood Grand Final sides between 1935–39, including two premierships in 1936–37, in an illustrious 196-game career.

Winner of the Copeland Trophy as Collingwood's best and fairest in 1936, he was also runner-up twice and represented Victoria every year between 1933–39.

Scrupulously fair, his duels with high-flying South Melbourne champion *Bob Pratt* were legendary. In the 1935 Grand Final, he outplayed another Swans star, centre half-forward *Laurie Nash*, to help

Collingwood emerge from a shaky start and win by 20 points.

Collingwood captain in 1940–41, his final year was 1946, when he was granted a 15-year certificate.

His 14 Victorian matches included three Australian carnivals. In 1941 he led a State team to Sydney.

Third in the 1934 Brownlow Medal, Collingwood's Jack Regan was a magnificent aerialist and a fine kick.

RENFREY, Russell

A tough Geelong follower and forward who was never dropped in his 11-season career, 180 cm 'Hooker' Renfrey inevitably had to battle against taller opponents. He revelled in the responsibility, playing in three Grand Finals in a row including the 1951–52 premiership double in his 201 matches from 1946–56.

In his debut season, he was Geelong's leading goalkicker and in 1948 represented Victoria.

REYNOLDS, Dick (1915–)

A teenage winner of the Brownlow Medal, Richard Sylvanus Reynolds was a golden great of the game, becoming known as 'King Richard'. He won three Medals (1934, 1937, 1938), seven Essendon best and fairests and represented Victoria 18 times, twice as captain in 1939 and 1946.

Dick 'King Richard' Reynolds, a triple Brownlow Medallist.

He finished in the Brownlow's 'top 10' votewinners in each of his first six seasons, an unprecedented effort. After his amazing 320 game career had ended—a record which stood for 20 years—he continued as Essendon's non-playing coach until 1959.

A grandstand at Windy Hill is named in his honour.

Originally a Carlton supporter, he wanted to play with the Blues but as his junior club, Woodlands, was in Essendon's territory, he had to go to Windy Hill.

Lifted straight into Essendon's senior team, Reynolds was not an eye-catching player—he was 179 cm and 83 kg and tended to lope after the ball—but he was deceptively fast, had superb reflexes, exceptional skill and was deeply loyal to his team-mates.

He was also very courageous, rarely being caught by the many rough-and-tumble merchants who gloried in crashing prized opponents to the ground.

Reynolds played in 10 Grand Finals, for four wins, including the 1949–50 Essendon teams which were among the best in the club's history.

His last game was in the 1951 Grand Final, when he played as a reserve. He was 36.

He kicked 437 goals in his 19 year playing career and gained more than 150 Brownlow votes. His No. 3 guernsey is one of the most famous in League football annals.

His 27-year association with Essendon, including 21 as coach, ended after the 1960 season when he was replaced by *John Coleman*. Essendon's historian, Michael Maplestone, said: 'When he bowed out from the club at the age of 45, it could truly be said that no man had served Essendon more loyally or had done so much for the club.'

Reynolds coached Essendon in 11 Grand Finals, for four wins and seven losses.

Shifting to Adelaide, he coached West Torrens for three years from 1961–62 before his return to Melbourne.

Dick's younger brother, Tom, who was taller and heavier at 180 cm and 92 kg, was also a fine player. In 1939, he kicked 71 goals to establish a new Essendon goalkicking record and in all played 113 games with Essendon from 1937–44. He also had a year with St Kilda in 1945.

RHYS-JONES, David (1962–)

Ian Stewart was adamant: 'Look at that kid over there. He'll play 200 League games, no question.'

The triple Brownlow Medallist, then coaching South Melbourne, was alerting reporters to the talents of 17-year-old David Rhys-Jones on the eve of the 1980 season.

David Rhys-Jones: a footballing firebrand.

Even then, the blond, pencil-thin winger had superb balance and ballhandling gifts.

Included in South Melbourne's senior team weeks later for a practice match against Collingwood at Hastings, the teenage prodigy was cleaned up several times, but made a contribution in his side's upset win against the reigning Grand Finalists.

Later he played at Carlton with great success, winning the Norm Smith Medal for being best afield in the 1986 Grand Final.

Injuries and a stream of suspensions cost him his chance at 200 and he announced his retirement from AFL ranks at the end of 1992, having played 182 games.

League football's most-reported player, he was charged 25 times for 12 'guilty' verdicts, 22 weeks suspension, a $5000 fine and a four-week suspended sentence.

Crossing to North Launceston as captain-coach in 1993, Rhys-Jones was reported in the grand final, but beat the charge after he produced medical evidence proving he could not clench a fist with his right hand due to a broken finger.

Lou Richards once said of him: 'David Rhys-Jones would be one of the best footballers around if he wasn't trying to be the middleweight boxing champion of Australia.'

RICHARDS, Lou (1923–)

An even bigger star off the field than he was on it, Lou Richards remains a household name in football-mad Melbourne almost 40 years after his retirement.

His multi-media duties, in television, radio and newspapers, ensure his high profile. In 1991, he even starred in his own music video.

The little Collingwood battler, who now lives in Toorak, is a one-man variety act. He's been King of Moomba, a TV star, author, comic, sports night funnyman and

Lou Richards was a fine rover who captained Collingwood to the 1953 premiership. He's pictured in action against Carlton in the early 1950s.

223

a friend to dozens of players, young and old. If they happen to play with Collingwood, so much the better!

In his first book, *Boots And All*, Richards said: 'In my younger days there was never any doubt that I would play with Collingwood if I was good enough—it was in my blood. I was born into a Magpie family and reared in the Magpie nest, kicking tin cans and paper footballs around the streets of Collingwood and Abbotsford'.

One of his proudest achievements was captaining Collingwood to the 1953 premiership against Geelong. It was his finest moment in 250 games and 15 seasons with the Magpies, which also saw him win Victorian representation three times.

Recruited from Collingwood Technical School, Lewis Thomas Charles Richards was a star rover in the rough and ready days of the '40s and '50s.

Cheeky and relentless, Richards was also tough and durable. He suffered nine broken bones in his 15 senior years, including three depressed fractures of the cheekbone.

But he handed out a lot of punishment, too. In 1949, Carlton officials claimed Richards had 'deliberately stomped' on Carlton players and kicked them in the head while they were down. Richards said he'd only been resting his knee on the back of a Carlton player's head!

Richards would deliberately taunt many of his opponents, even 'Captain Blood' *Jack Dyer*, one of the roughest and meanest players of his or any era.

If Dyer downed one of Richards' Collingwood team-mates, Richards would yell: 'Why don't you pick on someone your own size, you big bastard.'

RICHARDSON, Max (1948–   )

Two years younger than his celebrated brother *Wayne*, Max Richardson had a distinguished career in his own right, playing 211 games at Collingwood, 30 at Fitzroy and six with Victoria in 12 seasons from 1969–80.

Recruited from South Fremantle on his brother's recommendation—and without Magpie recruiters having ever seen him

kick a ball—he captained Collingwood in 1977, being renowned as a fierce, combative ruck-rover with good running skills.

He played in the memorable 1970 Grand Final in his first full year and in two Grand Finals in 1977.

RICHARDSON, Wayne (1946–   )

Another exceptional player from the rich footballing nursery of Fremantle, Richardson figured in more VFL club games, 279, than any other West Australian.

He captained Collingwood for four full years, played in four Grand Finals—three alongside his brother, *Max*—was twice best and fairest and a five-time Victorian representative. His son, Mark, first represented Collingwood in 1991.

A clearance tussle between Collingwood and East Fremantle kept Richardson out the entire '65 season. He was able to play for the Magpies only after an appeal to the Australian National Football Council at the start of 1966.

Richardson was in the seniors within a month of his first League year and roved in the thrilling '66 Grand Final which St Kilda won by a point. While he missed an easy goal in time-on of that historic game, he'd been one of the most impressive recruits of the season, showing agility, poise and determination.

Originally from WA country town Trayning, Richardson wasn't initially sure if he should accept the offer to shift east.

'My father (Arnold) made up my mind for me,' he said. 'He used to play with South Fremantle, which had a close relationship with Collingwood.

'If ever I played football in Melbourne, Dad wanted it to be with Collingwood. He told me, "Even if you stay there only a year, that's one year's coaching you have in top VFL football. You are sure to improve."

'It was the best piece of advice I ever had,' he said.

Collingwood paid for Richardson's air ticket and put 10 pounds towards his first two weeks' board.

Tall for a rover, he had great anticipation and along with Barry Price and his brother, *Max*, used to feed full-forward *Peter McKenna* with unstoppable, high-speed drop punt passes.

Richardson captained in five consecutive final series, but Collingwood never once qualified for the Grand Final.

At the start of 1976, when the club was heading for its first wooden spoon in history, he was dumped as skipper and within weeks of the opening of the season, dropped to the reserves. He fired a torrent of abuse at the club hierarchy, saying that 'the general committee selects the side instead of the coach' and that certain members of the Magpie board had him 'in the gun' after he beat *Len Thompson* for the captaincy in 1975.

Refusing to apologise or retract his statements, he was suspended for four weeks without pay and told not to attend training. It was yet another huge bust-up which characterised a club running fast out of control.

Richardson expected to be cleared, espe-cially after several clubs showed interest in his services, but he remained after the suspension was waived. The following season, under new coach *Tom Hafey*, he played in two Grand Finals and in 1978 extended his career into a 13th season.

RICHMOND

Formed in February, 1885, at Byrne's Royal Hotel, opposite the Punt Road Oval, Richmond successfully sought admittance into the senior Victorian football body, the Victorian Football Association. It played its first game, a trial match, at the Botanical Gardens against Cremorne Juniors in April, 1885.

The Richmond area quickly became renowned for its interest in the game. Among the XVIII representing Richmond cricket club were the founders of the game, *Henry Harrison* and *Thomas Wills*.

Richmond won two Association premierships, in 1902 and 1905, before being

Richmond's 1943 premiership team.
Back row (left to right): Jack Broadstock, Ron Durham, William Perkins, Arthur Kemp, Bob Bawden, Leo Maguire, Jack Scott, Len Ablett (reserve).
Middle row: Ray Hunt, Ray Steele, Jack Dyer (captain-coach), Dick Harris, Roy Quinn, Brian Randall, Bernie Waldron, Bert Edwards.
Front row: Max Oppy, Leo Merrett, Laurie Cahill.

admitted to the Victorian Football League in 1908, chiefly because of its proximity to public transport.

Former Collingwood player *Charlie Pannam snr* was the team's first captain.

The earliest Richmond teams wore blue outfits with a yellow and black sash and cap, until 1908, when yellow and black stripes and a yellow band around the waist were introduced. In 1914, the club's present colours were adopted.

Club officials of this era were renowned for their fashionable dress—boaters, white shoes and striped blazers. Bad language and misconduct were frowned upon, and members expelled from the club for swearing.

One of the team's best known early players was boxer Bill Lang who, in addition to spending two years at the club in 1908 and 1909, fought two of the world's best, Tommy Burns and Jack Johnson.

Straight-shooting forward Jack Hutchinson topped the VFA goalkicking lists five years in a row. Other star players included Charlie Ricketts, who later captained South Melbourne to a premiership, and George Johnson, who was also a fine player at Carlton.

The Tigers figured in the finals in two of their first 10 years, breaking through to win back-to-back premierships in 1920–21.

In the years before *Jack Dyer* joined in 1931, Richmond finished runners-up three seasons in a row from 1927–29, being beaten each time by Collingwood. Fourth in 1930 and second again in 1931, the club won the '32 flag. Its star-studded team included such greats as skipper *Percy Bentley*, Martin Bolger, Gordon and Doug Strang, Jack Baggott, Brownlow Medallist *Stan Judkins* and durable *Jack 'Skinny' Titus*.

The late 1920s, 1930s and early 1940s were the Tigers' halcyon years. The club won five premierships and appeared in nine other Grand Finals, in two and a half decades. From 1927–34, the side made the Grand Final in seven years out of eight.

Coach *'Checker' Hughes* was at least the equal of Collingwood's renowned leader *Jock McHale*, while Percy Page was regarded as the 'Prince of Secretaries'.

The architect of the Tigers' revival in the mid-1960s was Len Smith, coach in 1964–65, who insisted his players convert to a speedy, play-on style rather than the traditional mark-and-kick brand of football then in vogue.

Many believed Smith to be the greatest brain in football history. He is regarded as the most important figure in shaping the modern game.

The Tigers remained in the bottom four in Smith's first year but lifted to fifth in his second. Unfortunately he suffered from heart trouble and had to stand down on the eve of the fourth match against Essendon. Richmond was coached by club stalwart Titus for the remainder of the year.

The Tigers benefited from shifting from their Punt Road oval to become Melbourne's MCG co-tenant for the start of the '65 season.

The play-on game was ideally suited to the spacious MCG and attendances for Richmond home games more than doubled on the 1964 returns.

Ex-player *Tom Hafey* became coach at the start of 1966 and, with the dynamic off-field leadership of Graham Richmond, the club's revival continued.

Beaten only three times in the 18 home-and-away games in 1967, the superbly fit Tigers were favoured to win the flag and, after comfortably defeating Carlton in the second semi-final, won the Grand Final by just nine points in a cliffhanging finish from Geelong.

Richmond triumphed again in 1969, 1973 and 1974. Some of its star players were *Francis Bourke, Dick Clay,* Bill Barrot, *Kevin Sheedy, Michael Green* and perhaps the greatest of them all, Tasmanian *Royce Hart*.

Quick and courageous rover *Kevin Bartlett* was another brilliant newcomer. He later coached the club, before being replaced at the end of 1991 by *Allan Jeans*.

RICHMOND: THE STATISTICS

FORMED: February, 1885

JOINED LEAGUE: 1908
HOME VENUES: Punt Rd. Oval (1908–64), MCG (1965–   )
CURRENT HOME VENUE DIMENSIONS: 161 metres × 140 metres
COLOURS: Black guernsey with gold sash
TOTAL FINALS MATCHES: 72 (44 wins, 27 losses, 1 tie)
FINALS RECORD: Premiers: 10 (1920–21, 1932, 1934, 1943, 1967, 1969, 1973–74, 1980)
        Runners-up: 12 (1919, 1924, 1927–28–29, 1931, 1933, 1940, 1942, 1944, 1972, 1982)
PREMIERSHIP COACHES: Dan Minogue (2), 'Checker' Hughes (1), Percy Bentley (1), Jack Dyer (1), Tom Hafey (4), Tony Jewell (1)
NIGHT SERIES PREMIERSHIP: 1 (1962)
YOUNGEST PLAYER: Mick Maguire, 15 years 328 days (1910)
OLDEST PLAYER: Kevin Bartlett, 36 years 237 days (1983)
HIGHEST SCORE: 34.18 (222) v St Kilda, R.16, 1980, SCG
LOWEST SCORE: 0.8 (8) v St Kilda, R.16, 1961, Junction Oval
LONGEST WINNING SEQUENCE: 12 (1932–33)
LONGEST LOSING SEQUENCE: 14 (1961–62)
MOST FINALS: Kevin Bartlett 27, Jack Dyer 24, Jack Titus 24, Francis Bourke 23, Dick Clay 20, Kevin Sheedy 20
MOST SEASONS AS COACH: Jack Dyer 12 (1941–52)
MOST SEASONS AS CAPTAIN: Percy Bentley 9 (1932–40)
        Jack Dyer 9 (1941–49)

MOST GAMES		MOST GOALS	
Kevin Bartlett	403	Jack Titus	970
Jack Dyer	312	Kevin Bartlett	778
Francis Bourke	300	Michael Roach	607
Jack Titus	294	Dick Harris	550
Dale Weightman	274	Jack Dyer	440
Percy Bentley	263	Royce Hart	366
Vic Thorp	261	Ray Poulter	350
Kevin Sheedy	251	Dale Weightman	345
Roger Dean	245	Jeff Hogg	306
Mervyn Keane	239	Percy Bentley	275
Mark Lee	233	David Cloke	271
Jim Jess	223	Neil Balme	229
Dick Clay	213	Billy Wilson	226
Bryan Wood	209	George Bayliss	217
Kevin O'Neill	208	Pat Guinane	213
Michael Roach	200	Roger Dean	203

MOST GOALS IN A MATCH: Doug Strang 14 v North Melb., R.2, 1931, Punt Rd Oval
        Jack Baggott 12 v South Melb., R.9, 1928, Punt Rd Oval
        Michael Roach 11 v Footscray, R.7, 1980, Western Oval
        Michael Roach 11 v Hawthorn, R.5, 1985, Princes Park
BROWNLOW MEDALLISTS: Stan Judkins 1930; Bill Morris 1948; Roy Wright, 1952, 1954; Ian Stewart 1971
COLEMAN MEDALLISTS: Michael Roach 1981

RICHMOND: THE STATISTICS (cont)

LEAGUE LEADING GOALSCORERS: George Bayliss 63 (1920), Jack Titus 100 (1940), Dick Harris 62 (1943), Michael Roach 112 (1980), Michael Roach 86 (1981)

RECORD HOME VENUE ATTENDANCE: 46,000 v Carlton, R.9, 1949, Punt Rd Oval 91,936 v Collingwood, R.4, 1977, MCG

RECORD ATTENDANCE IN ANY MATCH: 119,165 v Carlton, GF, 1969, MCG

MOST RECENT PREMIERSHIP TEAM: 1980 Richmond 23.21 (159) d Collingwood 9.24 (78)
B: M. Malthouse, E. Dunne, G. Strachan. H.B: T. Smith, J. Jess, P. Welsh. C: S. Mount, G. Raines, B. Wood. H.F: M. Keane, D. Cloke, K. Bartlett. F: F. Bourke, M. Roach, R. Wiley. R: M. Lee, B. Rowlings. R: D. Weightman. Reserves: B. Monteath (c), D. Freame.

RIDLEY, Ian (1934–)

Born in Jeparit and recommended to Melbourne by the club's most notable goalkicker, *Fred Fanning*, who noticed his teenage talents while coaching Hamilton, Ian 'Tiger' Ridley was one of the first League footballers to wear contact lenses.

His premiership 'strike-rate' has rarely been equalled. In seven full seasons with the Demons, the jockey-sized rover played in six consecutive Grand Finals, for five wins and one loss.

The 170 cm Ridley played 130 games and kicked 230 goals with Melbourne from 1954–61. In 1992, he became club chairman.

ROACH, Michael (1958–)

A spectacular high mark and thumping kick, Michael 'Disco' Roach finally conceded to injuries in 1989, having kicked 607 goals in 200 games and 13 seasons with Richmond.

The gifted 193 cm athlete led the VFL goalkicking in 1980–81, including 112 in Richmond's '80 premiership year.

In 1979, he took the mark of the year, almost standing on the shoulders of Hawthorn ruckman Terry Moore.

'It was easily the highest I ever got up,' said Roach. 'I hit the ground head first on my way down and ended up with dirt all over my face, which was probably better than the beard I was trying to grow at the time.'

Best known for his prowess at full-forward, Roach also successfully played at centre half-forward, the ruck and late in his career, in defence.

Inheriting Richmond's No. 8 guernsey from *Dick Clay*, he twice kicked 11 goals in a game—against Footscray and St Kilda—and three times booted 10. He was Richmond's leading goalkicker seven times.

Representing Victoria three times, he was an All Australian in 1979.

Michael Roach began as a wingman before becoming a goalkicking force. He's pictured snap shooting for goal ahead of Carlton's Robbert Klomp.

ROBERTS, Neil (1933–)

One of many VFL champions to successfully switch from the forward line to defence in mid-career, Roberts won the 1958 Brownlow Medal from Hawthorn's Brendan Edwards and South Melbourne's *Bob Skilton*. He was accorded All Australian honours in 1958 and captained the

Saints from 1958 to his retirement at the end of the 1962 season.

In 1961, he led the club into its first final series for 22 years. He quit a year later, aged 29, having played 169 games. He said he'd lost pace and was tired of chasing younger players around.

Recruited from Melbourne High School Old Boys where he won a 'B'-grade amateurs best and fairest award, the 185 cm Roberts debuted as a teenager at St Kilda in 1952, playing seven games at full-forward. A brilliant mark but erratic kick in front of goal, he soon began to dominate after being shifted. His combination work with St Kilda's strongman Eric Guy across the half backline was a feature.

Nicknamed 'Coconut' because of his shock of blond hair, Roberts represented Victoria 11 times, playing in three carnivals. He is renowned as one of of St Kilda's greatest personalities. His son Michael wore his father's No. 10 guernsey at St Kilda and also represented his State. Neil's father, Ted, represented Manchester at soccer.

ROOS, Paul (1963–)

Fitzroy has had few more gifted footballers than accomplished key-position specialist Paul Roos who, in 1991, passed 200 games and played his 12th State match.

A five-time winner of Fitzroy's best and fairest, he captained the Lions from 1988–90 and again from 1992–94, before transferring to Sydney.

The 188 cm Roos became noted for his superb performances at centre half-back and, when he was needed, played at centre half-forward equally well.

In either position, he inspires, creates and commands total respect.

His superb marking is a particular strength. In 1987, he took 19 marks against the Brisbane Bears, just days after having represented his State.

Named an All Australian on five occasions, he also won the inaugural E. J. Whitten Medal in 1985.

He won the Whitten Medal again in 1988.

Paul Roos: five 'best and fairests' at Fitzroy.

ROSE, Bob (1928–)

Collingwood's master rover of the 1950s who later became the game's unluckiest coach, Bobby Rose was the most courageous player of his era, who starred in the 1953 final series, and helped Collingwood win its first flag in 17 years.

The eldest of four brothers to represent Collingwood, Rose was recruited from the tiny Wimmera town of Nyah West. Not only did he immediately appeal as a footballer, he was a prizefighter of note, winning six of his first seven fights as a teenage lightweight.

He made his debut for the Magpies in the 17th round of the 1946 season. He later overcame severe injuries, including two collarbone breaks, to win four Copeland trophies—a feat then unmatched at Collingwood. Three of his best and fairests were in consecutive years, from 1951–53.

A ruthless competitor with glorious stab-passing skills, the 174 cm rover became one of the most feared players in the game, at his best when the going was toughest. Collingwood fans loved to see him burst out of the centre, trading bumps with opponents before delivering the ball deep into the Magpie forward line.

Bob Rose during his coaching days at Footscray, with young Bulldogs Barry Round, Gary Merrington and Stewart Magee.

'Rose frequently tore into players bigger than himself,' said Collingwood historian Richard Stremski. 'He knew how to remove the glow from a rival player who was shining against Collingwood and was an inspirational leader.'

From 1948 to mid-season 1954, he played 132 consecutive matches including 15 interstate matches.

Not only was he best and fairest in Collingwood's 1953 premiership year, but runner-up in the Brownlow Medal and Collingwood's leading goalkicker. In the Grand Final against Geelong, his inspirational 60 metre torpedo punt goal from in front of the MCG members' stand is still remembered as one of post-war football's greatest moments.

In his last game, the 1955 Grand Final, Rose sparked a series of clashes with Melbourne toughman Noel McMahen, who had flattened him several times previously.

'Bob didn't know what the word defeat meant; he kept on fighting and fighting until he was exhausted,' said *Lou Richards*.

At 27, Rose joined a growing list of big-name VFL players to be lured to country football, while still in their prime.

Accepting a playing-coach role with Wangaratta Rovers at 30 pounds a week, he led his club into five Ovens & Murray grand finals in seven years for two wins and three losses.

He returned to Collingwood in 1963 as vice-president and coached the Magpies from 1964–71 and again in 1985, before stepping down early in the 1986 season. In 1967, he coached Victoria.

Rose was desperately unlucky not to win at least one premiership in his decade as coach. His teams made the finals in seven of his nine full seasons and three times were runners-up: in 1964 by four points, in 1966 by one and in 1970 by 10. Some said his teams didn't play with enough 'devil' but they were highly skilled and a match for almost any opposition.

The 1970 loss, to Carlton, was particularly humbling, however, as Collingwood had led 10.13 to 4.5 at half time.

Rose coached Footscray from 1972–75 before again becoming closely involved at Collingwood.

In all, he played 152 games in 10 years at Collingwood and coached 14 seasons and 281 matches for 163 wins, 114 losses and four ties. A stand at Victoria Park is named in his honour.

Rose's younger brother, Kevin, was also a prominent Collingwood player, with 159 games from 1958–67, including the '58 premiership. Later he coached Fitzroy for three years.

Bobby's son, Robert jnr, represented Victoria at cricket and was a League footballer with Collingwood and Footscray.

See: 'BROTHERS, Famous'

ROUND, Barry (1950–)

One of the oldest winners, at 31, of the Brownlow Medal and the first great hero of the Sydney Swans football club, Round's great career continued past his 41st birthday before he succumbed to a knee injury during the seventh round of the 1991 VFA season.

A self-proclaimed 'battler' the 195 cm strongman played 438 games, won a Brownlow and a Liston Trophy and captain-coached Williamstown to the VFA premiership, his only (daytime) flag in a 23 season career.

Recruited from Warragul in 1969, he had seven seasons at Footscray (for 135 games), 10 with the Swans (193) and six with Williamstown (110). No other big man has approached his enviable record or possessed his endurance.

When his reserves, representative and pre-season games are also included, he amassed almost 500 matches.

Shorter than many of the younger and more athletic ruckmen, Round compensated with clever body work, a telescopic reach and supreme fitness.

Captaining the Swans for the first of his five seasons in 1980, Round tied with ex-Bulldog teammate *Bernie Quinlan* for the 1981 Brownlow, both being awarded a Medal with the old countback system being discarded. Representing Victoria against Tasmania that season, he took 22 marks. In all, he represented the Big V four times.

For four seasons, Round was the idol of Sydney fans and deservedly made his 300 game milestone. He twice won the Swans' best and fairest award and in 1982 was captain when the Swans won the night premiership from North Melbourne. He played his last VFL game at 35. No battler ever had a bigger heart.

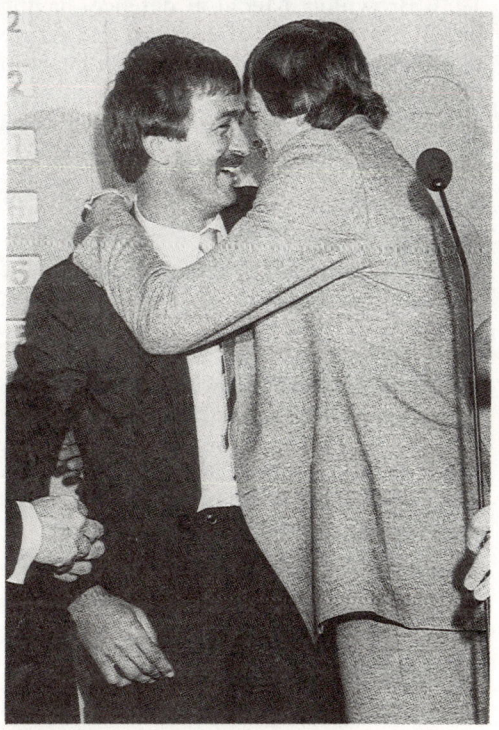

Bernie Quinlan (left) and Barry Round congratulate each other after tying for the Brownlow Medal in 1981.

ROWELL, Edward (1876–1965)

One of Collingwood's early greats who played successfully at both ends of the ground, pacy Teddy Rowell headed the League goalkicking, in tandem with Essendon's *Albert Thurgood*, in 1902, kicking 33 goals and being acknowledged as the 'Champion of the Colony'.

Recruited as a 23-year-old from Castlemaine via the Kalgoorlie goldfields, the 178 cm Rowell played 189 League games and kicked 175 goals from 1901–15, playing in three Collingwood premierships in 1902–03 and 1910 and being selected in Victoria's 1911 carnival team. He was 39 in his last game, the 1915 Grand Final.

In 1904–05, he played back at his old WA club, Kalgoorlie Railways, for whom he'd represented for five years before going to Melbourne. In 1907–08 he was Collingwood's playing coach, cementing his place at full-back.

In *Kill for Collingwood*, Richard Stremski says: 'His play on the half-forward line during his first season at Collingwood (1901) was dazzling. Rowell was a professional sprinter who place-kicked 60 yards accurately.'

He played seven games for Victoria and was a part of the first West Australian side to visit Victoria (1903).

ROWLINGS, Barry (1950–)

A member of four Grand Final sides, two at Hawthorn and two at Richmond, Rowlings played 234 League games including two premierships and represented Victoria five times.

He captained the Tigers in 1983–84, revelling in a ruck-roving role, after playing mainly on the wing at Hawthorn.

He returned to the Hawks in 1993 as assistant-coach after skills-coaching stints at Richmond and Hawthorn.

RUMNEY, Harold (1907–87)

A member of five Collingwood premiership sides, Harold Waldmere 'Dasher' Rumney played 171 games from 1927–37, playing mainly as a defender. He deeply loved Collingwood, once saying he would have paid for the privilege of representing the club.

Winner of the 1931 Copeland Trophy, he represented Victoria 10 times, having been recruited from Brighton, via Carlton, where he'd played 15 games in two teenage years in 1925–26.

A muscular, pacy placer he matched it with bigger players despite his slight physique, 170 cm and 71 kg.

RUSSO, Peter (1959–)

A member of five Hawthorn Grand Final teams—including two premierships—Russo spent 11 of his 13 League seasons at Glenferrie, amassing 162 games at Hawthorn before playing 33 in his last two years at St Kilda.

He was a skilled rover with immaculate left and right-foot kicking skills. In 1985, he represented Victoria against South Australia.

He remained in League football in the mid-1990s, as Melbourne's assistant-coach.

RUTHVEN, Alan (1922–)

Winner of the 1950 Brownlow Medal, by three votes from Geelong's Fred Flanagan, Alan 'Baron' Ruthven, so named for his flamboyant dress, was a magnificent rover for Fitzroy.

Quick off the mark, a perfect ball-handler, a deadly left-foot kick and blessed with amazing stamina. Ruthven was renowned for his liking to rove all day.

He played for Victoria 17 times, and was vice-captain in 1948, the first year of six in which he captained Fitzroy. On his retirement in August, 1954, he was carried off shoulder high by team members. Fitzroy's annual report of that year stated: 'No greater artist ever graced the football field and if any of the champions of the past can show a better record than Alan, we will certainly concede him pride of place. Alan's record shows 15 years' service, 222 games, 426 goals, Brownlow Medallist, carnival and state player for many years, best and fairest club player seven times, captain five years, coach three years and above-all, never a reprimand from an umpire for unfair play.'

The sturdily built 173 cm rover was a member of Fitzroy's 1944 premiership team. In the 1947 first semi-final against Richmond he ran around Tiger great *Jack Dyer*—who was on his mark—and went for a run. The veteran toughman couldn't catch him, but yelled: 'If I was 10 years younger, son, you wouldn't have done that.'

Ruthven employed quick, play-on tactics years before his time, often running past team-mates and calling for handballs.

RYAN, 'Dinny' (1917–80)

Another of Fitzroy's decorated stars from Albury, Denis 'Dinny' Ryan won the 1936 Brownlow Medal in defence, having begun his career at full-forward and centre half-forward, where he kicked 46 goals in his debut season, in 1935.

Shifted to centre half-back in his second season, his strong build (187 cm, 82.5 kg) and towering marking ideally complemented his long, if sometimes inaccurate, kicking.

On winning the Medal, Ryan said he was 'thunderstruck . . . I don't know if I'm on my head or my heels.'

He completed a VFL record for Fitzroy by being the third Brownlow Medallist to play together in the same side (along with *Haydn Bunton* and *'Chicken' Smallhorn*). Like Essendon great *Dick Reynolds*, he was just 19 when he won, being the youngest-ever winner.

He had only five seasons and 69 games with Fitzroy, his career being reduced by injury and the war.

SALMON, Paul (1965–)

One of the tallest men to play League football, 206 cm Salmon approached his 200th game milestone at the start of the 1995 season.

A follower/forward who debuted with Essendon as an 18-year-old from North Ringwood, Salmon's marking and ruck-work is of the highest standard.

A two-time premiership player and All-Australian, he remained loyal to the Bombers in mid-career despite a huge offer from Brisbane.

A knee reconstruction in mid-year, 1984—after he'd kicked 63 goals in half a year—was a major setback. He missed Essendon's 1984 premiership but played in 1985.

He was again full-forward in the 1993 premiership.

Topping Essendon's goalcharts for eight of his first 11 seasons, Salmon's speed off the mark and agility for such a tall man is exceptional.

He has twice kicked 11 goals in a match, against Richmond at Waverley in 1986 and against West Coast at the WACA Ground in 1987. He also kicked 10 against Geelong at the MCG, in 1993.

With Simon Madden's retirement, he assumed more rucking responsibility, but his form was restricted by a series of leg injuries, prompting some to query his worth.

Salmon had represented Victoria 13 times to the start of the 1995 season. He won the Tassie Medal in successive years in 1987 and 1988.*

SARAU, Jeff (1954–)

A tough and aggressive 191 cm ruckman renowned for the clever use of his body like another celebrated Saint follower, Alan Morrow, Sarau played 226 games in 11 seasons from 1973–83. He twice represented Victorian 'B' teams.

SCARLETT, John (1947–)

A free-running, fearless full-back who played in an era in which full-forwards

* see 'TALL TIMBER'

dominated, Scarlett played 212 games from 1967–78, including 183 in 10 and a half seasons at Geelong. In June, 1977, he crossed to South Melbourne in an unusual lease arrangement and stayed with the club until 1978. He represented Victoria once.

SCHIMMELBUSCH, Wayne (1953–)

Consistently outstanding, the inspirational Wayne Schimmelbusch played in North Melbourne's most glorious era when the Roos qualified for six Grand Finals in a row in the 1970s.

Amassing a club record 306 games from 1973–87, he figured in 29 finals, including the 1975 and 1977 premierships. There has been no more courageous modern-day footballer.

Wayne Schimmelbusch beats Geelong pair Bruce Lindner and Gary Ablett for the ball during his 300th game in 1987.

The 179 cm 'Schimma' represented Victoria 11 times and was State skipper in his final year, 1987, at the age of 34. He'd been named State skipper in 1981 but couldn't take his place in the side because of injury.

From 1990, Schimmelbusch replaced *John Kennedy* as senior coach of North.

Playing most of his early football on a wing or at half-forward, Schimmelbusch later became a fine defender.

Noted football writer Greg Hobbs said Schimmelbusch was as hard to control on a football field as a cage full of monkeys.

'He'd dance and weave his way around the North forward line, punching holes in opposition defences like a frenzied fighter on a rampage.'

Recruited from Brunswick where he'd won his club's best and fairest award and the Jack Field Medal in 33 senior games, Schimmelbusch was the outstanding recruit to League football in 1973 and played 92 games in a row before missing two matches late in the 1976 season after being injured against Collingwood.

'I didn't think I'd make it,' said Schimmelbusch. 'I was a bit hesitant and really didn't know what to expect or how to handle it.'

Representing Victoria every year from 1977–83, he played in the reserves only once, in 1977, when dropped because of poor form.

After being virtually injury-free for the first decade of his career, he averaged only 12 games a season in his final six seasons. During his celebrated career, he had five knee operations and surgery to a damaged achilles tendon.

As a mark of respect on his retirement, North didn't allocate his famous No. 20 guernsey for two years.

'He always has been an outstanding inspiration when things were at their toughest. We are sad and sorry his playing days are over,' said North administrator Ron Joseph.

Schimmelbusch captained North from mid-year 1979 until 1987. He was re-appointed in 1988, but didn't play a game, North being led by *John Law*.

Schimmelbusch's brother, Daryl, also represented North Melbourne in 47 games from 1978–81 and later played with West Torrens.

SCHULTZ, John (1938–   )

One of the elite players to represent Victoria in his very first season of VFL football as a teenager in 1958, Schultz was a Brownlow Medallist in 1960, an All Australian in 1961 and a five-time winner of Footscray's best and fairest.

A mobile, very fair ruckman, who expertly shared the ball to his rovers,

Schultz's spring, stamina and skill helped him win Big V selection on 24 occasions, a record surpassed by only one other Footscray player, his contemporary *Ted Whitten*, who played 29 times for Victoria.

Schultz played 160 games in a row during his 11 season, 188 game career. Known for his consistent marking in defence, he also kicked 39 goals.

He served for many years as an honorary member of the League tribunal.

SCOTT, Don (1947–   )

One of the most feared ruckman of his era, the 191 cm Scott is one of only four Hawthorn players to amass 300 club matches. He played 302 games from 1967–81, including three premierships, 1971, 1976 and 1978, being captain in two.

Don Scott with Carlton's John Nicholls in a rucking duel at Glenferrie Oval in the late 1960s.

Superbly fit and noted for setting an inspirational example, his commitment and big-hearted displays resulted in many Hawthorn victories.

Off the field, he was flamboyant—he carried a handbag, was once a fashion designer, and wore the trendiest gear. He was called the 'Beau Brummel' of Australian football.

Exuberant and volatile, he used to psych himself up tremendously before a match. There was no more competitive player in the game.

Scott did not possess great natural ability or style, but he had a fine spring and no one worked harder or offered more protection to smaller team-mates in and around the packs.

In the 1971 Grand Final, Scott and *Peter Crimmins* were among the players to push themselves to the point of exhaustion as Hawthorn overcame a persistent St Kilda to snatch the premiership by just seven points, after trailing by 20 points at three-quarter time. Scott was clearly best afield and a massive contributor in the biggest game (until then) of his career.

In 1973, he was Hawthorn's best and fairest. He also won State selection for the first time. The captaincy of Victoria in 1978 was reward for his sterling service. Many saw him as the most inspirational skipper of the decade.

Becoming disenchanted in his final years at Hawthorn, he stood down as skipper at the end of 1980, claiming a 'generation gap' had developed between himself and many of the club's younger players.

During his final troubled year, he was dropped for the first time in 13 seasons. He played two matches in the reserves and, in his final senior game against Melbourne, refused a directive from first-year coach *Allan Jeans* to come off the ground in the last term. Hawthorn historian Harry Gordon said: 'In a way it was a symbolic departure for a man who was both an inspiration and a rebel.'

SEPTEMBER SPECIALISTS

When Collingwood won the first AFL premiership in 1990, burying the dreaded 'Colliwobbles' which had seemingly afflicted the club since their previous flag in 1958, it ended an amazing run of ill luck which had seen the club lose eight Grand Finals in 22 years, several by less than a single kick.

Ironically, its 1900 flag came on the first Saturday in October, the '90 series having run an extra week because of an earlier tie between the Eagles and Collingwood.

The last Saturday in September is football's traditional day of the year, its answer to Melbourne Cup day and the Boxing Day Test cricket.

After taking more than 35 years to win its first premiership in 1961, Hawthorn has been a pacesetter in the last two decades, winning three flags in the 1970s, four in the 1980s and the second AFL flag in 1991.

The West Coast Eagles became the first interstate club to take the premiership in 1992. It came from fourth place at the end of the home-and-away rounds.

Since 1931, when the final four system was introduced—the forerunner to the current final eight—no team has won four finals in a row in the same year.

In 1900, however, Melbourne won the premiership from sixth position.

In 1916, when just four teams competed because of the First World War, Fitzroy won the flag from bottom position, having won just two of its 12 home-and-away matches.

The Lions defeated Collingwood in a semi-final and Carlton in the final. Because the Blues had finished on top, they were given a second chance, but Fitzroy beat them again to take the flag.

MOST LEAGUE FINALS, 1897–1994

39: M. Tuck (Hawthorn).
31: G. Coventry (Collingwood).
29: B. Doull (Carlton); L. Matthews (Hawthorn); W. Schimmelbusch (Nth Melb.).
28: W. Hutchison (Essendon); C. Mew (Hawthorn); G. Ayres (Hawthorn).
27: K. Bartlett (Richmond); H. Collier (Collingwood); R. Reynolds (Essendon).
26: A. Collier (Collingwood); D. Brereton (Hawthorn).

LEAGUE CLUBS' FINALS APPEARANCES: 1897–1994

CLUB	PREMIERS	SECOND	THIRD	FOURTH	FIFTH	SIXTH	SEVENTH	EIGHTH	TOTAL
Adelaide			1						1
Brisbane									0
Carlton	15	12	14	15	3				59
Collingwood	14	23	17	14	3				72
Essendon	15	13	7	10	6	1		1	52
Fitzroy	8	5	9	6	1				29
Footscray	1	1	4	6	2	1			15
Geelong	6	7	15	13	1				42
Hawthorn	9	5	4		1	2	1		22
Melbourne	12	4	7	9					32
North Melb	2	4	5	4	3				18
Richmond	10	12	3	7					32
St Kilda	1	3	5	7	1				17
SM/Sydney	3	8	6	6	1				24
West Coast	2	1	1	1	1				6
TOTAL	**98**	**98**	**98**	**98**	**23**	**4**	**1**	**1**	**421**

SHAW, Tony (1960–)

Captain of Collingwood's long-awaited 1990 premiership, Tony Shaw led the Magpies from 1987–1993 before retiring at the end of the 1994 season, having played a record 313 games.

Remaining loyal to the Magpies, he rejected a rich offer to be assistant-coach at Carlton and remained on staff as Collingwood's development coach.

Few have been as courageous or displayed as much loyalty and commitment to one club as Shaw.

In the 1989 elimination final against Melbourne, he hurt his knee in the first quarter but refused to come off, and was one of Collingwood's most gallant triers in a losing team. Three days later, he was in hospital for a knee operation.

At 170 cm, Shaw constantly conceded height to his opponents and rarely out-ran them. His kicking skills were mediocre, yet he became one of the first chosen each week.

'When I talk to groups of kids now, I tell them of my own experiences, that I was a battler just like most of them and that nothing can be achieved without training hard and then harder again. It's a simple philosophy but it works. If you train hard you'll be the same as everyone else. If you train harder, you'll be ahead of the rest.'

Being named the Norm Smith Medallist in 1990 capped off the greatest day of his sporting life. On that memorable Grand Final day against Essendon, Shaw had 22 kicks, 10 handballs and numerous tackles and knock-ons—an extraordinary effort after he was on the rubdown table for the entire half time interval having his bad back manipulated.

He was chaired off the MCG by his team-mates and cheerfully admitted that night to sleeping with the premiership cup. 'I woke up the next day, looked at the spoils of battle, sat up in bed and thought this is deadset heaven!' he said.

Shaw's courageous feats and loyalty to Collingwood made him the best known of the Shaw footballing brothers.

Ray and Neville also played with the Magpies, Ray winning a best and fairest, representing Victoria and captaining the club into successive Grand Finals, in 1979–80. He played 20 finals (compared with Tony's 21). In 146 games from 1974–81, Ray kicked 201 goals. Neville Shaw played 43 games from 1984–86.

SHEEDY, Kevin (1947–)

A self-made champion and one of the most successful player-coaches on record, the rough-and-tumble 180 cm Sheedy was associated with five premierships in his first 20 years in football, being a three-time premiership player at Richmond, before winning back-to-back flags as coach of Essendon, the team he'd followed as a youngster.

In 1993, he triumphed again, Essendon winning the premiership, Sheedy's third as coach.

In his days at Richmond he was one of the game's finest and most determined defenders. Later he ruck-roved with distinction. His awards include Richmond's best and fairest in 1976, the club captaincy in 1978 and premierships in 1969, 1973 and 1974, when he was best man afield.

Kevin Sheedy boots downfield against St Kilda at Moorabbin, 1974.

A belligerent and committed opponent, he overcame players with greater skill and superior strength through old-fashioned methods and sheer effort.

Winning the first of his eight State guernseys and playing in his first premiership with Richmond in 1969 are among his most treasured playing memories.

After 254 games with Richmond from 1967–79, he coached his 250th game at Essendon in 1991, maintaining his enviable winning ratio of almost 70 per cent.

Sheedy said his most satisfying games as coach were Essendon's consecutive Grand Final successes against Hawthorn in the mid-1980s. In 1984, he re-cast his side at three-quarter time and saw the Bombers charge home. 'I never played against the Hawks in a winning Grand Final side, so

the next best thing was being coach in a winning play-off,' he said.

A deep and innovative thinker, he coached Victoria in 1985 and 1986.

In 1992, he began his 12th season as Essendon's leader, having rejected lucrative offers to coach the Sydney Swans. He was scheduled to coach his 350th game late in the 1995 season.

SHELDON, Ken (1959–   )

A triple premiership player at Carlton, Sheldon lifted St Kilda into its first final series for almost 20 seasons in 1991. In 1992, the Saints made it again, finishing fourth, before Sheldon was surprisingly sacked just 12 months later, the club having slipped to 12th place.

An astute coach, known for his meticulous planning, Sheldon moved to Adelaide with immediate success.

He was one of the VFL's youngest-ever coaches when named *Darrel Baldock*'s successor in late 1989.

Recruited from Mitiamo, near Bendigo, he played 132 games with Carlton from 1977–86, having his first matches as a 17-year-old.

He also played 53 games with St Kilda from 1987–89.

Nicknamed 'Bomba', and known in his early days at Carlton as a fun-loving 'Court Jester' type, he was a skilled and versatile running player. In 1979, he led Carlton's goalkicking with 53 goals and in 1983 represented Victoria—one of his three State matches.

SHORTEST PLAYERS

When Footscray's midget rover *Tony Liberatore* won the 1990 Brownlow Medal, the first under the banner of the Australian Football League, he encouraged a new generation of teenagers to try football. Not only had he been rejected by his first League club, North Melbourne, he was the shortest player in the game since Kevin 'Skeeter' Coghlan.

Liberatore and Brisbane's Danny Craven are both around 164 cm, yet have had valued roles at their clubs for several seasons.

Footscray's 163 cm Tony Liberatore: one of the smallest-ever.

The shortest player in history is Collingwood's James 'Nipper' Bradford, who was just 152 cm and 52.2 kg.

The second-shortest, 156 cm Charlie Hardy, was one of the smallest of the truly great early Australian Rules footballers. Recruited from Trafalgar, he represented Victoria (VFA) six weeks after his North Melbourne debut in 1908.

Before joining Essendon in 1921, he played 224 games with North.

Among other 'midgets' to enjoy particularly illustrious careers are Richmond's Clarrie Hall, who played 150 games including the Tigers' 1920–21 premiership double; Essendon's Rowland Watt, 141 games from 1922–31 including the 1923–24 premiership teams and celebrated Aboriginal Doug Nicholls, 54 games with Fitzroy from 1932–37.

Speedy post-war rover, the 169 cm Bruce McMaster-Smith also played at a jockey's weight, of 57 kg. To help him win a trial at Fitzroy, he weighted his shorts with lead weights! After 23 games as a flanker with Fitzroy, he crossed to Carlton for 37 matches. He also played at St Kilda, figuring in the 1965 Grand Final.

SHORTEST PLAYERS

HEIGHT (cm)	NAME	CLUB	SPAN	MATCHES	GOALS
152	James 'Nipper' Bradford	Coll.	1943	7	11
		Nth.	1949	9	8
156	Charlie Hardy	Ess.	1921–25	36	21
157	Barcley Bailes	Fitz.	1905–09	79	29
157.5	Ray Horwood	Rich.	1950–52	27	26
		Coll.	1952	2	0
	Doug Nicholls	Fitz.	1932–37	54	2
	William Speakman	Ess.	1927–29	16	8
159	Tommy Downs	Carl.	1927–29, 1931, 1933	56	44
160	Jamie Lawson	Syd.	1991–94	61	29
	Clarrie Hall	Rich.	1912–22, 1924	150	169
	Rowland Watt	Ess.	1922–31	141	41
	Jack Carney	Geel.	1930–34	79	4
		Carl.	1936–41	84	6
163	Kevin 'Skeeter' Coghlan	Coll.	1949–52	31	25
		Haw.	1953–56	59	96
164*	Tony Liberatore	Foots.	1986–94	128	65
165*	Danny Craven	St K.	1989–92	33	10
		Bris.	1993–94	20	7

* current player.

SILVAGNI, Sergio (1938–)

A two-time winner of Carlton's best and fairest award, the nuggety 183 cm Silvagni, the son of Italian migrants, played 239 games from 1958–71. He led Carlton's goalkicking in his second year and represented Victoria twice.

Sergio Silvagni, a no-frills but highly effective ruck-rover, winning his kick, ahead of St Kilda's Carl Ditterich.

With champion ruckman *John Nicholls* and rover *Adrian Gallagher*, he helped form one of the VFL's most formidable following divisions in the 1960s. Silvagni's unselfish and creative play made him a favourite among his team-mates. He was far from a pretty footballer but was highly effective.

His son, Steve, is one of the AFL's modern-day champions. Taller and more athletic than his father, he debuted with the Blues in 1985 and played his 100th game early in 1991, having finished third in the Brownlow Medal as well as winning Carlton's best and fairest in 1990.

SIMMONDS, Roy (1928–)

A popular defender whose debut, in 1950, coincided with one of Hawthorn's bleakest periods—when it lost 27 matches in a row—Simmonds retired after the 1961 premiership season, having tallied 201 games in 12 seasons.

He'd missed selection in Hawthorn's historic Grand Final side after back problems sidelined him for six weeks late in the year. On return, he couldn't displace a younger player, Reg Poole, who'd substituted for Simmonds on the last line of defence.

Known as the 'Hawthorn tank', he represented Victoria four times from 1951–56 and won Hawthorn's best and fairest in 1956.

SKILTON, Bob (1938–)

Post-war football's No. 1 rover, Skilton became the most decorated small man of his era, winning the Brownlow Medal three times and South Melbourne's best and fairest a record nine times, in just 11 years. His 237 match tally was also a club record at his retirement, in 1971.

Renowned for his courage and habit of going as hard in the final minutes of a game as he had at the start, the team-orientated Skilton was a 25-time Victorian representative, being State captain in 1963 and 1965. His only regret was that South Melbourne finished in the finals only once in his time, in 1970, under the great *Norm Smith*.

Skilton said he would have gladly swapped one of his Brownlows for the opportunity to have played in a Grand Final. He considered his semi-final appearance the high point of his career.

'For years, I'd book holidays in the August–September school holiday period, and as much as it was great for the family, I would have liked to have had the opportunity of being on the MCG (instead),' he said. 'I'll never forget our first semi-final of 1970, against St Kilda; leading the team out, breaking the run-through and realising more than 100,000 people are in the ground yelling for you. It's a marvellous feeling—one you cannot imagine until you've been there.'

Recruited from South Melbourne fourths via Port Melbourne YMCA and Rossey Rovers, the 173 cm rover, known

Bobby Skilton: played just one final in an illustrious 237 game career.

with both feet and for hour after hour, he'd kick his battle-scarred footy against a factory wall. As it rebounded, he'd scoop it up and kick with his alternate foot until he became so proficient that he didn't know whether he was left or right-footed. His ability to kick with both feet became one of his greatest assets. He was more accurate with his left but could kick it further with his right.

Possessing great pace, especially off the mark, Skilton was fearless and often avoided trouble with his superb baulking ability. In 1962, however, he was shirt-fronted by St Kilda toughman Eric Guy and carried from the field. It remained one of the toughest knocks of his career.

During his celebrated career, he was concussed and had his nose broken four times, suffered 12 black eyes, dislocated his elbow, broke his right wrist twice and left wrist once, had a cartilage removed, tore his achilles tendon and had countless sprained and twisted ankles.

'I rate him a better footballer than (Haydn) Bunton,' said *Jack Dyer*. 'I never thought I'd see the equal of *Dick Reynolds* again—but I was wrong. Skilton is . . .

'He is God's gift to coaches and as an ex-coach I often wonder what you could do with two Bobby Skiltons in your side . . . he has personality and it is impossible to find a weakness in his football make-up.'

Skilton was playing coach of South Melbourne in 1965–66. He also coached Melbourne from 1974–77 for a best finish of sixth (in 1976).

Football has had no greater ambassador.

SMALLHORN, Wilfred (1911–88)

One of the smallest and most popular League footballers of the 1930s, Wilfred 'Chicken' Smallhorn won the 1933 Brownlow Medal. His pace and precise kicking were outstanding, along with his ability to leap with and outmark the tallest of opponents.

Smallhorn was renowned for his rigorous training—and temper, which almost resulted in his walking out in mid-career, saying that Fitzroy was not doing enough to find work for its local players. In 1936,

as 'Chimp', had one game with South under 19s and three with the reserves before being named, aged 17, for his senior debut in round five, 1956.

His habit of boring into packs and his grit and determination were immediately noticeable. In his second game, he kicked five goals.

'Skilts was one of the best of them all,' said one of his old coaches, Tommy Lahiff. 'He was the greatest because he gave you 100 minutes of guts, determination and complete dedication in every match he played.'

After one of Skilton's Brownlow victories, Collingwood legend *Lou Richards* said: 'Bobby is a football fanatic; he eats, sleeps and drinks football and the result is that his play is near faultless.'

Skilton learned the value of absolute dedication at a very young age from his father, who expected to win a Stawell Gift, but missed qualifying in the heats by trying to hide his true ability. He urged young Bob never to hold himself back. Bob snr insisted on Skilton learning to kick the ball when he injured a cartilage and was restricted to four games, he went 10 months without work.

'I enjoyed every bit of League football,' he said. 'I lived from one Saturday to another. I did my level best in League football and if a fellow beat me I would have to beat him back. I just loved every minute of it . . . the roar of the crowd and the thrill of being physically fit . . . '

During his 149-match career, Smallhorn joined the elite group to poll 100 Brownlow votes, represented Victoria nine times and gained carnival selection in 1933.

During the Second World War, he was taken prisoner and helped to organise football games at Changi.

SMITH, Bernie (1927–85)

One of the few non-Victorians to win a Brownlow Medal, Smith's victory in 1951 was particularly meritorious as he was a back-pocket player in a Geelong team which went on to win consecutive premierships and make another Grand Final, all in four years.

Originally from West Adelaide, where he had 55 games and represented South Australia—mainly as a defender—the 175 cm Smith first played in the VFL as a centreman, before in 1950—his third year—he began to play brilliantly in a back pocket.

His uncanny anticipation and daring often saw him leave his opponent and attack the ball. Only occasionally was he left stranded. Developing a fine understanding with Cats full-back Bruce Morrison, Smith helped turn defence into attack in exciting, vote-winning fashion.

He polled 23 votes in 1951 to win the Medal by three from South Melbourne's *Ron Clegg*. His semi-crouched, weaving running style made him a most elusive opponent. In a 183 game career which ended after the opening round of the 1958 season, he was twice Geelong's best and fairest, a member of the 1951–52 premiership teams and captain in 41 games.

In 1953, when he represented Victoria, he won All Australian status.

Geelong's Bernie Smith, a class act on the last line of defence.

SMITH, Norm (1915–73)

A fiery, iron-willed disciplinarian, Norman Walter Smith became the game's greatest coach by leading Melbourne into 11 consecutive final series, including five premierships in six years from 1955–60. His marvellous coaching record spanned four clubs and 35 years.

A great tactician, and a fluent and inspiring orator, he studied the opposition intently and was one of the first coaches to use statistics in his game strategies.

An integral part of 10 of Melbourne's 12 premierships, either as a player or a coach, Smith played 210 games at Melbourne and 17 at Fitzroy in his 16-year playing career from 1935–50. He was noted for his wizardry at full-forward, where he kicked 571 goals including 88 in 1941 and 86 in 1940.

He coached three clubs in 452 games, for 254 wins, seven draws and 191 losses. His 198/107 win-loss ratio at Melbourne is particularly impressive. His final senior years were spent at South Melbourne from 1969–72, although he did join his protégé *Ron Barassi* at North Melbourne as an assistant coach for a short time in 1973 until his death.

He'd been in ill health for some time and died of a brain tumor.

Melbourne diehards still vividly recall the scaring controversy when Smith was sacked mid-way through the 1965 season—only to be reinstated less than one week later.

Supremo Smith had argued with committeemen and selectors, and almost came to blows with a social-club committeeman during the tumultuous opening months of the '65 season. The reigning premiers won its first eight games for '65, before losing three of the next four. The dissenters gathered in force. On the eve of the round 13 game against North Melbourne, Smith was sacked. A messenger was sent to his Coburg home to break the news.

Celebrated former leader, 71-year-old *'Checker' Hughes* coached the Demons against North Melbourne the following day. The side lost and by Tuesday, Smith had been reinstated. But the damage was irrevocable, and Melbourne won only one of its last six games. Not only did it miss the finals for the first time since 1953, but was to forfeit its proud title of being Australia's leading football club.

On accepting the offer to coach Melbourne again, Smith said he owed it to the club and to those who had remained loyal to him during the crisis to continue.

SMITH'S COACHING RECORD

SEASON	MATCHES PLAYED	WINS	LOSSES	DRAWS	POSITION
FITZROY					
1949	19	10	9	—	7th
1950	18	10	8	—	5th
1951	18	10	6	2	5th
MELBOURNE					
1952	19	9	9	1	6th
1953	18	3	14	1	11th
1954	21	13	8	—	2nd
1955	20	17	3	—	1st
1956	20	18	2	—	1st
1957	21	14	6	1	1st
1958	20	16	4	—	2nd
1959	20	15	4	1	1st
1960	20	16	4	—	1st
1961	20	12	7	1	3rd
1962	19	14	5	—	3rd
1963	20	14	6	—	3rd
1964	19	15	4	1	1st
1965	17	10	7	—	7th
1966	18	3	15	—	11th
1967	18	8	10	—	7th
SOUTH MELBOURNE					
1969	20	7	13	—	9th
1970	23	14	9	—	4th
1971	22	3	19	—	12th
1972	22	2	20	—	11th
TOTALS	452	253	192	7	

Norm Smith, one of football's finest coaches, whose career spanned four clubs and 35 years.

Smith admitted that he'd often 'blown his top' and that he regretted his outbursts. 'I have always been fiery,' he said. 'Yet perhaps some of that fire would have played a part in the great success of the club. Weak men can't win premierships.'

While he left Melbourne at the end of the 1967 season, he still had a contribution to make. In 1970, he lifted South Melbourne into its first final since the war.

His proudest achievement was the 1964 flag, when Melbourne defeated Collingwood. In the rooms Smith not only congratulated his players, but apologised for his ferociousness during the year.

'As I stood at the victory dais, I thought back on my coaching through the year,' he said. 'Midway through the season I told my players I would spare nothing and nobody to get this premiership. If they didn't like it, they would be replaced. I've had my quarrels and been ruthless. At times I have been ashamed of things I have done. After the victory I apologised to the players and thanked them for their tremendous support. I am sure now when they think back, they will realise my ferocity was worth the reward.'

In 1979, the VFL moved to perpetuate Smith's memory. Each year, the player named as best afield in the Grand Final receives the Norm Smith Medal.

SMITH, Ross (1942–)

Like his great South Melbourne adversary *Bobby Skilton*, Ross Smith had limitless stamina and regularly roved all day,

amassing a club record 235 games with St Kilda. He was captain from 1970–72, and won the 1967 Brownlow Medal.

Recruited in 1961 from Hampton Scouts, he was courageous, clever and tenacious, a consummate team-man well known for his unselfish use of handball.

He had struggled, at first, to be part of St Kilda's best team, but blossomed during the 1966 final series when he was one of the best afield in the second semi and the preliminary finals.

He had an outstanding year in 1967, being club champion and a seven vote winner of the Brownlow Medal. His improvement had been stunning.

A fitness fanatic, the 173 cm Smith represented Victoria in 1967 and in 1972 was captain of the carnival squad.

Continuing his career as playing coach of Subiaco, in 1973, he lifted the club to its first premiership in almost 50 years.

He returned to St Kilda in 1975 as assistant coach to *Allan Jeans*. He hadn't intended playing again but after WA roving ace Bruce Duperouzel injured his ankle, Smith came out of retirement for the final 12 games.

In 1977, he was St Kilda's senior coach.

SMITH, Ross (1965–)

A determined and consistent half-back whose career at North Melbourne was rejuvenated under Denis Pagan, Smith played his 200th match in the opening month of the 1995 season.

Recruited from Jacana, he was third in North Melbourne's best and fairest in 1993, adding great rebound power to North's defence. He had represented Victoria three times to the start of 1995.

SMITH, Stephen (1956–)

A skilled key-position player noted for his marking, Steve Smith successfully combined his legal career with football, playing 203 games with Melbourne from 1974–85. He was the Demons' best and fairest player in 1981, and vice-captain to *Robert Flower* for his last seasons. He was recruited from Ormond Amateurs.

SOUTH AUSTRALIA

The obsession for football in Adelaide was highlighted in the first season of a South Australian team's participation in the national league, in 1991. Crowds of more than 40,000 regularly attended Football Park at Westlakes to see the Adelaide Crows go in against the big AFL names from interstate.

Even in the last game of the year, when the fledgling club played middle-of-the-list North Melbourne, the crowd was in excess of 36,000—in a match which had no bearing on the final six.

Revelling in the anti-Victorian rivalry, the Crows' defeat of powerful Hawthorn in their very first match in March was front-page news.

Key Victorian football officials had been trying to woo SA's involvement at national level for years, but a stand-off developed and it wasn't until Port Adelaide, SA's most successful club, made a bold approach and was accepted in as the 15th AFL club, that SA officials overturned their decision not to compete at AFL level until at least 1993.

Locals feared that interest in their own competition would be decimated. Less than 40,000 fans attended the 1991 SA league grand final, the poorest attendance since 1947.

The hugely successful State-of-Origin matches played in Adelaide in the 1980s had re-fuelled SA's appetite to be in the big time. As more of its star players accepted the professional monies on offer from Melbourne-based clubs—severely weakening local standards—the SA league attempted to arrest the flow by establishing the SA Players' Retention Scheme, rewarding the best and most promising Adelaide born-and-bred players for their loyalty in remaining home. Finding that much of the monies from the annual interstate games at Football Park were helping to fund the scheme, the AFL made alternative interstate arrangements in 1990, excluding a SA-Big V involvement. Within six months, Port Adelaide had made its bold attempt to join, triggering the greatest controversy in SA footballing history.

Triple Magarey Medallist Barrie Robran, the best player never to play in the VFL.

Lindsay Head also won three Magarey Medals. He played 364 games from 1952 to 1970 for West Torrens.

244

Port was not only the most successful club in SA, but its most followed. Its average crowds of 10,000 in the late 1980s were well ahead of anybody else. In 1994, the AFL agreed that Port could join the national league—if a place became available.

Their decision to leave the SANFL caused an enormous ruckus. After prolonged court squabbles and the reluctance of several Melbourne-based AFL clubs, most notably Collingwood, to accept Port's inclusion, the SA league's somer-

Russell Ebert, a stalwart Port Adelaide centreman and forward who played 400 games in SA.

saulting decision to become involved eventually won approval, the Adelaide football club being voted into AFL ranks for the '91 season.

Port Adelaide president Bruce Weber made no apologies for his club changing the direction of SA football. 'Football was deteriorating in this State,' he told journalist Ashley Hornsey. 'The proposal we put up was in the best interests of Port and SA football. We saw it as a good change—the other nine clubs didn't. They decided

to put a composite team in and I'm sure it is a positive one.

'Because SA was a feeder State, we were losing 20 recruits a year to the AFL and it wasn't the way to continue.'

Port had won almost 30 premierships in 120 years of SA football, a strike-rate unmatched by any senior football club in the country.

SA players were initially loath to cross to Victoria but the traffic increased after the summer of 1963–64 when four crossed the border: Don Roach, Jeff Bray, Steve Traynor and Bob Pascoe.

Earlier, the most notable South Australians to play in Victoria included Jimmy Dean (Richmond), Brownlow Medallist *Bernie Smith* (Geelong) and lanky Clayton 'Candles' Thompson (Hawthorn).

Name players from Victorian clubs to play successfully in South Australia after the war include Wally May, Len Fitzgerald—a two-time Magarey Medallist—Bob Shearman, Ted Langridge, Col Saddington, Malcolm Hill and Doug Long.

Later, Murray Weideman, *Noel Teasdale*, David Darcy, Bruce Stevenson, Stephen Clifford, Peter Cloke, Bob Keddie, Glenn Elliot, Barry Goodingham, Bill Barrot and for half a season, *Don Scott*, also had an involvement. Russell Johnston, a fringe ruckman from Collingwood, was one of the most successful, his long-running reign as Port Adelaide captain starting in 1986.

IMPORTANT DATES IN SOUTH AUSTRALIAN FOOTBALL

1860: A notice appears in the *Register* asking those interested in establishing a football club to meet at the Globe Inn. Three days later the first game, co-ordinated by the just-formed Adelaide football club, is played between teams captained by Mr J.B. Spence and John Acraman, who had brought out the first footballs from England.

1870: Port Adelaide plays its first competitive game on the Glanville Hall Estate, the property of its president, captain John Hart. Its first colours are blue and white. It is not until 1902 that the club is to adopt its now famous black and white colours.

1876: South Adelaide is formed, following a meeting in the Draper Memorial Church schoolroom. One of the conveners, Charles Cameron Kingston, is foundation secretary. Later he becomes an illustrious statesman. South's first game, on 10 June, 1876 against Woodville, finishes in a goalless draw.

1877: The South Australian Football Association is formed. Competing teams are: South Adelaide, North Adelaide, Port Adelaide, Adelaide, South Park, Kensington, Victorian, Willunga, Prince Alfred College, Gawler, Kapunda, Bankers and Woodville. Matches between Prince Alfred and St Peter's Colleges begin. Two Victorian teams, Melbourne and St Kilda, visit for matches against combined SA clubs.

1878: The Norwood club is established after a meeting at the Norfolk Arms hotel. Its home ground at East Parkland near the old Kent Town brewery has to be frequently cleared of cows before training and games can commence. Among its foundation players is 18-year-old George Giffen, who is to become one of Australia's 19th century cricket legends.

1879: The first intercolonial fixture is played against Victoria in Melbourne, the Vics kicking 7.14 to South Australia's 0.3. Norwood goes through the season undefeated.

1883: Victorian changes its name to North Adelaide. Norwood wins its sixth premiership in a row.

1888: Norwood hailed as champions of Australia after defeating South Melbourne in a challenge match. Port Adelaide's Jack McKenzie kicks the first 10 goals of the game against North Adelaide.

1889: A.E. 'Topsy' Waldron figures in his 10th premiership, one with Carlton (VFA) and the others at Norwood, including the six flags in a row from 1878–83.

1892: Port Adelaide's A.J. McKenzie place-kicks the ball 73 metres at the Adelaide Oval, the longest kick of its kind in competition by a South Australian on record.

1893: Norwood's Anthony 'Bos' Daly kicks a record 23 goals against West Adelaide at Kensington Oval, including his team's first 20 goals.

1894: Finals are introduced.

1897: Electorate football is introduced. Natives, once associated with Port Adelaide, become the West Torrens football club.

1898: The first Magarey Medal is awarded to Norwood's Alby Green, donated by sportsminded lawyer and chairman of the SAFA, Mr W.A. 'Bill' Magarey, who is later to serve for 26 seasons as vice-president of the South Australian cricket association.

1899: Norwood officials award J.D. 'Bunny' Daly a special trophy after he runs the entire length of the ground carrying the ball.

1900: Test cricketer Ernie Jones, aged 30, captains North Adelaide to its first premiership. Sturt forms, immediately adopting its now famous double blue colours.

1901: North Adelaide teenager Phil Sandland wins the Magarey Medal in his first season of open-age football.

1902: Top team Port Adelaide forfeits its semi-final against South Adelaide rather than play under field umpire Phil Kneebone. The association disqualifies the club, placing it third on the premiership ladder. North Adelaide takes the flag under the captaincy of legendary all-sportsman Jack 'Dinny' Reedman, who figures in his sixth flag as skipper.

1904: In an amazing recovery, Norwood comes from 35 points down at three-quarter time to defeat Port Adelaide. Tommy Gibbons scores a goal with one of the last kicks of the match to put his team ahead.

1906: Tom McKenzie of West Torrens is the first to win three Magarey Medals.

1907: League football begins, comprising seven teams: North Adelaide, Norwood, Port Adelaide, South Adelaide, Sturt, West Adelaide and West Torrens.

1910: Sturt team-mates Bert Renfrey and Albert Heinrichs brawl after the grand final in which Sturt had been beaten by Port Adelaide. Renfrey is accused of 'playing dead', the pair beating each other almost into insensibility. Later they shake hands.

1911: SA wins the second Australian championships, held in Adelaide, doubling Victoria's score.

1914: Port Adelaide is acclaimed as Australia's champion team after defeating VFL premiers Carlton. It remains undefeated throughout the season.

1915: Port Adelaide contests its seventh grand final in a row. Between 21 June, 1913 and 31 July, 1915, it wins 29 and draws one of its 30 matches.

1921: Glenelg joins the league. It takes the club four years to win a game. Dan Moriarty wins his third consecutive Magarey Medal. He is to become a prominent racehorse owner.

1929: South Australian Eric Tassie is named president of the Australian Football Council. The Tassie Medal is to be named in his honour.

1930: North Adelaide's Ken Farmer becomes the first South Australian to kick 100 goals in a season.

1936: Port Adelaide coach Samson 'Shine' Hosking makes a comeback for one game, aged 48. Twenty-six years previously, he'd become the first wingman to win the Magarey Medal.

1940: Goalkicking great Farmer equals Bos Daly's 23 goal record, against West Torrens. He kicks nine goals in the final quarter and amasses 100 goals for the season for the 11th year in a row.

1941: Norwood's Bruce Schultz kicks 19.2 against Glenelg. His two points are posters. Farmer retires having kicked 1419 career goals at an average of 6.33 a game.

1954: Port Adelaide win the first of six premierships in a row.

1958: West Adelaide shift to permanent headquarters at Richmond Oval.

1964: Woodville and Central Districts join competition.

1963: SA defeats Victoria for the first time at the MCG since 1936.

1966: Sturt wins the first of five flags in a row.

1968: South Adelaide's Peter Darley forfeits the Magarey Medal, to Barrie Robran, after a suspension earlier in the season, his only misdemeanour in a 284 game career.

1969: Norwood's Graham Molloy shares the Tassie Medal, with WA's Peter Eakins.

1970: Port Adelaide becomes the first South Australian club to celebrate its centenary. West Adelaide's Dexter Kennedy is the youngest player ever to play senior SA football at the age of 15 years, 11 months. West Torrens stalwart Lindsay Head retires, having played 327 games. He is awarded an MBE. Sturt wins its fifth flag on end.

1971: Agreement is made with West Lakes Limited for the development of a new ground, Football Park. The anticipated capacity is 80,000. North Adelaide's Mike Patterson becomes the first Victorian to coach a SA premiership side, declaring afterwards that the champion Barrie Robran, who was the outstanding player afield, is the best footballer he's seen.

1973: The last grand final is played at the Adelaide Oval, Glenelg winning its first flag since 1934.

1974: The first seating at the league-controlled Football Park is completed. Matches, including the grand final, are played on the new oval, which is 183 metres by 142 metres.

1976: A record 66,897 fans see Sturt defeat Port Adelaide for the premiership. It is coach Jack Oatey's 10th premiership, seven with Sturt and three with Norwood.

1979: Glenelg defeats Centrals by 238 points, the greatest winning margin in SA history. It kicks a record 49.23 (317) to 11.13 (79).

1980: Port Adelaide's Russell Ebert wins his record fourth Magarey Medal. Rick Davies is named captain of the All Australian team. Graham Cornes wins the Tassie Medal.

1982: Glenelg's Tony McGuinness is the youngest ever winner of the Magarey Medal at 18 years and four months.

1983: Glenelg's Stephen Kernahan forfeits the Magarey Medal despite finishing nine votes ahead of the field, after a disqualification during the season. Sturt's Rick Davies kicks 151 goals.

1985: Woodville's *Malcolm Blight* kicks 14 goals straight against West Adelaide and 12 in his last game, at Woodville Oval. Ebert plays the last of his 392 league games. Kym Dillon (West Torrens) has football's first cartilage transplant.

1986: Port Adelaide's Tim Evans becomes the second player (after Farmer) to boot 1000 goals in SA football.

1987: Norwood's Gary McIntosh finishes two votes clear in the Magarey Medal count only to forfeit the award because of a disqualification. Glenelg's Chris McDermott is named captain of the All Australian side.

1987: South Adelaide's Mark Naley wins the Tassie Medal.

1988: Peter Carey retires after his seventh losing grand final, having played a record 448 games with Glenelg—and 467 overall.

1989: Carey is awarded the Medal of the Order of Australia (OAM) for his services to football.

1990: South Adelaide announces it's in financial difficulty and may not see out the season. Woodville and West Torrens merge, its inaugural coach being Norwood's Neil Balme. *Mark Williams* becomes the first South Australian to play 200 VFL/AFL games—with Collingwood and the Brisbane Bears. An independent commission to administer football in SA is appointed. Port Adelaide's Scott Hodges kicks 153 goals, being the first full forward in more than 20 years to win the Magarey Medal. His club attempts to join the AFL, before its submission is superseded by a SA league package. In October, it is resolved that SA will field a new combined team— the Adelaide football club—in the AFL for 1991. In a great comeback, South Adelaide makes the finals.

Peter Carey: a record 448 games with Glenelg.

1991: The Adelaide Crows, under the coaching of Cornes, finish ninth with 10 wins and 12 losses in its first AFL year, attracting the biggest home ground attendances (at Football Park) of any AFL club.

1993: Glamour full-forward Tony Modra kicks 129 goals for the season as the Crows make the preliminary final.

1994: Cornes is sacked after the Crows slide to 11th.

Port Adelaide is confirmed as the second AFL team to operate out of Adelaide— once a vacancy occurs. Port wins the flag again under veteran coach John Cahill, who reaches his 500th game milestone on grand final day.

SA'S BEST POST-WAR EIGHTEEN

B: Bernie Smith, Paul Weston, Martin Leslie.

HB: Steven Stretch, Greg Phillips, Peter Motley.

C: Greg Anderson, Russell Ebert, Craig Bradley.

HF: Tony Hall, Stephen Kernahan, Tony Francis.

F: Phil Carman, Malcolm Blight, Mark Naley.

R: Matt Rendell, Tony McGuinness.

Rov: John Platten.

Team provided by Geoff Poulter.

Darryl Wakelin on his way to winning the Jack Oatey Medal for being best afield for Port Adelaide in the 1994 SANFL Grand Final.

MOST SANFL MATCHES, 1897–1994

Player	Matches	Club	Span
Peter Carey	448	Glenelg	1971–88
Russell Ebert	392	Port Adelaide	1968–85
Ralph Sewer	382	Woodville/Glenelg	1969–90
Graham Cornes	364	Glenelg/South Adelaide	1967–84
Paul Bagshaw	360	Sturt	1964–80
David Marshall	353	Glenelg	1978–93
Bruce Winter	351	Sturt/Norwood	1971–86
Rick Davies	350	Sturt/South Adelaide	1970–86
Greg Phillips	343	Port Adelaide	1976–93
Stuart Palmer	337	South Adelaide	1969–85
Grantley Fielke	332*	West Adelaide	1979–94
Lindsay Head	327	West Torrens	1952–70
Neil Craig	319	Norwood/Sturt/North Adelaide	1973–90
John Seebohm	319	Glenelg	1978–92
John Paynter	316	Sturt	1980–92
Michael Aish	307	Norwood	1979–93
Keith Thomas	304	Norwood	1979–93

* current player.

MOST VFL/AFL MATCHES BY PLAYERS FROM SOUTH AUSTRALIA
(150 matches or more)

PLAYER	MATCHES	TEAMS	SPAN	RECRUITED FROM
Craig Bradley	201*	Carlton	1986–94	Port Adelaide
Mark Williams	201	Collingwood/Brisbane	1981–90	Port Adelaide
John Platten	200*	Hawthorn	1986–94	Central Dist.
Stephen Kernahan	199*	Carlton	1986–94	Glenelg
Tony McGuinness	193*	Footscray/Adelaide	1986–94	Glenelg
Bernie Smith	183	Geelong	1948–58	W. Adelaide
Steven Stretch	183*	Melbourne/Fitzroy	1986–94	W. Torrens
George Bruce	181	Carlton	1903–13	W. Adelaide
Malcolm Blight	178	North Melbourne	1974–82	Woodville
Matt Rendell	177	Fitzroy/Brisbane	1981–92	West Torrens
John Mossop	171	Geelong/North Melb.	1979–88	Penola
Mark Yeates	154	Geelong	1980–86, 1988–90	West Gambier

* current player.

SOUTH MELBOURNE

Founded in 1867 from the amalgamation of the Albert Park and the Emerald Hill football clubs, South Melbourne was a foundation member of both the VFA and the VFL.

In 1880, South toppled an Australian Rules-trained rugby team from England. It became the dominant team in the Association, winning 56 of its 63 games under skipper 'Sonny' Elms in a golden period from 1888 to 1890. Crowds of more than 20,000 regularly attended games. A match against Essendon at the old East Melbourne ground attracted 30,000.

In these early years until 1890, South wore blue and white before the red and white colours of the Albert Park club were adopted. South teams played in red and white hoops until 1903, before a white guernsey with two or three broad vertical stripes was used in 1904 and 1905. In 1907, a white guernsey with red sash was

South Melbourne, 1905, captained by a former Port Melbourne champion Billy McGee. It came fifth with seven and a half wins in 17 matches.

used. From 1933, a red V replaced the red sash.

The club won its firs premiership in 1909—despite kicking only 4.14—and won again in 1918, the year it resumed in the competition after missing seasons 1915–17 because of World War One enlistments.

The 1918 South combination lost only one game all year and fielded such notables as 'Chook' Howell, *Mark Tandy*, Tom O'Halloran, skipper Jim Caldwell and *Vic Belcher*. Trailing Collingwood by two goals at three-quarter time of a low-scoring Grand Final, South kicked 3.2 to 0.3 in the final term to win by five points.

In a round 12 game in 1919, South kicked the then record VFL score of 29.15 (189) to defeat St Kilda 2.6 (18). South's 171 point winning margin remained a record for 60 years. In the final term, South kicked 17.4, St Kilda having been reduced to 15 players because of injury. In the last term, Saint numbers decreased even further when four men walked from the field in disgust!

In the last home-and-away round of the 1923 season, 40,441, the biggest crowd to attend a game at the Lakeside Oval, saw South defeat St Kilda in the battle for the 'Lake premiership'. Many believed the crowd was closer to 45,000 as parts of the outer fence on the bowling green side were broken down and thousands were able to enter free of charge. South needed to win to guarantee a place in the finals and, after an evenly fought match, ran away to win by 20 points.

The club's most famous teams were in 1933–34. They won 31 of their 41 matches, appeared in consecutive Grand Finals, and four in five years.

The star-studded South teams were headed by champion goalkicker *Bob Pratt* and super-skilled *Laurie Nash* who in 1934 helped the team kick 20 goals or more on a record eight occasions. Between them, they kicked 195 goals.

Recruits from interstate included Wilbur Harris and Ossie Bertram (West Torrens), Jack Wade (Port Adelaide), John Bowe, Brighton Diggins and Bill Faull (Subiaco), Jim O'Meara (East Perth) and Gilbert Beard (Kalgoorlie goldfields). Nash, who was Melbourne-born but had played most of his football in Tasmania, was one of the star newcomers. Tasmanian Fred Davies was another import.*

The club's failure to win more than one premiership in this era was a disappointment. Many thought South had the talent to win all four, but its team of champions could not always combine as a champion team.

Versatile and quick-thinking, Nash was one of the few surviving members of the teams of the mid-1930s who played in the club's next Grand Final, against Carlton in 1945. It proved to be a running brawl, the fieriest Grand Final on record.

South, known by many as 'the Bloods', fielded many of the best players in the competition, including Brownlow Medallists *Herbie Matthews* and *Ron Clegg*. But the club found difficulty in consistently matching the best teams.

After the war, the club played in just two final series and at the end of 1981, after a decline in membership and gate receipts, the VFL directors agreed to relocate the club to Sydney where it became the League's first privately owned club.

* see 'CROFTS, ARCHIE'

In 1979 and 1980, South incurred operating losses of almost $300,000, forcing the committee to either disband the club or shift. Following unsuccessful lobbying from the 'Keep South at South' faction—backed by old players such as Nash—the club's shift was complete after the joint Melbourne and Sydney training sessions ended. The entire squad, minus several notable 'defectors', was relocated.

From 1982, South Melbourne became known as 'The Swans', playing all its home games at the Sydney Cricket Ground, with direct television coverage back to Melbourne. Now the club is known almost exclusively as 'Sydney'. Only the basic colours remain, the red V having been altered to resemble the Sydney Opera House.

The VFL helped steady the club's unstable finances in the early 1980s, acting as an underwriter to allow it to continue in the 1983 season. The club's overall debt was estimated at $1.6 million. The AFL continues to take an active interest, guaranteeing funds important in the recruiting of big names including *Tony Lockett*.

SYDNEY/SOUTH MELBOURNE: THE STATISTICS

FORMED: July, 1874 (as South Melbourne)

JOINED LEAGUE: 1897 (South Melbourne), 1982 (Sydney)

HOME VENUES: Lake Oval (1897–1915, 1917–41, 1947–81); Princes Park (1942–43); Junction Oval (1944–45); SCG (1982–)

CURRENT HOME VENUE DIMENSIONS: 153 metres × 137 metres

COLOURS: White guernsey with red yoke incorporating Opera House insignia.

TOTAL FINALS MATCHES: 45 (18 wins, 27 losses)

FINALS RECORD: Premiers: 3 (1909, 1918, 1933)
Runners-up: 8 (1899, 1907, 1912, 1914, 1934–35–36, 1945)

PREMIERSHIP COACHES: Charlie Ricketts (1), Herbert Howson/H. Elms (1), Jack Bissett (1).

NIGHT SERIES PREMIERSHIPS: 4 (1956–57, 1960, 1982)

YOUNGEST PLAYER: Robert Hay, 16 years 285 days (1960)

OLDEST PLAYER (post-war players only): Barry Round, 35 years 187 days (1985)

HIGHEST SCORE: 36.20 (236) v Essendon, R.17, 1987, SCG

LOWEST SCORE: 0.5 (5) v Carlton, R.8, 1899, Princes Park

LONGEST WINNING SEQUENCE: 12 (1918); 12 (1933–34); 12 (1935)

LONGEST LOSING SEQUENCE: 29 (1972–73)

MOST FINALS: Vic Belcher 17

MOST SEASONS AS COACH: Charlie Pannam jnr 6 (1923–28)

MOST SEASONS AS CAPTAIN: Bob Skilton 10 (1961–68, 1970–71). He did not play in 1969.

MOST GAMES		MOST GOALS	
John Rantall	260	Bob Pratt	681
Mark Browning	251	Bob Skilton	412
Stephen Wright	246	Tony Morwood	397
Bob Skilton	237	Ted Johnson	386
Ron Clegg	231	Peter Bedford	327
Tony Morwood	229	Warwick Capper	317
Jack Graham	227	Len Mortimer	289
Vic Belcher	226	Austin Robertson snr	251
Dennis Carroll	219	Stephen Wright	247
Rod Carter	217	Laurie Nash	246
Jim Cleary	216	Jack Graham	234
David McLeish	213	Barry Mitchell	214
Mark Tandy	207	Bernie Evans	212
		Peter Reville	206

MOST GOALS IN A MATCH: Bob Pratt 15 v Essendon, R.3, 1934, Lake Oval.
Harold Robertson 14 v St Kilda, R.12, 1919, Lake Oval.
Bob Pratt 12 v Footscray, R.15, 1934, Lake Oval.
Lindsay White 12 v Melbourne, R.5, 1942, Princes Park.

BROWNLOW MEDALLISTS: Herbie Matthews snr 1940; Ron Clegg 1949; Fred Goldsmith 1955; Bob Skilton 1959, 1963, 1968; Peter Bedford 1970; Graham Teasdale 1977; Barry Round 1981; Greg Williams 1986; Gerard Healy 1988.

LEAGUE LEADING GOALSCORERS: Bob Pratt 109 (1933), Bob Pratt 150 (1934), Bob Pratt 103 (1935), Lindsay White 80 (1942).

RECORD HOME VENUE ATTENDANCE: 40,441 v St Kilda, R.18, 1923, Lake Oval.
16,000 v Carlton, R.2, 1942, Princes Park.
38,000 v Carlton, R.1, 1946, Junction Oval.
38,000 v Richmond, R.9, 1946, Junction Oval.
39,763 v Hawthorn, R.19, 1986, SCG.

RECORD ATTENDANCE IN ANY MATCH: 104,239 v St Kilda, FS, 1970, MCG.

MOST RECENT PREMIERSHIP TEAM: 1933 South Melb. 9.17 (71) d Richmond 4.5 (29).
B: R. McKenzie, H. McKay, J. Austin. H.B: W. Faul, L. Nash, H. McLaughlin. C: H. Clarke, L. Thomas, J. Bowe. H.F: J. O'Meara, B. Diggins, H. Reville. F: H. Matthews, R. Pratt, O. Bertram. R: J. Bissett (c), D. Kelleher. R: T. Brain. Reserve: G. Beard.

SOUTHBY, Geoff (1950–)

Carlton's greatest-ever full-back, and one of the most-decorated defenders of the post-war period, Geoff Southby achieved almost every possible VFL honour, playing in two premiership sides, 17 finals and representing Victoria 16 times between 1971–81.

But for injury, he could have played in four flags. He averaged more than 20 games a year in his first decade, but just 12 in his last four, finishing with 273 games in 14 years.

Southby represented Victoria in his very first year of football, as a 21-year-old from Sandhurst in 1971. He was also equal-best first-year player, with North Melbourne's *Keith Greig*.

At full-back, he won consecutive Carlton best and fairest awards, a magnificent feat for a specialist defender.

In mid-career, he attempted to switch to

Geoff Southby, a classic full-back, in action
late in his career against North Melbourne's
Ian Fairley.

South Melbourne and stood out of football
for the first eight games of the 1977
season, before returning. Carlton considered a full-back of his class irreplaceable.

At his best, his fingertip marking, judgement and pace made him a most formidable opponent. A magnificent kick, who
often unleashed 70-metre torpedoes, he
started many attacks with his handball and
precise passing.

STEPHEN, Bill (1928–)

One of post-war football's finest and
most reliable back-pocket players, Bill
Stephen played 162 games with Fitzroy
from 1947–57, won two best and fairests
and represented Victoria 14 times.

His influence at Fitzroy is profound. He
coached the Lions in 214 games in three
separate stints: 1955–57, 1965–70 and
1979–80.

A great gentleman and a magnificent
teacher of young players, he later coached
Essendon in 1976–77.

In his time with the Bombers, he introduced such notables as *Tim Watson, Paul*
Van der Haar and Shane Heard into
League ranks. His teams were known as
the 'Baby Bombers'.

STEWART, Ian (1944–)

One of only four players to win the
Brownlow Medal three times, Stewart
twice triumphed at St Kilda in 1965–66
and again at Richmond on his first of five
seasons with the Tigers, in 1971.

Stewart's deadly accurate left-foot
kicking was a feature of his game. He was
also a superbly-gifted aerialist, courageous
and equally at ease on wet or dry grounds.

He made his VFL debut as a winger in
1963, after just 13 games in the Tasmanian
football league. The 179 cm teenager won
St Kilda's club championship in his second
season.

He had a superb understanding with St
Kilda's captain and centre half-forward
Darrel Baldock, being able to hit him on the
chest from 50 metres, kicking either with
his left or right foot.

Injured in a car accident in 1967,
Stewart never again played with the same
consistency at St Kilda. When swapped for

Superbly-balanced Ian Stewart beats Hawk Des
Meagher in a 1973 contest at Glenferrie Oval.

Richmond's Bill Barrot in 1971, he regained his enthusiasm and poise, playing as a centreman and half-forward.

At St Kilda, Stewart played 127 games, being captain in 1969 and twice winning the best and fairest. He had 78 games with the Tigers for a total of 205. In 1971, as well as winning the Brownlow, he was Richmond's club champion and in 1973 played in another premiership.

He coached South Melbourne for five years, in 1976–77 and again from 1979–81. In 1978, he was appointed coach at Carlton but was forced to resign after the opening weeks because of a minor heart ailment.

ST KILDA

The club was formed in 1873 when several members of the South Yarra club joined with members of the St Kilda cricket club. The Saints were progressive, being the first Victorian team to visit South Australia and play at the Adelaide Oval. The club was also a foundation member of both the VFA and the VFL, but struggled to win games.

After three undistinguished years in the Association, the Saints were relegated to junior ranks.

But it was one of eight clubs admitted to the VFL for the initial 1897 season. St Kilda's headquarters at the already long-established Junction Oval were considered ideally located for the drawing of big crowds. Finals matches were first played at St Kilda in 1898 and 1899.

In 1897, the club failed to score a goal in three matches. It suffered 48 consecutive defeats until drawing with Melbourne in 1900 and being awarded the game on a protest.

Its most famous early player was Dave McNamara, a champion long kick, who had only one VFL rival, Essendon's *Albert Thurgood*. McNamara captained the club before he turned 21 and was twice voted 'Champion of the Colony', in 1907 and 1914.

The great *Wells Eicke* made his debut at 16 and played 197 games with two clubs from 1909–27. He was captain-coach in 1919.

The Saints suffered badly from in-fighting. Many leading players transferred elsewhere so they could be a part of stronger, united combinations.

McNamara moved to Essendon Town where he kicked 100 goals in a season, Jack Wells became Carlton's captain, Bert Renfrey led South Australia, Gerry Balme and Tom Soutar both captain-coached West Perth, *Roy Cazaly* went to South Melbourne and Bill Tymms and Harold Moyes to Melbourne.

The club first played in the finals in 1907, made the Grand Final in 1913 but didn't win its first premiership until 1966.

In 1914, at the outbreak of World War One, St Kilda changed its colours to red, yellow and black, but reverted to its original red, white and black in 1922.

The club crest, to signify courage, was added to the jersey in 1934, after a torrid match with North Melbourne in which it finished with 16 men. Opposing clubs were amazed. Richmond legend *Jack Dyer* said: 'If Collingwood and Richmond players were given a crest every time they displayed courage, we would have had 100 guernseys to fit the crests on. It made them (St Kilda) the laughing stock of the League.'

Wagga's *Bill Mohr* became one of the greatest goalkickers of his era, amassing 736 goals in 195 games from 1929–41.

The Saints made the finals in 1929 and 1939, having good all-round sides. It wasn't until the late 1950s, however, that the club assembled a truly competitive side. *Brian Gleeson* and *Neil Roberts* won back-to-back Brownlow Medals in 1957–58 under the emotional hot-gospelling coaching style of Alan Killigrew.

Until *Allan Jeans'* arrival in 1961, the Saints had been coached by 11 different men since the War, finishing last on six occasions. In 13 of Jeans' 16 years as coach, St Kilda was a top six side.

The club's move from St Kilda to Moorabbin in Melbourne's south-east suburbs for the start of the 1965 season was a great success. The Saints had always enjoyed good support, even in their poorest years, and not only maintained their consistent numbers, but attracted a ground record of

51,370 to the first game at Moorabbin, in April, 1965, when Collingwood was defeated by a goal.

Tasmanian recruits *Darrel Baldock, Verdun Howell* and *Ian Stewart* all made an instant impression.

Other champion players of the era included lion-hearted ruckman Alan Morrow; athletic *Carl Ditterich*; Sandringham's Bob Murray; another Medallist, rover *Ross Smith*; and 300-game forward, Mentone's *Barry Breen*.

In 10 years between 1965–74, the Saints played in the finals six times, but it wasn't until 1991 that the club again qualified, under Carlton premiership player *Ken Sheldon* and selection supremo *Peter Hudson*, boosted by full-forward and 1987 Brownlow Medallist *Tony Lockett*.

Late in 1994, the Saints lost the uncontracted Lockett to Sydney, having been unable to compete financially with the huge offers from rival clubs. Loyal captain Danny Frawley also announced that the 1995 season would be his last.

ST KILDA: THE STATISTICS

FORMED: April, 1873

JOINED LEAGUE: 1897
HOME VENUES: Junction Oval (1897–1915, 1917–41, 1944–64); Toorak Park (1942–43); Moorabbin (1965–92); AFL Park, Waverley (1993–)
CURRENT HOME VENUE DIMENSIONS: 180 metres × 142 metres
COLOURS: Vertical red, white and black striped guernsey with crest.
TOTAL FINALS MATCHES: 30 (12 wins, 18 losses)
FINALS RECORD: Premiers: 1 (1966)
　　　　　　　Runners-up: 3 (1913, 1965, 1971)
PREMIERSHIP COACH: Allan Jeans (1)
NIGHT SERIES PREMIERSHIP: 1 (1958)
YOUNGEST PLAYER: Wells Eicke, 15 years 315 days (1909)
OLDEST PLAYER: 'Vic' Cumberland, 43 years 48 days (1920)
HIGHEST SCORE: 31.18 (204) v Melbourne, R.6, 1978, MCG
LOWEST SCORE: 0.1 (1) v Geelong, R.17, 1899, Corio Oval
LONGEST WINNING SEQUENCE: 8 (1939); 8 (1966)
LONGEST LOSING SEQUENCE: 48 (1897–99)
MOST FINALS: Kevin Neale 16
MOST SEASONS AS COACH: Allan Jeans 16 (1961–76)
MOST SEASONS AS CAPTAIN: Danny Frawley 9 (1987–95)

MOST GAMES		MOST GOALS	
Barry Breen	300	Tony Lockett	898
Gary Colling	265	Bill Mohr	736
Kevin Neale	256	Allan Davis	306
Ross Smith	234	Barry Breen	305
Trevor Barker	231	Kevin Neale	304
Jeff Sarau	226	George Young	284
Danny Frawley	226*	Bill Young	275
Geoff Cunningham	224	Peter Bennett	259
Harry Lever	217	Stewart Loewe	254
Brian Mynott	209	Darrel Baldock	233
Carl Ditterich	203	Ross Smith	229
		Nicky Winmar	209

* current player.

ST KILDA: THE STATISTICS (cont)

MOST GOALS IN A MATCH: Tony Lockett 15 v Sydney, R.13, 1992, Moorabbin.
Tony Lockett 13 v Carlton, R.21, 1991, VFL Park.
Tony Lockett 12 v Melbourne, R.4, 1987, MCG.
Tony Lockett 12 v West Coast, R.9, 1989, Moorabbin.
Tony Lockett 12 v Adelaide, R.7, 1991, Moorabbin.
Tony Lockett 12 v Sydney, R.9, 1991, SCG.
Tony Lockett 12 v Brisbane, R.10, 1992, Moorabbin.

BROWNLOW MEDALLISTS: Colin Watson 1925; Brian Gleeson 1957; Neil Roberts 1958; Verdun Howell 1959; Ian Stewart 1965, 1966; Ross Smith 1967; Tony Lockett 1987.

COLEMAN MEDALLISTS: Tony Lockett 1987, 1991.

LEAGUE LEADING GOALSCORERS: Bill Mohr 101 (1936), Bill Young 56 (1956), Tony Lockett 117 (1987), Tony Lockett 127 (1991).

RECORD HOME VENUE ATTENDANCE: 46,973 v Carlton, R.5, 1950, Junction Oval.
10,000 v Richmond, R.3, 1943, Toorak Park.
51,370 v Collingwood, R.1, 1965, Moorabbin.
74,253 v Collingwood, EF, 1992, AFL Park, Waverley.

RECORD ATTENDANCE IN ANY MATCH: 118,192 v Hawthorn, GF, 1971, MCG.

MOST RECENT PREMIERSHIP TEAM: 1966 St Kilda 10.14 (74) d Collingwood 10.13 (73).
B: R. Head, R. Murray, B. Sierakowski. H.B: V. Howell, I. Synman, J. Bingley. C: J. Moran, I Stewart, J. Read. H.F: I. Cooper, D. Baldock (c), B. Breen. F: A. Morrow, K. Neale, A. Davis. R: B. Mynott, D. Griffiths. R: R. Smith. Reserves: T. Payze, K. Billing.

STONEHAM, Alan (1955–)

The fair-headed teenage star from Footscray had eight years and 129 games at the Western Oval, before crossing to Essendon for his final four seasons.

A skilled and able utility player, he did best when given the responsibility of playing in the centre or on the ball. He represented Victoria three times and, in all, played 201 games in his 12 years of League football. He was recruited from Sunshine.

STRATEGIES

When Hawthorn won its first premiership in 1961, its game was based on supreme fitness and discipline. Coach *John Kennedy* insisted his defenders punch the ball wherever possible. Players tackled fiercely and applied non-stop pressure. It was a close-checking and unattractive style, but proved highly effective, leaving a succession of opponents stunned.

After this, all sides added a new running dimension to the game, which for years had been based around stop-start, mark-and-kick football.

Len Smith, the brother of legendary *Norm*, developed teamwork patterns based round the rapid movement of the ball which negated Hawthorn's 'strength and spoil' approach.

The Smith brothers were among the most influential and innovative coaches of the period. Len coached at Fitzroy and Richmond without startling success, but his methods are still being copied. His position is undisputed as the father of modern football.

His thinking was radical for the time. He advocated the use of continuous movement through handball, long-kicking and players running in groups to assist each other—everything which occurs today.

He was the first to introduce the controversial flick pass, which was soon banned, but changed forever patterns of play, leading to a more running-orientated game.

'He was the founder of modern Richmond,' said Richmond's great administrator Graham Richmond. 'He was the first to have a coaching manifesto. Up until that stage coaching was very much a hand-me-down situation. But Len analysed it, wrote it down and edited it into a series of notes.'

Tom Hafey won four premierships in 11 years at Richmond, following Smith's basic ideas—one handball and one long kick—almost to the letter.

Others he particularly assisted included *Allan Jeans*, *Kevin Sheedy*, Col Kinnear and *John Northey*, who were all involved in the first year of AFL football in 1990.

The pace of the game has lifted so dramatically in recent times that many old-timers say the same skills, especially in marking, are not exhibited. However, a glance at old replays shows just how far the game has advanced, in almost every possible facet.

Coaches now have teams of specialist assistants from physical education experts to sports psychologists, dietitians and statisticians.

The most successful, like *David Parkin*—winner of four premierships—*Mick Malthouse* and Sheedy, study video tapes for hours, analysing and appraising.

Parkin's teams at Carlton and Fitzroy became renowned for being the best prepared in the competition. They didn't always win, but it wasn't through lack of knowledge of the opposition.

As coaches developed precise team plays, the old 'no-nos' of handballing on the backline and kicking across goal—once considered cardinal sins—became essential to teams changing the direction of play, and whipping the ball into the centre 'corridor'.

Carlton's successful use of non-stop handball in the 1970 Grand Final was the final nail in the coffin of the 'kick-and-mark' players who had thrived in the 1940s and 1950s.

As the game quickened, teams were able to accelerate the ball from the full-back line through the goals in a matter of seconds.

Umpires had trouble keeping up with the new running style and, in 1976, a two-umpire system was established. From 1993, three field umpires were used.

STYNES, Jim (1966–)

The first player from overseas to win the Brownlow Medal in 1991, Stynes' remarkable success story began in Dublin, Ireland, in October, 1984 when he was one of almost two dozen teenagers invited to try out for a sports scholarship to Australia. Melbourne wanted Irish boys younger than 18, taller than 183 cm, with above-average Gaelic football credentials.

Irishman Jim Stynes: a fine Melbourne and Big V representative.

Renowned coach *Ron Barassi* was convinced with the right coaching and patience the Irish could successfully adapt to Australian football. Eighteen-year-old Stynes, from Rathfarnham, eight km from Dublin, had played Gaelic football all his life at the encouragement of his father, Brian, who had trialled against the 1967 Australian Galahs.

The 199 cm Stynes immediately impressed Barassi and fellow recruiters. Along with James Fahey—another teenage scholarship winner—he arrived in Melbourne in November, 1984. The boys had been promised their air-fares, college fees for two years, accommodation and $60 a week spending-money.

It was a calculated gamble by the Demons. Neither Stynes nor Fahey had any background in Australian football, but the club had already recruited Irish pair

Paul Earley and Sean Wight and been sufficiently encouraged by their progress to continue their revolutionary recruiting.

Earley returned home after only one senior game and Fahey ended up playing local amateur football, but Wight proved to be a sensational import, making his senior debut in 1985.

Stynes enthusiastically threw himself into the task of learning the fundamentals, saying he'd been offered 'the experience of a lifetime'.

In 1987, he played 13 debut games in the Melbourne seniors, including the preliminary final, his most disappointing moment in football. Hawthorn won the last kick of the match after Stynes conceded a crucial 15-metre penalty in the final seconds to allow *Gary Buckenara* to move to within comfortable scoring distance.

Stynes said he resolved to make himself a better player after that match. 'I decided I wasn't going to be remembered as the man who ran over the mark. I changed my attitude towards football and became more competitive. I don't believe I would have won the Brownlow if it didn't happen. It is something that has become an inspiration for me. You don't realise how much you can learn from failure.'

He has repaid Melbourne many times over for that mistake. In 1988, he was first chosen for Victoria for the Bicentenary Carnival in Adelaide and in the 1988 Grand Final—won by a record margin by Hawthorn—was his team's best player.

His progress amazed everyone except the man himself who said that the similarities between Australian and Gaelic football mean players adept at one code should be able to adapt to the other.

He is one of the few current players to figure in more than 100 consecutive games.

SULLIVAN, Tony (1949–   )

Dependable and highly skilled, he had 192 games with Melbourne from 1967–79 after being recruited from St Pat's, Ballarat. He played mainly at half-back and represented Victoria once. His son, Chris, first represented Melbourne in 1992, before transferring to Richmond in 1995.

SUMICH, Peter (1968–   )

A convert from soccer who in 1991 joined the elite band to kick 100 goals in a season, Sumich rejected an offer from Collingwood to stay in Perth and play with the West Coast Eagles.

Topping the club goalkicking charts in each of his opening four seasons, his 111 goals in 1991 included a career best 13 against Footscray under lights in Perth. He also kicked five in the Eagles' losing Grand Final side. In 1992, he kicked six goals in a winning play-off, finishing with 82 goals in an injury-interrupted year.

A prodigious left-foot kick who often struggled for accuracy in his initial seasons, Sumich is best known for kicking a point on the siren from close range to force a tie in the 1990 qualifying final against Collingwood at Waverley. Many believe had he goaled, from an acute angle just 20 metres out, the Eagles could have gone all the way to win the first AFL flag.

In 1994, despite a disappointing season, he played in his second League premiership and lifted his career goal aggregate to 453 goals in 125 matches.

SUPERSTATS

(1) Most disposals in a match
Greg Williams (Sydney) 53 —25 kicks, 28 handballs, five marks, kicking 6.1 v St Kilda (Sydney), round 19, 1989.

Peter Featherby (Geelong) 51—43 kicks, eight handpasses, 12 marks, kicking 4.5 v Melbourne (MCG), round 16, 1981.

(2) Most kicks in a match
Bob Skilton (South Melbourne) 44 v St Kilda (Lake Oval), round 8, 1968.

(3) Most marks in a match
Alex Duncan (Carlton) 33 v Collingwood (Victoria Park), round 9, 1927.

Ron Clegg (South Melbourne) 32 v Fitzroy (Brunswick St.), round 9, 1951. He took 23 in the second half.

Harold Ball (Melbourne) 15 in the last quarter in damp conditions, v Essendon (MCG), 1940 preliminary final.

SYDNEY

An off-shoot of the old South Melbourne club, the Sydney Swans had a tough opening decade in Australia's biggest city, struggling on and off the field for recognition, despite several of the club's imported players being among the elite in the land.

Financially assisted by the VFL and given extra scope with new player drafting rules, the club has played home matches at the Sydney Cricket Ground since 1982 when it was known as The Swans. In 1983, the club became known as the Sydney Swans.

Despite the efforts of its marketers, the privately owned club found it difficult in rugby-orientated Sydney to attract a regular following and after the highs of 1986–87, when it made the finals and boasted crowds of more than 30,000, its attendances dropped below 10,000 in 1990 and 1991.

On-ball specialists *Greg Williams* (1986) and *Gerard Healy* (1988) both won the Brownlow Medal. *Bernard Toohey, Merv Neagle* and David Bolton were among other elite Melbourne-based players wooed to the club by its big-spending head, Dr Geoffrey Edelsten. They became the best paid group of players in the game. Healy and Williams received upwards of $200,000 a year.

Legendary Victorian coach *Tom Hafey* was in charge from 1986–88 when the side finished fourth, fourth and seventh. In 1987, the superbly fit Swans became the first team to kick 30 goals or more three weeks in a row—30.21 (201) against West Coast, 36.20 (236) v Essendon and 31.12 (198) v Richmond.

The three huge wins helped lift the club into top place, but it won only one of its final four matches, and lost both finals to finish fourth. It had also lost both finals in 1986.

Only a few players from the old South Melbourne club survived as the Swans entered the 1990s—skipper *Dennis Carroll*, who originally played with South in 1981, and rover *Stevie Wright*, who first appeared in 1979. He won the 1990 best and fairest, having also won in 1985.

The recruiting of *Dermott Brereton* (1994) and *Tony Lockett* and *Paul Roos* (1995) lifted the image of the Swans, which had finished bottom for three years running from 1992–94.

The Sydney Swans group together after a rare victory against Collingwood at Victoria Park. On the extreme right is Bernard Toohey, who crossed to Footscray in 1992.

TALL TIMBER

Essendon's crack ruckman Paul Salmon graduated to League under 19 ranks as a 15-year-old. He towered over opponents of his own age and wanted more competition so his game could more quickly advance.

Making his senior debut in 1983, aged 18, the 206 cm youngster joined Carlton's *Justin Madden* as one of the tallest men in the game. Later, much-travelled Romano Negri, who is also 206 cm, played League football, with the Crows.

Fitzroy's Dean Farnham was also 206 cm, but, unlike Salmon and Madden, had only a brief League career because of injury.

The tallest player ever to play senior Australian football is Fremantle's Matthew 'Spider' Burton at 210 cm. He originally played with Subiaco.

The tall and the short of it: Paul Salmon, circa 1984, with Essendon teammate Tony Buhagiar.

TANDY, Marcus

A speedy and skilful winger who figured in two Grand Finals, including South Melbourne's 1918 premiership, Marcus Tandy played 207 matches from 1911–26 and was captain in 1922. He represented Victoria 13 times.

TASMANIA

One of football's staunchest strongholds, which has produced some outstanding mainland champions, Tasmania should, in time, field its own AFL team. Fitzroy played several 'home' matches on the island from 1990–92, increasing expectation that a League side may relocate, given sufficient encouragement at AFL level and with the necessary corporate sponsorship.

Tasmanian football has so advanced in standard that regular games on a State-of-Origin basis are played against the Victorian 'B' team. In 1990, Tasmania defeated the Vics by 33 points at Hobart—

TALLEST LEAGUE PLAYERS

HEIGHT(cm)	PLAYER	CLUB/SPAN	MATCHES
210	Matthew Burton	Fremantle 1995	*
206	Ty Esler	Rich. 1991–93	12
	Dean Farnham	Fitz. 1974–75	17
	Justin Madden	Ess. 1980–82/Carl. 1983–94	286*
	Paul Salmon	Ess. 1983–94	196*
204	Trevor Mustey	Sydney 1982–83	2
	Romano Negri	Adel. 1991	5
203	Richard Lounder	Rich. 1989	4
	David Willis	Syd. 1988–9	25
	Damian Monkhurst	Coll. 1988–94	119*
202	Bob Heard	Coll. 1970–75/Rich. 1976–79	160

* current player.

only the second win against the Big V in its history. In 1991, it almost won again, but for poor kicking for goal.

Its most celebrated post-war champions to cross Bass Strait include *Darrel Baldock*, Ray Biffin, John Chick, *Brent Crosswell*, Mike Delanty, *Rodney Eade*, Michael and Brendon Gale, *Royce Hart*, *Verdun Howell*, *Peter Hudson*, *Tassie Johnson*, *Peter Jones*, Barry Lawrence, Peter Marquis, *Robert Neal*, Darrin Pritchard, *Michael Roach*, Paul Sproule, and *Ian Stewart*, a triple Brownlow Medallist.

One Victorian talent scout quipped to a Tasmanian friend one night: 'You know, we should chain the place (Tasmania) to our grandstand just in case it starts to float away!'

IMPORTANT DATES IN TASMANIAN FOOTBALL

1875: Launceston football club is founded in northern Tasmania, playing the first organised game at Windmill Hill.

1876: Football played in southern Tasmania between newly formed Railways and Cricketers clubs.

1879: Southern Tasmanian Football Association founded. Matches played on Upper and Lower cricket grounds on the Old Battery ground. City is declared competition premiers, even though there is no grand final.

1881: Games first played on north-west coast when Latrobe and Formby clubs formed. Teams are of 12 a side. Launceston organises first-ever intercolonial match in Tasmania between Hotham and a Northern Tasmanian side at Launceston. Scores: Hotham 4.18 d Northern Tasmania 0.2. Hotham also plays a game in Hobart.

1882: Essendon visits Tasmania, playing a northern combined team in Launceston and a combined Tasmanian team, chosen from the north and south of the island, in Hobart. Essendon wins 6.27 to Tasmania 1.8.

1883: North v South matches introduced. South wins the first match 6.18 to North 1.10.

1884: For the first time in an Australian

football match, scores are signalled via the waving of two white flags from one end of the ground to the other.

1886: The Northern Tasmanian Football Association formed in Launceston.

1887: Tasmanian colours of rose, primrose and black are adopted.

1892: NTFA meets a representative team from the North West Association for the first time.

1896: City changes its name to Hobart.

1897: The 'little mark' is abolished and the system of scoring points introduced with six points for a goal and one point for a behind, the team with the greater number of points winning; competition name is changed to Southern Tasmanian Football League.

1898: Name changed back to Southern Tasmanian Football Association.

1905: The NTFA engages an umpire from the VFL for the season.

1906: The Tasmanian Football League is formed, with three foundation clubs: North Hobart, Lefroy and Derwent.

1908: North Western Football League formed; Cananore wins the State premiership with a professional coach.

1909: Matches between the TFL and NTFA premier clubs are recognised as 'State premierships'. (The North West is not included until 1954.)

1913: Launceston, the northern premier, refuses to take the field in the State premiership match against southern premier Cananore, because of a dispute over the central umpire engaged for the game. Launceston is disqualified, and Cananore awarded the match on forfeit.

1922: After several years of negotiation, the Hobart City Council is granted use of North Hobart oval as its headquarters and for roster matches. One of the league's greatest administrators, W. H. Gill, dies, having served 14 years as league secretary.

1924: Tasmania stages its first ANFC carnival in Hobart. NTFA best and fairest is introduced, won by City's L. J. Keogh.

1925: TFL best and fairest introduced, won by Lefroy's E. R. Smith.

1927: TFL name changed to Tasmanian Australian National Football League.

1930: North Hobart's Allan Rait

becomes the first to kick 100 goals in a season. He notches 112, bettering Longford goalkicker Col Stokes' record.

1931: Collingwood's Brownlow Medalist, 'Leeta' Collier wins the William Leitch Medal, representing Cananore.

1936: The Burnie-Penguin match at West Park is completed despite blinding rain and a hurricane. Many players leave the field in the appalling conditions. Six Penguin players are left to battle 11 from Burnie. On the siren, the players cheer lustily. Burnie wins 8.10 (58) to Penguin's 2.5 (17).

1938: North Hobart's Len Pye becomes the first player to win the TFL best and fairest three times. Launceston wins sixth NTFA premiership in a row.

1945: North Hobart wins the TFL premiership, its fifth flag in a row and sixth in eight consecutive grand final play-offs.

1947: ANFC carnival staged in Hobart.

1950: Longford's Terry Cashion, vice-captain of the Tasmanian side, wins the Eric Tassie Medal for being the best and fairest player in the Brisbane carnival.

1951: Cashion wins the NTFA best and fairest for a third time, having previously won in 1948 and 1950.

1953: Lefroy Medal introduced for best and fairest player in Tasmanian teams; North Launceston's John Leedham becomes Tasmania's first-ever All Australian player.

1957: The first step towards a State competition is made where representatives of the three bodies, the TFL, NTFA and the TWFU combine for the first time.

1958: Rex Garwood becomes the second TFL player to win the best and fairest three times.

1960: In a historic victory, Tasmania defeats a Victorian No. 2 team at York Park, despite the absence of its champion, *Darrel Baldock*, who has to withdraw due to family bereavement.

1966: Australian carnival held in Hobart. New Norfolk's *Peter Hudson* is a sensation, winning an All Australian blazer.

1967: The State premiership match between Wynyard and North Hobart is declared a no-contest after the crowd encroaches onto the playing field and removes goal posts in the dying minutes of the game.

1969: Latrobe's Darrel Baldock becomes the first NWFU player to win best and fairest award three times.

1972: Latrobe wins its record fourth NWFU premiership in a row.

1974: Glenorchy's Kevin Baker sets a new Tasmanian post-war games record for one club when he plays his 312th senior game.

1978: Scottsdale's Ken Lette reaches his 300th NTFA games record. On June 12, Peter Hudson kicks his 100th goal for the season in all games on his way to an Australian-high 191 in all matches. The Tasmanian Football Council and the three senior football bodies agree to a Stateside roster in 1979.

1979: Peter Hudson creates a new Tasmanian high of 168 goals for Glenorchy. He wins his second consecutive William Leitch Medal.

1986: Launceston-based clubs, the North Launceston Robins and the South Launceston Bulldogs are admitted to the Statewide league (TFL). Glenorchy wins the grand final from Sandy Bay in a fiery affair, which sees a record nine players reported. The Bulldogs are an amalgamation of City South and East Launceston. The Northern Tasmanian Football League is formed, involving 12 teams.

1987: The first truly Statewide league is completed with the addition of two north-west clubs: the Devonport Blues and the Burnie Hawks, who join the six southern and two northern clubs in the TFL Statewide league.

1994: Clarence, coached by ex-Swan Stevie Wright, win back-to-back TFL premierships, spearheaded by an 84 goal contribution from full-forward Paul Dac.

TASMANIA'S BEST POST-WAR EIGHTEEN

B: David Grant, Verdun Howell, Tassie Johnson.

HB: Rodney Eade, Barry Lawrence, Daryl Sutton.

C: John Greening, Ian Stewart, Darrin Pritchard.

MOST VFL/AFL MATCHES BY PLAYERS FROM TASMANIA
(150 matches or more)

PLAYER	MATCHES	TEAMS	SPAN	RECRUITED FROM
Rodney Eade	259	Hawthorn/Brisbane	1976–87	Glenorchy
Peter Jones	249	Carlton	1966–79	North Hobart
Brent Crosswell	222	Carlton/North Melb.	1968–82	Campbelltown
Robert Neal	220	Geelong/St Kilda	1974–88	Wynyard
Ian Stewart	206	St Kilda/Richmond	1963–75	Hobart
'Tassie' Johnson	203	Melbourne	1959–69	N. Launceston
Michael Roach	200	Richmond	1977–89	Longford
Royce Hart	187	Richmond	1967–77	Clarence
David Grant	185*	St Kilda	1984–94	City South
Stephen Macpherson	180*	Footscray	1982–94	Clarence
'Vic' Cumberland	176	Melbourne/St Kilda	1899–1920	Tas.
Ray Biffin	170	Melbourne	1968–79	N. Launceston
Darrin Pritchard	167*	Hawthorn	1987–94	Sandy Bay
Craig Davis	163	Carlton/North Melb. Collingwood/Sydney	1973–88	Launceston
Scott Clayton	160	Fitzroy	1981–90	Hobart
Verdun Howell	159	St Kilda	1958–68	City South
Ian Paton	151	Hawthorn	1976–84	Scotch College
Eric Huxtable	150	Carlton	1930–38	Newtown

* current player.

HF: Darrel Baldock, Royce Hart, Laurie Nash.
F: Michael Roach, Peter Hudson, John Bonney.
R: Peter Jones, Brent Crosswell.
Rov.: Paul Sproule.
Team provided by Geoff Poulter.

TAYLOR, Richard

A winger in Melbourne's 1926 premiership team, 11 of Dick Taylor's 14 League seasons were at Melbourne. In all he played 207 matches from 1922–35. Forty of these were at North Melbourne from 1932–34.

He also had 18 State games with Victoria, being renowned for his superb ground skills.

TEASDALE, Graham (1955–   )

A much-travelled follower and forward with exceptional marking gifts, Teasdale embarrassed his first VFL club, Richmond, by winning the 1977 Brownlow Medal at South Melbourne.

Swapped with Tiger team-mates Brian Roberts and Francis Jackson in early 1975 for South Melbourne's John Pitura—who was to play just three seasons—Teasdale struggled for consistency in key-position roles before blossoming when becoming South's No. 1 ruckman in 1977 under the coaching of *Ian Stewart*. Replacing the injured Barry Goodingham from the seventh round, he had a magnificent year, lifting South into a rare finals appearance and polling a record 59 votes to defeat Richmond's *Kevin Bartlett*, who was second with 45.

Teasdale had played 128 games in his nine seasons at Richmond and South, winning South's best and fairest and the goalkicking in his golden '77 season, but many believed his knees were suspect and he wouldn't stand up. In 1982, he was cleared to Collingwood for almost $175,000. It was a recruiting misjudgement which Magpie coach *Tom Hafey*'s detractors used against him. In mid-season, 1982, Hafey was sacked.

The injury-plagued Teasdale had just 13 games with his new club in 1982 and one

263

in 1983 before breaking down and retiring. His three-year contract of almost $40,000 a year made him one of the highest paid players in the game. He was originally from Charlton.

TEASDALE, Noel (1938–)

One of seven champion players awarded a Brownlow Medal retrospectively by the VFL in early 1989, Teasdale was a powerhouse ruckman for North Melbourne from 1956–67. He played 195 games and represented Victoria 19 times, a feat unsurpassed by any other North player.

In 1965, he tied with St Kilda's *Ian Stewart* for the Brownlow, but lost on a countback as Stewart had polled one more best afield vote. He always felt he was a 'joint winner' of the Medal.

Recruited from Daylesford, the aggressive 184 cm ruckman played in only one final series, in 1958, when he helped North into the preliminary final by kicking the winning goal against Fitzroy in time-on of the first semi.

Noel Teasdale: a retrospective Brownlow Medallist.

He became famous for his protective head guard, 'Teasa's Turban', which he wore in his final three and a half seasons after suffering a fractured skull in a collision with team-mate Ken Dean and Melbourne's Barrie Vagg in 1964.

TEMPLETON, Kelvin (1956–)

Created VFL history in 1980 by being the first specialist key forward to win the Brownlow Medal. In the two previous seasons, he'd kicked 209 goals from fullforward before shifting to centre halfforward and becoming an even more valuable player.

Kelvin Templeton on arrival at Melbourne, with renowned coach Ron Barassi.

Leading Footscray's goalkicking for five consecutive seasons, he broke Jack Collins' 1954 record of 84 goals in a season in 1978 with 118 goals, including a club record of 15 goals against St Kilda. Only four players had ever kicked more in a League game.

Templeton perfected the skill of marking the ball out in front of him, by having team-mates rocket the ball at him from all angles from close range. Taking the ball in the hands rather than on the chest became second nature.

'As a kid I remember reading about *Tom Hafey* in the centre of the ground kicking the ball to *Royce Hart*, who marked it with his hands instead of on his chest,' he said. 'That's where I got the idea. I found that when I led I could take the ball on my chest against perhaps 10 full-backs but the others would always get through and punch it away.'

In 1981, Templeton was restricted to just six matches after severely injuring his knee in a pre-season match against Melbourne.

It was the first of a nightmarish run of leg injuries which forced his premature retirement.

In 1982, after 143 games at Footscray, he made front-page headlines, when he and fellow Brownlow Medallist *Peter Moore* agreed to join struggling Melbourne.

It was a once-in-a-lifetime offer which, had he gone injury-free, would have guaranteed him at least $500,000 for five years.

In three seasons with the Redlegs, he played just 34 games, including five in his last season, 1985. He attempted to play in 1986 and 1987 but without success and he retired. In 177 games he kicked 593 goals.

His record would have been even better but for the injuries which made his final seasons a misery.

In his final three seasons he had five operations for a total of 10, mainly to his legs. Years later it was discovered that a congenital hip misalignment was the root cause of his problems.

THOMAS, Len (d. 1943)

A South Melbourne stalwart who changed clubs twice in his final two years of League football, Thomas played 208 games from 1927–40, representing Victoria six times.

Twelve of his 14 VFL seasons were at South where he played 186 games and was twice best and fairest during the club's most powerful reign.

Playing in three Grand Finals, he was centreman and one of the best afield in the 1933 premiership.

Lured to Hawthorn as playing coach in 1939, he had 16 games before playing six matches in his final VFL year at North Melbourne in 1940.

In August 1943, while serving as a sergeant with the 'A' platoon of the 2/3 Independent commando company, he was killed by Japanese gun fire near Salamaua, New Guinea. He was 35.

THOMPSON, Len (1948–   )

One of football's tallest and most agile post-war followers, Thompson joined Collingwood from North Reservoir in 1964 as a 16-year-old. When his great career finished 16 years later, he'd amassed more than 300 games—267 with Collingwood, 15 with Victoria, 20 with South Melbourne and 13 with Fitzroy.

He won a record five Copeland trophies, captained Collingwood in 1978—his final season as a Magpie—and was named an All Australian in 1972.

As fast as most rovers, he not only had the ability to win the knockout, but sprint to the ball first. He'd been Victorian under 9 and under 10 champion over 80 yards and regularly beat most of his team-mates in training sprints.

He made his debut with Collingwood in the 1965 preliminary final—the day of the John Somerville 'K.O.'—and was one of Collingwood's best. In Thompson's second year, he was knocked out by

Len Thompson possessed amazing speed for such a tall man. He's pictured beating Carlton's David McKay for the ball.

Carlton strongman *John Nicholls* at a boundary throw-in. 'I didn't like this young kid putting it over me,' said Nicholls, 'particularly when he was just reaching up and taking the ball like a basketball from over the top of my head … unfortunately for "Thommo" he must have accidentally collided with my elbow that day!'

Skilled on both sides of his body and able to deliver searing stab passes on the run, Thompson worked hard at his athleticism and stamina, taking on gruelling summertime running programs.

He was at his best in 1972, when, encouraged by new Collingwood coach and former rucking giant Neil Mann, he won the Brownlow Medal.

'At his best, he wasn't far behind *(Polly) Farmer* and *(John) Schultz*,' said his great Carlton adversary, Nicholls. 'Perhaps because of injury, perhaps because of lack of concentration, perhaps because of too much money being involved at Collingwood and maybe through poor handling by Collingwood coaches, he never reached the heights he should have.'

After playing poorly in the Magpies' losing 1978 preliminary final side, Thompson was one of many big names placed on the 'unwanted' list. He was cleared to South Melbourne.

After just one year at South, his last games were at Fitzroy, which gave him and another veteran, *John Rantall*, an opportunity of breaking famous service milestones.

In all, Thompson played 305 VFL games and kicked 275 goals. He later coached Preston.

His biggest regret was having played in four senior Grand Finals at Collingwood and not winning one.

THOMPSON, Mark (1963–)

One of the unsung stars of the game of the 1990s with three day and three night premierships to his credit, 'Bomber' Thompson was scheduled to play his 200th AFL game at the end of the 1995 season.

Appointed Essendon's captain in 1992,

the 176 cm half-back from Airport West had resurrected his career after a knee reconstruction in 1988.

THORP, Vic

A dual premiership full-back with Richmond in 1920–21, 175 cm Vic 'Flippa' Thorp, played 261 games from 1910–25 as well as representing Victoria 14 times. Scrupulously fair and possessing magnificent judgement, he was the club's aggregate games record holder at his retirement, twice being voted the 'Champion of the Colony', in 1916 and 1919.

Recruited from Burnley via Yarra Park State, he was initially rejected by St Kilda without even a trial.

He served on Richmond's committee from 1927–35 having played with Prahran and Nhill. For several years he wrote for *The Sporting Globe*.

THORPE, David (1948–)

Realised his dream of playing in a VFL premiership team in his first of three years with Richmond in 1974, after nine years and 153 games at Footscray during which the club finished no higher than seventh.

A skilled and aggressive centreman who twice won Footscray's best and fairest, Thorpe was skipper in 1973, the year before he crossed to Punt Road. In all, he played 180 games.

THURGOOD, Albert (1874–1927)

Known as 'Albert The Great', the former schoolboy champion from Brighton Grammar was the first VFL footballer to score 50 goals in a season, a feat he achieved in his very first year, in 1892, from centre half-forward.

His brilliant high marking, speed and magnificent field-kicking were all match-winning strengths. At 183 cm and 85.5 kg he was a key-position player from his first matches, representing Victoria—and kicking four goals—in the intercolonial against South Australia.

He had splendid ball control and balance, could turn quickly on either foot

Albert Thurgood, the finest 19th-century footballer.

and according to football historian C. C. Mullen was the strongest and most spectacular high mark of his time.

His prodigious kicking records with either the drop, punt or place kicks have never been equalled. In June 1899 at the East Melbourne Cricket Ground, he sent a place kick 98.48 metres (107 yards, two feet, one inch) with a slight wind assistance and two years later kicked another 92 metres.

He frequently scored from 80 and 90 yards, while he was also a wonderful drop-kick for goal on the run.

His effort of scoring 64 goals for Essendon in the 1893 season was an Australian football record and a truly remarkable feat at a time when the game was not as fast as it is now and scores were much smaller.

In mid-career he went to Western Australia, before returning to Essendon in 1898. His last game was in 1906 when he emerged from retirement, but was hurt in a semi-final against Fitzroy and retired. In VFL ranks he played 46 games and kicked 89 goals.

TITUS, Jack (1908–78)

Richmond's most outstanding goal-kicker and third on the VFL all-time list, 'Skinny' Titus amassed 294 games and 970 goals in 18 seasons from 1926–43, including the 1932–34 premiership teams.

Remarkably durable, despite his slight build—177 cm and 77 kg—he holds the League record of notching 204 matches in a row, or the equivalent of 11 straight seasons, a run finally broken on 20 August 1943, because of an ankle injury.

A non-smoker and non-drinker, his capacity to recover from injuries was as well known as his liking to lob spit balls on the boot of his shadowing players.

Fiercely competitive and disdainful of the opposition, he was the cheekiest player of his era.

He was also known to abuse his own team-mates if they happened to drift into 'his' area.

Before a game against South Melbourne in the mid-1930s, Titus was offered a £50 bribe to 'play dead'.

The fiercely-loyal Titus abused the punter, reported the matter to the Richmond committee and gave a brilliant goalkicking display, lifting the Tigers to a comfortable win.

He represented Victoria on 14 occasions. His average of 3.3 goals a match was surpassed by only a few forwards of his era. Three times he kicked 10 goals in a match.

Leading VFL goalkicker in 1940 and Richmond's best and fairest in 1941, he

Jack Titus positions the ball for a place kick, 1935.

remained closely involved with the club following his retirement, coaching the reserves, and in 1965, the seniors, after Len Smith was forced to stand down because of ill health.

TODD, George (1903–86)

Three times Geelong's best and fairest and a member of the 1925 and 1931 premiership teams, George 'Jocka' Todd played 232 games from 1922–34 and represented Victoria 11 times.

Recruited from Queenscliff, he was a fine all-rounder, noted for his marking prowess and ability to punch the ball well clear of opponents. He played at full-back for the majority of his career but also was used at centre half-forward.

TODD, Ron (1916–91)

A full-forward with freakish ability who topped the VFL goalkicking lists in two of his five League seasons with Collingwood, Ronald Walford Todd created an Australian high of 188 goals with VFA club Williamstown in 1945.

Originally from the Heidelberg Railways team in 1935, Todd's high marking skills rivalled the great *Bob Pratt*. He was also fast and an enormous kick. A member of Collingwood's 1936 premiership team, he played in losing play-offs from 1937–39.

Some rated him an even better player than *John Coleman*.

After *Gordon Coventry*'s retirement at the end of the 1937 season, the 187 cm Todd became full-time full-forward and in 1938–39 twice headed the VFL goalkicking lists, kicking 120 goals in each season, before sensationally crossing to Williamstown without a clearance, aged 22. Its club president, bookmaker Bill Dooley, had personally contracted him for £500, exclusive of match payments.

Todd was an immediate sensation at Williamstown, kicking 99 goals from centre half-forward in 1940. A foot injury reduced his appearances in 1941 before the VFA went into recess, until 1945. Reappearing with Williamstown—despite Collingwood's offer for him to return—

Todd averaged 17 goals every two games, aggregating 188 for the year. He kicked 20 goals against Oakleigh, 13 against Preston and another 13 against Oakleigh. He broke Pratt's VFA record of 183 by kicking six goals in the grand final in which Williamstown comfortably defeated Port Melbourne. His weekly figures were: 9, 8, 13, 7, 20, 10, 6, 11, 11, 11, 7, 7, 5, 6, 5, 13, 10, 6, 9, 6, 3, 6.

He kicked 114 goals in 1946 and 95 in 1949. In his last game with Williamstown, he needed six goals to give him a combined tally of 1000 goals with Collingwood and Williamstown. He kicked five.

TOOHEY, Bernard (1963–   )

A tough and relentless defender who joined his third League club, Footscray, in 1992, Toohey had his first five seasons at Geelong and six with Sydney, where he played his 200th match in 1990.

Powerfully built and adaptable, he often was used in attack in Sydney and, in 1989, topped the club's goalkicking.

He first represented Victoria as a 19-year-old in 1982. He had four State games with the Vics.

In all club football, he played 263 games in 13 seasons.

TRAGEDIES IN FOOTBALL

Car accidents in the last 35 years have claimed the lives of three established League footballers at the height of their careers.

* Maurie Sankey (Carlton, 100 games, 1959–65), prior to the 1966 season;

* Doug Tassall (Essendon, 20 games, 1969–70), during the 1970 season;

* Darren Millane (Collingwood, 147 games, 1984–91), after the 1991 season.

Footscray teenager Ron James (16 games, 1987–89) was killed in a water skiing accident before the 1990 season. He'd made his senior debut, aged 14, in a VFA grand final.

Carlton's Peter Motley (19 games, 1986–87) never played again after being seriously injured in a car accident in mid-season, 1987.

Between the wars:

* Star Carlton rover Lyle Downs (47 games, 1917–21) suffered a fatal heart attack in July, 1921, after a light training run. Thousands attended his funeral.

* Another Blue, Les Witto (six games, 1926) broke his arm against Geelong in August, 1926. Tetanus set in and he died nine days later.

* Collingwood's Charlie Ahern (three games, 1929) was a shock selection in the 1929 Grand Final and was prominent before breaking his wrist. A severe infection developed and he died several weeks later.

* St Kilda star Fred Phillips (124 games, 1924–32) was appointed Hawthorn's coach at the end of the 1932 season. He died one week before the opening round of the new season, due to an infection believed to be caused by dye from his guernsey entering a boil on his arm.

See: 'CRIPPLING INJURIES'

TRIBUNAL, The

Some of the game's mightiest players including champion full-forwards *Gordon Coventry*, *John Coleman* and *Peter Hudson*, elite ruck-rovers *Ron Barassi* and *Michael Tuck* and Collingwood's celebrated *Collier* brothers, *'Leeta'* and *Harry*, are among those to have faced the League tribunal.

The suspensions of Coventry, Coleman and Barassi on the eve of final series provoked particularly emotional responses from 100s of fans waiting outside the League's old administrative headquarters, Harrison House.

Richmond was also seething in late 1967 when champion ruckman and reigning best and fairest Neville Crowe was suspended after a second semi-final incident in the third quarter with Carlton's *John Nicholls*.

Nicholls admitted he'd only been staging for a free kick, but Crowe was found guilty of striking, suspended for four weeks, and missed playing in Richmond's first Grand Final for almost 25 years. It was his first suspension in 10 years.

Even the game's longest-serving and seemingly-fairest players have not escaped

bookings. Of the 25 players to amass more than 300 League games, only five went unreported and more than one-third of the 62 players to win the Brownlow Medal were reported at least once in their careers.

TROTT, Stuart (1948–)

Best known for his service to St Kilda, where he played 160 games as a winger and rover from 1967–74, Trott transferred to Hawthorn for his final three seasons. In all, he had 199 games in 11 League years, including 105 in a row in mid-career.

His grandfather, Harry Trott, captained the Australian cricket team in eight Tests from 1896–98.

TUCK, Michael (1953–)

One of the legends of modern-day football and renowned for his record-breaking feats, Hawthorn's no-fuss superstar Michael Joseph Tuck was retired four weeks after the 1991 Grand Final, having played in 11 Grand Finals, seven premierships and 426 games—all League records.

Michael Tuck, in his 426th and final game, holds the 1991 premiership cup with coach Alan Joyce. Former League administrator Eric McCutchan (centre) presented the players with their medallions.

His extraordinary longevity allowed him to play 20 senior seasons. He was aged 38 years and 96 days in his final game, the 1991 premiership play-off in which Hawthorn defeated the West Coast Eagles.

Tuck was second in Hawthorn's club championship seven times and third twice. He captained the Hawks into five Grand

Finals in his final six seasons after succeeding *Leigh Matthews* at the start of 1986.

In all, he played 516 games, consisting of 426 day games, 29 night games, 11 State games and 50 reserves games. Another of his club records is his feat in amassing 138 games in a row from 1974–80.

Recruited as a shy, skinny full-forward from Berwick in 1971, he became the finest ruck-rover in the game in the late 1970s. Showing extraordinary enthusiasm, he remained a front-liner into the 1990s.

He was also proud to captain Victoria against Western Australia in 1983, a game which finished in near-heartbreak as he suffered a detached eye retina, an injury which sapped his confidence and made him consider retirement.

Twice selected as an All Australian, he helped change the role of the ruck-rover. He was still involved in packs, shepherding, blocking and assisting, but he also made himself a running target for his defenders coming out of the backline and, in his halcyon years in the late 1970s, regularly gained 25–30 possessions a game.

In his final years, he became a noted defender, his anticipation, tackling and personal pride helping him stay with players often half his age. His efforts in subduing Essendon's Michael Long in the 1989 second semi-final and a flying tackle on former Richmond rover Trent Nichols at the MCG in 1990 are remembered particularly fondly.

So is his courage from the memorable '89 Grand Final when he quietened the dangerous Geelong ruck-rover Mark Bairstow, despite split webbing of the hand.

In his final game, the '91 Grand Final, he recovered after an uncertain beginning against in-form Eagle Craig Turley, runner-up in the Brownlow Medal, to again be an important backline contributor.

His team-mates were genuinely sorry to see him stop. Officials hadn't wanted him to finish his celebrated career in the reserves. Tuck, however, had aspirations to become the first 40-year-old League footballer since St Kilda's 'Vic' Cumberland. In early 1992, he was awarded an OAM for his services to Australian football.*

His wife, Fay, is sister to Geelong great *Gary Ablett*. In 1995, he joined Ablett at Geelong, coaching the club's VSFL team.

TUDDENHAM, Des (1943–)

Few have matched Desmond Vincent Tuddenham's grit, willpower and commitment to winning. One of the game's most inspirational post-war half-forwards and captains, 'Tuddy' played 250 games from 1962–77, having 12 years at his beloved Collingwood and four at Essendon.

The inspirational Des Tuddenham: won Collingwood's best and fairest in 1963, only his second season.

Sandy-haired, chunky and one of the toughest players of the 1960s and early 1970s, he captained Collingwood in four seasons from 1966–69 and again in 1976 and was captain–coach of Essendon from 1972–75.

One of Tuddenham's few footballing regrets is that he never played in a premiership side. Collingwood made the Grand Final three times during his first 10 years at the club, only to lose by four points (to Melbourne, 1964), one point (St Kilda, 1966) and 10 points (Carlton, 1970).

Aggressive from the outset, he tore into packs, using his 178 cm and 82.5 kg frame to clear a path. Some opponents claimed he was unduly 'head-hunting' and he was regularly up on report.

* see 'VENUES'

In 1963, he was found not guilty on a kicking charge against Geelong's John Devine and later that year suspended for six weeks after being found guilty of striking Essendon's Barry Davis.

In 1967, he was reported for striking Geelong's Geoff Ainsworth during his 100th game and received a four week suspension. By the end of 1968, his record read: five reports in seven seasons; three suspensions.

The youngest-ever post-war Magpie skipper, he also regularly ruck-roved, developing a resilience to play with painful injuries.

Named by the Victorian selectors for his first of five representative games in 1965, he was State captain in 1971, even though he wasn't even Collingwood's skipper, having relinquished the position after a pre-season pay dispute.

Tuddenham's son, Paul, played 40 games in five seasons with Collingwood from 1987–91, before joining Carlton.

TURNER, Michael (1954–)

Like his father, Leo, a two-time Geelong premiership player, Michael 'Turkey' Turner wore No. 9. He was a fast, fiery and polished winger, who late in his career moved to the forward line with great success.

In addition to amassing 245 senior day games from 1974–88, the 183 cm Turner represented Victoria 12 times and was honoured with All Australian selection in 1979.

Geelong's leading goalkicker in 1982, he was captain from 1984–86. So confident did he become in his overhead marking that the Cats often switched him to centre half-forward.

TWOMEY, Bill jnr (1927–)

The most gifted of one of Collingwood's most-revered football families, match-winning centreman Bill Twomey made his debut as a 17-year-old in 1945 and played 189 games with the Magpies, as well as representing Victoria seven times.

A beautiful left foot kick, he played in Collingwood's 1953 premiership side and would have been in the 1958 triumph but for a knee cartilage injury which forced him out of the finals.

The injury flared again at training in the 1959 pre-season. He had a knee operation and never played again.

Twomey won interstate selection as a winger before cementing his reputation in the centre.

Occasionally he also played at full-forward, once kicking 11 goals in a game.

See 'BROTHERS, Famous'

Umpires

Field umpires have been controlling games since 1872. The one-umpire system was employed until 1976 when two were used at VFL level. From 1993, three were used, with talk of more.

Umpires first wore white uniforms from 1877, when George Coulthard appeared in an all-white uniform in the match between Melbourne and Norwood at the MCG.

Boundary umpires were first used in a match in Ballarat and in charity games in Melbourne in 1891, and at League level from 1903.

Goal umpires were introduced in Tasmania in 1884 and adopted by the VFA soon afterwards. VFL goal umpires wore white coats as part of their uniform from 1912.

Umpires were first paid in 1884—£1 1s for field umpires and 10 shillings for goal umpires. In 1975, payments were $90 for field, $43 boundary and $29 goal. In 1990 payments ranged from $475–$770 for field, $230–$320 boundary and $185–$275 goal. The Grand Final fee for the two field umpires was $4750. In 1995 all field umpires, no matter their experience received $1100 per game, with more for finals.

Umpires bounced the ball to start each quarter from 1887. Previously they'd thrown the ball in the air. From 1891 the central umpire was instructed to bounce the ball in the cleared area in the centre of the ground after every goal.

The first umpiring 'instructor', celebrated Grand Final umpire Jack Elder, was appointed in 1923. From 1911, the famous premiership coach and former Australian Test cricketer *Jack Worrall* had assisted. Bill Deller, who umpired five Grand Finals, has been the umpires director since 1982.

TWO HUNDRED MATCHES AS FIELD UMPIRE

Ian Robinson 352, Rowan Sawers 305, Jack McMurray snr 305, Kevin Smith 302, Jack Elder 295, Peter Cameron 292, Bill Deller 251, Neville Nash 216, John Sutcliffe 214, Jack McMurray jnr 211.

MOST FINALS MATCHES AS FIELD UMPIRE

Jack Elder 39, Ian Robinson 38, Rowan Sawers 25, Jack McMurray snr 23, Kevin Smith 23, Bill Deller 20, Bob Scott 19, Peter Cameron 19.

MOST GRAND FINALS AS FIELD UMPIRE

Jack Elder 10 (1908–13, 1918–20. 1922), Ian Robinson 9 (1973–74, 1977 (two), 1978, 1980–81, 1985, 1987), Bob Scott 7 (1929–35), Ivo Crapp 7 (1898–1902, 1904–05), Jack McMurray jnr 6 (1948 (two)–50, 1953–54), Jack McMurray snr 5 (1921, 1925–28), Jeff Crouch 5 (1963–65–66–68–69), Bill Deller 5 (1972–76–78–79–80).

UNIVERSITY

Known as VFL football's '13th' club, University had seven seasons in 1908–14 before disbanding at the start of World War One.

The club adopted a black jersey with a blue V, collar and cuffs, white shorts and black socks with blue tops. Eligibility was restricted to those holding a matriculation certificate or higher degree.

Action from the University v Geelong match at the East Melbourne ground, May 1909.

From 1908–10, the club shared the East Melbourne ground at Jolimont with Essendon, and from 1911–14, the MCG with Melbourne.

The club's finest year was in 1910 when it won 10 matches to finish sixth. It also was sixth in 1908.

It won only two games in its last four

FORMED: 1907

JOINED LEAGUE: 1908
HOME VENUES: East Melbourne C.G. (1908–10), MCG (1911–14)
OFFICIAL COLOURS: Black guernsey with a blue 'V'
HIGHEST SCORE: 13.18 (96) v Geelong, R.17, 1908 at the East Melbourne C.G.
LOWEST SCORE: 0.9 (9) v Collingwood, R.16, 1911 at the MCG
GREATEST WINNING MARGIN: 60 points v Melbourne, R.6, 1908, at the East Melbourne C.G.
GREATEST LOSING MARGIN: 89 points v Collingwood, R.16, 1911, at the MCG
                      89 points v Fitzroy, R.17, 1914, at the Brunswick St. Oval
LONGEST WINNING SEQUENCE: 5 (1908), 5 (1909)
LONGEST LOSING SEQUENCE: 5 (1910)
MOST GOALS IN A MATCH: Martin Ratz 5 v Geelong, at the EMCG, R.17, 1908;
                     Albert Hartkopf 5 v Geelong at Corio Oval, R.14, 1909
                     Dave Cumming 5 v Geelong at the MCG, R.18, 1911
                     Roy Park 5 (on seven occasions)

MOST GAMES		MOST GOALS	
Bert Hurrey	101	Roy Park	111
John Gray	85	Albert Hartkopf	87
Jack Brake	81	Martin Ratz	52
George Elliott	79		
Jack West	72		

years and its demise was not a surprise. Examinations, term holidays, a constantly changing XVIII and Australia's entry into the war were all obstacles the fledgling club could not overcome.

Leading players to represent the club include Dave Browning, Edward Cordner—father of the famous Melbourne quartet—Harry Cordner, Chris Fogarty, Tom Fogarty, Mark Gardner, Albert Hartkopf, Hubert Hurrey—the great schoolboy athlete, who played in six of the team's eleven seasons—Edgar Kneen, Tom Ogilvie, Martin Ratz and great all-rounder Leo Seward.

University won 27, tied two and lost 97 of its 126 matches. It never defeated Collingwood and had only one victory against Carlton and South Melbourne.

With University's withdrawal, the League reverted to a nine-team competition from 1915–24 until three Association clubs were included: Hawthorn, North Melbourne and Footscray.

UNLUCKIEST FOOTBALLERS

Two hundred games is an imposing milestone in any AFL footballer's career.

Five have come within one game of their double century: Steven Hocking (Geelong), Brian Royal (Footscray), *Basil McCormack* (Richmond), *Neville Fields* (Essendon/South Melbourne) and *Stuart Trott* (St Kilda/Hawthorn).

Royal was one of the unluckiest, rupturing an achilles tendon in his final match, in round 20, 1993, just days before his planned 200th game celebrations at the Western Oval the following weekend.

Players to retire with 198 League games are: *Roy Cazaly* (St Kilda and South Melbourne), Gary Cowton (North Melbourne, Footscray and South Melbourne), *Ken Fraser* (Essendon), *Des Meagher* (Hawthorn), Harvey Merrigan (Fitzroy) and Len Murphy (Collingwood and Footscray).

Five members of the League's 200-club never played in a final: long-serving St Kilda pair *Trevor Barker* and *Geoff Cun-*

ningham, Melbourne's *Gary Hardeman* and *Stephen Smith* and Hawthorn's *Ted Pool*.

Frank Tuck was Collingwood's captain in 1958, when the Magpies won the premiership. However, he never got to play, having been suspended for four weeks late in the home-and-away season and tearing a thigh muscle during the last minutes of training on the Thursday night before the play-off.

Fellow Collingwood player Rene Kink played in five Grand Finals without winning one. He also appeared in a losing Grand Final side at Essendon.

Among other leading footballers to be denied the ultimate premiership reward, despite distinguished service, include:

• Tony Buhagiar (108 games and 171 goals, Essendon and Footscray, 1981–85): Omitted from Essendon's 1984 Grand Final side after doubts about his knee. Bomber coach *Kevin Sheedy* said he'd never made a tougher decision in football.

• Neville Crowe (150 games and 85 goals, Richmond, 1957–67): Reported for the first time in his career in the 1967 second semi-final, Crowe was suspended for four weeks on a striking charge against Carlton's *John Nicholls* and never played at VFL level again. Nicholls admitted he had only staged to get a free kick; video-tape evidence of the incident proving Crowe's innocence was not then admissible at tribunal level.

• Neale Daniher (82 matches and 32 goals, Essendon, 1979–90): After playing his first 66 games in a row, Daniher injured his knee in round 21, 1981 and played only occasionally afterwards despite numerous operations. Was appointed Essendon's captain in 1982, but never played a game.

• Geoff Rosenow (147 games, Geelong, 1962–70): Omitted from Geelong's team late in the 1963 season. Not only did he miss the senior premiership, he was barred, on an eligibility rule, from playing with Geelong reserves in its premiership. Afterwards, he amassed 100 consecutive senior games from 1965–70, including the 1967 Grand Final, which Geelong lost.

VALLENCE, Harry (1905–71)

'Soapy' Vallence is Carlton's goalkicking recordholder, having amassed 722 goals in 204 matches from 1926–38, including four hauls of 11 goals. His most famous effort was in the 1932 preliminary final when he kicked 11 against Collingwood, to lift his beloved Blues into their first Grand Final in more than a decade. Critics remarked after that game that they had seldom seen a more brilliant display of high marking, anticipation and accurate kicking for goal.

A booming torpedo punt, he headed Carlton's goal charts eight times and was the leading VFL goalkicker in 1931, with 86. The following year, he kicked 97, including 20 in three finals.

At 183 cm and 80.5 kg, he was a fine mark and equally dangerous in wet or dry conditions.

Representing Victoria five times, he booted eight goals against South Australia in 1931. His last State game was in 1937 in Adelaide. On return, he found he'd been dropped to Carlton seconds!

One of football's most colourful characters and finest early goalkickers, Harry 'Soapy' Vallence.

VAN DER HAAR, Paul (1958–   )

Known as 'The Flying Dutchman', and famed for his spring-heeled high marking and flamboyance—on and off the field—Van der Haar played 202 games and kicked 278 goals from 1977–90, represented Victoria twice and was a member of four Essendon Grand Final sides, including the 1984–85 premierships.

Paul Van der Haar, a naturally athletic footballer with exciting high marking skills.

Named recruit of the year in 1977, he represented his State as a 20-year-old in his second season. His marking was astonishing, including one which he took standing on his head.

He suffered many injuries during his 14 season career—the most controversial being in the second semi-final in 1989 when he was knocked out by Hawthorn's *Dermott Brereton*. Despite suffering from concussion, he went back on to the ground late in the match, a move which triggered a rule change disallowing concussed players to return.

VENUES

Thirty-one different grounds hosted 10,802 matches in the first 98 years of League competition. The Melbourne Cricket Ground and Princes Park have each hosted more than 1000 matches. Collingwood's Victoria Park hosted its 850th match in the opening rounds of the 1992 season.

Record-breaking Hawk *Michael Tuck* played on 17 different grounds in five States—Carrara and the 'Gabba (Queens-

LEAGUE MATCH VENUES (1897–1994)

VENUES	MATCHES	TIES	1-POINT MARGINS	100-POINT MARGINS	CLUBS/SEASONS
Albury (NSW)	1	0	0	0	1952
Arden St. Oval	529	8	14	8	NM 1925–64, 1966–85
Brisbane E.G. (Qld)	1	0	0	0	1952
Brunswick St. Oval	612	13	20	3	Fitz. 1897–1966
Carrara (Qld)	61	1	1	2	Brisb. 1987–92
Coburg	9	0	1	0	North Melbourne 1965
Corio Oval	371	6	5	8	Geel. 1897–1915, 1917–40
East Melbourne C.G.	225	5	3	1	Ess. 1897–1915, 1918–21; Univ. 1908–10
Euroa	1	0	0	0	1952
Football Park (SA)	43	0	1	1	Adel. 1991–94
Glenferrie Oval	443	4	4	4	Hawthorn 1925–73
Junction Oval	734	5	15	6	St. K 1897–1915, 1918–41, 1944–64; Sth Melb. 1944–64; Fitz. 1970–84
Kardinia Park	477	2	13	9	Geel. 1941, 1944–94
Lake Oval	704	8	21	6	Sth Melb. 1897–1915, 1917–41, 1947–81
MCG	1608	16	28	27	Melb. 1897–1914, 1919–41, 1946–94; Rich. 1965–94; NM 1984–94; Ess. 1992–94; Coll. 1993–94
Moorabbin	254	2	4	8	St. K 1965–92
Motordrome	3	0	0	0	Melbourne 1932
North Hobart (Tas.)	5	0	0	0	1952; Fitz. 1991–92
Princes Park	1143	15	32	25	Carl. 1897–1994; SM 1942–43; Fitz. 1967–69; 1987–93; Haw. 1974–91
Punt Rd. Oval	543	6	9	6	Rich. 1908–64; Melb. 1942–46
Subiaco (WA)	57	0	3	0	W.C. Eagles 1987–94
Sydney C.G. (NSW)	154	0	3	7	1903–04, 1952, 1979–81, Syd. 1982–94
The 'Gabba (Qld)	26	0	1	2	1981; Bris. 1991, 1993–94
Toorak Park	13	0	0	0	St. K 1942–43
Victoria Park	866	5	22	18	Coll. 1897–1994; Fitz. 1985–86
WACA (WA)	36	0	1	3	W.C. Eagles 1987–94
Waverley Park	612	4	11	13	1970–89; Haw. 1990–94; St. K 1994–94
Western Oval	634	8	17	6	Foots. 1925–41, 1943–94; Fitz. 1994
Windy Hill	629	9	13	13	Ess. 1922–91
Yallourn	1	0	0	0	1952
Yarraville	7	0	0	0	Foots. 1942
Totals	10,802	117	242	176	

The MCG, looking towards the Great Southern Stand.

land), Princes Park, Victoria Park, Windy Hill, Western Oval, Kardinia Park, Glenferrie Oval, the MCG, Arden St., Junction Oval, Lake Oval, Moorabbin and Waverley Park (Victoria), Sydney Cricket Ground (New South Wales), Subiaco (Western Australia) and North Hobart (Tasmania). He was injured when the Hawks played the Adelaide Crows at Football Park, Westlakes, in the opening round of 1991 and didn't get another opportunity.

In 1995, Bruce Stadium in Canberra was used for the late autumn match between Fitzroy and West Coast.

VICTORIA

The Victorian Football League originated from key member clubs of the Victorian Football Association, formed in 1877, almost 20 years after the first recorded match in 1858.

The foundation members of the VFA— the oldest governing body for any code of Australian football—were South Melbourne, North Melbourne, Melbourne, St Kilda and Carlton. At various times over the next 20 years, Geelong, Essendon,

Footscray, Williamstown, Richmond, Port Melbourne and Collingwood also joined.

Since 1888, Geelong had been pushing for a new competition which was more representative of the State of Victoria. Initially it sought to embrace teams from Bendigo and Ballarat.

Some of the breakaway clubs believed the VFA competition had become too cumbersome and even when the sides were reduced from 18 to 13, resented travelling to out-of-the-way areas such as Footscray and Williamstown, especially as the grounds and amenities were inferior to their own. The inclusion of relatively unknown country teams in the competition wasn't seriously considered—even though the standard in areas such as Ballarat was comparatively high.

On the eve of the play-off for the 1896 premiership, representatives of the Association's wealthiest and strongest clubs, Essendon, Geelong, Melbourne, South Melbourne, Collingwood and Fitzroy, met at Buxton's Art Gallery rooms in Melbourne to form a new football body which was to become known as the Victorian Football League.

Boot inspection by field umpire A. Raven prior to the SA-Victoria match in Adelaide in July 1938. Among the Victorians pictured are Kevin O'Neill (left), Dick Reynolds (fifth from left), Jack Dyer (with the knee bandages on), flanked by Phonse Kyne.

These clubs, along with Carlton and St Kilda, left the Association and from 1897 shaped an eight-team VFL competition.

Essendon also won the inaugural VFL flag and played off for the second, being beaten by Fitzroy, the first club to snare two flags in a row.

Collingwood was a force from its early years, keen rivalry developing with Carlton which won three flags on end from 1906–08, under the game's first coach, ex-Test cricketer *Jack Worrall.*

Leading interstate players moved to Melbourne to be part of the already-thriving new competition. Among the most-notable imports were Tasmanian quartet Vic Cumberland and Fred McGinis (to Melbourne) and George Vautin and Colin Campbell (Essendon). Carlton's speedy defender *Norman 'Hackenschmidt' Clark,* from South Australia, was another early star.

From 1902, charity matches between the premier teams in the VFL and the VFA were played. Notable improvements included the use of boundary umpires from 1903.

In 1908, Richmond and University were admitted to the competition, the 10 teams being rostered 18, rather than 14, home-and-away rounds, plus play-offs.

Victoria won the first Australian Football Championships, held in Melbourne in 1908 to celebrate the 50th anniversary of the birth of Australian football. The competing teams were Victoria, Tasmania, Western Australia, South Australia, NSW, Queensland and New Zealand, the New Zealanders surprising by winning two matches, only to be drubbed by Victoria. At the end of the carnival, there was a 'monster smoke night' at the Melbourne Town Hall and the Prime Minister, Alfred Deakin, christened the game by proposing the Australian game of football. From that time football became known as 'Australian Rules'. Its more-popular current title is 'Australian football'.

IMPORTANT DATES IN VICTORIAN FOOTBALL

1858: The Australian game is initiated by *H. C. A. Harrison,* W. J. Hammersley, J. B. Thompson and *T. W. Wills* who form the Melbourne football club. The first recorded match is played between Scotch College and Melbourne Grammar School.

1859: Geelong club formed.

1866: First codification of rules made by a meeting of delegates from Melbourne, South Yarra, Carlton and Royal Park.

1872: Revision of rules. Umpires are introduced and ends changed at half-time.

1873: Uniforms are introduced.

1874: A new code of rules is drawn up.

1875: Spectators are charged sixpence a head to see Carlton play Melbourne, the first known charge for a football match in Australia.

1879: The first intercolonial match is played in Melbourne, between Victoria and South Australia. The first match is played under lights between East Melbourne and Collingwood Artillery at the MCG on 6 August.

1884: For the second time, Geelong wins its third consecutive premiership.

1892: The Britannia club merges into Collingwood.

1896: Carlton, Collingwood, Essendon, Melbourne, Fitzroy and South Melbourne secede from the Victorian Football Association. St Kilda and Geelong follow. The clubs combine to form the Victorian Football League.

1897: The first season of VFL matches. Essendon wins the premiership. For the first time, goals and behinds are counted.

1900: St Kilda's losing sequence balloons to 48 matches, before it defeats Melbourne, on a protest, in the opening round.

1902: Collingwood's *Charlie Pannam* becomes the first player to reach 100 games.

1903: A match for premiership points is played in Sydney for the first time. Collingwood plays Fitzroy.

1906: Carlton appoints *Jack Worrall* as the first VFL club coach.

1907: University is admitted to the League.

1908: Victoria wins the first Australian football carnival in Melbourne. Richmond admitted to the League. The ball is bounced in a five-yard square and no player is allowed closer than two yards until the ball touches the ground.

1910: Carlton loses the Grand Final to Collingwood by 14 points after it is alleged that three players had been paid not to win. The game is characterised by wild brawling and big bets.

1911: Payments to players approved by the League. The first wearing of numbers by Essendon and Carlton players in a semi-final.

1912: Player numbering is introduced. The *Football Record* is published for the first time. Stewards with the power to report players are introduced. Collingwood's great full forward *Dick Lee* has the first knee-cartilage operation.

1913: Independent tribunal instituted by the League. Jack Elder umpires his fifth consecutive final series.

1914: Lee kicks a record 11 goals in a score of 15.13 against University.

1915: University disbands on account of the Great War, having won just 27 of its 126 matches.

1919: South Melbourne kicks a record score of 29.15 (189) against St Kilda. A district scheme is adopted by industrial suburban clubs to stop player-trafficking.

1920: First morning VFL match held at the Punt Rd Oval.

1921: Carlton's Horrie Clover drop-kicks 95 yards, two feet, at the Punt Rd Oval.

1922: Essendon moves from the old East Melbourne ground to Windy Hill after railway authorities win approval to extend shunting yards at Jolimont.

1923: Jack Elder is appointed to the VFL's first umpires' adviser.

1924: Brownlow Medal introduced.

1925: Hawthorn, North Melbourne and Footscray join the VFL. Geelong wins 11 games straight and sets a new first-quarter record of 11.4 to South Melbourne's nil. The Geelong-Collingwood semi-final is broadcast by Mr A. N. Bishop on radio station 3AR.

1927: Collingwood corners major awards, winning the premiership, the goalkicking (through *Gordon Coventry*) and the Brownlow Medal (through *Syd Coventry*).

1928: A record crowd of 66,381 attends the Carlton-Richmond match.

1929: Collingwood goes through the home-and-away season unbeaten.

1930: Collingwood wins its fourth consecutive premiership, a record which still stands. Substitutes for injured players allowed for the first time. *The Coulter Law* regulating payments to players is adopted.

1931: The Page system of playing finals is introduced. Richmond creates new scoring record of 30.19 (199) against North Melbourne.

1932: Fitzroy's *Haydn Bunton* becomes the first to win the Brownlow Medal for the second consecutive season. The VFL becomes an incorporated company, composed of 12 clubs.

1933: A siren first used in a VFL game— Essendon v Geelong.

1934: *Laurie Nash* kicks 18 goals for Victoria against South Australia in Melbourne. His South Melbourne team-mate *Bob Pratt* kicks 150 goals for the year.

1935: 20,000 attend the first night match in Victoria under electric light: Richmond v South Melbourne at Olympic Park.

1936: Field umpire Jack McMurray snr officiates at his 300th League game. Round of 4 July postponed because of ground flooding. Essendon defeat St Kilda in the last morning match on Queen's Birthday.

1937: Collingwood goalkicking legend *Coventry* retires after 18 seasons, 306 games and 1299 goals, scored at an average of 4.25 a game.

1939: Matches postponed on 26 August due to bad weather. Melbourne's *Fred Fanning* drop-kicks a ball 105.5 metres in the reserves grand final against Richmond.

1940: Games conducted on a war-time basis. Payments to players and staff reduced by 50 per cent.

1941: Geelong transfers to Kardinia Park. Clubs allotted extra territory as recruiting districts.

1944: The finals are played at St Kilda (Junction Oval). Despite a general tramway strike, 43,000 attend the Grand Final.

1946: The laws of the game are amended to allow the replacement of two players. VFL Players' Provident Fund instituted. VFL under 19 competition starts.

1947: Melbourne's *Fred Fanning* kicks 18.1 against St Kilda on 30 August—a record which still stands.

1949: Essendon's *John Coleman* kicks 12 goals on debut against Hawthorn. Richmond's *Jack Dyer* retires after a record 310 games. He kicks six goals in his last match.

1950: North Melbourne wins its first ever game at Victoria Park. Essendon win the seniors, reserves and under 19 flags.

1952: Nineteen home-and-away rounds are played including an extra 'propaganda' round at interstate venues Brisbane, Sydney and Hobart and in country centres Yallourn and Albury. A night match is played at the Showgrounds between Essendon and Richmond.

1953: *Ron Barassi* makes his debut for Melbourne. Collingwood's 15-year-old forward Keith Bromage becomes the youngest player in League history. Geelong stretches its unbeaten record to 26 matches.

1955: Club runners are allowed.

1956: Resignations announced by W. C. McClelland, League president for 30 years and L. H. O'Brien, VFL secretary for 25 years. Eight clubs compete in the night football competition at South Melbourne's Lakeside Oval.

1957: VFL matches are televised (last quarter only).

1958: Under 19 matches played as curtain raisers to senior games for the last time.

1962: The VFL purchases approximately 200 acres of land in the City of Waverley for development of its own sports arena. VFL convenes first Australian football congress on 5–6 April.

1964: Fitzroy becomes only the sixth club to lose all 18 home-and-away fixtures.

1965: St Kilda plays 'home' matches at Moorabbin and Richmond at the MCG.

1968: The great *Bobby Skilton* has a VFL record 44 kicks in a match at South Melbourne. Carlton defeats Sturt in the first 'Championship of Australia'. Zoning introduced which sees Victoria and the Riverina divided into areas and allocated as country zones to clubs.

1970: VFL Park opens on 18 April, Fitzroy and Geelong contesting the first match. Footscray great *Ted Whitten* retires on 2 May, aged 36, after a record-breaking 321 senior games. First direct telecast of the Brownlow Medal. First Sunday match played in front of the visiting Royal family, at the MCG, between Fitzroy and Richmond. The second half of the game is televised live.

1971: Hawthorn's *Peter Hudson* equals

South Melbourne champion *Bob Pratt*'s season-best tally of 150 goals.

1972: The VFL introduces a final-five system of playing finals. In the highest-scoring game in history. Richmond kicks 22.18 (150) only to be beaten by Carlton's 28.9 (177) in the Grand Final.

1973: The League rules are altered prior to the season to allow players with 10 calendar years service with one VFL club to transfer to another without a clearance. Richmond wins the seniors, reserves and under 19 flags. Centre 'diamond' introduced.

1974: Colour changes to uniforms are approved in readiness for colour television.

1975: Television video-tapes made admissible as evidence at tribunal hearings.

1976: Hawthorn wins the first National Football League national series competition played during the day and under lights in Perth and Adelaide.

1977: The VFL Grand Final is televised live for the first time. Fitzroy kicks a home-and-away record of 36.22 (238) to defeat Melbourne. Hawthorn pair Hudson (110 goals) and *Leigh Matthews* (91) become the first pair to kick 200 goals or more in a VFL season. Lights are constructed at VFL Park.

1979: Two matches for premiership points are played in Sydney and televised live to Melbourne—North Melbourne v Hawthorn and Fitzroy v Richmond. Carlton's Wayne Harmes wins the first Norm Smith Medal.

1981: For the first time, the Brownlow Medal is shared between Fitzroy's *Bernie Quinlan* and South Melbourne's *Barry Round*. Richmond's *Michael Roach* wins inaugural John Coleman Medal. Perth's Alan Johnson is the first player named in the first interstate draft.

1982: South Melbourne changes its name to the Swans. All the club's home games are played at the Sydney Cricket Ground and televised live back to Melbourne. Patrons are banned from taking alcohol into VFL matches.

1983: The Swans undergo a second name change in as many years, becoming officially known as the Sydney Swans. Swans player Silvio Foschini successfully challenges the VFL rules to win a clearance to St Kilda. The Grand Final is telecast direct to the United States for the first time for cable television. Richmond's *Kevin Bartlett* becomes the first VFL player to amass 400 games.

1984: Ex-Collingwood player Jack Hamilton becomes the first full-time AFL commissioner. A club salary cap is also instituted.

1985: Alan Schwab is appointed executive commissioner of the VFL. The Sydney Swans become the first privately-owned club. The 12 clubs transfer to the independent commission the power to implement its plan for the long-term welfare of football.

1986: Two 'double-headers' are played at the MCG. North Melbourne plays five Friday night games at the MCG. Ex-St Kilda player Ross Oakley is appointed chairman of the VFL Commission. The first national draft is implemented.

1987: The West Coast Eagles and Brisbane Bears are included in the expanded 14-team competition. End-of-season matches are played in London, Tokyo and Vancouver. The first night match for premiership points is played at VFL Park between Fitzroy and North Melbourne.

1989: Victoria defeats South Australia for the inaugural Malcolm Blight Cup. Retrospective Brownlow Medals are awarded to players beaten previously on a countback.

1990: Hawthorn's *Michael Tuck* becomes only the second player, after Richmond's *Kevin Bartlett*, to play 400 club games. Collingwood wins its first premiership under the Australian Football League banner.

1991: The Adelaide Crows enter the competition. A final six is approved with extra time to be played in finals—bar the Grand Final—in case of any ties. Tuck figures in his record 11th Grand Final, seventh premiership and 426th match. Shortly afterwards, he announces his retirement. The first Grand Final is played at VFL Park.

1992: The League renames VFL Park as AFL Park, Waverley. Geelong kick a new League record of 37.17 (239) in Brisbane in round 7. First year teenager Ben Hart from the Adelaide Crows is named in the All Australian side. Hawthorn's *Jason Dunstall* kicks 145 goals for the season, just five short of the all time record. The West Coast Eagles become the first interstate side to win the flag. The number of reported AFL players drops by 30 per cent.

1993: Football legend *John Kennedy snr.* becomes chairman of the revamped AFL Commission. The AFL sells advertising space on its footballs to McDonald's. First final played at night. Channel Seven renegotiates AFL broadcasting rights for $80 million.

1994: A final eight is implemented. *Tony Shaw* announces his retirement after 313 games. *Tony Lockett* plays his last game with St Kilda. Geelong coach *Malcolm Blight* resigns after his Cats are thrashed in the Grand Final. The all-clear is given for Port Adelaide's entry into the AFL competition 'sometime after season 1995'.

1995: The 16th AFL team, Fremantle, is beaten by St Kilda in its first ever competition match, a first-round Ansett Cup pre-season match. *Paul Roos* joins Lockett in Sydney. *Dermott Brereton* joins his third club, Collingwood, after a season in Sydney. The AFL announces a dividend to clubs of $1.4 million each.

MOST LEAGUE MATCHES (1897–1994, club games only)

Michael Tuck	426	Hawthorn	1972–91
Kevin Bartlett	403	Richmond	1965–83
Simon Madden	378	Essendon	1974–92
Bernie Quinlan	366	Footscray/Fitzroy	1969–86
Bruce Doull	359	Carlton	1969–86
John Rantall	336	S.M./N.M./Fitzroy	1963–80
Kevin Murray	333	Fitzroy	1955–64, 1967–74
David Cloke	333	Richmond/Collingwood	1974–91
Leigh Matthews	332	Hawthorn	1969–85
Gary Dempsey	332	Footscray/North Melbourne	1967–84
Doug Hawkins	329*	Footscray	1978–94

* current player.

MAJOR RULE CHANGES

1872: Umpires introduced—rival captains had previously been responsible for awarding free kicks; ends changed at halftime; it's agreed that goals must be kicked not forced.

1873: Uniforms introduced. Previously, caps had been the only distinguishing mark.

1903: Boundary umpires appointed.

1912: Numbering of players introduced. Stewards appointed with power to report players.

1913: Independent tribunal instituted.

1922: Free kick for forcing ball out of bounds introduced.

1924: Black shorts for home team and white shorts for visiting team introduced.

1930: 19th man introduced, to help cover the possible loss of players through injury.

1939: Throw-in from boundary re-introduced; players to be free kicked when dropping the ball after being held.

1946: 19th and 20th man allowed.

1955: Runners first allowed to convey messages from coaches.

1964: Coaches allowed to enter arena at quarter time to address players.

1968: Zoning introduced—Victoria and Riverina are divided into areas and allocated as country zones to clubs for an initial three year period.

1969: Players free kicked for kicking the ball out of bounds on the full.

1973: Centre square established where

only four players a side are allowed for centre bounces.

1976: Two field umpires used in matches for the first time.

1986: First national draft takes place. Fifty metre arcs in goal areas introduced.

1988: Players awarded a free kick obliged to kick the ball, rather than hand-ball or kick. Replacement of 15-metre penalty with 50-metre penalty.

1990: Players awarded frees again given option of taking a kick or hand-passing.

1991: In case of ties, extra time is introduced in the first three weeks of the finals series, with two five-minute halves being played, with time-on added.

1993: Introduction of third interchange player and third field umpire.

1994: Quarters reduced to 20 minutes each, plus time-on.

WADE, Doug (1941–)

Few have kicked the torpedo punt as prodigiously or with the unerring precision of Douglas Graeme Wade, whose goalkicking feats in a 15-year period produced more than 1000 goals and were surpassed by only one man, *Gordon Coventry*.

In 267 games from 1961–75, Wade amassed 1057 goals, heading the VFL goalkicking three times and averaging 3.96 goals a match. Geelong's leading goalkicker in all but one of his 12 seasons, he topped North Melbourne's lists three years in a row from 1973 until his retirement after figuring in North's first premiership in 1975.

A strongly built 183 cm and 86 kg, he was a fast lead and fine mark.

He could be surly and aggressive on the field, but was a mild-mannered, gentle character off it.

Playing in two premierships, his first with Geelong in 1963, he also figured prominently in the 1967 Grand Final, kicking four goals in Geelong's narrow loss to Richmond.

First chosen for his State against Western Australia in 1964, he kicked six goals to three-quarter time before injuring his knee. It took him 15 months to fully recover.

During the 1967 season, when he amassed 96 goals, he booted 13 against South Melbourne at the Lakeside Oval, a new Geelong club record and one hailed as one of the best performances ever because of the boggy conditions. He also kicked 13 goals against North Melbourne, in 1971.

His conversion rate was initially criticised. But later he straightened his kicking through hours of practice. On debut for Victoria, he kicked 10 goals against Western Australia in the greatest exhibition of forward play since the days of *John Coleman*.

Wade was easily upset by opposing fullbacks and received a four week suspension in one of his first seasons. He learned to curb his temper and became an inspirational leader, winning the best and fairest in 1969 and captaining the Cats in 1972.

He was at the centre of a bitter controversy resulting from the cliffhanging Geelong-Carlton 1962 preliminary final. Wade had kicked six goals and marked within easy range, 30 metres out, in the final minutes of the game, when the kick was taken off him and awarded to his opponent, Carlton full-back Peter Barry.

Geelong was trailing Carlton by five points and most thought Wade had fairly out-manoeuvred his opponent. But umpire Jack Irving refused to pay the mark, saying Wade had infringed by hanging onto Barry's shorts.

After an illustrious career at Geelong, Doug Wade was involved in North Melbourne's historic 1975 flag.

Carlton won, 10.18 (78) to 10.13 (73), but the Barry incident was debated for days.

Umpires' adviser Allan Nash said it was the most courageous decision he'd ever seen from an umpire.

Wade's finest year was in 1969, when he kicked a personal-best 127 goals, a clear-cut Geelong record, to win the League goalkicking for a third time, just ahead of Hawthorn's *Peter Hudson*, with 120.

After 12 years at Geelong, he transferred to North Melbourne. In 1974, he became the first North player to reach the 100 goal milestone, when he kicked 103, including his 100th in the '74 Grand Final.

WALLACE, Terry (1958–)

Many were quizzical when Hawthorn vice-captain Terry Wallace left Glenferrie at the height of his powers at the end of 1986, having just played in his third premiership team. The courageous centreman with the rare ability to average 30 possessions a game had been one of the best afield and was next-in-line for the captaincy. But his pride had been irreparably hurt. Selected in the 1986 preliminary final side against Fitzroy, he was told on the eve of the match that he wouldn't be playing. After an angry discussion, a stunned Wallace vowed to leave.

Later that tumultuous Friday, he found he'd been reinstated. He was best afield the next day and a motivator, too, in Hawthorn's Grand Final victory, but he didn't feel a part of the celebrations that night. 'It was obvious that someone within the match committee had decided that my style of football wasn't what they required,' he said. 'I saw no point in hanging about.'

It took three clearance applications and $175,000 before he was released to Richmond after the start of the '87 season. In his first game, he was best afield, triggering the Tigers' surprise win against Essendon.

But he was to play just half the season (11 games) before joining Footscray where he immediately became a key player again, averaging 24 possessions in his first year, 27 in his second and 25 in his third.

He won back-to-back best and fairest awards with Footscray in 1988–89, to go with his two best and fairests at Hawthorn, in 1981 and 1983—a premiership year in which he amassed a record 540 kicks, at almost 22 a game.

Persistent injuries finally forced him out early in the 1991 season and he retired, having amassed 255 games in 14 seasons,

including 175 at Hawthorn.

A consummate team man, he countered his natural lack of speed with courage and anticipation. He also developed his handball skills expertly. Team-mates called him 'Plough' for his hard-work ethics and habit of always being at the bottom of packs. The bigger the game, the better the durable and committed 183 cm centreman liked it.

WALLIS, Steve (1964–)

A three-time Victorian representative, Wallis played his 200th game for Footscray in the 1992 first semi-final, being one of the best afield in a tagging role against St Kilda's in-form centreman Robert Harvey.

Originally from Leongatha, he debuted as an 18-year-old, playing mainly at halfforward and in the centre before enjoying great success at half-back. Captain of Footscray in 1989, he was runner-up in the best and fairest in 1985 and third in 1987 and 1989.

He continued into his 13th League season in 1995.

WALLS, Robert (1950–)

A three-time Carlton premiershp centre half-forward and coach of the club's 1987 premiership team, Robert Walls' career has involved three clubs extended over almost a 30 year period.

Season 1995 is his 14th as a senior coach. He had five years at Fitzroy and three and a half at Carlton before being sensationally sacked in mid-season, 1989. In 1991, he joined Brisbane and coached his 200th match.

His teams appeared in finals in six of his first 10 years. The Blues made the Grand Final in 1986 before winning in '87.

Astute, shrewd and calculating, his coaching methods are consistently innovative.

He was 16 when named as a replacement for full-forward John Gill for Carlton's second match of the 1967 season against Hawthorn at Glenferrie Oval. He'd never played at full-forward previously, but scored a goal with his first kick in the game—and two for the day in a winning

Robert Walls beats North Melbourne's Frank Gumbleton for the ball at VFL Park during the mid 1970s.

team. Later that season he was used at full-back after Wes Lofts was suspended for four weeks, before settling into the centre half-forward post where he played in two premierships before he'd turned 21.

His leadership abilities were recognised by Carlton's senior coach *Ron Barassi* in 1971, when he was named Carlton's vice-captain, aged 20. A year later, he was helping to select the teams. In 1974, he shared the captaincy with *John Nicholls* and was skipper in 1977 and early 1978, before switching to Fitzroy in May, 1978, after 219 games at Princes Park.

Extremely athletic and mobile, Walls was a good mark, very aggressive and a fine team player. His accuracy in front of goals was a further asset and in 1975–76 he headed Carlton's goalkicking charts in successive years. He wore No. 42 throughout his career at Carlton, an uncommonly high number for such an elite player.

The following year, he became the youngest player (at 23) to reach 150 games, beating Geelong and Footscray forward *Ken Newland* by four months.

In all, he played 260 League games and kicked 243 goals. He represented Victoria four times.

WANGANEEN, Gavin (1973–)

One of the youngest winners of the Brownlow Medal, in 1993, the Adelaide-born part-Aboriginal was just three months past his 20th birthday when he finished ahead of celebrated pair *Greg Williams* and Garry Hocking.

Joining Essendon as a 17-year-old after playing in Port Adelaide's 1990 SANFL premiership, Wanganeen's athleticism and poise under pressure is a feature of his game.

While only 177 cm and 75 kg, he has the leap to outmark the tallest player afield and the balance to remain on his feet and in the contest despite the firmest battering.

He approached his 100 game milestone late in the 1995 season, another prodigy wooed to the club by star recruiter Noel Judkins.

WARE, Norm (1911–)

Footscray's second Brownlow Medallist, Norman Maurice Ware was a scrupulously fair and gifted all-round ruckman from Sale who played 200 games with the Bulldogs from 1932–46.

At 193 cm, he was one of the tallest players of his era and his strong marking was a boon to Footscray's forward line. He kicked 222 goals in 15 years, including 51 in 1942.

He was a four-time best and fairest winner and also tied for the award in 1939.

He was placed in the Brownlow top 10 on six occasions and from 1940–42, captain-coached Footscray, being stationed at Royal Park in the early stages of the war as a member of the Southern Command postal unit.

He tied for the Argus Cup with Collingwood's Marcus Boyall in 1938. One of his most memorable moments was in the final round of 1945, when, playing his first game of the year, he kicked six of Footscray's eight goals against eventual premier Carlton.

His father, George, was a professional swimming champion of Australia. His brother, Wally, played 63 games with Hawthorn from 1930–34.

WARNE-SMITH, Ivor (1897–1960)

The first player to twice win the Brownlow Medal, in 1926 and 1928, Warne-Smith was a 182 cm follower with pace and exceptional skill on both sides of his body. In the 1925 preliminary final, which Melbourne lost to Collingwood, he took nine marks in 11 minutes, after injuries reduced his team to just 15 fit men.

After just eight debut matches with Melbourne in 1919, he shifted to LaTrobe, Tasmania, to manage an apple orchard. He won the Cheel Medal with the LaTrobe club in 1924 and represented Tasmania.

Returning to the mainland, Warne-Smith, then 29, intended to play with Richmond, but Melbourne blocked the move. Less than two years later, he won the first of his Brownlows, eventually playing 146 games, being vice-captain to 'Bert' Chadwick in Melbourne's 1926 premiership win. He was captain-coach from 1928–31. In 1932, he retired, to become Melbourne's non-playing coach, but was enticed into playing again, acting as vice-captain to F. S. 'Pop' Vine, one of the few cases in the VFL where a coach has played under another captain.

One newspaper of the day described him as: 'An astute leader, who makes some daring moves and inspires his players by his own brilliance. He can play anywhere. The ruck, defence, attack or centre positions all come alike to this brainy, sterling footballer.'

WATSON, Colin (1900–70)

The year after winning the 1925 Brownlow Medal when he was voted best afield in nine of his 15 matches, Watson asked for a clearance to country football, which was refused. The following year, he

Sydney-born Ivor Warne-Smith was the first to win two Brownlow Medals.

St Kilda's Colin Watson, the 1925 Brownlow Medallist.

crossed to Maryborough without a clearance and was immediately disqualified. His ban was lifted in 1930 and he transferred to South Warrnambool.

His career at St Kilda spanned 16 seasons, from 1920–35. He was captain in 1933 and captain-coach in 1934. He represented Victoria in 1923–24.

His brilliance at the 1924 Hobart carnival was highlighted in the play-off match against Western Australia when he kept highly-rated Jack 'Snowy' Hamilton kickless for the entire match.

WATSON, Tim (1961–)

Essendon's youngest-ever player at 15 years and 10 months, Timothy Michael Watson had 307 games in 17 seasons with Essendon. A dominant footballing force from day one, Watson had a year off in 1992, before returning for Essendon's premiership year in 1993 and continuing into 1994.

Tim Watson: speed, strength and skill.

Few possessed his exhilarating ability and explosive speed, rivalled his popularity or matched his achievements which included the Essendon captaincy, 10 State matches, four club best and fairest awards

and a top three placing in the 1989 Brownlow Medal.

The 185 cm Watson overcame a knee reconstruction in 1986 to recapture his very best form, winning consecutive best and fairests in 1988–89 with all his renowned flair and dash. Teammate *Gary Foulds* said: 'There is probably no-one else in the League who can take a game on like Tim can.'

His feat of playing 16 consecutive games in his first season after breaking into the team for the seventh round was truly noteworthy. His natural skills, exciting running and sheer zest for the game were immediately evident.

Before he was old enough to vote or drive a car, Watson several times kicked five goals in a game. Against St Kilda at Windy Hill in 1979, he notched seven.

By 19, he'd won Essendon's best and fairest and also represented Victoria. At 20, he became the youngest VFL player to amass 100 games and by 21 was regularly captaining Essendon in the absence of Neale Daniher—who didn't play at all in 1982 because of injury—and Ron Andrews, who missed many matches with suspension and injury.

The 1983 Grand Final against Hawthorn remains a bitter-sweet memory as Watson, Essendon's potential matchwinner, was knocked out behind play before quarter time and the Bombers were drubbed.

But Watson and his team-mates gained their revenge, winning each of the next two flags, Watson being unstoppable in the finals.

In the 1984 second semi, which Hawthorn won narrowly, Watson carried the ball from deep into defence, around the members' wing, to half-forward before his long shot at goal just missed. It was a stirring individual effort which almost changed the game.

It took two years after his knee reconstruction in early 1986 for him to recapture his best. He'd fallen heavily on his knee in the third-round game against Footscray at VFL Park, didn't play again that season and had only seven matches in 1987.

Coach *Kevin Sheedy* retained supreme

faith in him and was rewarded late in '87 with glimpses of Watson's best. In the final game of the season against Collingwood, he 'clicked', being one of the best three or four players afield. His confidence and form returned, he re-won State selection and snared back-to-back club championships.

Rewarded for his outstanding form with the Essendon captaincy, he led the club into the Grand Final in his first year, only to see the side beaten by Collingwood in the first-ever play-off under the AFL banner.

His brother, Larry, also played VFL football with Essendon and Fitzroy.

WEIGHTMAN, Dale (1959–   )

A dominant interstate player and captain whose performances for Victoria rivalled

Dale 'Flea' Weightman overcame diabetes to be one of Richmond's post-war greats.

the greatest Big V players of the post-war era, including *Ted Whitten* and *John Nicholls*, Dale 'Flea' Weightman retired at the end of the 1993 season having played 274 games and kicked 345 goals in 16 seasons.

His feats at Richmond included back-to-back best and fairests. His precise passing and extraordinary handball skills, coupled with his goal-sense and commitment, made him Tigerland's most popular and admired player of the 1980s.

He weighed just 57 kg on arrival at Punt Road. He made his senior debut in 1978, only to be dropped after three games, his coach Barry Richardson saying he was being knocked off the ball too easily.

From early in his career, he had to contend with diabetes which requires daily doses of insulin.

He played in two Richmond Grand Finals, including the 1980 premiership. In the Tigers' losing 1982 Grand Final side, he had 25 possessions to be his side's best player. Weightman's uncanny anticipation in winning the ball off packs is a feature of his game. At his best on big occasions, he revels in the atmosphere of interstate games.

Winner of the Tassie Medal after the 1985 Australian carnival, he's also won the Simpson and Whitten Medals, and captained Victoria thrice, including successive years in 1987–88. In 1985, he kicked six goals against South Australia at Football Park to lift Victoria to a memorable 57 point win. A three-time All Australian representative, in 1991 he represented his State for the 20th time.

'He is one of those rovers who was born great,' said fellow Richmond legend *Kevin Bartlett*. 'He doesn't fumble, he has quick reflexes and sure ballhandling.'

In mid-career he was offered lucrative terms to leave Richmond but refused, saying players who transfer clubs tend to lose their identity.

He captained the Tigers from 1988–1992. Later he played in Tasmania.

WELLS, Greg (1950–   )

One of Melbourne's few superstars in a barren era, the blond, showy and tigerish

175 cm centreman played 226 games with Melbourne from 1969–80 before crossing to Carlton for 33 further games, including the 1981 premiership.

Few worked harder or more furiously on the training track. He played six consecutive seasons without interruption, amassing 131 games in a row from 1971–77.

Twice winner of Melbourne's best and fairest in 1971 and 1976, he represented Victoria four times and was captain in 1977–78.

In 1972, he finished runner-up in the Brownlow Medal, behind Collingwood's *Len Thompson*. In 1976, he was equal fourth.

WEST COAST EAGLES

Formed in 1987 as a virtual 'best of' West Australian team, the Eagles played in six final series in their first eight years,

Dean Kemp: best afield in the 1994 Grand Final.

winning premierships in 1992 and 1994.

The club won 15 of its first 16 games in 1991. Fourteen of its members represented the State team in a runaway victory against combined Victoria.

The club's blue and gold colours featured royal blue eagle wings, monogram and numbers. The name and logo were adopted partly because of the travelling involved, but also because of the eagle's size and ferocity.

From 1995, it successfully sought permission to have two guernseys, with a darker blue version with a bold white border featuring its WA-based sponsor SGIO for home matches. For away games, it incorporated white into the traditional club colors, with the naming rights being taken by Hungry Jack's.

The Eagles' inaugural coach was highly regarded former ruckman Ron Alexander who had just one year. Its first captain was another expatriate, *Ross Glendinning*.

The club won only one of its first five finals, struggling to come to terms with the travelling. In 1990, it played a draw against Collingwood in the qualifying final, but lost the replay.

WESTERN AUSTRALIA

The quest for gold at the turn of the century in Western Australia was a catalyst for the game's rapid growth and expanding popularity in its most western outpost.

Thousands of hopeful prospectors from the east moved to the goldfields in Kalgoorlie, the Federation drought of the 1890s severely cutting employment and forcing many off farms and out of office jobs.

Football stars from Victoria and South Australia were among those searching for gold and the Goldfields competition soon flourished—being almost as strong as its Perth counterpart at the turn of the century.

By World War One, Australian Rules had become by far the State's major football code. The Roaring Twenties helped the game win even more popularity, WA breaking through for its first interstate vic-

WEST COAST EAGLES: THE STATISTICS

FORMED: December, 1986

JOINED LEAGUE: 1987
HOME VENUES: Subiaco (1987–), WACA (1987–)
CURRENT HOME VENUE DIMENSIONS: Subiaco: 173 metres × 129 metres
                                WACA: 165 metres × 129 metres
COLOURS: Royal blue guernsey with gold eagle wings incorporating emblem.
TOTALS FINALS MATCHES: 27 (19 wins, six losses, 1 tie)
FINALS RECORD: Premiers: 2 (1992, 1994)
              Runners-up: 1 (1991)
PREMIERSHIP COACHES: Mick Malthouse (1992, 1994)
YOUNGEST PLAYER: Chris Lewis, 18 years 159 days (1987)
OLDEST PLAYER: Dwayne Lamb, 32 years 229 days (1993)
HIGHEST SCORE: 29.18 (192) v Brisbane, R.3, 1988, WACA
LOWEST SCORE: 1.12 (18) v Essendon, R.15, 1989, Windy Hill
LONGEST WINNING SEQUENCE: 12 (1991)
LONGEST LOSING SEQUENCE: 6 (1989)
MOST FINALS: Chris Lewis 17, Guy McKenna 17, John Worsfold 17
MOST SEASONS AS COACH: Mick Malthouse 5 (1990–94)
MOST SEASONS AS CAPTAIN: John Worsfold 4 (1991–94)

MOST GAMES		MOST GOALS	
Michael Brennan	163*	Peter Sumich	453*
Chris Mainwaring	161*	Chris Lewis	195*
John Worsfold	156*	Brett Heady	160*
Chris Lewis	153*	Ross Glendinning	111
Dwayne Lamb	151	Peter Matera	110*
Guy McKenna	148*	Karl Langdon	106*
David Hart	137*		
Peter Sumich	125*		
Chris Waterman	111*		
Dean Kemp	110*		
Don Pyke	103*		
Peter Wilson	101*		

* current player.

MOST GOALS IN A MATCH: Peter Sumich 13 v Footscray, R.13, 1991, WACA
                        Peter Sumich 11 v Essendon, R.15, 1992, MCG
RECORD HOME VENUE ATTENDANCE: 42,209 v St Kilda, R.15, 1991, Subiaco
                              32,121 v Geelong, R.22, 1993, WACA
RECORD ATTENDANCE IN ANY MATCH: 95,007 v Geelong, GF, 1992, MCG
MOST RECENT PREMIERSHIP TEAM: 1994 West Coast 20.23 (143) d. Geelong 8.15 (63)
                              B: D. Hart, M. Brennan, A. McIntosh. HB: G. McKenna,
                              G. Jakovich, J. Worsfold (c). C: P. Matera, D. Pyke, C.
                              Mainwaring.
                              HF: P. Wilson, J. Ball, B. Heady. F: C. Lewis, P. Sumich,
                              S Bond. R: D. Hynes, D. Kemp. R: T. Evans.
                              Interchange: R. Turnbull, D. Banfield, C. Waterman.

tories against Victoria and in 1921, defeating South Australia for its first Australian championship—under the captaincy of distinguished all-sportsman and ex-Goldfields champion W. J. 'Nipper' Truscott, who represented WA in five carnivals, playing until he was 41.

In the 1924 carnival, WA's 'Bonny' Campbell kicked 33 goals in an Australian record score of 49.19 (277) against

Barry Cable played more than 400 games of senior football, his highly-tuned handball and kicking skills a feature.

Pint-sized Kevin Taylor takes one of the great marks in the post-war WA football. He later joined South Melbourne briefly before returning to Perth in the early 1980s.

South Fremantle's John Gerovich was an exciting aerialist who topped the WA League goalkicking three times in his 221-game career. He's pictured marking ahead of East Fremantle's Ray French.

Queensland in a game played in continuous rain. He amassed 51 goals in five matches and remains one of football's most celebrated goalkickers.

While WA was not to win another Australian championship for 40 years, its own competition prospered.

IMPORTANT DATES IN WESTERN AUSTRALIAN FOOTBALL

1868: The Fourteenth Foot regiment arrives on the *Virago* from Hobart-town and on 19 September, plays a team of locals on the Bishop's Collegiate school grounds. The best-of-three goals game goes into a second day, the military team winning after kicking two goals consecutively. It is the first known game in WA.

1883: First games played in Perth by the Swans club.

1885: The Western Australian Football Association is formed at a meeting at the John Bull (now the Criterion) Hotel. Three clubs join: Fremantle Union, Victorians and Rovers, paying one guinea each for the privilege; Hugh Dixson (later Sir Hugh Denison) is appointed secretary; the first official WAFA game is played on 6 June at the Esplanade between Victorians and Rovers.

1886: Fremantle Union splits into two clubs: Fremantle and Unions, who combine with Victorians and Rovers to form a four-team competition.

1889: Metropolitans replace Victorians in the competition.

1890: Victorians become West Perth.

1891: West Perth, East Perth and Centrals enter the competion to join Rovers and Fremantle in a five-team contest.

1895: Essendon recruit *Albert 'The Great' Thurgood* heads the goalkicking for Fremantle, the first of three consecutive seasons of his goalkicking dominance. Imperials join the competition.

1898: East Fremantle founded.

1899: Fremantle disbands, having dominated the 19th century competition, winning 11 premierships—the first three under the name of Unions. South Fremantle emerges, under the guidance of visionary Griff John. Rovers change name to

Perth. West Perth's Herb Loel kicks 14 goals (out of 15) against Perth.

1900: District football emerges, each club bearing the name of a district, with the majority of their players coming from their own individual districts.

1904: The first interstate game against Victoria is played, in Melbourne, the Vics winning 14.10 (94) to WA's 8.11 (59). WA also meets SA for the first time, winning 10.7 (67) to 8.10 (58).

1906: WA football celebrates its 21st birthday with six clubs involved: West Perth, South Fremantle, East Fremantle, Perth, Subiaco and East Perth. North Fremantle and Midlands Junction also compete, before dropping out at wartime.

1908: The association becomes known as the WA Football League. Subiaco Oval first used for Australian football.

1911: Ballarat-born David 'Dolly' Christie plays his last of 27 seasons and 16th in WA (including 14 at East Fremantle, a club he helped co-found). East Fremantle rover Dick Sweetman dies after his spine is badly injured by an opponent's knee.

1913: Renowned centreman W. J. 'Nipper' Truscott arrives from the Goldfields and the Mines Rovers club for the first of 13 seasons with East Fremantle.

1921: WA wins its first Australian carnival, held in Perth, defeating arch-rival Victoria by five points; Subiaco ruckman Tom Outridge wins the first Sandover Medal—on the casting vote of the league chairman.

1922: Administrator A. A. Moffat becomes the first West Australian president of the Australian National Football Council.

1923: East Perth win its fifth consecutive premiership under the guidance of Phil Matson—an Australian record until 1959.

1924: South Fremantle's Bonny Campbell kicks 23 goals for WA against Queensland in Hobart, playing the first three quarters at full-forward and the last at full-back. He amasses a record 51 goals for the series.

1926: Claremont joins.

1930: Sandover Medal voting system is changed from one vote for the best player to a 3–2–1 system.

1931: The Page system of finals football

is adopted, in line with the VFL.

1932: The WAFL becomes the WA National Football League.

1933: East Fremantle rookie George Doig becomes the first player in the WA league to kick 100 goals in a season. He is to become known as the 'Bradman' of WA full-forwards.

1934: Swan Districts joins. Doig kicks 152 goals for the season—an Australian record—including 19 (out of 22) against Claremont-Cottesloe. He is to amass 100 or more goals in every season from 1933–41, a WA and Australia record.

1935: Claremont-Cottesloe shortens its name to Claremont.

1937: Five players reach a century of goals: Doig, West Perth's Ted Tyson and Frank Hopkins, Swan Districts' Ted Holdsworth and Perth's Bert Gook. Mick Cronin becomes the first West Australian to win the Tassie Medal.

1938: Fitzroy's immortal *Haydn Bunton snr* wins the first of his three Sandover Medals, having joined Subiaco along with fellow Victorian top-liners in Geelong's Les Hardiman and Carlton's Keith Shea. Tyson kicks 126 of his team's 259 goals for the season. In Melbourne, WA-born Brighton Diggins (ex-Subiaco) becomes the first West Australian to coach a League team to a premiership. He is successful with Carlton.

1940: Claremont's *George Moloney* becomes the first player to kick 100 goals in two competitions. Having returned from Geelong, he wins the '36 Sandover Medal and in 1940, boots 113 goals.

1941: Young star Stan 'Pops' Heal, who had joined the Royal Australian Navy, plays in two premiership sides in the same year, with Melbourne (VFL) and West Perth (WAFL).

1945: Relayed free kicks allowed down the field for infringements incurred after a player has disposed of the ball.

1947: Claremont's Les McClements wins the Tassie Medal. A players' provident fund is introduced. East Fremantle extends its unbeaten sequence to 35.

1949: Ern Henfrey becomes the first West Australian to captain Victoria—in 1949 against SA and WA.

1951: District boundaries re-allocated.

1953: South Fremantle's Bernie Naylor amasses an Australian record 167 goals for the season, including 23 goals in one game against Subiaco, South scoring a record 35.18 (228). Perth ruckman Merv McIntosh wins the Tassie Medal and Sandover Medal in the same year.

1955: South Fremantle's John Todd wins the Sandover Medal at the age of 17 years and four months. Perth breaks a 47-year drought by defeating favourites East Fremantle in the grand final. McIntosh retires, having been supreme in Perth's two point grand final win after a distinguished 218 game career which includes three Sandover Medals and three Simpson Medals.

1956: East Perth's *Graham Farmer* wins the Tassie and Sandover Medals.

1958: A 14-a-side trial game between members of the WA State squad is played at Subiaco Oval, but is not a success. The WA league votes against a move by the standing committee of the ANFC to introduce 14-a-side teams into football. A lightning premiership is played as part of celebrations for the centenary of Australian football. Five country leagues come to Perth for the series: South-West, Great Southern, Goldfields, Eastern Districts and Great Northern. West Perth's Ray Schofield plays his 274th game, breaking the league record held previously by Claremont's Ken Caporn.

1959: Subiaco kicks a record 16.8 in the third quarter of its semi final match against Perth, winning the match 26.23 (179) to 7.8 (50).

1960: East Perth's Jack Sheedy becomes the first West Australian to play 300 games. A year later, he is to break legendary *Dick Reynolds'* Australian record of 321 matches.

1961: WA wins the Australian championship for the first time since 1921. Ruckman-defender Jack Clarke from East Fremantle gains selection in his fourth All Australian team.

1962: Swan Districts' Haydn Bunton jnr clinches the Sandover Medal, becoming the only son of a Sandover Medallist to win the award. Perth's Roy Harper wins the Simpson Medal in his first State appearance, against SA. The grand final attracts a crowd of 42,000—representing about one ninth of Perth's entire population.

1964: Jim Davies becomes president of the league, the only Sandover Medallist to be WA league president.

1966: Three time East Perth premiership full back John Watts has the distinction of playing in premierships in three different States, after being a part of Hobart's flag. He'd previously played in Geelong's 1963 winning Grand Final side. Fitzroy great *Kevin Murray* leads East Perth into the grand final in the second of his two years of WA football. *Barry Cable* wins the Tassie Medal.

1967: Swan Districts' Billy Walker wins his third consecutive Sandover Medal.

Billy Walker, one of WA's finest rovers, who won three Sandover Medals in a row from 1965 to 1967.

1968: Subiaco's Austin Robertson jnr beats Naylor's goalkicking record, with 162 goals, including 15 against East Fremantle.

1969: Graham Farmer plays his 300th league game in the match between West Perth and South Fremantle at Leederville oval. In that game, Garry Scott plays his 200th consecutive match for South Fremantle. He goes on to play 205 in a row,

breaking *Jack Titus*' Australian record. Subiaco's Peter Eakins ties for the Tassie Medal.

1970: Boundaries Commission announces new boundaries of eight league clubs to extend 30 miles from the GPO.

1972: East Perth's Malcolm Brown is named All Australian captain.

1975: West Perth centreman Mel Whinnen wins his ninth Breckler Medal, his club's best and fairest award. No other player in WA history has ever been as successful at one club. For the first time, all games are played on ovals free of cricket pitches. West Perth's Barry Day kicks seven goals in the final quarter against South Fremantle.

1976: West Perth's Bill Dempsey plays the last of 343 matches in the 1976 first semi-final. Claremont's *Graham Moss* becomes the first West Australian to win the VFL's prestigious Brownlow Medal, representing Essendon.

1977: WA defeats Victoria in the first State-of-Origin challenge match, in a game which attracts 44,891. Sandover Medal count is opened to the public and conducted at the Perth-Sheraton hotel for the first time.

1979: WA wins the inaugural State-of-Origin football championships, in Perth. Brian Peake is honoured with the All Australian captaincy. Barry Cable plays his 400th game in Australian senior football. Mr Justice Northrop rules in the High Court that the league's clearance rules are in contempt of common law, clearing West Perth's Brian Adamson to play with Norwood. A record grand final crowd of 52,781 witness East Fremantle's defeat of South Fremantle. League drops 'national' from its official title.

1981: Aboriginals Stephen Michael, Phil Narkle and Jim Krakouer finish first, second and third in the Sandover Medal count—Michael polling a WA-record 37 votes.

1983: The State Government appoints a three-man taskforce to investigate the long-term financial needs of WA League Football. East Perth's *Ross Glendinning* wins the Brownlow Medal, representing North Melbourne.

1984: Former Collingwood player John Walker is appointed chief executive of the WAFL. He later becomes the first chief executive for the West Coast Eagles. *Brad Hardie* wins the Tassie Medal. He is to repeat his success in 1986. An independent Board of Directors is appointed to administer WA football.

1985: East Fremantle wins the Centenary grand final— its 26th flag. A new 5–4–3–2–1 voting system in the Sandover is introduced.

1987: The West Coast Eagles are formed, playing 11 games in WA in their first season of VFL competition. Football returns to the WACA ground with both day and night matches.

1989: Subiaco becomes the permanent WA headquarters of the West Coast Eagles. The WA Football Commission assumes control of the Eagles.

1990: The WAFL changes the competition name to the WA State Football league, to differentiate between State and national competitions.

1991: In the first year of truly national football, the Eagles make the AFL Grand Final for the first time, under the coaching of a former Victorian, *Mick Malthouse*. Eagle utility Craig Turley is runner-up in the Brownlow Medal. League name reverts to the WAFL.

1992: Peter Matera becomes the first wingman to kick five goals in a Grand Final as the Eagles defeat Geelong for a historic first AFL pennant.

1994: East Fremantle wins its second WAFL flag in three seasons under coach Ken Judge. Mark Amaranti is best afield with four goals in a 24-possession performance.

MOST WAFL MATCHES, 1885–1994

Mel Whinnen	371	West Perth	1960–77
Bill Dempsey	343	West Perth	1960–76
Jack Sheedy	332	East Fremantle/East Perth	1942–63
Brian Peake	308	East Fremantle/Perth	1972–80, 1985–90
Bill Walker	305	Swan Districts	1961–76
Alan Watling	284	West Perth	1969–83
Les Fong	284	West Perth	1973–87
Stan Nowotney	279	Swan Districts	1966–83
Ray Schofield	277	West Perth	1942–58
Ken Caporn	273	Claremont	1943–58
John Hayes	272	East Perth/Claremont/South Fremantle	1970–84
Darrell Panizza	271*	Claremont	1979–94

* current player.

MOST VFL/AFL MATCHES BY PLAYERS FROM WESTERN AUSTRALIA
(150 matches or more)

PLAYER	MATCHES	TEAMS	SPAN	RECRUITED FROM
Wayne Richardson	278	Collingwood	1966–78	Trayning
Max Richardson	244	Collingwood/Fitzroy	1969–80	S. Fremantle
Ross Glendinning	230	North Melb./W.C. Eagles	1978–88	East Perth
Stephen McCann	226	North Melbourne	1977–88	Geraldton
Ted Pool	200	Hawthorn	1926–38	Kalgoorlie
Ted Rowell	189	Collingwood	1901–03; 1906–15	Kalgoorlie
Wally Buttsworth	188	Essendon	1939–49	West Perth
Alec Epis	180	Essendon	1958–68	Boulder

PLAYER	MATCHES	TEAMS	SPAN	RECRUITED FROM
Gary Malarkey	172	Geelong	1977–86	East Perth
Earl Spalding	170*	Melbourne/Carlton	1987–94	Perth
John Annear	166	Coll./Rich./W.C. Eagles	1981–90	Claremont
Bruce Duperouzel	164	St Kilda/Footscray	1974–84	Claremont
Michael Brennan	163*	W.C. Eagles	1987–94	E. Fremantle
Chris Mainwaring	161*	W.C. Eagles	1987–94	E. Fremantle
Ray Gabelich	160	Collingwood	1955–60; 1962–66	Mt Hawthorn
Neil Balme	159	Richmond	1970–79	Subiaco
Ron Cooper	157	Carlton/North Melb.	1932–43	Claremont-Cottesloe
Michael Richardson	156	Collingwood/Essendon/Bris.	1983–90	Swan Dist.
John Worsfold	156*	W.C. Eagles	1987–94	S. Fremantle
Peter Wilson	155*	Richmond/W.C. Eagles	1987–94	E. Fremantle
Gary Buckenara	154	Hawthorn	1982–90	Subiaco
Chris Lewis	153*	W.C. Eagles	1987–94	Claremont
Nicky Winmar	153*	St Kilda	1987–94	S. Fremantle
Dwayne Lamb	151	W.C. Eagles	1988–94	Subiaco
Mike Fitzpatrick	150	Carlton	1975–76; 1978–83	Subiaco
Brad Hardie	150	Footscray/Bris./Coll.	1985–92	S. Fremantle

* current player.

WA'S BEST POST-WAR EIGHTEEN

B: Guy McKenna, Gary Malarkey, John McIntosh.
HB: Ken Hunter, Ross Glendinning, Denis Marshall.
C: Peter Matera, Maurice Rioli, Chris Mainwaring.
HF: Nicky Winmar, Graeme John, Gary Buckenara
F: Graham Moss, Brian Taylor, Wayne Richardson.
R: Graham Farmer, Mark Bairstow.
Rov.: Barry Cable.

Team provided by Geoff Poulter.

WHELAN, Marcus (1914–73)

A superbly gifted centreman known as Collingwood's 'quiet achiever', Whelan helped form a formidable goal-to-goal line, playing in the pivot in the Magpies' five consecutive Grand Finals from 1935–39.

Recruited from Darley, just outside Bacchus Marsh, he played eight games in his debut year (1933) before winning a permanent place with his accurate kicking and polished high marking, which surprised many a taller opponent. Just 173 cm, he had the ability to leap, being regarded as an exceptional high mark for his height. He won the Brownlow Medal in 1939, playing 172 games in a career which spanned from 1933–47. He represented Victoria on three occasions.

'He had great skill and did everything with great polish,' said teammate *Bob Rose*. 'Everything about him was immaculate. He was never ruffled and always seemed to have plenty of time to decide what to do with the ball. He also had a superb football brain and was one of the most skilful players I have ever played with.'

After retiring in 1947, he coached St Kilda seconds for a season.

His son, Shane, also represented Collingwood in the late 1960s.

WHITTEN, Ted (1933–)

Post-war football's unchallenged genius, Edward James 'Ted' Whitten was a fabulously gifted and charismatic key-position player who became the darling of Footscray and Victorian crowds with his flair, class and exuberance.

In a supreme 20-year career, he amassed 350 club and interstate matches and countless honours and distinctions. The only major award to elude him was the Brownlow Medal—irrefutable evidence that the best footballer doesn't always win. In 1959, he was equal third and in 1961, equal fifth, years in which he helped advance the flickpass into a potent weapon. It was later outlawed.

Umpires claimed he was too aggressive and talked too much, yet he was reported only once in 321 club games from 1951–70 and won five Footscray best and fairests, being captain for 14 years and 212 games (second only to *Dick Reynolds* who led Essendon in 224 matches).

Ted Whitten lets one go at practice.

Playing coach of the Bulldogs for 12 years, he was also non-playing coach in 1971, his final season, before being cleared to North Melbourne where he didn't appear in an official match.

'I thought I could go on longer (at North),' he said.

'*Brian Dixon* was coach. After playing 20 years (in the seniors at Footscray), he said to me, "We'll run you in the reserves for six weeks and see how you go."'

'I said, "You can stick it up your a..."'

Whitten's tri-coloured No. 3 Footscray guernsey is one of the most famous of them all.

Representing Victoria on 29 occasions and three times winning All Australian status, his devotion, input and love of State football was unparalleled. In 1958, he tied with North Melbourne's *Allen Aylett* for the Tassie Medal, only to lose on a countback.

In 1961, Whitten considered offers from three West Australian clubs to coach, but remained in Melbourne after a job offer from Adidas Footwear's John Van Hoboken who was responsible for outfitting some of the most famous names in football in streamlined new boots.

Whitten has remained with Adidas ever since, a larger-than-life figure, whose contribution to the game at all levels is unsurpassed.

A proud son of the western suburbs, hero-worshipped by thousands, Whitten rose to legendary status from a tough, materially-deprived childhood, playing in Footscray's only VFL premiership in 1954 and captain-coaching the club into the 1961 Grand Final. For years, his novel way of preparing for a match, was to take his mother to the pictures.

In his first game, in 1951, he was knocked out by Richmond toughman Don 'Mopsy' Fraser.* He said Fraser did him a favour that day, hardening his attitude and making him realise that League football was a no-nonsense game that only the toughest could consistently succeed at.

A magnificent high mark, he could run with the rovers and split open packs. His

* see 'FIVE FAMOUS INCIDENTS'

athletic 183 cm physique, skill and anticipation allowed him to play at centre half-forward or centre half-back equally effectively.

His peers regarded him as the greatest player of his time. Of post-war champions, only Hawthorn's *Leigh Matthews* rivals his record.

Geelong's *Bob Davis* said Whitten was a footballer in a class rarely seen: 'He was the master craftsman. I well remember him drop-kicking two 65-yard goals on the Western Oval to beat Geelong. He could stab, drop, torpedo or flat punt. He could baulk and blind turn. His marking could be safe or spectacular and there was his strength applied properly or improperly (only occasionally, and then to return some earlier misdemeanour). And his full loyalty was given to the jumper he was wearing.'

In the early 1970s, the VFL's magazine *Football Life* conducted a poll among press, radio and television commentators to find the best players in their positions since 1950. Whitten won both the centre half-back and centre half-forward categories.

Truly versatile and an architect of so many Victoria State team victories, Whitten regarded State selection as the ultimate honour, first sporting the famous Big V in 1955. He was Victoria's captain-coach, against arch rivals SA and WA in 1962.

'In our day, playing for the State was like a dream come true,' he said. 'If you offered the guys selected a choice of winning Tatts or playing for Victoria, nine out of 10 blokes would choose the jumper.'

Long-time VFL administrator Eric McCutchan said Whitten's leadership at State level was remarkable: 'Sometimes when a band of brilliant players get together in a State side, there is no talking, little cohesion.

'Somehow Whitten had the knack of getting these players together as if they were playing in a club match. The results, when he was in our State sides, speak for themselves.'

Whitten became only the fourth player to reach the 300 game milestone in the opening round of the 1969 season. Originally it was thought that No. 300 would coincide with the final home-and-away match of the previous year. The club was inundated with telegrams and a huge party arranged before it was found that Whitten had played just 298 matches and not 299.

When Whitten passed Reynolds' mark of 320 League games, he was immediately retired. He could not hold back the tears as he was chaired off. One commentator wrote of the Bulldog legend: 'The sporting arena farewells the greatest showman, clubman, all-rounder, personality . . . and footballer . . . of all time.'

Whitten continued a frontline football role in the media and as the Victorian State selection chairman. The E. J. Whitten Medal for the best Victorian player afield in interstate competition is named in his honour.

Whitten's son, Ted jnr., also played for Footscray and in 1980 represented Victoria.

Don Whitten, Ted's brother, played 21 games with Footscray from 1956–58 and with Yarraville from 1961–64.

WILDMEN OF FOOTBALL

Don 'Mopsy' Fraser was as ferocious a footballer as anyone to play at League level. His turbulent post-war career included 12 reports, at least 51 confirmed weeks of suspension—and as many as 84. In eight years and 124 games at Richmond, he was booked six times, being outed for 16 weeks.

'Sometimes I was fitted for offences that didn't happen, plenty of times I got away with murder,' he said.

Possessing an explosive temper, he thought nothing of steamrolling opponents, fairly or unfairly. Team-mate *Jack Dyer* said Fraser was the most hated player in the game. 'I doubt if he ever played in a match without being the centre of controversy . . . When he went berserk he went deaf. I couldn't get through to him at all. He was the most rugged and vicious footballer I have encountered.'

Fraser captain-coached Port Melbourne into three consecutive grand finals before coaching in Tasmania. He played his last games, aged 38, in the 1958 Australian carnival.

Ironically, he could play brilliant football. He was a breathtaking mark and could roost the ball 70 metres. However, his use of vigour is best remembered.

More recently, the most-reported players have included West Australian Mal Brown (25 tribunal appearances as a player and a coach), and Victorians *Dermott Brereton, David Rhys-Jones, Carl Ditterich* and *Tony Lockett.*

Brereton incurred two seven-match penalties in the 1994 season.

The heaviest suspension, of five years, belongs to Alex 'Bongo' Lang, a member of three Carlton premiership sides.

In 1910, he was involved in a bribery scandal on the eve of the second semi-final against South Melbourne. An hour before the game, the names of Lang and two

'Mopsy' Fraser, a ferocious defender with an explosive temper. Even Jack Dyer couldn't control him.

THEY SERVED LENGTHY SUSPENSIONS

PLAYER	CLUB/S	SEASONS	NUMBER OF CHARGES	FOUND GUILTY	MATCHES SUSPENSION
Alex Lang	Carl.	1906–10, 1916–17	1	1	101
Doug Fraser	Carl.	1910	1	1	99
Fred Rutley	NM	1925, 1930	1	1	89
Dermott Brereton	Haw/Syd./Col.	1982–95	16*	8	37†
Tommy Downs	Carl.	1927–29, 1931, 1933	2	2	31
Rod Grinter	Melb.	1975–94	10	7	31
Ken Boyd	SM	1957–61	7	7	30
Carl Ditterich	SK/M	1963–80	19	11	30
Rod McLean	Carl.	1935–46	6	4	29
James Shorten	Coll.	1909–10, 1912–13	1	1	29
Stan Thomas	Geel.	1915, 1917–25	3	2	29
Arthur Coghlan	Geel.	1922–25, 1927–32	2	2	29
William Gent	SM	1903–04, 1906–08	2	2	27
Jack Williams	SM	1939–40, 1942–46	6	4	27
Jim Krakouer	N/SK	1982–91	16	9	27
Ron Andrews	E/Co	1973–84	9	7	24
Phil Carman	Co/M/E/N	1975–82	9	4	24
Ted Bryce	Ess.	1935–42	2	2	23
Ted Whitfield	SM	1939–41, 1944–45	7	5	22
Robert Muir	SK	1974–78, 1980, 1984	12	9	22
David Rhys-Jones	SM/Carl.	1980–92	25	12	22
Greg Williams	G/Syd/C	1984–94	15*	9	21#
Tony Lockett	St K/Syd	1983–95	11*	6	21

* current player.
# —plus a $3000 fine.
† —plus a $5000 fine.
Prior to 1926, a few players were found guilty of serious offences and given a life sentence. In each case, such a penalty was later rescinded.

others were removed from the team sheet, news circulating that they had allegedly been offered £100 bribes to 'play dead'.

After serving his time, he again represented the Blues in 1916–17.

St Kilda's Glenn Middlemiss, the son of Russell Middlemiss, a former Geelong premiership player, holds the record of most reports, five, in the 1984 season.

Geelong's Mark Jackson was reported four times in 1984 and in mid-season 1985 received an eight-week suspension after being reported on four different charges against Hawthorn.

WILLIAMS, Don (1935–   )

A superb athlete and spirited athlete best known for his dashing displays at half-back, Williams played for Melbourne in seven VFL Grand Finals, including five premierships in 12 years and 210 games from 1953–68.

Williams represented Victoria eight times.

WILLIAMS, John (1947–   )

A reliable centre half-back from Rochester who had 12 League seasons, Williams represented Essendon for nine years and Collingwood for three. He was vice-captain of the Bombers in 1971 and 1973 and a member of the club's 1968 Grand Final side, playing 161 of his 197 VFL games at Windy Hill. He also represented Victoria.

WILLIAMS, Greg (1963–   )

A fearless, offensive centreman who holds the recent League record of 52 possessions in a match, Greg 'Diesel' Williams won the 1986 and 1994 Brownlow Medals during his tumultuous first 12 years in the game.

The master ballwinner had an uncertain start, having to wear calipers as a child to help straighten his legs. His first VFL club Carlton believed he was too slow and twice sent him back to country club, Golden Square.

After he'd won consecutive Bendigo league best and fairests, Geelong coach *Tom Hafey* gave him a second chance. When Hafey joined Sydney, Williams was one of three ex-Cats to go with him. He'd been offered $100,000 to play with Sydney, but said he'd stay at Geelong, where he'd just won the best and fairest, if he was paid $50,000. The Cats offered only $45,000 and he left.

Greg Williams.

Williams won his Brownlow in his first year with his new club, the privately-owned Swans, clinching All Australian selection in 1986–87 and captaining Victoria in 1988.

In 1986, he created an Australian record for possessions, having 311 kicks and 379 handballs, an average of amost 30 a game. His match record is 53 possessions (including six goals) against St Kilda, at the Sydney Cricket Ground in 1989.

His extraordinarily quick handball skills —on both sides of his body—even surpassed the standard of the modern game's most-renowned handball exponents, Geelong's *Graham Farmer* and North Melbourne's *Barry Cable*.

His combination work with teammate *Gerard Healy* became a feature, Healy also winning a Brownlow Medal, in 1988.

Throughout his brilliant career, Williams had to contend with taggers who often strayed outside the rules. Sometimes they exposed the only chink in his armour, his temper, and he had several long suspensions, including eight weeks for striking Carlton's *David Rhys-Jones* in 1989, and six more in 1990, for striking Essendon's David Grenvold.

A further suspension in 1991, this time for striking West Coast Eagle tagger Dwayne Lamb, cost him Victorian selection and probably the State captaincy. His seven State appearances were top-class efforts, highlighted by his 50-possession game against Western Australia in Perth in 1988 when he won the E. J. Whitten Medal.

Many of his peers regarded him as the player they'd most like to have in their team. Collingwood's *Tony Shaw* said: 'Greg has the quickest hands of any footballer I've ever played against. He has peripheral vision and seems to know where everyone is on the field. Diesel is a very aggressive bastard. I've had run-ins with him. But I don't hold grudges and he'd be in any side that I had.'

Despite his lack of natural speed, Williams' great fitness allowed him to run at three-quarter pace throughout his matches and his uncanny anticipation and skills made him Public Enemy No. 1 for most opposing sides.

In 1992, he joined Carlton—the club which had first rejected him—on a huge contract claimed by some to be worth more than $300,000 a year, making him the highest paid player in the game.

Despite knee injuries which made it difficult for him to train, he was a dominant figure in helping lift the Blues under the second-time-around coaching of *David Parkin*.

In 1994, he won the club's best and fairest, as well as the Brownlow, in a close finish from West Coast's Peter Matera.

WILLIAMS, Mark (1958–)

The first South Australian to play 200 League games, Mark Williams amassed 201 matches from 1981–90 with Collingwood and Brisbane before returning to Adelaide, saying he couldn't enjoy his football while his team, the Bears, were being flogged almost every week.

A lead member of one of South Australia's most decorated football families, he approached 400 senior games at the start of the 1992 season, having previously had 66 with his first club, West Adelaide, and almost 100 at Port Adelaide, including the 1979–80 and '90 premierships. He represented SA eight times, winning All Australian status in 1980.

Mark Williams: the first South Australian to play 200 VFL/AFL games.

Best known in the VFL for his achievements at Collingwood, Williams joined the Magpies in 1981, aged 22, winning the Copeland Trophy, representing Victoria and playing in the '81 Grand Final in his maiden year. He captained the Magpies from 1983–86, playing 135 matches and kicking 178 goals before becoming No. 1 recruit for the newly-formed Brisbane Bears in 1987, where he played 66 matches.

WILLS, Tom (1835–1880)

The first captain of Melbourne Football Club, Wills, a third generation Australian, is regarded as one of the 'founding fathers' of Australian Rules football. His cousin,

Henry Harrison, was also an important figure in the game's evolution.

Born on 19 August, 1835 at Molonglo, near Canberra, Wills was the son of a rich English sheep-owner, who was sent to boarding school in England to further his education. His father hoped he'd become a lawyer. Young Tom was more interested in games.

Tom Wills (top left) with three of the men also responsible for the foundation of Australian football, H. C. A. Harrison, W. J. Hammersley and J. B. Thompson.

An exceptionally gifted and colourful sportsman, he captained Victoria at cricket and helped sponsor the first All Australian cricket touring team to England in 1878.

Just returned from England where he'd been playing sport and finishing his schooling, 22-year-old Wills had a burning desire to develop an Australian version of the football he had seen while attending Rugby School and Cambridge.

Appointed secretary of the Melbourne Cricket Club at the age of 22, he quickly became well known for his flashy dress, drive and determination. Writing to Melbourne's sporting journal *Bell's Life in Victoria*, he suggested cricketers should keep fit for their summer sport by playing football. The turf would also benefit from the traffic, becoming 'firm and durable'.

His now famous letter was published on 10 July 1858 and is regarded as the most important document in the game's early history.

Within weeks, Wills had co-umpired the first match, between Melbourne Grammar and Scotch College, a 40-a-side affair played at Richmond paddock, site of the present Punt Road Oval. Luncheon was taken in the pavilion, where the present Melbourne Cricket Club members' stand is located.

The maiden match was an epic affair, being played over three days, on 7 and 21 August and 4 September. The goals were 990 yards apart and there were virtually no rules. Scotch scored the first goal and Grammar the equaliser. As neither side had scored the requisite second goal, the contest was declared a draw, the weather being considered too warm.

Later, Wills, his cousin Harrison, the editor of the *Herald* newspaper J. B. Thompson and Mr W. J. Hammersley, a noted cricketer, combined with other members of the Melbourne Cricket Club committee to draw up rules for a football game later to be known as Victorian or Australian Rules.

Harrison said: 'It was a rather go-as-you-please affair at first but a set of rules was gradually evolved which experience taught us to be the best.'

The founding fathers considered that certain features of the English football codes were unsuitable for the harder grounds and warmer weather of Victoria. Wills believed that a new Australian code should not be too different from that played in England as he envisaged international competition between the two countries, just as was soon to occur with cricket.

He particularly liked the idea of players

'running with the ball' as invented by schoolboy William Webb Ellis at the Rugby School, in 1823.

A keen player himself, the 180 cm Wills figured in more than 200 games, mainly for Geelong, until his retirement in 1876, aged 41. Four years later, he suicided. An inquest found that his excessive drinking had been a factor. 'For one who had been called "The Grace of Australia" and "a model of muscular Christianity" it was a sad end,' said the *Australian Dictionary of Biography*.

WILSON, Brian (1961–)

The 1982 Brownlow Medallist and one of the few to play League football at four AFL/VFL clubs, 20-year-old Wilson was the youngest winner of the Medal since *Bob Skilton* in 1959. He was in his fifth season of League football and first with Melbourne.

Originally from Braybrook, he played his first games at Footscray as a 16-year-old, being renowned for his skill, if not his dedication.

The 188 cm Wilson developed into a top-rate centreman afer playing mainly as a flanker in his teenage days. His goal sense made him a particularly dangerous opponent, but attracted criticism, some claiming him to be selfish.

Notorious for his dressing room pranks and not always popular with his coaches for his tendency to individualise, Wilson's ability to kick 'impossible goals' helped his longevity. Playing only his third game for St Kilda in 1991—against his old side, Melbourne—he kicked six goals at the MCG.

Months later, however, he forfeited his chances of playing in St Kilda's first finals team in almost 20 years by retiring midway through the season.

Wilson played 209 games in his 14 years, including nine matches at Footscray, 39 at North Melbourne, 154 at Melbourne and seven at St Kilda. He kicked 245 goals.

Gary Wilson.

WILSON, Gary (1953–)

When Fitzroy's paperweight rover Gary 'Flea' Wilson was named State captain in his final year in 1984, he said it was the pinnacle of his career. Wilson won the Big V guernsey 12 times in a celebrated 14-year, 270-game career from 1971–84, which included All Australian honours in 1979.

He won Fitzroy's best and fairest five times, was skipper in his final three years and leading goalkicker in two. Twice kicking seven goals in a game, his career aggregate of 450 goals places him high among Fitzroy's leading goalscorers.

Many felt he should have won a Brownlow Medal. In 1978, he finished third after being one of the hottest favourites in years. In 1979, when he won Fitzroy's best and fairest by a record 151 votes, he was second, just one vote behind Collingwood's *Peter Moore*.

A skilful, big possession winner with fine running skills, the 176 cm Wilson was tall for a first rover and a fine high mark. A fitness fanatic, he gave up his schoolteaching job so he could train every day and his level of consistency was equalled by few.

For many years, Wilson was a champion in a weak team and was often singled out for 'rough' treatment. He was concussed on many occasions and resorted to wearing a bicycle helmet for protection.

In his final years, knee injuries forced him to play more of a forward-pocket role and he retired at the end of 1984, aged 31, realising he could no longer perform at his best.

WILSON, Percy (1889–1941)

A member of Collingwood's 1910 premiership team and captain of the 1917 team which defeated Fitzroy in the Grand Final, Percy Wilson was a rugged centreman/forward who played 183 games for the Magpies from 1909–20 before crossing to Melbourne for his final four seasons and an additional 51 matches. He represented Victoria three times.

WOOD, Bryan (1954–)

Playing in four premierships in 15 years, three at Richmond and one at Essendon, Bryan Wood's illustrious career stretched from 1972–86 and included 253 matches, two State matches and the Richmond captaincy, in 1981.

WORRALL, Jack (1863–1937)

A three-time Carlton premiership coach known for his autocratic methods, Worrall also led Essendon to two premierships. He was the game's first acknowledged coach.

Worrall won 60 per cent of his 267 matches in 15 seasons. His record of five premierships was surpassed by only two men, Collingwood's *Jock McHale* (eight) and Melbourne's *Norm Smith* (six).

An Australian cricketer of note, he played 11 Tests over a 14-year period, including two tours of England. In January, 1896 he made 417 not out for Carlton in a then world record score of 922.

Short and wide-shouldered with a touch of belligerence, he was 39 when appointed secretary at Carlton in 1902.

He immediately insisted on being in charge of the team in all matters, from recruiting, training and selection to directing the team's on-field fortunes. He was a rigid disciplinarian, who enjoyed wonderful results.

Worrall donned football gear and trained with the players well into his 40s. He was inundated with offers when he let it be known publicly that Carlton would seek the best players in the land. He demanded teamwork, discipline and loyalty. Those who didn't conform were cleared.

At the start of 1904, Worrall was sacked over his book-keeping methods. He had paid gate receipts from three games into his own account before paying his own cheques to the club in exchange. There was never any question of dishonesty but he was sacked by the committee. The players rallied behind him, ousted the committee and Worrall was reinstated. The Blues went on to win the premiership each year from 1906–08, the club's first VFL pennants.

Mid-way through the 1909 season, Worrall resigned, the players having turned against him. 'For the sake of the club and for peace and quietness, I consider it best to resign from the position (as coach) and thus remove any unpleasantness,' he said.

He was inundated with coaching offers. He joined Essendon and helped the Same Old win premierships in each of his first two years, 1911–12.

He retired from football after seven seasons at Essendon to concentrate on sports journalism. As 'J.W.' of *The Australasian* he is credited with coining the term 'Bodyline' during cricket's most infamous summer, in 1932–33.

WRIGHT, Roy (1929–)

A gentle giant, one of an elite few to win dual Brownlow Medals, Wright took six seasons and was into his 23rd year before he commanded a regular rucking spot at Richmond.

His late development may have been triggered by boyhood bouts of rheumatic fever and weak knees, which necessitated the use of splints.

Using his great spring and 10-inch hand-span to great effect, he won Brownlow Medals in 1952 and 1954. In 1954, he won by 10 votes from Collingwood's Neil Mann, a record Brownlow margin, surpassing *Haydn Bunton*'s eight vote victory in 1935.

Wright wasn't as good a mark as his mentor *Bill Morris*, but he was a better kick and a magnificent palmer of the ball, forming a potent combination with rover Billy Wilson.

First earning Victorian honours in 1953, he played 18 State games in seven seasons, including the 1953 and 1956 canrivals. Named an All Australian in '56, he would have played for Victoria again in 1958, but for injury.

A knee complaint finished his career half-way through the 1959 season.

WRIGHT, Stevie (1961–)

Wright overcame serious injury–including several knee operations–to play his 250th game during 1992.

Winner of two Sydney best and fairest awards in 1985 and 1990, his courage, skill and leadership were an integral factor in helping the Swans remain competitive.

See: 'TASMANIA'

WYND, Scott (1970–)

The 1992 Brownlow Medallist and Footscray best and fairest, the 201 cm Wynd's rapid improvement under the expert eye of one of the most decorated post-war ruckmen in *Gary Dempsey* helped Footscray into the last three in 1992.

The athletic, likeable blond became the game's No. 1 follower in 1992, representing Victoria with distinction and winning All Australian selection.

His strong marking drifting across half-back and rucking skills enabled him to poll Brownlow votes in 10 of his 22 games.

'I just came along to enjoy the night and see what happened,' said Wynd, when asked of his Medal expectations.

He'd originally been tied to North Melbourne, but slipped across to Footscray on his 18th birthday without having played a game at North. Embarrassed North officials signed Wynd's brother, Paul, as a 16-year-old.

Their father, Gary, played two games with Melbourne in 1966.

Zeds, A team of

Seventeen League players have had surnames beginning with 'Z', the most successful being much-travelled Shane Zantuck, who played 149 games from 1974–86 with three clubs, North Melbourne, South Melbourne and Melbourne.

A team of 'Zeds' is complete with the inclusion of Footscray defender Zeno Tzatzaris (pronounced Tat-zaris), who played 34 games with Footscray from 1984–90:

A TEAM OF 'ZEDS'

B: Z. Tzatzaris, M. Zanotti, C. Zinnick.
HB: T. Zeltner, N. Zunneberg, D. Zeunert (vice-capt.)
C: D. Zanoni, E. Zschech, S. Zantuck (capt.).
HF: L. Zimmer, R. Zander, B. Zorzi.
F: H. Zucker, P. Zychla, M. Zemski.
R: M. Zeuschner, J. Zimmerman.
Rov.: O. Zinko.

ZEDS, A TEAM OF

PLAYER	CLUB	SEASONS	GAMES	GOALS
Roy Zander	Hawthorn	1933–34	14	13
Denis Zanoni	Geelong	1960–62	14	0
Mark Zanotti	West Coast	1987–88	36*	6
	Brisbane	1989–92	64	4
	Fitzroy	1993–94	35	7
Trevor Zeltner	Footscray	1970, 1972	18	3
Mike Zemski	Hawthorn	1973–74	8	1
Denis Zeunert	Carlton	1954–60	110	11
Murray Zeuschner	Footscray	1962–67	64	4
L. Zimmer	Fitzroy	1918	1	0
J. Zimmerman	Footscray	1937–39	14	2
Owen Zinko	Melbourne	1963–64	3	3
Charles Zinnick	Essendon	1921	13	0
	Footscray	1925	1	0
Bruno Zorzi	Fitzroy	1957–58, 1960	18	0
Eric Zschech	Richmond	1930–35	102	16
Harold Zucker	Hawthorn	1942	3	3
Noel Zunneberg	Fitzroy	1967–72	69	3
Peter Zychla	Geelong	1982–83, 1985	12	1

* current player.

BIBLIOGRAPHY

Books consulted include:

Aborigines in Sport, Colin Tatz (The Australian Society for Sports History, 1987)

A Century of Tasmanian Football, 1879–1979, Ken Pinchin, ed Allan Leeson (Tasmanian football league, 1980)

A Century of the Best, Michael Roberts (Collingwood football club, 1991)

A Game of Our Own, Geoffrey Blainey (Information Australia, 1990)

A Shaw Thing, Tony Shaw, with Daryl Timms (1990)

Allen Aylett: My Game, a life in football, as told to Greg Hobbs (Sun Books, 1986)

Arden St '79 (Official publication of the North Melbourne Football Club)

Australian Football Life, magazine

Australian Rules Football, an illustrated history, ed John Dunn, written by Jim Main (Lansdowne Press, 1974)

Big Nick, John Nicholls with Ian McDonald (Garry Sparke & Assoc, 1977)

Blood, Sweat & Tears, West Adelaide Football Club, 1887–1987, ed Merv Agars (West Adelaide football club, 1987)

Blues, Blinders & Ballbursters, Ken Piesse (Sun Books, 1991)

Boots and all! Lou Richards, as told to Ian McDonald (Stanley Paul, 1963)

Captain Blood, Jack Dyer as told to Brian Hansen (Stanley Paul, 1965)

Carlton 1864–1989, 125 years, (Carlton F.C., 1989)

Cats' Tales, the Geelong football club, 1897–1983, ed Col Hutchinson (The Geelong Advertiser Pty Ltd, 1984)

Courage Book of Brownlow Medal Records, written and compiled by Peter R Blair (Allsport Publications, 1976)

Encyclopedia of Australian Sport, Jim Shepherd (Rigby, 1980)

Flying High, the history of the Essendon Football Club, Michael Maplestone (EFC, 1983)

Football Australia, magazine

Football Close-up 1973 (Inside Football, 1973)

Football Fan, magazine

Football Headlines, (An Argus Publication, 1955)

Football Life, magazine

Football with the stars, Ken Piesse and Daryl Timms (Wedneil Publications, 1983)

Footy Annual, 1967 ed John Dunn and Jim Main (Lansdowne Press, (1967)

Footy Annual, 1968, ed John Dunn and Jim Main (Lansdowne Press, 1968)

Footy Facts, All Australian Guide to Aussie Rules 1987–88, Ray Young and Dave Pincombe (Information Australia, 1988)

Football's 50 Greatest (in the past 50 years), Greg Hobbs and Scot Palmer (Bradford Usher and Assoc., 1976)

Football's who's who, 1989 edition, ed Alan East (Indian Pacific Ltd)

From the Outer, watching football in the '80s, Garrie Hutchinson (McPhee Gribble/ Penguin Books, 1984)

High Mark, the complete book of an Australian football, ed Jack Pollard (K. G. Murray Publishing Company Pty Ltd, 1964)

Just Crackers, Keenan and Football, Ray Carroll (RayRon Books, 1982)

Kill for Collingwood, Richard Stremski (Allen & Unwin, 1986)

Old Easts 1948–75, Jack Lee (Read's Printing & Publishing, 1976)

Red And Blue Blooded, Mike Coward (Norwood Football Club, 1977)

Ron Barassi's Football Book, (Rigby Limited, 1978)

Running with the ball, A Mancini and G. M. Hibbins (Lynedoch Publications, 1987)

SA Greats, the History of the Magarey Medal, John Wood (self published, 1987)

Southern Saints, 1986, Russell Holmesby

Sporting Life, magazine

The A to Z of Football, your favourite footy stars, Jim Main and Ken Piesse (Wedneil Publications, 1982)

The Australian Football Business, a spectator's guide to the VFL, Bob Stewart (Kangaroo Press, 1983)

The Coach—a season with Ron Barassi, John Powers (A Sphere Book, 1978)

The Complete Book of SANFL Records, 1990 edition, compiled by Dion Hayman (1990)

The Complete Book of VFL Finals, from 1897 to The Present, Graeme Atkinson (The Five Mile Press, 1989)

The Dominator, Wayne Johnston, with Ron Reed (Caribou Publications, 1991)

The First One Hundred Seasons, Fitzroy Football Club, 1883–1983, Mike Sutherland, Rod Nicholson and Stewart Murrihy (Fitzroy Football Club, 1983)

The Footballers, from 1885 to the West Coast Eagles, Geoff Christian (St George Books, 1988 edition)

The Great Grand Finals, George Handley (Walshe Publishing, 1989)

The Greatest Game, ed Ross Fitzgerald and Ken Spillman (William Heinemann Australia, 1988)

The Hard Way, the Story of Hawthorn Football Club (Lester-Townsend Publishing, 1990)

The North Story, Gerard P. Dowling (The Hawthorn Press, 1973)

The Paddock That Grew, the Story of the Melbourne Cricket Club, Keith Dunstan (Cassell Australia, 1962)

The Pioneers, 100 years of Association Football, Marc Fiddian (Victorian Football Association, 1977)

The Proud Champions, Australia's Aboriginal Sporting Heroes, Bret Harris (Little Hills Press, 1989)

The Royce Hart Story, Royce Hart (Thomas Nelson, 1970)

The Speed Guide to Football, ed Peter Bye (1962)

The Top 240, the greats of the VFL 1925–82, Greg Hobbs and Alf Brown (Herald & Weekly Times, 1982)

The Wild Men of Football, Jack Dyer and Brian Hansen (Southdown Press, 1968)

Tigerland, the History of the Richmond Football Club from 1885, Brian Hansen (RFC Past Players Associaiton, 1989)

Toohey's Guide to Every Game Ever Played, VFL results 1897–1982, compiled by Stephen Rodgers (Lloyd O'Neil Pty Ltd, 1983)

Victorian Country Football League Annual Reports

Victorian Football League Yearbooks and Annual reports

Violent Saturday, ed Neill Phillipson (Garry Sparke & Assoc., 1976)

WA's Fabulous 40, the best footballers for 40 years, ed Alan East (Presented by the Commonwealth Bank, 1984)

125 years of the Melbourne Demons (1958–1983), Greg Hobbs (MFC, 1983)

3AW Book of Footy Records, Graeme Atkinson and Michael Hanlon (Matchbooks, 1989)

Newspapers consulted included *The Age, The Australasian, The Argus, The Sporting Globe, The Sunday Observer, Sunday Press, Sunday Sun, The Sun, The Sun News-Pictorial, The Herald* and *The Sunday Herald.*

INDEX

(page numbers in **bold** indicate a main entry)

Banfield, D. 291
Banks, Denis 65
Banks, Tom 101
Barassi, Ron jnr 3, 12, **14–17**, 35, 43, 46, 47,
    53, 55, 60, 74, 79, 81, 83, 85, 127, 128,
    130, 131, 132, 145, 150, 158, 160, 163,
    164, 168, 185, 186, 201, 204, 205, 242,
    257, 264, 269, 280, 286
Barassi, Ron snr 15, 152
Barham, Rick 133
Barker brothers (Lou & Gilbert) 32
Barker, Syd 95, 105
Barker, Trevor **17–18**, 112, 255, 273
Barling, Tim 66
Barrett, John 86
Barrot, Bill 23, 50, 123, 226, 245, 254
Barry, Peter 284
Bartlett, Kevin **18–19**, 24, 36, 40, 53, 84, 89,
    90, 102, 119, 135, 142, 156, 198, 226,
    227, 228, 235, 263, 281, 282, 289
Barwick, Doug 65
Bawden, Bob 225
Baxter, Ken 46, 126
Bayes, Mark 19
Bayliss, George 109, 227, 228
Bayliss, Mark 211
Beames, Percy **19–20**, 152, 185, 196
Beard, Gilbert 250, 252
Beasley, Simon 110, 120
Beckwith, John 16, **20**
Bedford, Bill 20
Bedford, Peter **20**, 252
Beecroft, Bob 103, 191
Beers, Brian 87
Belcher brothers (Vic & Alan) 29 30, 32
Belcher, Alan 29–30, 32
Belcher, Vic **20**, 29–30, 102, 103, 250, 251,
    252
Bennett, Darren 19, 173, 186
Bennett, George 21
Bennett, Jack 126
Bennett, Peter 87, 211, 255
Bentley, Percy **21**, 43, 46, 53, 55, 87, 226,
    227
Bertram, Ossie 74, 250, 252
Betts, Gerard 133
Beveridge, Jack 21
Bewick, Darren 96
Bews, Andrew **21**, 116, 134
Bickerton, L. 104
Bickford, George 127
Bickley, Mark 6
Biffin, Ray 261, 263
Bigelow, Doug 127
Billing, Kevin 129, 256
Bingham, Lawrence 211
Bingley, John 129, 256
Birt, John **21**, 75, 95, 96

Bisset, George 21
Bissett, Jack 53, 251, 252
Blackwell, Wayne 211
Blethyn, Geoff 96
Blew, Russell 198
Blight, Malcolm 1, 17, **22–3**, 68, 131, 132,
    173, 204, 205, 206, 247, 248, 249, 282
'Bloodbath' Grand Final 124–5
Bolger, Martin **23**, 209, 210, 226
Bolton, David 259
Bond, Shane 133, 291
Bone, Mick 127, 128
Bonney, John 87, 263
Boon, David 86
Borthwick, 'Jerry' 123
Bos, Mark **23**, 134
Bourke, Barry 127, 128, 150, 186
Bourke, Damian 134
Bourke, David 24
Bourke, Francis **23–4**, 36, 50, 54, 226, 227,
    228
Bourke, Frank 23
Bowe, John 250, 252
Bowman, Gordon 127, 209
Bowyer, Percy **24**, 124
Box, Peter 16, **24**, 110, 111
Boyall, Marcus 124, 286
Boyd, Ken 105, 203, 300
Boyle, Stephen 73
Boyne, Peter 129
Bradbury, Peter 133
Bradford, James 'Nipper' 171, 238
Bradley, Craig **24–5**, 46, 47, 86, 93, 166, 248,
    249
Bradley, Robert 127
Brain, T. 252
Branton, Ron 137
Bray, Harold 36
Bray, Jeff 245
Breckler Medal 295
Breen, Barry **25**, 128, 129, 255, 256
Bremner, Ian 131
Brennan, Dan 217
Brennan, Michael 291, 297
Brereton, Dermott 13, **25–7**, 85, 88, 105–6,
    118, 133–4, 144, 145, 169, 200, 235, 259,
    282, 300
Brereton, Harry 186
Brewer, Ian 65
Briedis, Arnold 131, 132, 155, 206
Bright, Terry **27**, 116
Brisbane Bears Football Club 27–9
Britt, Con 131
Brittingham, Bill **29**, 96, 126, 127, 155
Broadstock, Jack 225
Bromage, Keith 64, 280
Brooks, Sir Norman 87
Brosnan, Gerald 103

Dac, Paul 262
Daicos, Peter 64, 65, **75**, 120
Dalton brothers (Don, Pat & Barry) 31
Dalton brothers (Jack & Bill) 30, 32
Dalton, Denis 128
Daly brothers ('Bos' & 'Bunny') 32
Daly, Anthony 'Bos' 32, 119, 123, 246, 247
Daly, J.D. 'Bunny' 32, 246
Danckert, Jack 126
Daniher brothers 31, 32, 33, 76, 77
Daniher, Anthony 33, **76**, 201
Daniher, Chris 31, 33, 76, 96
Daniher, Neale 33, 66, 76, 77, 177, 274, 288
Daniher, Terry 31, 33, 43, **76–7**, 95, 96, 100, 133, 177, 201
Darcy, David 245
Darcy, Tim 134
Dargie, Ian 211
Darley, Peter 247
Darren Millane Perpetual Memorial Shield 187
Davie, Harry 121, 186
Davies, Fred 251
Davies, Jim 295
Davies, Rick 247, 249
Davis, Allan 77, 129, 190, 255, 256
Davis, Barry 36, **77–8**, 43, 94, 96, 131, 271
Davis, Bob 1, **78–9**, 98, 99, 100, 115, 116, 299
Davis, Craig 64, 66, 263
Davis, Frank 128, 186
Davis, Michael 107
Dawson, S. 104
Day, Barry 295
Daykin brothers (Richard & Perce) 32
De Lacy, Hec 91, 92, 143
Deacon, Bert 37, 47, 52, 59, **79**, 126
Dean, Jimmy 245
Dean, Ken 264
Dean, Peter 47
Dean, Robert 131
Dean, Roger 16, **79–80**, 227
Deans, William 127
Dear brothers (Greg & Paul) 31, 32
Dear, Greg 31, 32, 134
Dear, Paul 31, 32, 145
Deas brothers (Jack & Robert) 32
Decoit, Dave 109
Delanty, Mike 261
Deller, Bill 80, 272
Dempsey, Bill 4, 295, 296
Dempsey, Gary 20, 36, 37, **80–1**, 110, 217, 282, 306
Dempsey, Jack 126
Dench, David 45, **81**, 131, 132, 164, 204, 205, 206
Denham, S. 96
Denning, Clem 104

Dennis, Richard 47
Devine, John 117, 271
Dibbs, Charlie 64, **81**
Dickerson, Glen 11
Dickson, 'Delicate' Des 100
Diggins, Brighton 46, 53, 250, 252, 294
Dillon, Jerry 10
Dillon, Kym 247
DiPierdomenico, Robert 36–7, **81–2**, 133, 134, 144
Ditchburn, Ross 47
Ditterich, Carl **82–4**, 195, 214, 217, 239, 255, 300
Dixon, Brian **84**, 127, 128, 185, 186, 298
Dixson, Hugh 293
Dockett, Len 127
Doherty, Vin 124
Doig family 31, 119, 294
Doig, George 119, 294
Domburg, Terry 220
Donald, Wally **84**, 111
Donaldson, Graham 100
Donnellan, S. 102
Donohue, Larry 116, 117, 196
Doolan, B. 198
Dorotich, J. 47
Dougherty, George 124
Doull, Bruce 46, **84–5**, 88, 142, 235, 282
Dowling, Reg 124
Downs, Tommy 238, 300
Downs, Lyle 269
Dredge, E. 102
Drop Punt 85–6
Dual Sportsmen 86–7
Duckworth, Bill 133
Duffy, Roger 10, 57, 111
Dugdale, Dean 87
Dugdale, Glenn 87
Dugdale, John **87**, 174, 203, 205
Dullard, Adrian 126, 127
Dummett, Rosey 62, 63
Duncan, Alex 258
Dunell, Frank 133, 217, 218
Dunne, E. 228
Dunne, Ross 64, **87–8**, 131, 132, 133
Dunstall, Jason 26, 36, 38, 48, 81, **88–9**, 118, 119, 120, 121, 134, 144, 145, 151, 169, 189, 217, 218, 282
Duperouzel, Bruce 243, 297
Durable Players 89–90
Durham, Ron 225
Dwyer family 90
Dwyer, Anthony 90
Dwyer, David 90
Dwyer, Laurie 36, 87, **90**, 205
Dwyer, Leo 90
Dyer, Jack 16, 21, 35, 43, 44, 52, 56, 57, 59, 60, 62, 67, 79, 83, 84, 85–6, **90–2**, 101,

Hamill, G. 102
Hamilton, J. 102
Hamilton, Jack 281
Hamilton, Shane 134
Hamilton, W. 102
Hammersley, W.J. 278, 303
Hammond, Charlie 138
Hammond, Tom 174
Hampshire, Ian **138**, 142
Hands, Ken 16, 46, 125, 126, **138–9**, 202
Hank brothers (Bob, Bill & Ray) 33
Hank, Bob 33, 198
Hanna, Milham 210, 211
Hansen, Brian 191, 192
Hanson, Jack 109
Hardeman, Gary 136, **137**, 185, 274
Hardie, Brad 27, 28, 29, 109, 110, **139–40**, 176, 296, 297
Hardiman brothers (Les & Harold 'Peter') 32
Hardiman, Harold 'Peter' 32, 124
Hardiman, Les 32, 116, 124, 294
Harding, Paul 211
Hardy, Charlie 95, 171, 208, 209, 238
Harmes, Wayne 281
Harper brothers (Roy & Keith) 31
Harper, Albert 127
Harper, Roy 31, 294–5
Harris, Bernie 29
Harris, Bill 109
Harris, John D. 'Jiggy' 143
Harris, 'Dick' 120, **140**, 225, 227, 228
Harris, Leon 140
Harris, Wilbur 250
Harrison, Barry 'Hooker' 16, 168
Harrison, Henry Colden Antill 94, **140**, 184, 225, 278, 303
Hart, Ben 6, 282
Hart, David 291
Hart, Eddie 103
Hart, John 245
Hart, Royce 54, 135, 137, **140–2**, 149, 182, 226, 227, 261, 263, 264
Hartkopf, Albert 273
Hartridge, Ron 126
Harvey, Mark 96, 133
Harvey, Robert 86–7, 285
Hassell, George 127
Hawke, Neil 86
Hawker, Glenn 96, 133, **142**
Hawking, Fred 124
Hawkins, Doug 110, 140, **142**, 282
Hawkins, Jack 202
Hawthorn football club 142–5
Hay brothers (Phil & Sted) 31, 32
Hay, Phil 31, 32, 65
Hay, Robert 251
Hayes, John 109, 296
Head, Lindsay 198, 244, 247, 249

Head, Roger 129, 256
Heady, Brett 291
Heal family 31
Heal, Stan 'Pops' 31, 141, 294
Healey, Des 5, 104–5
Healy brothers (Gerard & Greg) 31
Healy, Gerard 31, **145–6**, 185, 199, 200, 252, 259, 302
Healy, Greg 13, 31, 145, 146, 175
Healy, Matthew 146
Heard, Bob 131, 260
Heard, Shane 66, 133, 253
Hearn, M. 104
Heath, Kevin 146
Heathcote, John 105
Heavyweights 146–7
Hebbard brothers (Robert, Colin & Neville) 31
Heinrichs, Albert 246
Henderson, Herbie 84, 111
Henderson, John 128, 129
Hendrie, Gil 147
Hendrie, John 131, 144, **147**, 155
Henfrey, Ern 44, 294
Henshaw, Ross 131, 132, 202, 206
Heywood, Doug 126, 127
Hickey, Harry 147
Hickey, John 138
Hickey, Reg 43, 56, 81, 115, 116, 121, 124, **147–8**
Hickinbotham, David 115
High Fliers 148–9
Hill, Laurie 128, 129, 198
Hill, Malcolm 245
Hillard, N. 104
Hillis, Ron 87
Hills, P. 96
Hird, J. 96
Hiskins brothers (Fred, Albert 'Paddy', Stan & Rupert) 32, 33
Hiskins, Fred 32, 33, 96
Hobbs, Greg 193, 233
Hocking brothers (Steve & Garry) 31
Hocking, Garry 31, 134, 286
Hocking, Steve 31, 134, 273
Hodges, Scott 6, 248
Hodgson, Arthur 197
Hogg, Jeff 227
Holden, George 103
Holdsworth, Ted 294
Holmesby, Russell 173
Hopkins, Allan 37, 109, 110, **148–9**, 162
Hopkins, Frank 294
Hopkins, Ted 130
Horan, Tom 86
Hore, Bernie 124
Horwood, Ray 238
Hosking, Samson 'Shine' 247

Hoskins, G. 104
Hovey, Ron 115
Howell, Jack jnr 46, 68
Howell, 'Chook' 250
Howell, Verdun 66, 129, **149–50**, 255, 256, 261, 262, 263
Howson, Herbert 251
Hudson, Paul 145, 151, 155
Hudson, Peter 9, 58, 86, 88, 93, 118, 119, 120, 144, **150–1**, 169, 172, 179, 183, 189, 215, 216, 255, 261, 262, 263, 269, 281, 285
Hughes, Danny 6
Hughes, Frank jnr 152
Hughes, Frank V. 'Checker' 53, 55, 89, **151–2**, 184, 185, 193, 226, 227, 242
Hughes, Les 'Flapper' 64, 123, **152–3**, 208, 209
Hughson, Fred 43, 101, 103, 104
Hunnibell, Michael 199
Hunt, Ray 225
Hunt, Rex 87, **153**
Hunter, Ken 47, 297
Hurrey, Bert 273
Hurst, Paul 45
Hutchesson, Errol 129
Hutchinson, Col 148
Hutchinson, Jack 226
Hutchison, Bill 36, 43, 50, 59, 95, 96, 122, 126, 127, **153–4**, 198, 235
Hutton, John 29
Huxtable, Eric 263
Hyde, Bert 144
Hyde, John 115
Hyde, Robert 133
Hynes, D. 291
Hynes, G. 117

Ibrahim, John 198
Icke, Steven 19, 132, **155**, 206
Inaccurate kicking 155
Interstate football *See* National Australian Football Council
Ireland, Andrew 133
Ironmonger, John 146
Irving, Jack 284
Irwin, Warwick 103, 155
Ishchenko, Alex 146

Jackson, Eddie 3, 127
Jackson, Francis 146, 263
Jackson, Mark 120, 123, 301
Jackson, Syd 3–4, 130
Jacobs, Graeme 128, 186
Jakovich, Allen 30, 120, 175
Jakovich, Glenn 30, 291

James brothers (Hugh & William) 32
James, Des 199
James, Edward 117, 155, **156**
James, Glenn 4
James, John 47, **156**
James, Michael 156
James, Ron 268
Jameson, Rod 6
Jarman, Andrew 6, 30
Jarman, Darren 30, 145
Jarvis, Noel 101, 104
Jaworskyj, Bohdan 131
Jeans, Allan 13, 15, 19, 38, 53, 54, 55, 83, 129, 133, 134, 135, 147, 150, **156–8**, 178, 226, 235, 243, 254, 255, 257
Jencke, R. 145
Jenkin, Graeme 131, 158, 159
Jenkin, H. 102
Jenkins, Harry 141
Jesaulenko, Alex 10, 17, 35, 36, 46, 47, 53, 54, 75, 88, 130, 149, 155, **158–9**, 161, 210, 211, 217
Jess, Jim 159, 173, 227, 228
Jewell, Tony 23–4, 54, 172, 227
John Coleman Medal 60, 281
John, Graeme 297
John, Griff 293
Johnson, Alan 281
Johnson, Bob jnr **159–60**, 164, 186
Johnson, Bob snr 160, 185, 186
Johnson, Brian 73
Johnson, Chris 3
Johnson, George 226
Johnson, Joe 3
Johnson, Robert 'Tassie' 128, **160**, 186, 198, 261, 262, 263
Johnson, Ted 252
Johnson, Trevor 160
Johnson, W. 102
Johnston, Russell 245
Johnston, Wayne 46, 47, **160–1**, 167
Johnstone, Norm 51, 103, **161**
Jones, Bernie 131
Jones, Ernie 246
Jones, Jack 127
Jones, Peter 'Perce' 46, 130, **161–2**, 163, 261, 263
Jordon, Ray 57
Joseph, Ern 101
Joseph, Ron 136, 234
Joyce, Alan 13, 53, 269
Judge, Ken 133, 296
Judkins, Noel 162, 286
Judkins, Stan 37, 61, 122, 149, **162**, 226, 227

Keane, Merv **163**, 227, 228
Keddie, Bob 245

McIntosh, Merv 198, 294
McIvor, Scott 28, 29, 217, 218
McKay, David 46, 130, **182–3**, 265
McKay, H. 252
McKellar, Craig 137
McKenna, Guy 172, 291, 297
McKenna, Peter 64, 65, 86, 119, 120, 123, 129, 131, **183**, 225
McKenzie, A.J. 246
McKenzie, Bob 186
McKenzie, Don 78, 96, **183–4**
McKenzie, R. 252
McKenzie, Tom 246
McKenzie, Warren 47
McKernan, Corey 87
McLaughlin, H. 252
McLean, Colin 127
McLean, Kevin 128
McLean, Michael 4, 206, 207
McLean, Peter 128, 186
McLean, Ricky 182
McLean, Rod 126, 300
McLeish, David **184**, 252
McMahen, Noel 127, 185, 230
McMahon, David 103, **184**
McMahon, Kevin 90
McMaster, Bill 115
McMaster–Smith, Bruce 171, 238
McMurray, Jack jnr 272
McMurray, Jack snr 272, 280
McNamara, David 148, 155, 173, 254
McNeill, H. 102
McNicholl, Dermott 211
McRae, Dean 218
McShane brothers (Jim and Joe) 30
McShane, Paddy 101
McSpeerin, W.J. 102
Meagher, Des 131, **184**, 253, 273
Melbourne football club 184–6
Meldrum, Paul 47
Melesso, Peter 66
Melling, E. 102
Mercuri, M. 96
Merrett, Leo 225
Merrett, Roger 28, 29, 133, **186**, 217
Merrett, Thorold 5, 86
Merrick, Robert 102, 103
Merrigan, Harvey **186**, 273
Merrington, Gary 230
Merryweather, Andrew 66
Metherell brothers (Len & Jack) 32
Metherell, Jack 32, 116, 124
Mew, Chris 66, 133, 134, 144, 145, **187**, 235
Michael, Stephen 3, 4, 90, 290
Mickan, Mark 6, 27, 44, 186
Middlemiss, Glenn 301
Middlemiss, Russell 115, 301
Millane, Darren 19, 65, **187**, 268

Miller, Alan 54
Miller, Keith 86
Miller, R. 102
Mills, Andrew 11
Mills, Bert 187
Minogue, Dan 43, 53, 55, 123, 143, 152, 227
Misiti, J. 96
Mitchell, Barry **187–8**, 252
Mitchell, Hugh 50, 66, 96, **188**
Mithen, Laurie 185, **188**
Modra, Tony 5, 6, 120, 149, 248
Moffat, A.A. 293
Moffatt, Hugh 146
Mogg, Les 50
Mohr, Bill 119, 120, **188**, 196, 202, 254, 255, 256
Molloy, Graham 247
Moloney, George 116, 117, **188–9**, 294
Monahan, Jack 148
Moncrieff, Alan 189
Moncrieff, Michael 81, 120, 131, 144, **189**
Monkhorst, Damian 65, 260
Monteath, B. 228
Montgomery, Ian 129
Montgomery, Ken 132, **189**, 206
Montgomery, William snr and jnr 189
Moody, John 11
Moore, Colin 199
Moore, Frank 98
Moore, Kelvin 81, 131, 144, **189–90**
Moore, Peter 36, 63, 64, 65, 80, 132, 133, 138, 163, 186, **190**, 265, 304
Moore, Roy 74
Moore, Terry 228
Mooring, Jim 126
Moran, Jeff 129, 256
Morey, Sonny 4
Moriarty, Dan 247
Moriarty, Jack 101, 103, 104, 120, **191**
Moroney, Jack 209
Morris brothers (Stan & Mel) 32
Morris, Bill 68, **191–2**, 227, 306
Morris, Russell 202
Morrison, Alby 109, 110, **192**, 208, 209
Morrison, Bruce 115, 241
Morrissey, James 134, 145
Morrow, Alan 129, 198, 233, 255, 256
Morrow, Tom 115
Mortimer, Len 252
Morwood brothers (Tony, Paul & Shane) 19, 31, 192
Morwood, Shane 65, **192**
Morwood, Tony **192**, 252
Moss, Graham 96, 136, 167, **192–3**, 198, 295, 297
Mossop, John 249
Motley, Geof 198
Motley, Peter 24, 73, 248, 268

Palmer, George 86
Palmer, Stuart 249
Panizza, Darrell 296
Pannam brothers (Charlie snr & Albie) 32, 212
Pannam, Albie 124, 212
Pannam, Albie jnr 64
Pannam, Charles jnr 212, 251
Pannam, Charles snr 32, 65, **212**, 226
Parer, P.A. (Dr) 102
Park, Roy 273
Parker, Geoff 86
Parker, J. 198
Parkin, David 46, 55, 114, 142, 144, 146, 161, 165, **212–13**, 257, 302
Parkin, Jack 208
Parratt, Percy 53, 102, 103, 112, 208, 209
Pascoe, Bob 245
Paton, Ian 133, 263
Patterson, Mike 247
Patterson, Peter 129
Paynter, John 249
Payze, Travis 129, 256
Peake, Brian 3, 198, 295, 296
Pearson, Charlie 94
Peart, Neil 220
Peck, John 144, **213**
Pekin, Tim 214
Penberthy, Stan 109
Peoples, Darryl 83
Perkins, Polly 211
Perkins, William 225
Pert, Brian 214
Pert, Gary 214
Peterson, Robert 205
Phelan, Jim 201
Phillips, Fred 269
Phillips, Greg 248, 249
Phillis brothers (Wayne & 'Fred') 33
Phillis, D.K. 'Fred' 33, 118, 119
Pianto, Peter 115
Picken, Bill 64, 132, 133, 149, **214**
Pinnell, Phil 130, **214**
Pitt, Max 129
Pittman, David 6
Pitura, John 146, 263
Platten, John 22, 36, 68, 134, 144, 145, **214–15**, 248, 249
Player payments (& the Coulter Law) 68–70, 280
Polinelli, A. 117
Pool, Ted 144, **215**, 274, 296
Poole, Reg 239
Potter, Ted 128, 129, 131
Poulter, Ray 227
Pratt, Bob 58, 59, 70, 86, 118, 120, 121, 148, 151, 172, 196, **215–16**, 221, 250, 252, 268, 280, 281

Price, A.L. 198
Price, Albert 126
Price, Barry 131, 183, 224
Price, Noel 104
Prior, Butch 144
Pritchard, Darrin 134, 145, 261, 262, 263
Pryor, Geoff 78
Pye, Len 262
Pyke, Don 211, 291

Quade, Ricky 202
Queensland 217–18
Quinlan, Bernie 36, 84, 86, 103, 104, 109, 119, 173, **218–19**, 231, 281, 282
Quinn family 33
Quinn, Roy 225
Quinn, Tommy 33, 124

Raines, Geoff 109, 123, **220**, 228
Rait, Allan 109, 119, 261–2
Ramsay, Sam 112
Randall, Brian 225
Rankin, Cliff 42, 53, 116
Rankin, Teddy 116
Rantall, John 77, 131, 217, **220–1**, 252, 266, 282
Rattray, Gordon 102
Ratz, Martin 273
Rawle, Keith 127
Rayson, Noel 115, 116, 117
Read, Jim 129, 256
Reedman, Jack 'Dinny' 42–3, 246
Reeves, Ron 128
Regan, Jack 124, 182, **221**
Rehn, Shaun 6
Reid, Jim 61
Reid, Norman 74
Rendell, Matt 248, 249
Renfrey, E.L. 'Bert' 246, 254
Renfrey, Russell 115, 116, **222**
Reville, H.J. 'Peter' 252
Reynolds brothers ('Dick' & Tom) 31, 32
Reynolds, Richard 'Dick' 29, 31, 36, 37, 42, 43, 50, 53, 55, 58, 59, 95, 96, 108, 111, 127, 154, 176, 193, 216, **222**, 232, 235, 240, 278, 294, 298
Reynolds, Tom 31, 96, 222
Rhys-Jones, David 13, 47, 82–3, 215, **223**, 300, 302
Ricciuto, Mark 6
Rice, C. 117
Rice, Leon 131
Richards brothers (Lou & Ron) 31, 32, 212
Richards, Lou 31, 64, 79, 91, 108, 179, 212, **223–4**, 230, 240
Richards, Reg 126
Richardson brothers (Max & Wayne) 30

324

Richardson twins (Mike & Steve) 34
Richardson, Barry 289
Richardson, Mark 224, 296
Richardson, Matthew 149
Richardson, Max 30, 64, 131, 133, **224**, 225
Richardson, Wayne 30, 43, 64, 69, 129, 131, 133, 183, **224-5**, 296, 297
Richmond football club 225-8
Richmond, Graham 226
Ricketts, Charlie 53, 226, 251
Ridley, Ian 9, 168, 186, **228**
Ridley, Todd 113
Rigney, Roger 4
Rioli, Maurice 3, 4, 87, 206, 207, 220, 297
Roach, Don 245
Roach, Michael 120, 159, 227, **228**, 261, 263, 281
Roberts, Brian 'Whale' 137, 146, 194, 263
Roberts, Michael 229
Roberts, Neil 135, **228-9**, 254, 256
Robertson brothers (Harold & Austin snr) 30
Robertson, Austin jnr 30, 118, 119, 295
Robertson, Austin snr 30, 87, 119, 252
Robertson, Colin 133
Robertson, Harold 30, 252
Robertson, Ian 45, 130
Robertson, Shane 47
Robinson brothers (William, Alex, Fred & Gordon) 34
Robinson, Ian 272
Robran, Barrie 244, 247
Robran, Matthew 6
Rocca, Saverio 146
Rodda, Alby 127, 152
Roet, Dr Brian 66, 128, 186
Romero, Jose 211
Roos, Paul 103, 201, **229**, 259, 282
Rose brothers (Bob, Bill, Kevin & Ralph) 31, 32, 34, 229
Rose, Bob 12, 34, 56, 64, 87, 180, 183, **229-30**, 297
Rose, Kevin 31, 34, 127, 128, 129, 250
Rose, Robert jnr 73, 230
Rosenow, Geoff 274
Ross, Jack 124
Round, Barry 36, 37, 109, 218, **230-1**, 251, 252, 281
Routley, H. 117
Rowe, Des 43
Rowell, Edward 65, 112, **231**, 296
Rowlings, Barry 131, 228, **231**
Royal, Brian 110, 273
Ruddell, Cec 126, 127
Rule, Stan 127
Rumney, Harold 124, **231-2**
Ruscuklic, Peter 119
Rush family (Bob, Brian, Gerald, Kelvin & Leo) 30, 33

Rush, Bob 30, 33, 182
Russell, S. 65
Russo, Peter 133, **232**
Ruthven, Alan 43, 89, 103, 104, **232**
Rutley, Fred 300
Ryan family 33
Ryan, Bill 116, 149
Ryan, 'Bulla' 33
Ryan, Denis 'Dinny' 37, 101, 104, **232**
Ryan, Nick 87

Sachse, Neil 73
Saddington, Col 245
Salmon, Paul 96, 146, **233**, 260
Sampson, Vic 109
Sandland, Phil 246
Sanger, Arthur 126
Sankey, Maurie 100, 268
Sarah, Paul 116
Sarau, Jeff 84, **233**, 255
Savage, Ron 124, 126
Sawers, Rohan 272
Sawley, Brian 213
Scales, J. 102
Scarlett, John 233
Schache, Laurie 29
Schaffer, Keith 218
Schimmelbusch, Daryl 234
Schimmelbusch, Wayne 42, 43, 107, 131, 132, 165, 204, 205, 206, **233-4**, 235
Schmidt, Paul 46
Schofield, Ray 198, 294, 296
Schultz, Bruce 247
Schultz, Graeme 66
Schultz, John 36, 89, 90, 110, 198, **234**, 266
Schulze, Michael 106, 134
Schwab, Alan 281
Schwab, Peter 133, 144
Schwass, Wayne 202, 210, 211
Scott, Bob 272
Scott, Don 43, 69, 131, 144, 163, 180, **234-5**, 245
Scott, Garry 90, 295
Scott, I. 117
Scott, Jack 225
Scott, Mark 135
Scott, Robert 134
Scott, Walter 198
Searl, Doug 129
Seebohm, John 249
Sellwood, Joe 124, 211
September specialists 235-6
Serong, Bill 87
Seward, Leo 273
Sewer, Ralph 249
Sexton, Ben 211
Sharp, A. 102

Walker, Billy 41, 198, 295, **296**
Walker, John 296
Walker, Max 86
Walker, Peter 116, 117
Wallace, Terry 133, **285**
Wallis, D. 96
Wallis, Gary 129
Wallis, Steven 89, 110, **285**
Walls, Robert 27, 28, 45, 46, 54, 56, 85, 130, 159, 218, 219, **285–6**
Walsh, Kevin 133
Wanganeen, Gavin 3, 5, 37, 96, **286**
Warburton, Keith 73, 87
Wardill, Ben (Major) 62
Wardill, Robert 185
Ware, George 287
Ware, Norman 36, 109, 110, 209, **286–7**
Ware, Wally 287
Warne–Smith, Ivor 21, 89, 108, 184, 186, 209, **287**
Warren, Les 102
Waterman, Chris 291
Waters, Terry 69, 128, 129, 131, 149
Watling, Alan 296
Watson, Colin 256, **287–8**
Watson, Larry 289
Watson, Tim 66, 95, 96, 133, 253, **288–9**
Watt, Ricky 128, 131
Watt, Rowland 171, 238
Watters, Scott 113
Watterston, Roy 11
Watts, J. (Geelong) 117
Watts, John 295
Waverley Park 8
Way, Alex 126
Waye, Tom 109
Wearmouth, J. 44
Wearmouth, Ron 64, 133
Weatherill brothers (Robert & George) 32
Weber, Bruce 245
Weideman, Murray 64, 168, 245
Weidemann, Wayne 6
Weightman, Dale 289
Wells, Greg 36, 185, 186, **289–90**
Wells, Jack 254
Welsh, P. (Richmond) 228
Welsh, Peter 131
West Coast Eagles football club 27, 290
West, Peter 115
West, R. 117
Western Australia 290, 292–7
Weston, Paul 133, 248
Wheeler, Sandford 211
Wheeler, Terry 171
Whelan, Marcus 65, 124, **297–8**
Whelan, Shane 298
Whinnen, Mel 295, 296
White, Jeff 113

White, Lindsay 10, 116, 117. 120. 252
Whitfield, Ted 124, 126, 198, 300
Whitten, Don 299
Whitten, Ted jnr 299
Whitten, Ted snr 25, 35, 36, 42, 43, 51, 56, 104, 109, 110, 111, 155, 173, 177, 194, 198, 203, 234, 281, 289, **298–9**
Wight, Sean 210, 211, 258
Wigney, Stuart 6
Wigraft, Len 102
Wildmen of football 299–301
Wiley, R. 228
Williams family 33
Williams, Billy 126
Williams, Darren 26, 133
Williams, Don 66, 128, 185, 188, **300**
Williams, Doug 126
Williams, F. 102
Williams, Fos 44, 54, 57, 197, 198
Williams, Geoff 115
Williams, Greg 36, 47, 68, 70, 81, 82, 122, 145, 188, 189, 199, 252, 258, 259, 286, **300–1**
Williams, Jack 'Basher' 124, 126, 300
Williams, Mark 249
Williams, Mark 3, 29, 43, 248, 249, **302**
Williamson, Michael 114
Willis, David 260
Wills, Jim 124
Wills, Thomas Wentworth 10, 114, 140, 184, 225, 278, **302–4**
Wilson, Billy 227, 306
Wilson, Brian 109, 110, 123, 155, 186, **304**
Wilson, Gary 35, 36, 103, 190, **304–5**
Wilson, Percy **305**
Wilson, Peter 291, 297
Wilson, Tom 43
Wines, Clinton 126
Winmar, Nicky 2, 3, 4, 149, 255, 297
Winneke, Sir Henry 174
Winter, Bruce 249
Wise, Graeme 127, 128, 186
Wittman, Chris 134
Witto, Les 269
Wollard, Jack 123
Wood, A.M. 102
Wood, B. (Richmond) 228
Wood, Bill (South Sydney) 119
Wood, Bill (Footscray) 110
Woods, Bervyn 124
Woodward, George 65
Wooller, Fred 116, 117
Worrall, Jack 45, 46, 47, 53, 56, 86, 95, 101, 272, 278, 279, **305**
Worsfold, John 29, 291, 297
Worsfold, Peter 29
Worthington, Kevin 133
Wraith, Frank 62–3